FEEDING THE BYZANTINE CITY

* * *

MEDIEVAL AND POST-MEDIEVAL

MEDITERRANEAN ARCHAEOLOGY SERIES

M · P · M
A · S
· V ·

Cover illustration
JOB'S CHILDREN
Miniature, St. Catherine's Monastery *gr. 3* (fol. 17v), Sinai – 11th century
After K. Weitzmann and G. Galavaris 1990,
The Monastery of Saint Catherine at Mount Sinai; The Illuminated Greek Manuscripts.
Vol. 1: From the Ninth to the Twelfth Century,
Princeton, NJ, 37

* * *

FEEDING THE BYZANTINE CITY

*

THE ARCHAEOLOGY OF CONSUMPTION

IN THE EASTERN MEDITERRANEAN

(CA. 500 – 1500)

*

EDITED BY

JOANITA VROOM

*

BREPOLS

* * *

MEDIEVAL AND POST-MEDIEVAL
MEDITERRANEAN ARCHAEOLOGY SERIES – V
*
Series editor
PROF. JOANITA VROOM
Leiden University (NL)
*
EDITORIAL BOARD
Prof. John Haldon, *Princeton University* (USA)
Dr. Archibald Dunn, *University of Birmingham* (UK)
Prof. Sauro Gelichi, *University of Venice* (IT)
Prof. Scott Redford, *SOAS, University of London* (UK)
Prof. Enrico Zanini, *University of Siena* (IT)
*

Editorial consultant
SEBASTIAAN BOMMELJÉ
*

Typesetting & book design
STEVEN BOLAND
*

© 2023
BREPOLS PUBLISHERS N.V., TURNHOUT, BELGIUM
All rights reserved.
No part of this publication may be reproduced, stored in a retrieval system
or transmitted, in any form or by any means, electronic, mechanic, photocopying,
recording or otherwise, without the prior permission of the publisher.
PRINTED IN THE EU ON ACID-FREE PAPER
D/2023/0095/48
ISBN (*print*) 978-2-503-60566-1
E-ISBN (*online*) 978-2-503-60567-8
DOI (*book*) 10.1484/MPMAS-EB.5.133277
ISSN 2565-8719
E-ISSN 2565-9723

Contents

List of contributors   7

JOANITA VROOM (SERIES EDITOR) – *Preface*   11

PRODUCTION AND CONSUMPTION IN BYZANTIUM
GENERAL INTRODUCTION

ARCHIBALD DUNN   19
The Medieval Byzantine town: Producers, suppliers, and consumers

EARLY BYZANTINE & MIDDLE BYZANTINE PERIODS

VESNA BIKIĆ   57
Caričin Grad (Justiniana Prima) as a market:
Searching for an Early Byzantine model of pottery production and consumption

MYRTO VEIKOU   79
Geographies of consumption in Byzantine Epirus:
Urban space, commodification, and consumption practices from the 7th to the 12th century

NATALIA POULOU   113
Production and consumption in Crete from the mid-7th to the 10th century AD:
The archaeological evidence

EVELINA TODOROVA   139
Mapping Byzantine amphorae: Outlining patterns of consumption in present-day
Bulgaria and the Black Sea Region (7th-14th century)

MIDDLE BYZANTINE & LATE BYZANTINE PERIODS

PHILIPP NIEWÖHNER 171
Not a Consumption Crisis: Diversity in marble carving, ruralisation, and the collapse of urban demand in Middle Byzantine Asia Minor

STEFANIA S. SKARTSIS & NIKOS D. KONTOGIANNIS 195
Central Greece in the Middle Byzantine and Late Byzantine periods: Changing patterns of consumption in Thebes and Chalcis

JOANITA VROOM, ELLI TZAVELLA & GIANNIS VAXEVANIS 223
Life, work and consumption in Byzantine Chalcis: Ceramic finds from an industrial hub in central Greece, ca. 10th-13th centuries

ELLI TZAVELLA 261
Consumption patterns of ceramics in town and countryside: Case-studies from Corinth and Athens in central Greece

*

EARLY BYZANTINE TO LATE BYZANTINE PERIODS
AN OVERVIEW

JOANITA VROOM 283
Production, exchange and consumption of ceramics in the Byzantine Mediterranean (ca. 7th-15th centuries)

*

LIST OF FIGURES 339
INDEX OF GEOGRAPHICAL NAMES 349

List of contributors

*

VESNA BIKIĆ is a Principal Research Fellow at the Institute of Archaeology, Belgrade. Her research and publications focus on Medieval and Early Modern archaeology of the Balkans, including regional, Byzantine, Central European and Ottoman cultural phenomena, with an emphasis on pottery studies. She directs the Scientific Research Project for the Belgrade Fortress, and participates in several national and international projects and networks. Among her many publications, the most recent one is 'Pottery assemblages and social contexts in the Early Middle Ages: Examples from Serbian archaeology', in: V. Ivanišević, V. Bikić and I. Bugarski (eds.), *The Medieval World of Fortresses, Towns and Monasteries. Hommage to Marko Popović* (Belgrade 2021), 287-307.

ARCHIBALD DUNN is Research Fellow in Byzantine Archaeology at the Centre for Byzantine, Ottoman and Modern Greek Studies, University of Birmingham; PI in collaboration with the Ephoreia of Antiquities of Thebes in the Survey of Thisve-Kastorion; and Acting Director of the excavations of 'Saranta Kolones' (Byzantino-Frankish Paphos, Cyprus). He has published numerous reports and studies about his surveys in Greece (The Strymon Delta; Thisve/Kastorion), and is member of the editorial board of the journal *Byzantine and Modern Greek Studies*. His forthcoming publications include *Byzantine Greece: Microcosm of Empire* (editor); *The Byzantine and Frankish Seals from the Excavations of Corinth* (editor, The American School of Classical Studies at Athens).

NIKOS D. KONTOGIANNIS has studied Archaeology and History of Art at the Universities of Athens (Greece) and Birmingham (UK). He has worked as archaeologist at the Hellenic Ministry of Culture, as lecturer at the University of Peloponnese, and as associate professor at Koç University,

Istanbul. Since 2021, he is the Director of Byzantine Studies at Dumbarton Oaks Research Library and Collection (Washington, DC). His recent work includes *The Venetian and Ottoman Heritage in the Aegean: The Bailo House in Chalcis* (Turnhout, 2020; co-editor S.S. Skartsis); and *Byzantine Fortifications: Protecting the Roman Empire in the East* (Barnsley 2022).

PHILIPP NIEWÖHNER has surveyed and excavated the city of Aezani in Phrygia, the pilgrimage site of St Michael in Galatia, and the city of Miletus in Caria (Turkey). Minor research projects include various other sites and monuments in Asia Minor, at Constantinople (present-day Istanbul), and in the Balkans. After Istanbul and Oxford, Philipp is currently teaching at Göttingen University in Germany. Recent publications include reference books on the *Archaeology of Byzantine Anatolia* (Oxford, 2017) and on *Byzantine Ornaments in Stone: Architectural Sculpture and Liturgical Furnishings* (Berlin & Boston 2021). For more of his publications, see: http://www.uni-goettingen.de/de/pd-dr-philipp-niew%C3%B6hner/115262.html and https://independent.academia.edu/Philipp-Niewoehner

NATALIA POULOU is Professor of Byzantine Archaeology at the School of History and Archaeology at the Aristotle University of Thessaloniki (Greece). Since 2014, she is Director of the University of Thessaloniki excavations at the Byzantine site of Loutres, Mochlos/Crete and since 2019 she is the Director of the University of Thessaloniki excavation at Philippi. Among her many publications, she co-edited *LRCW4: Late Roman Coarse Wares, Cooking Wares and Amphorae in the Mediterranean* I-II (Oxford 2014; co-editors E. Nodarou, V. Kilikoglou). See https://qa.auth.gr/en/cv/npoulou. Currently she is the President of the administrative board of the European Center of Byzantine and Post-Byzantine Monuments.

STEFANIA S. SKARTSIS is currently Head of the Department of Large-Scale Works, Hellenic Ministry of Culture (Athens). Her interests lie in the fields of Byzantine archaeology, ceramics, and commercial networks in the eastern Mediterranean. Her most recent publications include *The Venetian and Ottoman Heritage in the Aegean: The Bailo House in Chalcis* (Turnhout 2020; co-editor N.D. Kontogiannis), as well as studies on the Medieval and Post-Medieval material culture of Euboea and Boeotia, on Chalcis as a major ceramic production and distribution centre in the Byzantine and Frankish periods, and on the finds from excavations for the Transadriatic Pipeline in northern Greece.

EVELINA TODOROVA is an Assistant Professor at the Department of Medieval Archaeology, National Institute of Archaeology with Museum, Bulgarian Academy of Sciences. Presently, she is the Editor-in-Chief of the journal *Contributions to Bulgarian Archaeology*. Her most recent publication is 'One amphora, different contents: The multiple purposes of Byzantine amphorae according to written and archaeological data', in: S.Y. Waksman (ed.), *Multidisciplinary Approaches to Food and Foodways in the Medieval Eastern Mediterranean* (Lyon 2020), 403-16.

LIST OF CONTRIBUTORS

ELLI TZAVELLA is Archaeologist at the Ephorate of Antiquities of Boeotia, Hellenic Ministry of Culture (Thebes). Both her monograph *Byzantine Attica: An Urban and Rural Landscape in the Early and Middle Byzantine Period, 4th.-12th Century AD*, Medieval and Post-Medieval Mediterranean Archaeology V (Turnhout, *forthcoming*) and the co-authored volume *The Christianization of Athens, Attica, and Adjacent Areas: From Paul to the End of the Reign of Justinian I (527-565)* (Leiden & New York *forthcoming*) are currently under publication. Recent contributions include 'Material culture from Early Byzantine to Ottoman times', in: Y. Lolos (ed.), *Sikyon I. The Urban Survey, Vol. 1: Text*, Μελετήματα Series 82 (Athens 2021), 234-306; 'Defence in Early Byzantine Attica (4th-7th centuries): Fortified towns, forts, and guard posts', in: H. Saradi (ed.), *Byzantine Athens: Proceedings of a Conference, October 21-23, 2016* (Athens 2021), 154-69.

MYRTO VEIKOU is Researcher at Uppsala University within the Project Retracing Connections – Byzantine Storyworlds in Greek, Arabic, Georgian, and Old Slavonic, ca. 950-ca. 1100 (Dir. I. Nilsson, UU/Riksbankens Jubileumsfond), and cooperation partner within the project 'Medieval Smyrna/İzmir: The Transformation of a City and its Hinterland from Byzantine to Ottoman Times' (Dir. A. Külzer, öaw/fwf). She has published a wide range of studies on spatial topics in the Byzantine period, including Medieval settlement theory and practice, among which *Byzantine Epirus: A Topography of Transformation: Settlements of the Seventh-Twelfth Centuries in Southern Epirus and Aetoloacarnania, Greece* (Leiden & New York 2012); *Byzantine Spatialities: From the Human Body to the Universe* (co-editor I. Nilsson; Leiden & New York 2022).

GIANNIS VAXEVANIS has worked as an archaeologist at the Ephorate of Byzantine Antiquities at Chalkida, and is currently a PhD student at the Department of Archaeology and History of Art of the National and Kapodistrian University of Athens. His publications include 'Investigating the origins of two main types of Middle and Late Byzantine amphorae', *Journal of Archaeological Reports: Science* 21 (2018), 1111-21 (co-author).

JOANITA VROOM is Professor of the Archaeology of Medieval and Early Modern Eurasia at the Faculty of Archaeology, Leiden University (NL), specializing in Medieval and Post-Medieval archaeology in the eastern Mediterranean and the Near East (including the Byzantine, Islamic, Crusader and Ottoman periods). She takes a particular interest in the socio-economic (production and distribution) and cultural aspects (cuisine and eating habits) of ceramics in these societies. Currently, she is Head of the World Archaeology Department of the Faculty of Archaeology at Leiden University, as well as Scientific Director of the 'Hinterland of Medieval Chalcis Project' (HMC). For further information on her research projects and international field projects, see: www.universiteitleiden.nl/en/stafmembers/joanita-vroom. For her publications, see: www.academia.edu/JoanitaVroom and/or https://www.researchgate.net/profile/Joanita_Vroom.

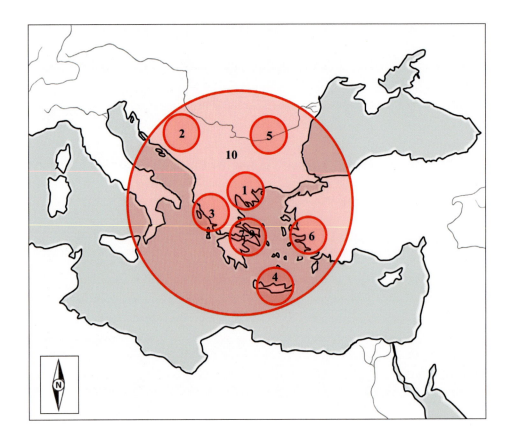

FIG. 1 – Map with most important regions mentioned in the contributions in this volume, ordered by chapter sequence: 1 – Eastern Macedonia (e.g., Thessaloniki); 2 – Serbia (e.g., Caričin Grad); 3 – Epirus; 4 – Crete; 5 – Bulgaria; 6 – Western Anatolia (e.g., Miletus); 7-9 – Central Greece (e.g., Thebes, Chalcis, Corinth, Athens); 10 – Eastern) Mediterranean (drawing J. Vroom).

Preface

Joanita Vroom

*

Throughout the history of the Byzantine Empire, with its various periods of expansion and stagnation, Constantinople remained in every sense of the word its capital. Apart from being the political and military heart of the empire, the city on the Bosporus was also a prime hub in a trading and exchange system which extended across large parts of Eurasia and North-Africa. The nodal points in this commercial network consisted of provincial cities and towns, which functioned as foci of Byzantine urban civilisation and of economic activity, being both centres of production and of consumption in their respective regions.

After the focus had been quite some time on the production side of the economy, in recent decades an increasing interest has been devoted to the study of consumption in the Byzantine world, both of the consumptive demands of cities and their hinterland in general, and of the functioning of the supply of goods to urban and rural areas in particular. There existed in fact a wide range of these Byzantine consumption goods, varying from durable products (e.g., furniture, ornaments) to non-durable products (e.g., food, beverages, clothing, footwear, perishable objects) as well as to services (work done by one person or a group that benefited others).

The focus in this volume is on the Byzantine city and its hinterland as centres of consumption in the broadest sense, although the production side of Byzantine life is never out of sight, as there is no consumption without production. Some of the questions which will be discussed are: can long-term patterns of consumption be established, or did consumption change fundamentally over time? What do the archaeological, literary and iconographical sources reveal about consumption behaviour in Byzantine cities and towns? May provincial towns such as Çaricin Grad, Miletus, Corinth, Athens or Chalcis be compared with the metropolis Constantinople as far as their function as centres of consumption and manufacture is concerned? How was the day-to-day distribution of goods from and to the Byzantine cities organized? And is it possible to determine the consumptive reasons why in one category of goods some objects were apparently more desired by Byzantine town dwellers than others?

Originally these questions – and many more – were addressed at a round table session with the title 'New Perspectives on the Byzantine City as Consumption Centre', which was held at the 23rd International Congress of Byzantine Studies on the 23rd of August 2016 at Belgrade. Most contributors to this volume did participate in that session, and they have set out to answer these questions here in more detail, from various perspectives, using and comparing different sources of information, such as archaeological artefacts, literary texts and visual arts.

Throughout the contributions special attention is paid to the developments and changes of urban consumption behaviour over time during the rise and fall of the Byzantine Empire. One instance of this approach is by comparing the centralized economy of the Early Byzantine society, characterised by its heavy handed state interference, with the flourishing of long-distance trade and the growing appetite for luxury goods in the Middle Byzantine and Late Byzantine world after the 9th and 10th centuries.

The volume *Feeding the Byzantine City: the Archaeology of Consumption in the eastern Mediterranean (ca. 500-1500)* starts with a general introduction by Archibald Dunn, aptly titled 'The Medieval Byzantine town: Producers, suppliers, and consumers'. Initially, this contribution started out as a shorter paper written for a plenary session at the 22nd International Congress of Byzantine Studies, which was held in the week of 22-27 August 2011 at Sofia (Bulgaria), but was unfortunately never published since then. As I happened to be the one asked to read the text of Dunn (who was unable to be present in person at this conference) to a clearly very interested audience, I knew the content of the paper very well and was convinced that it would be perfect as a general introduction to the other chapters in this volume.

In fact, in the current (extended and updated) version of his text Dunn explores characteristics of Byzantine provincial urban markets, the products which were available there, and the wide range of potential suppliers on the basis of literary sources (among which Byzantine and Ottoman records of regional products and exported merchandises). He discusses not only provincial markets as regional importers and inter-regional exporters in the Byzantine world, but also sheds light from a more mundane viewpoint on villagers and pastoralists as suppliers of foodstuffs, raw materials and artisanal goods. His case-study concentrates mostly on records of towns in south-eastern Macedonia, in particular on Thessaloniki and the twin *skalai* (ports) of Krysoupolis and the Strymon Delta from Middle Byzantine to (Late) Ottoman times.

After this thought-provoking introduction by Dunn on demand and supply in a Byzantine provincial rural economy, mainly based on literary sources, the following contributions mostly cover archaeological regional case studies, and are therefore presented as much as possible in a chronological order. The locations in the Byzantine world of the regions discussed in these case studies, as well as their province-specific consumption patterns, are indicated in Fig. 1 (by the red numbered circles in this map). Although various types of material culture are discussed, the focus in this volume is primarily on ceramic finds (because these are ubiquitous in most archaeological projects in the Mediterranean).

The first part of *Feeding the Byzantine City* encompasses both the Early Byzantine and the Middle Byzantine periods, and contains four chapters. In the first one, titled 'Caričin Grad (Justiniana Prima) as a market: Searching for an Early Byzantine model of pottery production and consumption', Vesna Bikić discusses the 6th-century Byzantine provincial town Caričin Grad which was situated in the vast Prefecture of Illiricum (western Balkans). The town was also known as 'Justinana Prima', a name which referred to the fact that the settlement was founded as a '*Neustiftung*' by the Byzantine Emperor Justinian I near his birth-place. In order to sketch the socio-economic contexts of this town, Bikić focuses on the organisation of the production and distribution of pottery, based on the functional analysis of the ceramics found here. The site of Caričin Grad (in present-day Serbia) stands out as a time capsule due to its mere 75 years-existence (it functioned only between circa 530 and 615), its extraordinary archaeological indicators (especially its precise chronology), its spatial layout and inner (architectural) structures, as well as its contextual ceramic assemblages. In her chapter Bikić presents unknown excavated ceramic finds (among which imported tablewares and amphorae as well as locally made cooking pots and storage jars) from this *polis* and uses these finds to create general models of production and consumption behaviour in an Early Byzantine provincial town.

In the second case study, 'Geographies of consumption in Byzantine Epirus: Urban space, commodification, and consumption practices from the 7th to 12th century' Myrto Veikou direct our attention southwards, to the Byzantine province of Epirus (present-day western Greece). Using the results of her earlier research on various types of Byzantine material culture (either still *in situ* or part of museum collections) during an extensive archaeological survey project, she currently investigates 'consumption geographies' in this region. Veikou shows special interest in spaces and practices which can be partly considered as 'urban environments'. Her approach is based on a comparison of archaeological evidence from these environments (such as pottery, metal and glass artefacts, art, coins, sculptures) with Byzantine texts referring to these manifestations of material culture. In this perspective, she explores the intricate relations between imported and locally produced symbolic goods, durable goods, non-durable goods and services in the region under study.

In the third contribution, 'Production and consumption in Crete from the mid 7th to the 10th century AD: The archaeological evidence', Natalia Poulou considers in what way cities and small rural settlements in Crete participated in the commercial network of the Byzantine Empire. More specifically, she focuses on the production and consumption of specific commodities on the island, as well as on the exchange of goods between Crete and other isles in the Aegean. The objects discussed in her chapter include various types of imported pottery, among which Glazed White Wares and Polychrome Ware from Constantinople and glazed wares from the Islamic world, as well as locally made ceramics (not only amphorae but also painted ware and utilitarian vessels), metal artefacts (bronze and golden belt buckles; golden earrings) and silk textiles. It appears that during the 8th and 9th centuries, even after the conquest by Andalusian Muslims in 827/28, agricultural and commercial activities in most cities on Crete continued to be linked to the Byzantine network, in particular those in the area of Heraklion (by then known as Chandax/Al-Khandaq).

In the fourth chapter, 'Mapping Byzantine amphorae: Outlining patterns of consumption in present-day Bulgaria and the Black Sea region (7th-14th century)', Evelina Todorova shows how plotting different find spots of amphorae and their respective quantities can be valuable to outline distribution patterns of these ceramic transport jars and their contents (mostly wine or oil). She argues that despite certain practical shortcomings the approach makes it possible to identify consumption centres which imported such vessels. To proof her point, Todorova persuasively identifies several such consumption centres by mapping quantities of published imported amphora types along the western Black Sea coast, along the Danube River, as well as in north-eastern Bulgaria (along the Maritsa and Struma rivers). Furthermore, she points to the fascinating variety of stamps and *graffiti* on these transport jars, and offers a new interpretation of 7th- to 14th-century amphora distribution in the eastern Mediterranean and the wider Black Sea region.

The second part of this volume deals with the Middle Byzantine and Late Byzantine periods, and consists of four chapters. In the first, titled 'Not a consumption crisis: Diversity in marble carving, ruralisation, and the collapse of urban demand in Middle Byzantine Anatolia', Philipp Niewöhner discusses Byzantine marble carvings for churches and other buildings in present-day Turkey. Such stone carvings were employed throughout Byzantine times, and their production and distribution in towns and countryside seem to reflect settlement patterns and the way these changed over time. The Early Byzantine period was, for instance, dominated by the supra-regional production of three quarries that had already been active during the Roman period and continued to set the example for various local workshops. These were Docimium in Phrygia for the central Anatolian High Plateau; Proconnesus/Constantinople for the Mediterranean Basin, and Sivec near Prilep in Macedonia for the central Balkan region. The Middle Byzantine production, on the other hand, was characterised by countless local workshops making products which could end up in remote rural locations. Niewöhner argues that the difference between the Early and the Middle Byzantine patterns may be explained by a collapse of urban consumption, as has become apparent through his research at the city of Miletus on the western coast of Turkey.

In the second chapter Stefania S. Skartsis and Nikos D. Kontogiannis debate in their contribution 'Central Greece in the Middle Byzantine and Late Byzantine periods: Changing patterns of consumption in Thebes and Chalcis' the consumptive habits of two vibrant Byzantine cities They discuss not only ceramic finds from these two urban centres (situated in Boeotia and on the Island of Euboea), but also finds of luxury products which were either produced or consumed by their inhabitants under Byzantine and Frankish rule. The finds of precious goods included silk textiles, minor objects from burial contexts (such as religious amulets, dress accessories, jewels and jewel boxes), as well as high-quality luxury objects which apparently belonged to local magnates. Skartsis and Kontogiannis argue that these objects were often linked to the social standing and the identity of their owners, and may help to get a better understanding of social and economic circumstances, production models and consumption patterns at Thebes and Chalcis from the 11th century onwards.

In the third contribution, 'Life, work and consumption in Byzantine Chalcis: Ceramic finds from an industrial hub in central Greece, ca. 10th-13th centuries' by Joanita Vroom, Elli Tzavella and Giannis Vaxevanis, the emphasis is on one specific, important production zone in an extramural neighbourhood of Byzantine Chalcis. The authors present and discuss the very significant finds from a recent rescue excavation at Orionos Street in the eastern part of this city. During this dig remains of building structures were unearthed which seemed to have functioned as a waste dump for several workshops which were active from Middle to Late Byzantine times. The excavated material included huge amounts of ceramic finds, as well as significant amounts of bone, shell, metal and glass finds. The first processing of the extraordinarily large quantities of finds was carried out between 2013 and 2016, and the initial research already yielded fascinating insights in the development of local pottery production of

Byzantine glazed and unglazed wares dated between ca. the 10th and 13th centuries in this important harbour city.

In the last chapter of the second part, Elli Tzavella explores in her contribution 'Consumption patterns of ceramics in town and countryside: Case-studies from Corinth and Athens in central Greece' the meaning of the term 'consumption' in relation to Byzantine cities and their rural surroundings. She reminds us that a considerable part of the Byzantine elite resided, or was at least also active, in the countryside. Consequently, consumption above subsistence level was an economic habit which was not exclusively linked to urban settlements. On the other hand, the lower social strata of towns (such as Corinth and Athens) consumed goods which were transported to the city from the surrounding countryside, which indicates that provisioning held a special place in the Byzantine urban economy as a whole. In addition, Tzavella raises the question to what extent the Byzantine urban centres of Corinth and Athens showed comparable developments in dining habits, food storage, and cooking.

In the third and final part of *Feeding the Byzantine City*, 'Production, Exchange and consumption of ceramics in the Byzantine Mediterranean (ca. 7th-15th centuries)', the author of this Preface sets out to present a general outline of various levels of production, circulation and consumption of ceramic products from Early Byzantine to Late Byzantine times. The emphasis is on two consumer goods in particular, namely glazed tablewares and amphorae, as these belong to the better traceable types of pottery in ceramic distribution systems. Some of the topics discussed in this chapter include innovations in Byzantine pottery production (exemplified for instance by Glazed White Wares from Constantinople), transmission of iconographical styles, as well as excavated shipwrecks as evidence for distribution patterns of Byzantine amphorae and glazed tablewares. The chapter finishes with 'exotic' ceramic imports from the Islamic world. All this makes it quite clear that throughout the entire Byzantine period changing consumer demands encouraged potters to actively investigate new techniques for potting and decoration, and thus induced new ways of production.

Last but not least, I would like to mention the operational website *'The Archaeology of a Byzantine City'* at http://www.bijleveldbooks.nl/ResearchSeminar/ (which was made together with some of my RMA students at Leiden University). This online forum/exhibition serves as an additional tool to the current book as it provides information on topics such as architecture, daily life, entertainment and religion in key Byzantine cities in the eastern Mediterranean (with a focus on Athens, Butrint, Ephesus and Tarsus).

Leiden, January 2022

PRODUCTION AND CONSUMPTION IN BYZANTIUM

GENERAL INTRODUCTION

* * *

Servant handling a Late Roman amphora in Constantinople during Early Byzantine times, Great Palace Mosaic Museum, Istanbul (after J. Vroom 2014², *Byzantine to Modern Pottery in the Aegean – An Introduction and Field Guide, Second & Revised Edition*, Turnhout, 56, fig. EBYZ 15.4).

The Medieval Byzantine town: Producers, suppliers, and consumers

Archibald Dunn

*

CHALLENGES TO AN UNDERSTANDING OF PROVINCIAL MARKETS, AND AN OPPORTUNITY

There are good reasons for attempting a collective study of the supplying of urban markets in the Byzantine world, not least the need to present and evaluate the growing quantity and rising quality of relevant archaeological evidence. The task of this contribution to the collective effort in this volume however will be the necessary, but tentative, one of building upon historical enquiries in this area, and one which will concentrate on the Medieval Byzantine centuries. The organisation of urban markets is remarkably obscure after the demise of the Late Roman or Early Byzantine *polis*, languishing somewhere off a historiographic stage occupied by the *Thema*, imperial treasuries' officials, and evidence of tax-farmers.

Meanwhile a rich secondary literature about the Middle Byzantine *Book of the Eparch*, or civil governor, of the city of Constantinople, draws attention away from the fact that his *operational* equivalents in the Medieval Byzantine provinces at the level of towns and cities have never been identified, and the arguments against their existence are reasonable.[1] Meanwhile too the roles and relative strengths of the potential suppliers of Medieval urban markets remain as obscure or contentious as the markets' organisation on the ground, owing to the loss of provincial records of most kinds, but also to that 'pessimism' (now superseded) about the Byzantine economy, or more specifically about the provincial rural economy at its base.

The real organisation of the Medieval markets may therefore remain as hidden from us historically as it still is archaeologically.[2] And it is not truly illuminated by apparently evocative seals of *kommerkiarioi* and *apothekai*. So this contribution can only be an exploration of some ways of negotiating the evidential *impasse* insofar as it affects the supplying of Medieval 'markets' (however constituted), which is arguably less intractable than the *impasse* which affects their administrative organisation (or the lack of one: the sets of local 'customs' encountered by the Fourth Crusaders). But the sources, such as they are, do suggest an opportunity to explore further not only the feeding but the clothing and the heating of Medieval Byzantine townspeople.

The evidence, direct or often indirect, for supply and suppliers, grows with the editing of monastic archives of the 9th to 15th centuries, and yet there remain wide gaps in the documentation of supply, the addressing of which looks not only to the right kinds of urban and rural archaeology, but also to other broadenings of approaches to Byzantine economic history. Still within the conventional discipline of history, very early Ottoman evidence (e.g., of the 1470s) about local and regional suppliers of markets, and retailers in markets, will be explored, with a focus, for practical reasons, on just one range of products (mostly to do with textiles), to see whether this can illuminate in several ways the relatively obscure Late Byzantine picture.

Broader perspectives – But a methodologically broader approach is also necessary. The evaluation of more general Byzantine references to products supplied to markets, e.g., to the production of necessities without which urban life would have been degraded or impossible, needs to correlate these with secure 'pre-industrial' evidence (be it earlier or later Ottoman) for specific geographical spaces. This involves reference to both the traditional economic values of landscapes captured for us by Western 'Travellers', geographers and map-makers before the East Mediterranean Agricultural Revolutions of the 20th century, and reference to their spatial relationships to markets where multi-faceted continuities are traceable between Byzantine and Ottoman times.

Some such broader approach needs to be explored if the real functionality, distribution and hierarchy of Byzantine provincial markets is to be studied. For only on this kind of basis can haphazardly preserved references to supplies to known markets, and references to the circulation there of famous luxuries and/or items with remote origins (e.g., Asian) start to be seen in something akin to a realistic perspective. It is worth highlighting a typical kind of distorted interpretation of the markets of an important Middle Byzantine city (in this case, of Greece), based only on references to its famous luxuries. Angeliki Laiou asserted that Boeotian Thebes' 'trade' was in silk, and even that 'it does not seem to have functioned as a regional or inter-regional centre for other trade'.[3] The surviving references do not lead to this conclusion at all, which anyway makes no sense in terms of physical and administrative geography. It in fact creates a new *impasse* (while drawing our attention to the methodological challenges that await).

Records for the supplying of Byzantine urban markets, as we know, survive only in rare fragments before the 15th century (e.g., from Trebizond), and would only ever have captured some of the integral processes of supply (such as specific urban tolls, their rates, and takings), or some of the contextual phenomena (such as fiscal censuses, including comprehensive records of occupations, or artisanal or other associations' records). Byzantine urban supply, and its prerequisite, 'urban demand', will never therefore be studied like those of some 16th-century towns. They can – and can only – be approached in less direct ways, some of which are therefore explored here. The shortcomings of the Byzantine sources also more or less dictate that what we can explore are somewhat generalised historical structures and patterns, not quantities, real trajectories, or economic 'league tables' of any kind. At the same time, the actual state of research into the supplying of Medieval Byzantine markets in a sense 'dictates' that the focus move to the provincial world or level, despite its challenges, challenges which arguably defeated a recent attempt to engage with the provincial level of markets.[4]

This shifting of focus is also fairly necessary because the relevant (and great) recent achievements of historians of trade, Byzantine and related (e.g., the Mercantile Republics') have retained a great focus, with regard to urban markets, upon long-distance trade, much of it only passing through the Byzantine space; upon merchants in major ports, Constantinople in particular, and the mercantile activities of Late Byzantine aristocrats in and around Constantinople;[5] the roles of Byzantine agents in 'international' trade;[6] and, in several important works, upon the feeding of Constantinople.[7] Significant exceptions to these tendencies are studies of the markets of Thessaloniki and Trebizond, relatively great provincial markets, the second of which cannot, for practical reasons, be considered here.[8] But these achievements overall leave us with very sparse examples of and hazy ideas about the great mass of provincial markets and their arguably most important supplying relationships, those with their geographical hinterlands.[9]

The growth of enquiries into the Medieval Byzantine economy has been so extensive however, in terms for instance of new general economic histories;[10] of studies of the roles of Western, Muslim and Jewish merchants in Constantinople and the provinces;[11] of the ongoing editing of provincial estates' archives; and of Venetian and early Ottoman archives that refer to late Medieval production, trade, and taxation in ex-Byzantine lands, that, despite the less-than ideal preservation of many kinds of sources (especially, sadly, urban ones), it is possible to explore some quite general historical questions, such as the one in hand, without finding oneself always 'at square one', trying to lay foundations.[12] And it is helpful methodologically, in view of this loss of relevant sources, that studies of the feeding and wider logistical support of Constantinople have now successfully integrated a multidisciplinary approach, in which long-term demographic, technological and geographical factors, but also cultural behaviours, can be shown to have operated across conventional eras (i.e., the Byzantine and Ottoman). This aligns approaches to aspects of Byzantine urban economic life with a long-established multidisciplinary strand in the reconstruction of aspects of the Byzantine rural economy in the light of pre-Byzantine and post-Byzantine and/or Early Modern evidence, for instance considering the evidence for Byzantine farmers' productivity in the light of the better evidence for early modern, unmechanised farmers' productivity in the same landscapes.[13] Such multidisciplinary approaches are also demonstrably valuable for the necessary reconstruction of the 'economic hinterlands' of Medieval Byzantine provincial markets.

The 'early optimism' of Vryonis – While framing Byzantine sources in such ways, it is necessary, practically, to explore mainly the supplying of Byzantine provincial urban markets whose hinterlands are relatively well documented archivally, such as parts of the Greek mainland. But there is every reason to think that these reflect in terms of historical structures, while varying in illustrative details, the lively, if 'spare', tableau of Medieval provincial Byzantine markets spread throughout Anatolia sketched by Speros Vryonis.[14] He conscientiously extracted the salient and highly relevant characteristics of these markets, paying close attention to vocabulary, including reference to the 'farmers' and 'inhabitants' as sellers,[15] from a remarkable range of non-archival sources, including contemporary non-Byzantine Muslim sources, and then summarised in the following words:

'The towns served as markets for the produce of the peasants [,] most important items of which were grain, fish, wine, fruit, legumes, nuts, livestock, and lumber. Each town had its group of villages, the inhabitants of which brought these products to town, very often during the big fairs held on the feast day of the saints. Here the villagers sold their produce and bought the products of local or foreign industry. Many of these villages were quite large and thriving. Thus, parallel to the larger movement of trade, there was generated also this smaller local trade between the villages and the towns, which was just as important in some respects as the larger scale trade. In this manner the farmers and herdsmen received cash for their goods. The towns in turn were able to dispose of the villagers' produce both by sale among the townsmen and by selling it to merchants of Constantinople and other cities.'[16]

After fifty years this synthesis remains refreshing for its 'optimism'. It is a scholarly position, although one reached without the aid of the limited Byzantine Anatolian archives; one which concerns important aspects of the supplying of provincial markets in major regions of the Middle Byzantine empire in, essentially the 8th to 12th or 13th centuries, and which identified 'farmers and herdsmen', and implicitly their economic conditions, as dynamic drivers of markets. It thereby posited an 'optimistic' view of rural producers' capacities to engage advantageously with markets, which was by no means the consensus either in 1971, when Vryonis published this, or even in 1997 when Alexander Kazhdan stated that 'it remains unclear to what extent the Byzantine countryside was involved in trade'.[17]

One could quibble about Vryonis's 'single vision', which seems to over-emphasise Anatolian markets' relationships with Constantinople, or about the absence of an overt challenge to the then prevalent pessimistic models of Byzantine agriculture and exchange, but Vryonis's own interpretation of the economic capacities of Medieval Byzantine farmers and herdsmen is clear enough. Far from assuming that the supplying of urban markets, or topographically rural fairs, was monopolised by the secular and ecclesiastical elites, while farmers remained stuck in autarkic mode (the old but enduring consensus which retained adherents at least until the 1990s), Vryonis implicitly puts Anatolian farmers and herdsmen at the heart of this business, or at least not in a marginal position. This was recognised by 2002.[18] It is therefore with this clear (but early) forerunner of more recent views about engagement with markets and fairs in mind that some relevant characteristics of the supplying of provincial urban markets in regions to the west of Constantinople will be reviewed or explored; regions where luckily this subject can also be explored in comparatively more detail beyond the *de facto* Middle Byzantine timeframe of the relevant part of Vryonis's study of Anatolia.

Although the essence of the conclusions made by Vryonis about the supplying of provincial markets was somewhat 'overlooked', historians were tending to recognise a potentially relevant aspect of the supply-side: a Medieval Byzantine 'individualised' approach to rural production.[19] That individualism is probably more apparent than real though. However, in the same period (the 1960s to 1980s) authoritative contributors to then-innovative explorations of this supply-side, specifically assessments of the suitability of eastern Mediterranean landscapes for non-subsistence agriculture, and assessments of their configurations and conditions in the Byzantine Era, authors such as André Guillou, Alexander Kazhdan, Michael Hendy, Johannes Koder, and Bernard Geyer, all agreed, or implied, that these landscapes were seriously constraining the ability of the Byzantine farmer (and herdsman, implicitly) to produce surpluses for the state and/or the market. So, by a then-methodologically novel route, an 'updated' explanation was 'found' for the supposed 'stagnation' of Byzantine agriculture.[20]

Mediterranean landscapes – In fact, scholars such as these had not recognised the many economically gainful yields of 'unimproved' Mediterranean landscapes such as traditional floodplains and wetlands, Mediterranean woodlands, and scrubland; therefore they had not recognised the pre-industrial farmers' and herdsmen's gainful exploitation of the entire Mediterranean landscape; and therefore that the household incomes of most Byzantine farmers would never have been limited by conventional agriculture. Luckily, the surviving archives of Medieval Byzantine estates reveal the Byzantine farmers' comprehensive approach towards land-use, while Western Europeans' observations of 16th-to-19th-century land-use in the former Byzantine world, taken together, allow us to trace the continuation of almost every aspect of this wider use of the landscape. The people who recorded these observations (the 'Travellers') also recorded details which make sense of laconic Byzantine archival references, for instance to the widespread and varying kinds of fisheries of the 'unimproved' floodplains and wetlands.[21]

In other words, several assumptions about Byzantium, including the teleological one about the 'seeds of long-term decline', reinforced by misconceptions about Mediterranean landscapes and their supposed fragility,[22] reinforced too by a clear empirical unawareness of pre-modern economic lifeways, were impeding recognition of the Byzantine farmer's and herdsman's ability to engage with and supply markets (and therefore the mass of provincial markets which we know existed in some form). Nevertheless, almost without reference to post-Medieval pre-industrial Mediterranean land-use and lifeways, other historians, perhaps studying the surviving estates' cartularies more holistically, have tended to recognise that numerical totals of farms' economic installations, as well as of their animals of all kinds, and of the taxes upon their productive installations of all kinds, are indicative of their engagement with markets. Less clear, however, is their understanding of references to economic installations that might have belonged to communities rather than to individuals (for instance *linovrokheia*: flax washeries). And the wide range of commercially gainful exploitations of Mediterranean woodland and scrubland, rivers and wetlands, both within and beyond (but especially beyond) the shared rights (*dikaia*) of villages had still to be established.[23]

But a turning point in the use of the archives was reached in 1989 with Alan Harvey's study of the Middle Byzantine economy.[24] He for instance recognised that not only provincial landowners must have been supplying wine to markets, but that villagers were able to do so too.[25] He could argue also that pulses (of fundamental importance in traditional Mediterranean diets) were being supplied to the market by Middle Byzantine farmers.[26] By 1991 Jacques Lefort had put the recognition of a Middle Byzantine rural artisanate, and its later growth, on a firm footing, and later strengthened the argument that farmers were engaging successfully with markets by the 12th century.[27]

The assumed bigger picture was that, as Michel Kaplan argued, the Middle Byzantine elite was investing in viticulture, olive cultivation, and the pastoral economy for markets.[28] And he and others could argue persuasively that Middle Byzantine farmers in general could not have safely sought to sell their grain harvests at markets.[29] But let us not assume that the *higher* fiscal bands of farmers were marginal figures. Again, Kaplan could argue that the Byzantine farmer required about twelve olive trees and at least ten beehives for self-sufficiency, but without mentioning that the richer *Late* Byzantine archives record significantly higher numbers of hives among some farmers' possessions.[30] The problem is really the extremely limited survival of Middle Byzantine detailed cadastral or equivalent records. Harvey could also argue that the Middle Byzantine *elite* was rearing cattle and other animals for markets (for instance Thessaloniki).[31] But Lefort could later argue that independent Middle Byzantine herdsmen were also breeding animals for the markets of southern Macedonia.[32] And let us not assume that the quite well-documented Vlachs and, later, Cumans of the Middle Byzantine Balkans and Greece, were just marginal figures at urban markets or rural fairs either.

The overarching framework will therefore be one in which Vryonis's mostly viable Middle Byzantine farmer and herdsman could successfully achieve both self-sufficiency and gainful engagement with markets by exploiting the entire Mediterranean landscape and contiguous inland zones on fiscally amenable terms. For neither the long-term rural demographic growth which Harvey and Lefort identified, nor the increasingly recognised and archaeologically documented revival of urban life, can be explained within a framework of simple rural autarky.

There is an opportunity here to identify, with hopefully a little more clarity and breadth than has been the case, some important characteristics of Medieval Byzantine urban provincial markets; namely, the *range* of producers supplying these markets, and thus the range of products available there; the *extent* of the supplying hinterlands of such markets; and the relative significance of city- and town-dwellers in the supply of provincial urban markets and/or communities. This should involve thinking about supply in terms of, ideally, a wide range of players: the sub- and non-elite producers, big landowners, merchants, and monopolistic officials selling foodstuffs levied in kind, all of whom are historically identifiable. But, because of their widely assumed insignificance I will concentrate upon the sub- and non-elite producers. On this basis the currently relatively neglected, and yet organisationally central, element of provincial or regional economic life, the market, or fair, may begin to lose its 'default' assumed characteristic as a setting somehow dominated by big landowners and (increasingly) foreign merchants.

VILLAGERS AND PASTORALISTS AS SUPPLIERS OF FOODSTUFFS, RAW MATERIALS, AND ARTISANAL GOODS

To begin with, let us concentrate upon, the historically 'silent majority', the sub- and non-elite producers, whose household economies, as captured in the fiscal registers of estates, the *Praktika*, and acts of pious benefaction, indicate that these people were supplying markets. Ten significant specialising types of market-orientation are identifiable in the archives of monastic estates, Middle-to-Late Byzantine, among their tenant farmers. And two more are identifiable in some of the earliest Ottoman fiscal documents, a group which however has deep roots in the Medieval Byzantine economy. It is most important that, whether paying rents and privatised taxes, or whether paying access-charges and shares of their production to managers or lessees of imperial monopolies such as lakes, rivers, and forests, sometimes locally significant percentages of Medieval Byzantine farmers were investing enough of their surpluses to supply markets. Access-charges for the *Incultum* presuppose commercially gainful productions.

Foodstuffs – Sheep- and goat-rearing for the purposes of exchange has been identified in the most extensive Macedonian *Praktika*, those of the first half of the 14th century. In one village for instance 15.6 percent of households had more than 20 sheep.[33] Jacques Lefort established that in the region nearest to Thessaloniki one *fifth* of the tenants of one monastery had on average thirty sheep each.[34] Meanwhile, in the well-documented settlement of Gomatou (about 80 kilometres to the east of Thessaloniki) four families had *on average* one hundred and ninety sheep each.[35] The numerous products of the sheep guaranteed several incomes in a pre-industrial economy. You will remember at this point the χωρίται (countrymen), who according to the Middle Byzantine *Book of the Eparch,* were not to be impeded by livestock-traders from bringing their sheep directly to the markets of Constantinople.[36]

Other farmers specialised in pig-rearing. The Bulgarian scholar Nikolai Kondov showed that one third of households in a well-document village in eastern Macedonia kept about 20 pigs each.[37] Ferjančić corroborates this with four other eastern Macedonian case studies, but can argue that this was not a common specialisation.[38] At the relevant point the *Book of the Eparch* makes no distinction among those bringing pigs to Constantinople. All are χοιρέμποροι.[39] Cattle-breeding and larger-scale sheep-breeding have meanwhile been identified as businesses dominated by elite landowners, secular and ecclesiastical.[40]

Others specialised in the production of honey and wax. It has been observed that, while every rural household in the *Praktika* kept a couple of beehives, nearer to Thessaloniki fourteen per cent of the tenants of *one* monastery had *on average* 14 beehives each and one had 60.[41] The proximity of the urban market is surely the key to this level of investment.

Probably the largest proportion of those investing in commercial production invested in vineyards and winemaking. I draw here upon the research of Kondov and Lefort (but this research has been amplified by Angeliki Laiou). It has been calculated that anyone planting more than two *modioi* of vines was, in the third *modios*, investing for trade.[42] One study of six well-documented villages shows that *more than two thirds* of the farmers could have served the market. The largest vineyard in this sample would have produced 6600 kilos of grapes for drying, and making wine and vinegar. In several well-documented villages around the year 1300 the average holding of vines was five *modioi,* so there was huge variation in the *individual* level of investment.[43]

Another highly significant area of specialisation for communities located by lakes, permanent rivers and the sea, was in the sale of fresh and salted fish. Salted fish was an article of long-distance trade. The urban marine fishermen of Constantinople and the Sea of Marmara, and that city's markets for fresh and salted fish, have been well studied by Matschke, Dagron, and others.[44] But for present purposes we need to assess a complementary phenomenon: the scale of the service provided by freshwater-fishing villages in the provinces to meet this major dietary requirement. The service provided to Thessaloniki by inland fishing villages is evoked by Ioannes Kameniates in the 10th century with reference to the lakes of Agios Vasileios (Langadas) and Volvê (their 'great [...] service' – μεγάλην [...] χρείαν – and 'most abundant provision' – δαψιλεστάτην τράπεζαν.[45] The supplying of Thessaloniki by these lakes is also recorded throughout the Ottoman era,[46] and in 1918 we learn from official figures that these two lakes yielded together 993, 280 kilos of fish, in other words about one million kilos – several million individual dishes.[47] The other lakes of Macedonia also still produced several million kilos of fish in 1918, and by traditional means,[48] and the Macedonian rivers' nutrients fed rich marine fishing grounds, which also appear in the Late Byzantine monastic archives among imperial income-yielding concessions.[49]

As regards specialisation by freshwater-fishing communities, wherever lakeside and riverine villages occur in the monastic archives for south-eastern Macedonia (Fig. 1), there are references to *aleiai,* that is fishing grounds *demarcated* for tax-assessing purposes, and frequent references to the fishermen's boats.[50] Associated with many of these are manmade *vivaria* – fishponds. Around one well-documented village, a monastic landowner, the Great Lavra, was granted by the Palaiologoi the tax upon the villagers' 60 fishing boats, and owned 60 *vivaria* itself, while 39 households (nearly a quarter of all households) owned *vivaria*, between 2 and 30 per household, making 364 *vivaria* altogether, on the sale of whose catches they were clearly paying commercial taxes, which were also granted to the Lavra.[51] Most of these 39 households (which could also exploit the contiguous lakes, and exploit the Lavra's own local *vivaria*, will have been producing fish and fish products for markets, and perhaps for exportation by merchants from the nearby maritime *skalai*. Their village, Toxompous, was adjacent to Kaisaroupolis (Fig. 3), and was situated between the city of Serres, whose fish-market is recorded in the 14th century,[52] and the port and imperial saltpans of Khrysoupolis. The siting of this immense cluster of ponds towards the 'seaward' end of the floodplain probably reflects the accessibility of salt, as salted fish was a very important part of the Byzantine diet.[53] Many villagers around the lakes and marshes also bred fish in cuttings called variously *avlakia, kháradrai,* or *strougai* .[54] Landowners were, by the 14th century, also being granted the right to the tax of one third upon the villagers' catches. But it is quite clear from foreign travellers' observations of the same villages and installations in the 16th century that they managed to earn good livings from these installations (whoever their masters were).[55]

Textile products – The raw materials for cloth-making, and the semi-finished and finished products, could have formed another type of village-based specialisation. Sheep-rearing for the sale of their products has already been mentioned. In terms of the significance of the input of villagers, it is likely, besides the well-documented involvement of the elite in the pastoral economy,[56] that transhumant pastoralists, who were numerous throughout the western provinces,[57] were also major suppliers, particularly to the great seasonal fairs such as that of Saint Demetrius outside Thessaloniki, which was a great market for animals,[58] and which coincided with the transhumants' autumnal descent to the plains. It is surely relevant that the post-Byzantine-to-Early Modern fairs of Greece are well-documented as markets for wool, at which 'yarn markets' would be found next to the animal markets.[59]

Such seasonal wool and yarn markets could have supplied some households' own private weaving, as well as artisanal workshops and 'domestic artisans'. A prosperous urban head of household for instance in Byzantine southern Italy in the 11th century (owner of several urban dwellings, and of farmland) bequeaths eight skeins of woollen yarn for the weaving of curtains or hangings (βίλα) for a church, while leaving the loom to his two great nephews.[60] This suggests a domestic scale of production that could be switched between the family's requirements, business, and *psykhika*. But it is not clear whether an urban family might own enough sheep and goats, kept in the countryside, to really meet more than private needs, such as the three 12th-century Thessalonican brothers who share out their parents' unquantified animals (*zôa*).[61] Some villagers probably could do so. However the absence (to my knowledge) of any reference to looms as taxable fixtures in the Byzantine 'rural' *Praktika* (in contrast to their inclusion in Early Ottoman fiscal surveys) could imply a lack of commercially significant woollen manufacture in the countryside. It certainly existed on a small scale outside of Thessaloniki in the Late Byzantine period.[62] But perhaps it could not compete with dedicated transhumant groups and urban workshops, and only supplied rural fairs.

Clearer, in terms of rural engagement with the supply of thread or cloth to markets, is the case of linen. Flax-washeries (*linovrokheia*) were most definitely taxable fixtures in late Byzantium. Linen was a highly desirable multi-purpose cloth which is recorded, as is well known, in the *Book of the Eparch*, along with two of its major areas of production and commercial supply: eastern Macedonia ('[the Thema of] the Strymon') and the Pontus.[63] Tax-*concessions* for flax-washeries are frequently recorded from the mid-13th century, and refer (so far) to the whole Khalkidiki, the Lower Strymon Valley and its foothills, and to the foothills of Mount Menoikion.[64] These were village-based investments, whose taxes could be conceded by the emperor to landowners as part of a village, which would have necessarily been operated by expert villagers. But of course they could be created by both landowners and villagers. Interestingly, in the period when references to *linovrokheia* multiply in Macedonia so too do references to hemp-growing (*kan[n]avotopia*),[65] and cotton-growing (*vanmpaki*: the crop; *vamvakiai*: cotton fields),[66] followed by the recording of cotton as an item available in the markets of Late Byzantine Thessaloniki.[67] And in the same period, that of the cadastral *Praktika*'s topographically best coverage, across 40 well-documented villages, nine include 'weavers' (*yphantai*), at least some of whom may be presumed to have been active at the dates of surveys.[68]

The preparation of wool for 'yarn markets', and of flax for the linen industry (wherever that was located, within and/or beyond a given region), probably via fairs both rural and urban, and via middlemen at such events, will not have been the limit of the rural sub-elite and non-elite producers' involvement in the range of textiles amenable to production. We should not assume that stages, and grades, of silk preparation were beyond their competence. Byzantine silk is a subject on which so much has been written that cannot be rehearsed here, but we must in the present context question the tendency to assume that, at least in the Byzantine provinces such as those of Greece, silk-supply to markets was simply in the hands of an elite. In fact David Jacoby, proponent of an 'aristocratised' supply of luxurious silks to Constantinople, had to recognise that his putative aristocratic suppliers would have relied greatly upon farmers to produce cocoons, thread, and even raw silk.[69]

Ottoman Qanuns and the continuity of the Byzantine rural artisanate – Ottoman sources (of the 15th to 16th century) enable us to assess some of the gaps in the Byzantine documentation: to think about the economic range and variety of consumers' requirements, about continuity with Late Byzantium, and about the very wide provincial distribution of silk products, revealed by them. And this, I suggest, enables us in its turn to question the still pessimistic narrative of the fate of the Byzantine internal market in finished goods, including silk articles, which has been extrapolated from the evidence of later Medieval *Western* supply to Byzantine markets. In other words, the only slight traces of Late Byzantine silk production beyond the Peloponnese are, given the state of the Byzantine sources, not evidence of Late Byzantine products' general absence from provincial markets.

Some material in the *Qanun*s for Greece and the southern Balkans of the period 1477-1613 – regulations *including* the taxes and privileges of (mostly) urban markets which were often added to fiscal surveys – deserves to be considered in the context of the supply of Late Byzantine provincial markets.[70] Throughout these regions at the end of the Middle Ages silk was being produced, from the Peloponnese to Thrace. The *Qanun*s distinguish, in terms of their respective rates of taxation, between silk cocoons (at varying rates);[71] silk yarn or thread;[72] bales of plain silk;[73] 'coarse silk';[74] and *ivladí*.[75] This last is clearly a loanword derived from the Byzantine *vlattion* or *vlattín*, which we might translate here as 'dyed silk'.[76] The *Qanun*s also itemise a highly-valued silk dye: the unprocessed *prinokok*, as a raw material requiring special documentation.[77] This is Byzantine *prinokokkion*, harvested in woodland and scrubland, and still an imperial tax in kind in Late Byzantine Greece.[78] And they taxed the processed product of that in many parts of Greece (the editor and translator use the words 'carmine dye').[79]

Besides references to cloth-looms there is also a province-wide reference to the taxing of silk-spinning wheels.[80] And while we know that the Early Ottoman administration encouraged artisanal production, some of the most complex fiscal regulations concerning this production are described specifically as 'in accordance with custom', which is probably indicative of fiscal arrangements inherited from Byzantium (including the Despotate of the Morea).[81] This would not have been strange as the Early Ottomans maintained important Late Byzantine urban market-taxes too.[82] In urban markets and in the countryside the *Qanun*s distinguish, in practice, four stages of production (silk cocoons, thread, undyed silk, and dyed silk), each of which involves merchants, stages which are already recognisable in the 10th-century *Book of the Eparch*.

More generally, the same *Qanun*s' determinations of the annual taxes on a range of productive installations – including mills, olive-presses, flax-washeries, hemp-presses, and pottery-kilns – further support a picture of a widely distributed provincial commodity-production for local and more distant markets, at least of necessities and middle-range articles (such as their 'coarse silk'). The taxation of installations *not* established to produce saleable goods would simply have led to their destruction or (where feasible) secretion.

The *Qanun*s also reinforce the idea of the unbroken continuity of widely dispersed production since Byzantine times when they state that the 'old laws' are applied to the pottery-kilns of Ganos on the Sea of Marmara.[83] These will be the kilns whose empire-wide Mid-to-Late Byzantine significance has been demonstrated by Nergis Günsenin and others.[84] And the allusion to now-lost regulations concerning this particular commercial artisanal industry is a useful sign that the Byzantine administration had in fact exploited this major provincial industry, one which historians have liked to observe is *missing* from the Constantinopolitan *Book of the Eparch*. Indeed 'Pottery works' in the Peloponnese are itemised as objects of a special tax like those on silk-spinning wheels and hemp-presses.[85] We can already detect documentary traces of a widely dispersed provincial production of pottery by the early 14th century (the time of the Byzantine cadastral surveys' topographically best-preserved coverage): seven out of 40 well-documented villages in central and southern Macedonia included persons called 'potter' (*Tzykalas*), and one village (Radolivos) included two familial workshops with which seven *Tzykaladai* were associated.[86]

Overlapping in some landscapes with some of the pastoral village-based productions that were organized to varying degrees for the market were the market-focussed activities of villagers and whole villages that exploited the products of arboreal vegetation itself. Firewood was needed by every urban household and institution of course.[87] Urban self-supply may have been the main source for this however (for which see the part below). But timber, charcoal, resin, pitch, and dyes – including highly prized sources of red and black dyes – were primarily extracted for the urban artisanate (and its village-based equivalents) in exchange for access charges and renders in kind to the administration or to beneficiaries of tax-concessions.[88] Meanwhile the elite, including for instance the monasteries of Mount Athos, could also compete with villages to produce surpluses of these kinds of products for the market on the vast *incultum* which they in practice controlled.[89]

The extramural/intramural kitchen-garden – Finally, in the Byzantine sources there is a locally significant producer for urban markets who could be both rural and intra-urban: the grower of vegetables and fruits, the cultivator of the *kêpos*.[90] But we are dealing here with the 'market garden', whose great range of products is so instructively described in the Middle Byzantine (as preserved) *Geoponica*, and so instructively glossed by Johannes Koder, not the normally untaxed plots of villagers.[91] Landowners could even be involved as ultimate owners of the ground (documented in the late period at Thessaloniki), but the suppliers to the urban markets remained the tenants themselves.[92]

This survey could not be exhaustive of course. Questions about the relative inputs of different socio-economic groups of suppliers, including urban officials as sellers of staple foodstuffs pre-empted as renders in kind, and ethnically distinct transhumant groups, are unanswerable as yet. More might be said about the range of village-based crafts and apparent 'industries' on the basis of syntactical differentiation in documents between craft-descriptors as patronyms and as designators of actual specialisations.[93] The possibilities for the engagement of minor landowners with provincial markets have become clearer, while the economic importance of this group, though numerically considerable, remains ill-understood.[94] The socially and strategically important grain market may have become dominated by the elite during the Middle Byzantine period.[95] But the ability of some tenant farmers to engage with it by the early 14th century, as argued by John Nesbitt and later by Angeliki Laiou, hints at almost 'counter-intuitive' changes within a broader response to rising levels of commercialisation.[96] But a concentration upon the socio-economic variety of *suppliers* to markets helps to redress the narrative bias that is created by a concentration on the supposed eclipse or downgrading of the Byzantine merchant, and on the rise and subsequent fall of the great Byzantine landowner, between the 11th and 15th centuries, both of which stories by default have served to promote the significance of the Western merchant as supplier of Byzantine markets.

PROVINCIAL MARKETS AS REGIONAL IMPORTERS AND INTER-REGIONAL EXPORTERS

If the roles of farmers, herdsmen, some rural artisans, and other village-based makers, as suppliers of Medieval Byzantine urban markets, can now be delineated a little more clearly as the result of many scholars' efforts, this has been temporarily at the expense of any clarity about specific historically attested urban markets, including loci of maritime traffic that may have primarily 'fed' more developed centres of retail exchange. So, it is important to try and extrapolate (again with a focus on the Greek mainland) case studies of probably fairly stable characteristics of specific centres of exchange and/or maritime traffic.

The characteristics currently identifiable at specific sites are *minimum* ranges of regionally derived goods, and *minimum* ranges of extra-regional goods, brought to them in the Medieval Byzantine period. But the hypothetical mitigation of such minimal tableaux, which reflect the many problems of the primary sources, deserves to be explored by reference to post-Medieval observations of such markets and in the light also of the configurations and recorded resources of the pre-modern 'unimproved' landscapes of the hinterlands of such markets (Fig. 1).[97]

Thessaloniki as a case study – This visualisation of the state of current research presents many important primary and secondary products which are explicitly described in Medieval Byzantine or Ottoman or Early Modern sources as entering Thessaloniki; or, in the case of salt, as produced by Byzantine Thessalonicans (Fig. 2).[98] *Timber*, which was being brought from north and south over considerable distances, was already probably not available near to the city in Kameniates' day, the 9th-to-10th century. Freshwater fish was brought in the 10th century and throughout the Ottoman era from as much as 60 kilometres' distance (for which see the part above); charcoal from forty-to-sixty kilometres, for which some of the evidence is of the 17th century.[99] Important products first explicitly recorded as entering the city's markets from its hinterland in Late Ottoman times, such as silk and wool, are already recorded *without provenance* as Thessalonican exports in Late Byzantine times.

The Thessalonicans' Petition of 1425 to their temporary Venetian masters for the protection of the Kassandra Peninsula illustrates these and other characteristics of supply to urban markets: this peninsula, up to 100 kilometres distant from the city, supplied it with a wide range of important products. It illustrates the size of a larger urban market's supply-base, but also the equally important factor of urban self-supply (for which see the part below). The Kassandra Peninsula's agricultural productivity is singled out by one of the Western travellers in 1692, when he observed that it 'produces wine, oyl, honey & with store of wheat'.[100] Finally, as you can see, the whole of central Macedonia, whether through the agencies of villagers, town-dwellers, pastoralists, and of course, estate-owners, supplied Thessaloniki.

References to foreign merchants' purchases in Thessaloniki, and more generally to the significant availability there of specific products, in the 13th-to-15th centuries, lengthens the list of the market's major products (Table 1).[101] The peculiar absence of some of Macedonia's principal ancient and Medieval products – iron, fish, and wine – from the 13th-to-15th century published references is rectified in 17th-century ones.[102] Iron however had been a traditional imperial *kekolymenon* (forbidden item), which might, conceivably, explain the lack of late Medieval references.[103]

Other case studies – Something like the exercises visualised in Fig. 2 and Table 1 could be profitably repeated for several major provincial markets. From Charis Kalligas's studies of three of the imperial charters of privileges for the great commercial town of Monemvasia, those of 1301, 1336, and 1390-91, can be extrapolated a list of the city's and (as the author rightly stresses) its hinterland's, known products, all of them, even the humble acorn, being commercially highly desirable (Table 2).[104]

The relationship of the Medieval Byzantine towns of the lower Strymon valley to the network of rivers and lakes is clear. These were the arteries of Byzantine inland trade and redistribution, which was achieved using pontoons, hence 'The Skala of the Pontoons' at one of the mouths of the river. The wetlands and seasonal floodplain supported vast fisheries, reedbeds, and prime grazing land, and were surrounded by what the geographer Angus Ogilvie defined in 1916 as 'permanent agriculture' before Macedonia's well-documented Agricultural Revolution (as opposed to the 'intermittent agriculture' of the then-normal fallow system).[105] This valley should have been a great exporter of agricultural surpluses of many kinds therefore.

However, it remains much easier to identify or extrapolate *probable regional suppliers* of products, than to identify specific products at specific markets, owing to the destruction of Byzantine records. In most case-studies it will be essential to study the Ottoman era's evidence systematically, and correlate it with the Byzantine evidence for *regional suppliers*. To illustrate this, I correlate the still-exiguous Medieval Byzantine references to the supply of Macedonia's products to the twin *skalai* of Khrysoupolis and the Strymon Delta ('Of the Pontoons') *with* the Ottoman era's references to the region's exports from exactly the same locations (Table 3). The 'Ottoman' references I extract from Western travellers' and Western diplomatic Consuls' observations. Many of the later Ottoman regional exports correspond to the range of twelve types of Medieval Byzantine and Early Ottoman market-specialisation that were identified above (Part 2) in central and south-eastern Macedonian villages or, in the case of silk, in the settlements of Greece and the southern Balkans in general in the 15th or 16th centuries.[106] It draws attention to many provincial products which, not being luxuries, have a very low historical profile, yet will have stimulated the establishment of trading towns. This is therefore another visualisation of the model-building challenge of the origins and development of Byzantine provincial markets.

THE IMPORTANCE OF URBAN SELF-SUPPLY

Urban self-supply will presumably have been interwoven with gainful enterprises like the ones already mentioned, the intramural or extramural *kêpos* for instance, but also, at a very different point on the economic scale, some Thessalonicans' ownership and/or leasing of farmland and woodland even 100 kilometres from their city. Perhaps more typical, at least in terms of the proximity of their rural investments to their city, would be the Thessalonican brothers Leon, Konstas, and Romanos, who in 1110 AD divided in several ways these investments and their intramural properties, their familial inheritance.[107] The wide range of rural terrains, types of land-use, and of productive installations, inherited by them together, looks like a set of enterprises developed to both feed a household and to generate significant surpluses (which before the year 1110 may have grown enough to pay for their fully furnished privately owned church).[108]

For besides urban properties (houses and workshops) they had inherited fields, grazing lands (*topion, khersotopion, kherson*), vineyards both maintained and neglected, animals (*zôa*), a vegetable garden (*perivolion*), one or possibly two reedbeds with an associated workshop, two watermills, a winepress (*patêtêrion*), and a rural dwelling, together with 'uncultivated wooded lands' (*ylôdesi khersois*).[109] The 'wooded lands' (which they continued to share rather than split), but also the *topia*, will have provided the firewood for heating and cooking, a characteristic included within the meaning of *topia*, and one meaning of the derived term *topiatikon*, in other, later, documents.[110]

Looking further along the social spectrum, Charalampos Bouras, who strove for decades to synthesise and interpret the excavations of Middle Byzantine Athens (but also of other sites), established that, throughout the settlement, archaeologically non-elite households stored grain, olive oil and wine, the 'Mediterranean Triad' (from, presumably, their own or rented fields, vineyards and small groves), in *pithoi* and *bothroi* below their houses. So this was normal practice in then-prospering towns (for whose prosperity and economic complexity there is much evidence today).[111] And many city- and town-dwellers' ability to supply themselves with a wide range of foodstuffs, and some firewood from their trees or other woody plants, need not be doubted. Less clear however are the economic conditions and circumstances of the suppliers of all the artisanal goods that also helped to make urban life possible. How did they 'supply themselves' (if they are distinguishable)?

The significance of this internal urban market (as opposed to the rising volume of long-distance trade that historians have identified during the Medieval Byzantine period), and the viability and even the distinctiveness of urban craftsmen and probably -women have been questioned. The range of artisanal skills available in a city such as Thessaloniki in the 7th to 10th centuries has been emphasised by Charalampos Bakirtzis on the basis primarily of a wide variety of contemporary literary texts, which however is qualified by the argument that 'autarky' (his 'autarchy') must then have been an important precondition.[112] But others seem to accentuate the importance of autarky or self-supply across almost the whole of urban society, rather than a widespread professionalisation of the urban sectors of production. Gilbert Dagron for instance characterises Medieval Byzantine urban industries as 'a system of social complementarity and not an urban economy in a strict sense', which also evokes the world of barter (a practice which cannot be discussed here, but which even autonomous late Medieval merchants used).[113]

Meanwhile Klaus-Peter Matschke evokes 'a relatively low density of artisanal establishments and activities in Late Byzantine cities'.[114] Neither cites texts (or archaeology) that substantiate their suggestions, but the extensive excavations of the sealed deposits of a 13th-century phase of Cherson in the Crimea seemed to reveal a world in which, in a sense, craftsmen and -women were in fact everywhere, and yet of ambiguous status. Synthesising the excavations' overtly most relevant findings, the minor objects, L.A. Golofast identifies a wide distribution in 'domestic' contexts of the tools for, or the installations of, agriculture, woodworking, building, wool-carding (everywhere), fishing, small-scale intramural animal-keeping, small-scale iron-working, and of course milling and baking.[115] They also observe that 'practically in every household there were found *pithoi* with salted fish remains', and characterise all these deposits as 'domestic' or neighbourhood-based artisanal activities whose scale suggests 'production […] as required'. Indeed they argue that 'there are no traces of workshops specifically for markets in the city'.[116]

The inference would be that demand for many artisanal goods was at too low a level to sustain many fully specialised professionals, and that these makers would have needed to practise some mixture of agriculture, herding, fishing, and gardening, to survive. But the *total* domestic archaeological assemblages of these 13th-century levels contain a wide range of imported fine wares and metal wares; and the now advanced palaeobotanical and archaeozoological studies indicate access to vegetable plots, a wide range of pulses, grains, wild fowl, and dairy products (but not a 'rich' diet). A fuller referencing of features finds two-storeyed dwellings with stone upper storeys, roof tiles, and stone-framed windows, which fundamentally distinguishes them from the houses of the urban poor (the emperor Theodore II's 'mouses' nests'). Among the non-domestic entities were found the excavated neighbourhood's own church where the stages of life were ritualised, including burial, and a well-stocked general store.[117] These would not suggest that the residents were *defined* by autarky or by 'a system of social complementarity'. Palaeobotany, archaeozoology, and many tools, clearly indicate important roles for fishing, pastoralism, hunting, and kitchen gardens in a household's economy, but the total archaeological record presupposes surplus production for commercial markets in other parts of Cherson (e.g., in the archaeologists' 'commercial centre') and/or in the terrestrial and marine hinterlands, and multi-faceted engagements with production, supply, and exchange. In many ways it resembles the total records of Pergamon's Late Byzantine *Wohnviertel* and Byzantino-Frankish Corinth's excavated neighbourhoods. Provincial towns and their constituent districts were therefore only *in extremis* defined by autarky and poverty, and were distributed along a spectrum of economic scale and complexity, to which we shall return.

So, we can glimpse in outline probably significant degrees of self-supply within most if not all classes of the *epoikoi*, the residents of provincial towns, in agricultural, pastoral (broadly defined), and sylvan products of almost every kind, but also an increasingly useful non-numismatic archaeological basis for arguing that city- and town-dwellers engaged in non-socially reciprocal exchanges to meet both important dietary needs and socio-cultural goals. And barter, if involved, could have been purely transactional. Households' supplies, gained from the land or the water, were of course not left to chance. Providing much of them would have been the legally defined terrains of each Medieval urban community (*ta synora tou kastrou*).[118] These were distinct from any provincial subdivision (e.g., *enorion*) of which it was the administrative centre. The *synora* enclosed the urban community's economic rights (*dikaia*), both private and communal, and were necessarily attached to towns and cities of all sizes (so for example Smyrna).[119] At coastal sites these included fishing rights, which might be distinguished, for any coastal settlement, as their *paraigialika dikaia* or *paralia dikaia*.[120] These fishing rights were clearly more colloquially known as a town's *Thalassa* ('sea').[121] But whilst being 'theirs', these various rights and resources were not necessarily (unless explicitly excused) tax-free.[122]

TRACES OF THE COMPLEXITY OF PROVINCIAL MARKETS

In exploring the daily business of urban provincial markets, the wide range of suppliers, and the geographical extent of their supply-base for staple products, one risks conveying the impression that supply, self-supply, and implicitly demand, were all about the bare necessities. To correct this impression, it could be argued that regionally distributed artisanal skills could always bring products made with good, though not necessarily luxurious materials, to provincial markets. The 15th-to-16th century *Qanun*s for Greece document this, implicitly, socially broad phenomenon in a way that no fiscal document from Byzantine Greece can do. But the *Qanuns*' evidence for the dispersed production of three qualities or grades of silk for regional markets, 'coarse', an unqualified or intermediate grade, and the *ivladí*, recalls the world of Middle Byzantine provincial supply and consumption of silk goods of three approximate qualities that is already revealed in the 11th-to 13th century wills of Byzantine and Early Norman southern Italy, and in other sources.

The Byzantino-Norman wills reveal a wide range of women's and some men's clothes, and various hats, made of *serica*, identified as lower-grade silk.[123] They reveal a small range of clothes made of higher-grade *sendais* silk.[124] But garment-linings, bed-quilts, and bed-coverlets are also made of *sendais*.[125] This was a kind of silk which probably originated in the Middle East, but came to be made in Greece.[126] And then there are a few references to luxurious silk articles distinguished by technical Byzantine descriptions (e.g., *examitum, cataxamitum, vlattium*).[127] But the point to stress is that these uniquely surviving collections of wills mostly reflect a provincial industry serving provincial markets, something which is not contradicted by references to luxurious grades of silk. A large Middle Byzantine market for lower grades of silk was identified by David Jacoby.[128] This is the same industry whose echo we catch in occasional references to silk of more than one grade among the Late Byzantine exports of Macedonia, Monemvasia, and more generally the Peloponnese.[129] It is that broad range of qualities which the Early Ottoman *Qanun*s indicate was ubiquitous. Therefore even providing urban markets with silk goods was largely not about luxuries imported over great distances, but about logically enduring regional artisanates.

The *Qanun*s also record a complex world of provincial mercantile middlemen, buying and selling the materials of each stage of the process of silk production from cocoons to finished articles, whose Byzantine predecessors at the heart of provincial economies should not be doubted.[130] Angeliki Laiou assumed that Byzantine merchants were a declining presence in all Byzantine markets from the 12th century onwards.[131] But the traditional pre-industrial structures of supply militate against their displacement. The 11th-to-12th-century wills of Byzantine-to-Norman southern Italy also hint at specialisation within a regional textile industry (in this case silk), while the later Medieval evidence indicated a still very widely dispersed and semi-ruralised supplying system (which Jacoby admitted would have always underpinned much of his putative 'aristocratised' supply of luxurious fabrics).[132] It is these ultimately Medieval Byzantine, but more broadly pre-industrial, systems of supply that are 'recaptured' (for us) by the first Ottoman censuses and regulations.

These arguments for enduring continuities and dispersed Medieval Byzantine provincial artisanates specialising in different stages of production and qualities of products, and working largely to supply regional urban markets (and rural fairs), are consistent with the enormous range of Medieval Byzantine makers (and retailers) that has now been identified in literary texts and documents.[133] While many of their crafts are not easily studied, the whole sphere of fabric and clothing production has been demonstrated, on the basis of archival and literary evidence, and now archaeological evidence, to have flourished in Late Byzantine towns or cities, such as those of Macedonia.[134]

Staying close, as we must, to the Macedonian records, and to the sphere of fabrics and fibres which has served as an example of the multi-faceted regional and rural supply of urban markets, the progress of the publication of records for Early Ottoman Serres offers one of several similar opportunities for a future correlation of the historical range of Medieval Byzantine makers and retailers with the evidence for specific mid- or late 15th-century urban markets. A Macedonian city such as Serres has already been shown to have prospered economically and been the home of a provincial aristocracy in the Late Byzantine period.[135] The differentiated demands of this class and of other classes, steady, of several qualities, and at scale, could collectively have generated degrees of complexity in supply, both wholesale and retail, not unlike those first captured systematically (for us) by the earliest comprehensive fiscal *Defter* for 15th-century Serres, which itself continued to be an important provincial city.[136]

The economic census of the province of Serres for the *city* of Serres in the year 1478 records seventeen distinct groups of artisans and specialist retailers in textiles and fibres, from silk to rope;[137] and thirteen distinct groups of artisans and retailers in leather and leather goods.[138] More generally, it records about 130 groups of artisans and retailers in the city.[139] Probably a 'confessional' multiplier-effect raises the total number of groups involved (since there are Muslim groups and Christian groups of many a given specialist). But much of the numerical total will reflect that other parameter of specialisation to which we have been referring, namely differentiation on quality and price (which is clear throughout the wider Byzantine archaeological record), rather than representing people making or purveying 'more of the same'. So, the 30 types of maker and dealer in textiles and fibres, leather and leather goods, provide, I suggest, just one of several opportunities for a 'mitigated' correlation of the synthesised Medieval Byzantine evidence with Early Ottoman evidence for artisanal and retailer specialisation in specific urban markets, which would inform further discussion of the models of the 'under-development' of Medieval Byzantine markets that are on offer.

CONCLUSION

As a working conclusion then, in thinking about Medieval Byzantine provincial urban markets as a whole, there are already reasons for 'de-dramatising' the narrative of their steady 'conquest' by Western merchants and craftsmen, and for historians and archaeologists to work together towards a more multi-faceted model. This is partly achievable by characterisations of long-term regional environmental and socio-economic frameworks of production; partly by characterisations of the material cultural 'horizons' or expectations of consumers that are being revealed by archaeology; and partly by emphasising the range of dispersed, semi-professional and professional production for provincial markets, which, in different but complementary ways, the progress of Middle Byzantine and Late Byzantine urban archaeology and essentially 'rural' archival publications, also reveals.[140]

But it is helped too by the ways in which the survival of Early Ottoman province-wide records for urban (and some rural) markets, and urban and rural artisanal production, reveals topographically widely dispersed production for markets, and specific economic practices, terminology, and historical references to continuity of organisation, which reflect, clarify, or complement unevenly preserved Late Byzantine evidence. They also reveal suppliers such as provincial mercantile middlemen connecting villages and towns whose Byzantine predecessors require much more research. They therefore still invite us to propose more complex, specialising, and wide-ranging levels of provision in Medieval Byzantine provincial markets than the minimalist and pessimistic assumptions would allow (however important self-supply surely was).[141]

Syntheses of the ranges of artefacts and artisans to be found in specific important Medieval Byzantine towns such as Thessaloniki already offer a corrective point of reference and 'bridge', I suggest, towards the levels of specialisation only captured *systematically* for us in the first fiscal *Defters*.[142] What Western producers and merchants brought was a relatively increasing degree of professionalisation in specific crafts such as textile- and glass-production from the 13th century onwards, for which there was surely room, commercially, within an economy and market that were, over the long term, despite fluctuations (as in the mid 14th century), expanding.[143]

THESSALONIKI: RECORDS OF EXPORTED PRODUCTS					
	13TH C.	14TH C.	15TH C.	16TH C.	17TH C.
Cotton		■	■		■
Wax		■			
Grain	■	■			■
Silk	■	■			■
Silver			■		
Luxuries		■			
Timber					■
Textiles					■
Tanned leather					
Hides			■		
Wool			■		
Iron					■
Fish					■
Wine					■

TABLE 1 – Thessaloniki: Records of exported products (Archibald Dunn).

MONEMVASIA	
PRODUCTS AND/OR ITEMS OF EXTERNAL TRADE (14TH CENTURY)	
Livestock	Wine
Salted meat	Olive oil
Hides	Raw silk
Felt	Kermes
Linseed	Acorns
Fish	Fruits

TABLE 2 – Monemvasia: Products and/or items of external trade in the 14th century (Archibald Dunn).

KRYSOUPOLIS AND THE STRYMON DELTA EXPORTS	
MID-BYZANTINE TO EARLY OTTOMAN	LATE OTTOMAN (18TH-19TH CENTURY)
Grain	Wheat, barley
Salt	Salt
?	Linseed
Flax	Raw cotton
Textiles (16th century)	Cotton cloth
Hides (16th century)	Raw cattle hides, tanned hides, sheepskins, goatskins, rabbit skins
?	Wool
?	Silk
Salted fish?	
?	'Animals'
?	Raw suet
?	Honey
?	Wax
?	Timber
?	Firewood
?	Charcoal
?	Materia medica
x	Maize
x	Tobacco

TABLE 3 – Khrysoupolis and the Strymon Delta: Records of exports (Archibald Dunn).

NOTES

1. Gerolymatou 2008, 115-16.
2. Bouras 2002, 512-13; *Idem* 2017, 123-24; Gerolymatou 2008, 270-73; Matschke 2002b, 778-79.
3. Laiou 2002c, 747.
4. Laiou 2012.
5. Oikonomidès 1979.
6. Laiou 2002c, 723-24.
7. Koder 1993; Lefort 1998; Mango 2000; Kislinger 2007; Jacoby 2010; Matschke 2010.
8. Matschke 1989; Laiou 1995; Harvey 2000; Jacoby 2003; Bakirtzis 2007.
9. Kalligas 2002; Dunn 2009.
10. Laiou 2002a; Laiou and Morrisson 2007.
11. Jacoby 1979; 1989; 1997; 2001; 2005; 2009; 2014; 2018.
12. Dunn 2005a.
13. Dunn 2007, 104-105.
14. Vryonis 1971, 6-24.
15. Vryonis 1971, 12, 13.
16. Vryzonis 1971, 24.
17. Kazhdan 1997, 56.
18. Laiou 2002c, 730-31; see also Gerolymatou 2008, 266-70.
19. Kazhdan and Constable 1982, 57; Svoronos 1976.
20. Dunn 2007, 106-109.
21. Dunn 2005b, ch.2; *Idem* forthcoming b.
22. Dunn 1992, 240-42; Rackham and Moody 1996; Grove and Rackham 2001.
23. Dunn 1992.
24. Harvey 1989, ch. 4-6.
25. Harvey 1989, 142, 131.
26. Harvey 1989, 141-42, 148.
27. Lefort 2006b (2nd edition of article 1rst published in 1991); Lefort 2002, 265, 305.
28. Kaplan 1992, 71-72, 565-67.
29. Kaplan 1988; Kaplan 1992, 493-573; Svoronos 1976.
30. Kaplan 1992, 505.
31. Harvey 1989, 152-53, 157.
32. Lefort 2002, 264.
33. Kondov 1977/3, 82-83.
34. Lefort 2002, 246.
35. Laiou 2002b, 347.
36. *The Book of the Eparch*, XVI.4.
37. Kondov 1977/3, 83-85.
38. Ferjančić 1993, 35-124; Ferjančić 1993, 97, 99, 104, 124.
39. *The Book of the Eparch*, XVI.2; Hendy 1985, 562-63.
40. Kaplan 1992, 343-45.
41. Lefort 2002, 246.
42. Lefort 2002, 256.
43. Kondov 1973/1, 67-76; Lefort 2002, 254.
44. Matschke 1980; Dagron 1993; Maniatis 2000.
45. *Kameniates*, v.11.
46. Dunn 2005b, 70-73.
47. *Megalê Ellênikê Enkyklopaideia*, 3, 798.
48. Dunn 2005b, 71-73.
49. Dunn forthcoming a.
50. Smyrlis 2006, 106, and 275: 'Carte 11. La région du Strymon aux XIIIe-XIVe siècles'.
51. *Actes de Lavra II*, no.104 (1317 AD), lines 16-180.
52. Lefort 2002, 263.
53. Shepard 2014, 426-27; Vryonis 1971, 17, n.18 for the salting of lacustrine fish.
54. Dunn 2005b, 69.
55. Dunn 2005b, 70-73.
56. Kaplan 1992, 343-45.

57 Kaplan 2005, 82-85.
58 Vryonis 1981, 203.
59 Vryonis 1981, 220, 223.
60 *History and Cartulary of the Great Monastery of St Elias and St Athanasius II,I*, no. IV (1049 AD), lines 377-79.
61 *Actes de Lavra I*, no.59 (1110 AD), lines 42-43.
62 Laiou 2002b, 348.
63 *The Book of the Eparch*, IX.1.
64 *Actes d'Iviron III*, no.58 (1259 AD), lines 67-68; *Actes de Xéropotamou*, no.18B (ca.1300 AD), line 56; *Actes d'Iviron III*, no.70 (1301 AD), lines 30, 155, 317 (twice), 323, 360; *Actes de Lavra II*, no.94 (1302 AD), lines 15-16; *Actes de Lavra II*, no.104 (1317 AD), line 167; *Actes de Lavra II*, no.105 (1317 AD), lines 4-5, 23; *Actes de Xénophon*, no.15 (1321 AD), line 24; *Actes de Lavra II*, no.111 (1321 AD), line 6; *Actes de Docheiariou*, no.19 (1338 AD), line 29; *Actes de Philothée*, no.9 (1346 AD), lines 69-70.
65 *Actes de Docheiariou*, no.15 (1315-1316 AD), lines 17-18; *Actes de Xénophon*, no.19 (1322-1323 AD), lines 14, 20, 32, 76.
66 *Actes de Docheiariou*, no.10 (1307 AD), line 55; *Actes d'Iviron III*, no.70 (1301 AD), line 233; *Actes d'Iviron III*, no.75 (1318 AD), line 358; *Actes d'Iviron III*, no.79 (1320 AD), line 344.
67 Thiriet 1961, vol.III, no.1204 (1406 AD), no.1340 (1409 AD).
68 Lefort 2006b (2nd edition of article 1st published in 1991), 261-62.
69 Jacoby 1991-1992, 478, 484.
70 Alexander 1985.
71 Alexander 1985, 264 (TD 34); 305, 317 (TD 367); 325 (TK 157); 370-71 (TD 367); 388 (TD 367); 237 (TD 424); 251-252; 56 (TD 25); 258 (TD 434); 259 (TD 307); 262 (TD 75).
72 Alexander 1985, 327 (TK 157); 360-62 (PFTA 35): some dyed, some presumably undyed, and some 'from abroad'.
73 Alexander 1985, 235 (TD 424).
74 Alexander 1985, 366 ('Kanunname of the Scales of the Morea').
75 Alexander 1985, 327 (TK 157).
76 *Lexikon zur byzantinischen Gräzität*, Cf./sub verbis βλαττίον, βλαττίτζιν and βλαττοπώλης (seller of vlattia).
77 Alexander 1985, 283 (TD 367).
78 Dunn 1992, 290-92; *Idem* 1996, 491-92.
79 Alexander 1985, 318 (TK 157); 327, 332; 324, 325 (TK 367); 341, 351 (the 'Carmine dye of Cephalonia').
80 Alexander 1985, 370 ('The Kanunname of the Scales of the Morea').
81 Alexander 1985, 361 ('The Kanunname of the Scales of the Morea').
82 Cvetkova 1970, 295-99.
83 Alexander 1985, 246.
84 Vroom 2020. I would like to thank Joanita Vroom for her guidance on this bibliography.
85 Alexander 1985, 370.
86 Lefort 2006b (2nd edition of article 1st published in 1991), 261-62.
87 Morrisson 2013, 783-91.
88 Dunn 1996, 486-596.
89 *Actes du Prôtaton*, no.8 (1045 AD), lines 57-62.
90 Laiou 2002b, 364; Lefort 2002, 253-54.
91 *Geoponica sive Cassiani Bassi de Re Rustica Eclogiae*; Laiou-Thomadakis 1977, 172; Koder 1993.
92 Lefort 2002, 254.

93 Laiou-Thomadakis 1977, 120-27; Lefort 2006b (2nd edition of article 1st published in 1991).
94 Harvey 1989, 142, 231; Laiou 2002b, 321; Lefort 2002a (2nd edition of article 1st published in 1986).
95 See note 29.
96 Nesbitt 1972; Laiou 2002b, 346-47.
97 Ogilvie 1920; Dunn 2005b, Map 2 'Chief vegetation divisions of Aegean Macedonia'.
98 Laiou 1995; Harvey 2000; Jacoby 2003; Bakirtzis 2007.
99 Dêmêtriadês 1980, 414-15, 416-18; Dunn 2005b, 62-63.
100 Roberts 1699, 33.
101 Matschke 1989; Laiou 1995; Harvey 2000; Jacoby 2003.
102 Coronelli 1687, 224; Dapper 1703, 347.
103 Laiou and Morrisson 2007, 55.
104 Kalligas 2002, 879-97; *Idem* 2010, 156-63; Dunn 1992, 287, 288-89.
105 Ogilvie 1920.
106 Dunn 2005b, ch.2; Dunn 1998; Dunn 2009.
107 *Actes de Lavra I*, no.59 (1110 AD).
108 *Actes de Lavra I*, no.59, lines 71-74.
109 *Actes de Lavra I*, no.59, lines 4-52, 75-78.
110 *Actes d'Iviron I*, no.4 (982 AD), lines 65-67 ('akhreia topia'); *Mega lexikon olês tês ellênikês glôssês*, vol.9, 7238 ('topiatiko').
111 Bouras 1974, 32-36; *Idem* 1981, 625-26; *Idem* 2017, 54-115 and Figures 24-64; see also for these Athenian pithoi, Vroom 2020, fig. 5 and tables 1a-b.
112 Bakirtzis 2007.
113 Dagron 2002, 395-96.
114 Matschke 2002a, 471.
115 Golofast 2008, 345-67.
116 Golofast 2008, 360, 348.
117 Rabinowitz, Sedikova and Hennenberg 2011.
118 *Actes d'Iviron I*, no.30 (ca. 1095-1100 AD), line 12; *Actes d'Iviron I*, no.28 (1047 AD), line 55; *Actes d'Iviron I*, *Idem*, line 21.
119 *Acta et diplomata graeca medii aevi sacra et profana*, vol.4, Lembiotissa ii (1235 AD), 12, line 23; *Actes d'Iviron III*, no.70 (1301 AD), lines 186-187.
120 *Actes de Vatopédi II*, no.107 (1356 AD), line 16.
121 *The Mediaeval Greek and Bulgarian documents of the Athonite monastery of Zographou*, Falsified Act no.7 (1378 AD), line 21; *Idem*, Falsified Act no.8 (1366-1378 AD), lines 17-18.
122 Dunn forthcoming b.
123 Ditchfield 2007, 397-99.
124 Ditchfield 2007, 401-403.
125 Ditchfield 2007, 403.
126 Jacoby 2000, 22-23.
127 Ditchfield 2007, 403-405, 409, 415-16.
128 Jacoby 1991-1992, 474-75.
129 Jacoby 1994; *Idem* 2000.
130 Alexander 1985, 360-61.
131 Laiou 2002c, 751-52.
132 Jacoby 1994; *Idem* 1991-1992, 462-92 and 478.
133 Koder 2016, 133-53.
134 Matschke 1989; Antonaras 2016, 79-80.
135 Laiou 1998.
136 Lowry 2008.
137 Lowry 2008, 191: Tables II and III.
138 Lowry 2008, 193, Tables V and VI.
139 Lowry 2008, 196-99, Table VIII.
140 Matschke 1989; Antonaras 2016, 89-92.
141 See notes 113-116.
142 Antonaras 2016, 89-92.
143 Abulafia 2011, 366-404.

BIBLIOGRAPHY

PRIMARY SOURCES

Acta et diplomata graeca medii aevi sacra et profana, ed. by F. Miklosich and J. Müller, 6 volumes, Vienna 1860-1890.

Actes de Lavra I: Première partie des origines à 1204, ed. by P. Lemerle, N. Svoronos and D. Papachryssanthou, Paris 1970.

Actes de Lavra II: De 1204 à 1328, ed. by P. Lemerle, N. Svoronos and D. Papachryssanthou, Paris 1977.

Actes de Dionysiou, ed. by N. Oikonomidès, Paris 1984.

Actes d'Iviron I: Des origines au milieu du XIe siècle, ed. by J. Lefort, N. Oikonomidès and D. Papachryssanthou, Paris 1985.

Actes d'Iviron II: Du milieu du XIe siècle à 1204, ed. by J. Lefort, N. Oikonomidès and D. Papachryssanthou, Paris 1990.

Actes d'Iviron III: De 1204 à 1328, ed. by J. Lefort, N. Oikonomidès, D. Papachryssanthou and V. Kravari, Paris 1994.

Actes de Philothée, ed. by W. Regel, E. Kurtz and B. Korablev, *Vizantiiskii Vremennik* 20, Appendix 1, 1913.

Actes du Prôtaton, ed. by D. Papachryssanthou, Paris 1975.

Actes de Vatopédi II: de 1330 à 1376, ed. by J. Lefort, V. Kravari, Ch. Giros and K. Smyrlis, Paris 2006.

Actes de Xénophon, ed. by D. Papachryssanthou, Paris 1986.

Actes de Xéropotamou, ed. by J. Bompaire, Paris 1964.

Book of the Eparch: Das Eparchenbuch Leons des Weisen, ed. by J. Koder, Vienna 1991.

Geoponica: Geoponica sive Cassiani Bassi De Re Rustica Eclogiae, ed. by O. Beckh, Leipzig 1897.

History and Cartulary of the Great Monastery of St Elias and St Anastasius II, 1. Cartulary, ed. by G. Robinson, Rome 1929.

Kameniates: Ioannis Cameniatae De Expugnatione Thessalonicae, ed. by G. Böhlig, Berlin 1973.

The Mediaeval Greek and Bulgarian Documents of the Athonite Monastery of Zographou (980—1600): Critical Edition and Commentary of the Texts (University Library No. 512), ed. by C. Pavlikianov, Sofia 2014.

Mega lexikon olês tês ellênikês glôssês [*Great Lexicon of the Whole Greek language*], ed. by D. Dêmêtrakos, 9 volumes, Athens 1953-1958.

LITERATURE

Abulafia, D. 2011. *The Great Sea: A Human History of the Mediterranean*, London.

Alexander, J. 1985. *Towards a History of Post-Byzantine Greece: The Ottoman Kanunnames for the Greek Lands, circa 1500-circa 1600*, Athens.

Antonaras, A. 2016a. *Arts, Crafts, and Trades in Ancient and Byzantine Thessaloniki: Archaeological, Literary and Epigraphic Evidence*, Mainz.

Antonaras, A. 2016b. Artisanal production in Byzantine Thessaloniki (4th-15th century), in: F. Daim and J. Drauschke (eds.), *Hinter den Mauern und auf dem offenen Land. Leben im Byzantinischen Reich*, Mainz, 113-40.

Bakirtzis, Ch. 2007. Imports, exports and autarchy in Byzantine Thessalonike from the seventh to the tenth century, in: J. Henning (ed.), *Post-Roman Towns, Trade and Settlement in Europe and Byzantium*, Berlin & New York, 89-118.

Bouras, Ch. 1974. Katoikies kai oikismoi stê vyzantinê Ellada [Houses and settlements in Byzantine Greece], in: O. Doumanis and P. Oliver (eds.), *Oikismoi stên Ellada [Shelter in Greece]*, Athens, 30-52.

Bouras, Ch. 1981. City and village: Urban design and architecture, in: *Akten. XVI Internationaler Byzantinistenkongress 1,2*, Vienna, 611-53.

Bouras, Ch. 2002. Aspects of the Byzantine city, eighth – fifteenth centuries, in: A. Laiou (ed.), *The Economic History of Byzantium from the Seventh Through the Fifteenth Century, Vol. 2*, Dumbarton Oaks, 497-528.

Bouras, Ch. 2017. *Byzantine Athens, 10th-12th centuries*, London.

Coronelli, P. 1687. *An Historical and Geographical Account of the Morea and the Maritime Places as far as Thessalonica*, London.

Cvetkova, B. 1970. Vie économique des villes et ports balkaniques aux XVe et XVIe siècles, *Revue des Études Islamiques* 38.2, 267-356.

Dagron, G. 1993. Poissons, pêcheurs et poissonniers de Constantinople, in: C. Mango and G. Dagron (eds.), *Constantinople and its Hinterlands: Papers from the Twenty-seventh Spring Symposium of Byzantine Studies, Oxford*, Aldershot, 57-73.

Dagron, G. 2002. The urban economy, seventh – twelfth centuries, in: A. Laiou (ed.), *The Economic History of Byzantium from the Seventh Through the Fifteenth Century, Vol. 2*, Dumbarton Oaks, 393-461.

Dapper, O. 1703. *Description exacte des isles de l'archipel et de quelques autres adjacentes*, Amsterdam.

Dêmêtriadês, V. 1980. Phorologikes katêgories tôn khôriôn tês Thessalonikês [Taxational categories of the villages subject to Thessaloniki], *Makedonika* 20, 375-462.

Ditchfield, Ph. 2007. *La culture matérielle médiévale. L'Italie méridionale byzantine et normande*, Rome.

Dunn, A. 1992. The exploitation and control of woodland and scrubland in the Byzantine world, *Byzantine and Modern Greek Studies* 16, 235-98.

Dunn, A. 1996. The control and exploitation of the arboreal resources of the Late Byzantine and Frankish Aegean region, in: S. Covaciocchi (ed.), *L'uomo e la foresta secc. XIII-XVIII. Atti della 'ventisettesima settimana di studi'*, Istituto internazionale di storia economica F. Datini, Florence, 479-97.

Dunn, A. 1998. Loci of maritime traffic in the Strymon Delta (IV-XVIII cc.): Commercial, fiscal, and manorial, in: Demos Serrôn, *Oi Serres kai ê periokhê tous apo tên arkhaia stê metavyzantinê koinônia. Diethnes Synedrio* [Community of Serres, Serres and its Region from Ancient to Post-Byzantine Society. International Congress], Vol. 1, Serres, 339-60.

Dunn, A. 2005a. Review of: A. Laiou (ed.), *The Economic History of Byzantium from the Seventh Through the Fifteenth Century*, 3 Volumes, Dumbarton Oaks, 2002, in: *Speculum* 80.2, 616-21.

Dunn, A. 2005b. The Interaction of Secular Public Institutions and Provincial Communities in the Political and Economic Spheres in Late Antique Aegean Macedonia, *unpublished* doctoral thesis, University of Birmingham.

Dunn, A. 2007. Rural producers and markets: aspects of the archaeological and historical problem, in: M. Grünbart, E. Kislinger and A. Muthesius (eds.), *Material Culture and Wellbeing in Byzantium (400-1453)*, Vienna, 101-109.

Dunn, A. 2009. Byzantine and Ottoman maritime traffic in the estuary of the Strymon: Between environment, state and market, in: J. Bintliff and H. Stöger (eds.), *Medieval and Post-Medieval Greece. The Corfu Papers,* BAR International Series 2023, Oxford, 15-31.

Dunn, A. forthcoming-a. The control and exploitation of the resources on the Aegean and Ionian littorals in the Middle and Late Byzantine era [article commissioned for conference].

Dunn, A. forthcoming-b. The management of the *incultum* in Byzantine Macedonia: The archives and the comparative perspective, *Proceedings of the 53rd Spring Symposium of Byzantine Studies, University of Birmingham, 2021.*

Ferjančić, B. 1993. Stočarstvo na posedima svetogorskikh manastira u srednjem veku [Animal husbandry on the estates of the Athonite monasteries in the Middle Ages], *Sbornik Radova Vizantološkog Instituta* [Recueil des Travaux de l'Institut d'Études Byzantines] 32, 35-124.

Gerolymatou, M. 2008. *Agores kai emporio sto Vyzantio (9os-12os ai.)* [Markets and Trade in Byzantium (9th-12th centuries)], Athens.

Golofast, L. 2008. Remesla i promisli Khersona v XIII v. (po nakhodkam iz sloya požara) [Crafts and trades in Cherson in the 13th century (on evidence of finds from [the] fire layer)], *Materialij po Arkheologii, Istorii, i Etnografii Tavrii* [*Materials Concerning the Archaeology, History and Ethnography of Tauris*] 14, 345-84.

Grove, A. and O. Rackham 2001. *The Nature of Mediterranean Europe. An Ecological History*, Yale.

Harvey, A. 1989. *Economic Expansion in the Byzantine Empire 900-1200*, Cambridge.

Harvey, A. 2000. Economic conditions in Thessaloniki between the two Ottoman occupations, in: A. Cowan (ed.), *Mediterranean Urban Culture, 1400-1700*, Exeter, 118-21.

Hendy, M. 1985. *Studies in the Byzantine Monetary Economy, c. 300-1450*, Cambridge.

Jacoby, D. 1979. *Recherches sur la Méditerranée orientale du XII au XV siècle: peuples, sociétés, économies*, Aldershot.

Jacoby, D. 1991-1992. Silk in western Byzantium before the Fourth Crusade, *Byzantinische Zeitschrift* 84-85, 452-500.

Jacoby, 1994. Silk production in the Frankish Peloponnese, in: H.Kalligas (ed.), *Travellers and Officials in the Peloponnese: Descriptions – Reports – Statistics*, Monemvasia, 41-61.

Jacoby, D. 1997. *Trade, Commodities and Shipping in the Medieval Mediterranean*, Aldershot.

Jacoby, D. 2000. The production of silk textiles in Latin Greece, in: *Tekhnognôsia stê latinokratoumenê Ellada* [*Technological Knowledge in Western-controlled [Medieval] Greece*], Athens, 22-35.

Jacoby, D. 2001. *Byzantium, Latin Romania and the Mediterranean*, Aldershot.

Jacoby, D. 2003. Foreigners and the urban economy in Thessalonike, c. 1150-c. 1450, *Dumbarton Oaks Papers* 57, 85-132.

Jacoby, D. 2005. *Commercial Exchange Across the Mediterranean: Byzantium, the Crusader Levant, Egypt and Italy*, Aldershot.

Jacoby, D. 2009. *Latins, Greeks and Muslims: Encounters in the Eastern Mediterranean, 10th-15th centuries*, Aldershot.

Jacoby, D. 2010. Mediterranean food and wine for Constantinople: the long-distance trade, eleventh to mid fifteenth century in: E. Kislinger, J. Koder and A. Külzer (eds.), *Handelsgüter und Verkehrswege. Aspekte der Warenversorgung im östlichen Mittelmeerraum (4. bis 15. Jahrhundert)*, Vienna, 127-47.

Jacoby, D. 2014. *Travellers, Merchants and Settlers in the Eastern Mediterranean, 11th-14th centuries*, Aldershot.

Jacoby, D. 2018. *Medieval Trade in the Eastern Mediterranean and Beyond*, London.

Kalligas, H. 2002. Monemvasia, seventh – fifteenth centuries, in: A. Laiou (ed.), *The Economic History of Byzantium from the Seventh Through the Fifteenth Century, Vol. 2*, Dumbarton Oaks, 879-97.

Kalligas, H. 2010. *Monemvasia: A Byzantine City State*, London.

Kaplan, M. 1988. Pour un modèle économique de l'exploitation agricole byzantine. Problèmes de méthode et premiers résultats, *Histoire et Mesure* 3, 221-34.

Kaplan, M. 1992. *Les hommes et la terre à Byzance du VIe au XIe siècle. Propriété et exploitation du sol*, Paris.

Kazhdan, A. and G. Constable. 1982. *People and Power in Byzantium. An Introduction to Modern Byzantine Studies*, Dumbarton Oaks.

Kazhdan, A. 1997. The peasantry, in: Guglielmo Cavallo (ed.), *The Byzantines*, Chicago, 43-73.

Kislinger, E. 2007. Lebensmittel im Konstantinopel. Notizen zu den einschlägigen Marktorter der Stadt, in: K. Belke, E. Kislinger, A. Külzer and M. Stassinopoulou (eds.), *Byzantina Mediterranea. Festschrift für Johannes Koder zum 65. Geburtstag*, Vienna, Cologne & Weimar, 303-18.

Kondov, N. 1973. Produktionsorganisatorische Verschiebungen bei dem Weinbau in der ersten Hälfte des XIV. Jahrhunderts im Gebiet des unteren Strymons, Études Balkaniques 9.1, 67-76.

Kondov, N. 1977. Das Dorf Gradec II. Die demographisch-wirtschaftliche Gestalt eines Dorfes aus dem Gebiet des unteren Strymons vom Anfang des 14. Jahrhunderts, Études Balkaniques 13.3, 71-91.

Laiou-Thomadakis, A. 1977. *Peasant Society in the Late Byzantine Empire: A Social and Demographic Study*, Princeton, NJ.

Laiou, A. 1995. Thessalonikê, ê endokhôra kai o oikonomikos tês khôros stên epokhê tôn Palaiologôn [Thessaloniki, its hinterland, and its economic space in the Palaeologan period], in: Society of Macedonian Studies, *Diethnes Symposio. Vyzantinê Makedonia 324-1430 m. Kh.* [*International Symposium. Byzantine Macedonia 324-1430 AD*], Thessaloniki, 183-94.

Laiou, A. 1998. Koinônikes dynameis stis Serres sto 14o aiôna [Social forces in Serres in the 14th century], in: Dêmos Serrôn, *Oi Serres kai ê periokhê tous apo tên arkhaia stê metavyzantinê koinonia. Diethnes Synedrio* [Community of Serres, *Serres and its region from Ancient to Post-Byzantine society*], Vol. 1, Serres, 203-19.

Laiou, A. 2002a. (ed.), *The Economic History of Byzantium from the Seventh Through the Fifteenth Century*, 3 volumes, Dumbarton Oaks.

Laiou, A. 2002b. The agrarian economy, thirteenth – fourteenth centuries, in: A. Laiou (ed.), *The Economic History of Byzantium from the Seventh Through the Fifteenth Century, Vol. 1*, Dumbarton Oaks, 311-75.

Laiou, A. 2002c. Exchange and trade, seventh – twelfth centuries, in: A. Laiou (ed.), *The Economic History of Byzantium from the Seventh Through the Fifteenth Century, Vol. 2*, Dumbarton Oaks, 697-770.

Laiou, A. 2007. Regional networks in the Balkans in the Middle and Late Byzantine periods, in: C. Morrisson (ed.), *Trade and Markets in Byzantium*, Dumbarton Oaks, 125-46.

Laiou, A. and C. Morrisson. 2007. *The Byzantine Economy*, Cambridge.

Lexikon zur byzantinischen Gräzität besonders des 9.-12. Jahrhunderts, ed. by E. Trapp, 8 Fascicles, Vienna, 2001-2017.

Lefort, J. 1998. Le coût des transports à Constantinople, portefaix et bateliers au xve siècle, in: ΕΥΨΥΧΙΑ. Mélanges offerts à Hélène Ahrweiler, Vol. 2, Paris, 413-25.

Lefort, J. 2002. The rural economy, seventh – twelfth centuries, in: A. Laiou (ed.), *The Economic History of Byzantium from the Seventh Through the Fifteenth Century, Vol. 1*, Dumbarton Oaks, 231-310.

Lefort, J. 2006²a. Une exploitation de taille moyenne au xiiie siècle en Chalcidique, in: J. Lefort (ed.), *Société rurale et histoire du paysage à Byzance*, Paris, 201-209 [2nd edition of article, 1st ed. published in 1986].

Lefort, J. 2006²b. Anthroponymie et société villageoise (xe-xix siècle), in: J. Lefort (ed.), *Société et histoire du paysage à Byzance*, Paris, 249-263 [2nd edition of article, 1st ed. published in 1991].

Lowry, H. 2008. *The Shaping of the Ottoman Balkans, 1350-1550: The Conquest, Settlement and Infrastructural Development of Northern Greece*, Bahçeşehir.

Mango, M. 2000. The commercial map of Constantinople, *Dumbarton Oaks Papers* 54, 189-209.

Maniatis, G. 2000. The organizational setup and functioning of the fish market in tenth-century Constantinople, *Dumbarton Oaks Papers* 54, 13-42.

Matschke, K.-P. 1980. Situation, Organisation und Aktion der Fischer von Konstantinopel und Umgebung in der byzantinischen Spätzeit, *Byzantinobulgarica* 6, 281-98.

Matschke, K.-P. 1989. Tuchproduktion und Tuchproduzenten in Thessalonike und in anderen Städten und Regionen des späten Byzanz, *Vyzantiaka* 9, 68-84.

Matschke, K.-P. 2002a. The Late Byzantine urban economy, thirteenth – fifteenth centuries, in: A. Laiou (ed.), *The Economic History of Byzantium from the Seventh Through the Fifteenth Century, Vol. 2*, Dumbarton Oaks, 463-95.

Matschke, K.-P. 2002b. Commerce, trade, markets and money, thirteenth – fifteenth centuries, in: A. Laiou (ed.), *The Economic History of Byzantium from the Seventh Through the Fifteenth Century, Vol. 2*, Dumbarton Oaks, 771-806.

Matschke, K.-P. 2010. Rechtliche und administrative Organisation der Warenversorgung im Byzantinischen Raum: die Strukturen der 13. bis 15. Jahrhunderts, in: E. Kislinger, J. Koder and A. Külzer (eds.), *Handelsgüter und Verkehrswege. Aspekte der Warenversorgung im östlichen Mittelmeerraum (4. bis 15. Jahrhundert)*, Vienna, 205-21.

Megalê Ellênikê Enkyklopaideia [*Great Hellenic Encyclopaedia*], ed. by P. Drandakês, 28 Volumes, Athens, 1957.

Morrisson, C. 2013. Feu et combustible dans l'économie byzantine, in: Fondazione Centro italiano di studi sull' alto medioevo, *Il fuoco nell' alto medioevo. Settimane di Studio LX*, Spoleto, 777-803.

Nesbitt, J. 1972. Mechanisms of Agricultural Production on Estates of the Byzantine Praktika, *unpublished* doctoral thesis, University of Wisconsin.

Ogilvie, A. 1920. A contribution to the geography of Macedonia, *The Geographical Journal* 55/1, 1-34.

Oikonomidès, N. 1979. *Hommes d'affaires grecs et latins à Constantinople (XIIIe-XIVe siècles)*, Montreal.

Rabinowitz, A., L. Sedikova and L. Hennenberg 2011. Daily life in a provincial Late Byzantine city: recent multidisciplinary research in the South Region of Tauric Chersonesos, in: F. Daim and J. Drauschke (eds.), *Byzanz – Das Römerreich im Mittelalter. Teil 2,1 Schauplätze*, Mainz, 425-78.

Rackham, O. and J. Moody. 1996. *The Making of the Cretan Landscape*, Manchester.

Roberts, Mr. 1699. *Mr Roberts' adventures among the corsairs of the Levant; His account of their way of living; description of the Archipelago islands, taking of Scio, & c.*, in: W. Hacke (ed.), *A Collection of Original Voyages*, London.

Shepard, J. 2014. 'Mists and portals': The Black Sea's north coast, in: M. Mango (ed.), *Byzantine Trade, 4th-12th Centuries: The Archaeology of Local, Regional, and International Exchange*, Farnham, 421-41.

Svoronos, N. 1976. Remarques sur les structures économiques de l'empire byzantin au XIe siècle, *Travaux et Mémoires* 6, 49-67.

Thiriet, F. 1958-1961. *Régestes des délibérations du Sénat de Venise concernant la Romanie*, 3 volumes, Paris & The Hague.

Vroom, J. 2020. Eating in Aegean lands (ca 700-1500): Perspectives on pottery, in: S.Y. Waksman (ed.), *Multidisciplinary Approaches to Food and Foodways in the Medieval Eastern Mediterranean*, Archéologie(s) 4, Lyon, 275-93.

Vryonis, S. 1971. *The Decline of Medieval Hellenism in Asia Minor and the Process of Islamization from the Eleventh Through the Fifteenth Century*, Berkeley.

Vryonis, S. 1981. The Panēgyris of the Byzantine saint: a study in the nature of a medieval institution, its origins and fate, in: S. Hackel (ed.), *The Byzantine Saint: University of Birmingham. Fourteenth Spring Symposium of Byzantine Studies*, The Fellowship of St Alban and St Sergius, London, 196-227.

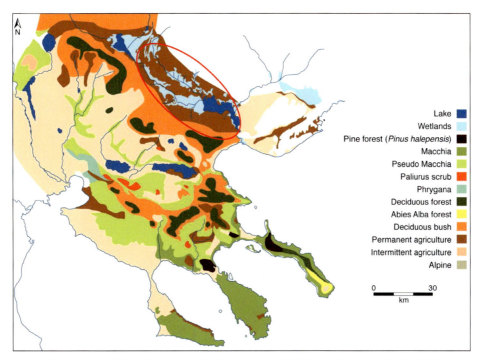

FIG. 1 – South-eastern Macedonia (part): Lakes and wetlands (fisheries) *ca.* 1900 (Archibald Dunn).

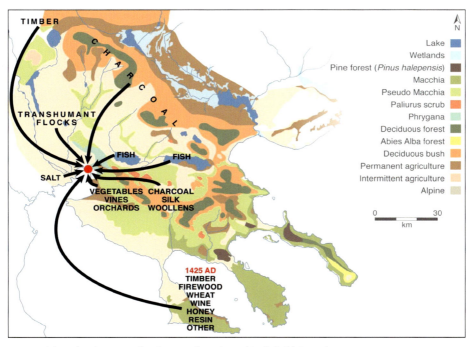

FIG. 2 – Thessaloniki: Records of regional products (Archibald Dunn).

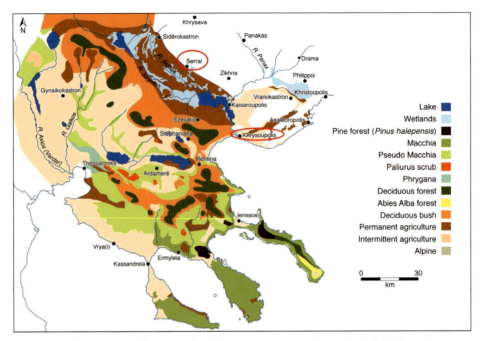

FIG. 3 – South-eastern Macedonia: Medieval Byzantine towns and cities (Archibald Dunn).

* * *

EARLY BYZANTINE &

MIDDLE BYZANTINE PERIODS

* * *

Slip-painted Ware dish of Middle Byzantine times (after J. Vroom 2014², *Byzantine to Modern Pottery in the Aegean – An Introduction and Field Guide, Second & Revised Edition*, Turnhout, 80, fig. MBYZ 6.2).

* * *

Caričin Grad (Justiniana Prima) as a market: Searching for an Early Byzantine model of pottery production and consumption

Vesna Bikić

*

INTRODUCTION

In order to reconstruct everyday life in the Byzantine city, archaeology gradually has shifted its focus from the analyses of objects and their spatial distribution to the wider study of political and socio-economic patterns. The past decades showed in particular significant advances in Late Roman archaeology, which thus became a sort of testing ground for various theoretical models addressing the organisation of different activities and the nature of socio-economic developments. The study of pottery production, distribution, and functional analyses has proved to be of huge importance for these models. In this respect, pottery consumption should be seen as resulting from the choices driven by many factors, including tradition, fashion, market demands, and social and cultural identities.[1]

Previous contextual analyses underlined the important role of production and distribution for the study of pottery consumption, and its theoretical and disciplinary developments drew from the research of urban centres, as was the case at Sagalassos in south-western Turkey.[2] A number of major surveys conducted in other regions of the Mediterranean yielded material that persuasively testified to the processes of renewal during Early Byzantine times, i.e. the 6th and the early 7th centuries, including ceramic production trends and consumption patterns.[3]

The archaeological evidence from the Balkans is similar. Owing to their cultural and economic histories, towns in the vast Prefecture of Illyricum (including mostly the area along the eastern coast of the Adriatic Sea and its inland mountains, with its Dioceses of Dacia and Macedonia stretching from the Danube to the Peloponnese) were different in size and structure.[4] These towns are all well-known from the written sources, but among them Caričin Grad stands out for its archaeological values because of its well-studied urban plan and architecture, its narrow chronology and its indicative contexts containing reference pottery assemblages. Hence, the case study of Caričin Grad should provide parameters for creating a wider model of pottery production and consumption behaviour in the Early Byzantine city.

THE CITY

Caričin Grad is situated in the province of Dacia Mediterranea, close to its border with Dardania (in the central Balkans). It was founded *ex nihilo* around the year 530, in an isolated area away from the main communication routes, but still with good access to the road system. It was located almost half way between Naissus and Scupi; main roads led from these cities either north to the Danube border or south to Macedonia.[5] The city is believed to be the site of Justiniana Prima, founded by Emperor Justinian I (527-565) near the village of his birth, Taurision. Due to the intrusions of the Gepids, the Kutrigurs and especially the Slavs in North Illyricum the Emperor's intention to transfer the seat of the Praetorian Prefect of Illyricum from Thessalonica to Justiniana Prima, announced in Novel II of the Codex Justinianus,[6] was not fulfilled. Justiniana Prima remained primarily the ecclesiastical administration centre of the Dacian Diocese, and a military city. Judging by the latest coin-find, Caričin Grad was abandoned ca. 615 or shortly afterwards.[7] In line with this, Justiniana Prima disappeared from the historical records already after the end of the pontificate of Gregory the Great (590-604).

The layout of the city shows classical traditions and Early Byzantine innovations. The urban area was divided into several fortified quarters, each with its own plan. The Acropolis was a sacral complex with the cathedral, baptistery and administrative buildings. The Upper Town was the seat of the military administration, whereas the Lower Town accommodated public facilities, among which several basilicas, the cistern and baths, and a residential quarter with small workshops and private houses (Fig. 1).[8] On the slopes around the city, large suburbs were built, encircled by defensive ditches, opus mixtum and dry-stone walls, earth ramparts, and wooden palisades. Following the ideas of Julian of Ascalon, brought together into the so-called 'Urban Treatise' by the middle of the 6th century,[9] the main workshop area, where brick kilns and a melting furnace were found, was situated at the foothill of the city, where two rivulets came together (see in Fig. 1 the yellow circle on the right).

In the course of its 80 year-long life-span, extending from the time of Emperor Justinian I (483-565) to the second decade of the 7th century, Caričin Grad underwent three stages of development: its establishment, its prosperity, and finally its decline.[10] The transformation of its urban matrix and the de-urbanisation processes was illustrated by the excavated pottery assemblages, comprising vessels with distinct typological features and formal attributes.[11] The differences enabled a thorough study of pottery from Caričin Grad in the context of Early Byzantine production trends, and made it possible for me to determine the consumption matrix and to analyse it in relation to the socio-political realities of that time.

THE MAIN FEATURES OF LOCALLY MADE POTTERY

Due to its clearly defined context (with a chronology lasting no more than around 80 years) and the vessel amount, the ceramic finds from Caričin Grad became an important reference assemblage in the study of Early Byzantine pottery in the Mediterranean.[12] This assemblage appeared to be uniform in fabric, colour, dimensions and shapes, but showed variations with respect to the vessels' function. All the pottery types were made in a similar looking fabric, compositionally corresponding to lithological units in the local area, and thus strongly indicating that their production was organised in the immediate city surroundings.[13] In fact, a relatively fine fabric with fine inclusions of sand and mica was characteristic for all the pottery types found in the city, although firing procedures for the various types were different as they were often closely related to the vessels' function.[14]

For this reason, pottery from Caričin Grad can be described as being of a standardised category, with respect to its technological and its formal features. Its specific style follows trends that were common in Early Byzantine pottery, but the overall character is quite regional, with a representative selection of cooking pots and glazed jugs. The reconstruction of the pottery production process clearly points to intentional standardisation, conscientiously controlled by the craftsmen. This is best testified to by the use of particular raw materials for specific purposes, the techniques used to form vessels and the application of glazes and pottery firing procedures, as well as by the morphology, which is related to vessel function and size, and in some cases by the type of decoration and the selection of motifs.

The pottery assemblage comprises all functional classes of vessels: not only cookware, storage ware, and tableware, but also open and closed cooking forms are both represented (Figs. 2a-b, nos.1-6,7). Cooking pots were made on the potter's wheel. They have all the same dimensions/volume, and in most cases they have relatively thin, symmetrical walls. Furthermore, in contrast to other Balkan sites, Caričin Grad produced a number of baking covers, also known as 'bells' or *clibani* for baking bread or buns (Figs. 2a-b, no. 7).

Nearly all the city quarters yielded storage containers, or pithoi.[15] They were found *in situ*, put in holes dug into the earthen floors, as it is in the '*maison* aux *pithoi*' on the Acropolis (Figs. 3a-b), in a building in the western part of the Lower Town (Sector 5), and in building 15c at the Upper Town's northern plateau.[16]

In addition to morphology, other features are uniform as well (Fig. 4). This is most evident in the thick walls of the containers, made of clay with inclusions of sand, mica, and occasionally gravel. Except for large storage vessels, houses primarily used 'pithoid'-looking pots in which small quantities of food were kept. These are similar to cooking pots, but larger in volume; many of them were even partially covered with an olive green glaze.

The tableware is typologically quite diverse, especially the jugs and ewers (Figs. 5a-b). Open forms occur sporadically, represented by only a few types of bowls. Although their fabric looks similar to the cooking pot' fabric, some vessels have a more compact fracture and are biscuit-fired red. Most of the tableware is glazed in olive green, yellow or brown; the lead glaze is transparent and is applied directly to the vessel surface. Certain regularity in the correlation between the vessel function and the thickness of the glaze can be observed: the tableware has thick glaze coatings, but the majority of the pithoid-looking pots have thinner ones.

Handmade pots also appear at Caričin Grad (Figs. 6a-b), but mainly in contexts pre-dating the final destruction of the city. These vessels are made of clay, with a lot of coarse non-plastic inclusions, sand and gravel. As opposed to the distinctive brown-, red- and grey-fired colours of wheel-thrown cooking pots, handmade vessels are of an uneven colour, often dullish brown and grey-brown, which indicate firing in a reducing atmosphere with lower temperatures.

CARIČIN GRAD ON THE POTTERY DISTRIBUTION MAP

The analyses done so far support the view that the region of Central Illyrycum and Caričin Grad as its most important centre have an important place in the distribution map of pottery types indicative of considering flows of supply of basic commodities and trade of luxurious items during the 6th century (Fig. 7).[17] Although overall low, the percentage of imported pottery in the Caričin Grad assemblage (some 3 percent) is still considerably higher in comparison to other sites in North Illyricum (1 percent).[18] This group comprises products of two functional classes: food transport containers (i.e. amphorae) and tableware. The most frequently found vessels of the first group are *spatheia* from North Africa (Fig. 8, nos. 1, 2) and examples of the Late Roman Amphora 2, followed by those of the Late Roman Amphora 1 and the Late Roman Amphora 4.[19] These last ones were frequently used to transport olive oil and wine, that is to say: bulk goods.[20] Locally made amphorae were also found at Caričin Grad, but in much smaller numbers. Yet, given the wine-growing traditions of the Leskovac Valley,[21] their presence can be explained in the context of local trade and regional wine supply patterns. Orders for the import of tableware were restricted to a few products only: African Red Slip Ware (ARS) from North Africa and, to a significantly lesser extent, Late Roman C from Asia Minor/modern Turkey (Fig. 8, nos. 3-5).[22]

Also indicative is the distribution of the finds within particular spatial units. Amphorae have been found throughout the city, with the highest concentration in buildings in the northern part of the Lower Town. The finds of imported tableware provide an entirely different picture at Caričin Grad. While in the Upper Town only six different red slip wares have been recovered, some 30 finds came from the Lower Town, almost all of them African Red Slip Ware plates.[23] These types of transport vessels and tableware are 6th-century trade markers. Large quantities of amphorae on Early Byzantine sites are a genuine testimony of the important role of the *annona militaris* and the *annona civica*[24] in the economy of that time.[25] The evidence from Caričin Grad shows the city's active role in the supply system of Byzantium. The imported tableware originates, for instance, from workshops in North Africa and Asia Minor. The origins of the traded goods and the imported pottery are not uncommon at 6th-century sites (including those from Central Illyricum),[26] while locally made amphorae prove on the other hand the existence of a local market. The ceramic markers of regional and long-distance trade finally show that Caričin Grad was well connected with other regional centres by way of important transit routes and a local road network.[27]

THE SOCIO-ECONOMIC CONTEXT OF THE POTTERY

All these aspects refer to certain socio-political consequences of the reciprocity between pottery demand and production in this Illirian city.[28] Due to the political background of its establishment and its general economic, architectural and settlement features, Caričin Grad can be seen as an urban role model of this era, and by all means as a representative case study for such issues.

The above described features, and above all the uniformity across various functional classes, made me think that pottery specialists were involved in setting up the production of ceramics at Caričin Grad. This was in particular the case during the first two construction phases of the city. Regrettably, the exact location of the workshops has not been found yet, but I would like to suggest that they were probably situated on the bank of the Svinjarička Rivulet, near the brick kilns.[29]

Nevertheless, the pottery itself also provides certain clues about the organisation of this production. The assemblage presented here reveals clear technological choices (bearing in mind some previously studied examples from that time[30]): pottery production at Caričin Grad was most likely organised within a complex of several separate units, working together on a high level. Even if this assumption is not speculative, we still lack field data. However, one should keep in mind that on-going surveys at Caričin Grad (including archaeopedological and archaeogeological analyses) focus precisely on the study of the resources and the organisation of different crafts within the city area.[31]

Judging by already established parameters of pottery use and consumption, ceramic production at Caričin Grad may have been organised according to some of earlier suggested models, particularly those of C. L. Costin (*nucleated workshops*)[32] and K. Sinopoli (*centralized production*).[33] When combined together, this new model defines specialised production in a workshop complex, organised primarily for one particular community, but with unconstrained regional consumption. The system of market, supply and demand was of crucial importance for such workshop organisation, but also for selecting products and their distribution; lastly, state administration had a significant impact on these processes. This new (combined) model of production organisation can be applied to the total period of Late Antiquity, when the state's involvement in all life spheres was so substantial that it affected not only the monumental building projects, the large estate management and the supply and market organisation, but also the control over certain crafts through the guilds system.[34]

Given the specifics of Caričin Grad, which was a place of both production and consumption, one should not exclude the possibility that the state elite (in this case the ecclesiastical and military elite) played an important role in creating the needs for consumption, which could have led to some kind of administered production.[35] However, the new supposed model of production organisation should certainly be discussed in the wider discourse of the 'ruralisation' of Late Antique towns, a process that clearly became visible from the middle of the 6th century. This would imply that pottery specialists could be engaged full-time or part-time, next to their farming activities in the countryside.[36]

The results of studies on pottery contexts carried out so far at Caričin Grad show functional differences between assemblages from different spatial units. Significant was, for instance, the study of the distribution of cooking pots, because these vessels dominated in all the units, accounting for almost 70 percent of all the finds. It revealed that pots with flat bottoms were more abundant in the Lower Town, whereas those with rounded bottoms and with spouts in the Upper Town. These morphological differences are quite reliable indicators of different ways of food preparation.[37] Vessels with flat bottoms were used for cooking in ovens, and the pots with rounded bottoms were used for the preparation of meals over the fire and in the hearth. On the other hand, baking covers appear in both units,[38] demonstrating the common way of baking flat loaves of wheat or millet bread throughout the city.

In the context of spatial/functional structures at Caričin Grad, distribution of pottery types may even be indicative of the organisation of everyday dining: communal dining of the military elite and the soldiers in the Upper Town, while household dining (a family meal in the house) was taking place in the residential and trading quarter of the Lower Town. On the other hand, the finds of pithoi illustrate the economic role of the city. In addition to a *horreum* (a type of public warehouse) on the Upper Town's northern plateau, where large containers are expected,[39] the quantities and the distribution of pithoi in other quarters and archaeological contexts show complex economic activities in the city area.

There are clear indications that different types of cooking pots were used in different parts of Caričin Grad. However, given the quantitatively and qualitatively uneven samples (notably from the Upper and Lower Towns), this distribution pattern still cannot reliably reflect the occupation of different social groups in the city.

The issue of the social structure of Caričin Grad can therefore only be discussed with the study on locally made and locally used pottery.[40] The reason for the establishment of this city and its general appearance is often related to the idea that its inhabitants must have been members of the ecclesiastical and, to a lesser degree, military elite. The seals of Archbishop John and Bishop John[41] and the finds of the Baldenheim-type helmets[42] speak in favour of this option.[43] On the other hand, the pottery finds show a different picture, namely that of a modest milieu in which luxury objects were few. The everyday pottery used at Caričin Grad is evidently functional: either cooking pots and table wares, or large food and drink containers, pithoi and amphorae. A similar functional impression is to be seen in the Red Slip Ware bowls and plates, which are also low in numbers.

Yet, the contrast between the monumental architecture and the objects of everyday use at Caričin Grad is firstly instigated by the chronology of the archaeological contexts, and secondly by the chronology of the pottery. The majority of the ceramic finds can be dated to the second half of the 6th and the beginning of the 7th century. Stratigraphically excavated material from the oldest horizon (i.e. from the time of the city's foundation) comes from the Lower Town.[44] Although its volume is not very large, this pottery assemblage displays some production differences in details but not in essence, as I will show you.[45] A concentration of pithoi and amphorae around the Acropolis and in the Upper Town[46] points to a solid organisation of food supply, storage and distribution activities. In such a setting, it is not surprising that luxurious pottery shows up as well, but in a relatively small amount (around 1 percent).[47] Nonetheless, the distribution of Red Slip Ware throughout the city points to social differentiation within residential quarters. A good example is the building complex with an atrium in the Lower Town. With approximately 30 African Red Slip Ware plates and a number of amphorae, it may well have been the residence of a wealthy trader.[48]

The situation is somewhat different during the final stages of the city's history. Starting with the last decades of the 6th century, a process of de-urbanisation is evident in the Upper Town, where huts were built on locations of earlier churches and administrative buildings. This is followed by the introduction of very different ceramics.[49] The most peculiar assemblage of handmade pottery comes from the *'maison aux pithoi'* from the city's last construction phase.[50] As the appearance of this pottery more or less coincides with Slavic incursions, it was long believed to have been made by the Slavs.[51] However, the Caričin Grad material clearly indicates that the emergence of handmade ceramics was in fact the result of what has been described as 'a substantial decline in demand for professionally produced pottery'.[52] One can observe not only the imitation of the main types of cooking and storage pots in a handmade fashion, but also the introduction of new coarse pottery forms, mostly of cooking pots. Eventually, some of these may have had a connection with the Slavs, among which perhaps mercenaries in Byzantine service.[53] The features of these vessels show a regression in pottery trade, a decline of urban commerce and craft, as if scaled-down pottery consumption resulted from the impoverishment of the city's inhabitants.

CONCLUDING REMARKS

The data, which are shortly presented in this chapter, make Caričin Grad (Justiniana Prima) one of the key sites for studying models of pottery production and of consumption behaviour in an Early Byzantine city. The case study of Caričin Grad, a large administrative stronghold, sheds light on patterns of production, trade and consumption that can also be observed in other, smaller settlements in Illyricum and beyond. Regarding its morphological features, pottery from Caričin Grad fits into the general trends of the Early Byzantine era.[54] It is clear that there is a prevailing presence of locally made wares, and a uniform production of a limited number of types of products. A significant percentage of pots with rounded bottoms is also present, as well as a wide application of glazes on both tableware and cookware. Another trend is the active engagement in the state supply of strategic food and in trade with luxury goods, mostly originating from North Africa and Asia Minor.

A high level of pottery standardisation is reflected both in technological choices (the composition of raw materials, techniques and procedures) and in a small number of forms in all functional classes (cooking pots, storage, transport and table wares). These trends imply that the production was organised in workshop units, by professional potters, to meet predominantly the needs of the city's inhabitants. At Caričin Grad, an administrative centre (primarily ecclesiastical), an important role is believed to have been played by the elite in organising pottery production and consumption. With the find of many cooking pots, covers for baking bread and pithoi for keeping cereals, these activities resemble those performed according to the model of administered production, where potters worked under the 'control' of the state administration, which both employed them and addressed them as their main consumers. At the same time, craftsmen were controlling each other's work to meet the standards of specialisation, daily demands, and production volume requirements, thus creating a dynamic pottery market. The exchange and trade of olive oil and wine (and their ceramic containers) should be considered in the same context.[55]

The most important observations made in connection with pottery consumption behaviour at Caričin Grad may be summarised as follows:

— Caričin grad, an important 6th-century centre in Illyricum, represents a consumer's zone highly influenced by representatives of the state administration; that is to say, the ecclesiastical elite.

— A causal link can be established between the socio-economic background of the city and the consumption of pottery.

— The selection of wares in separate city districts suggests a slightly different diet in these parts of the city: communal dining of the military administration and the garrison in the Upper Town, and household dining in the residential and trading quarter in the Lower Town. Different economic functions of specific districts and the tight organisation of strategic food supply, storage and distribution activities may also be suggested on the same basis.

— The pottery consumption is strongly based on locally produced, very good quality pottery vessels. The production was standardised in both technological and formal terms, including a number of glazed vessels. As such, it followed production trends of the Early Byzantine period.

— Various finds of locally-made pithoi and baking covers mark economic activity zones (i.e. grain storage and bread/buns making areas), while imported pottery for storage was mostly used to contain oil and wine.

— African Red Slip Ware is practically the only kind of fine tableware at Caričin Grad. Its on-site distribution indicates that it was used by wealthy inhabitants, such as administration officials, craftsmen, merchants etc., who lived in a well-defended quarter of the Lower Town.

In contrast to other classes of archaeological finds from Caričin Grad, and due to the fact that luxurious dishes are very rare, the pottery finds show (at least at first sight) a quite modest standard of living of its population. But is this really so? Does standardised pottery production, performed by skilled artisans, paint a picture of a community of picky consumers more vividly than other, more obvious luxuries do? In other words, can the acknowledgement of quality of everyday, utilitarian products be seen as a criterium for a society's pickiness? By all parameters, Caričin Grad may be seen as an ideal model for the Emperor Justinian's 'new city for a new society'.[56] As convincingly demonstrated by J. L. Quiroga, this new society, intimately connected with the official Church, stimulated mostly local and regional economies, because these last ones were essential for its survival.[57] Could it be, then, that the pottery consumed at Caričin Grad might be regarded as the *best* choice of all the production standards of the era? The assemblages recovered and analysed so far strongly support the view that this pottery was indeed representative from different (production, formal-typological, and socio-political) points of view. Thus, it can be stated that the finds from Caričin Grad illustrate the best trends in Early Byzantine pottery production and consumption.

ACKNOWLEDGEMENTS

This paper results from the research project of the Institute of Archaeology *Urbanisation Processes and Development of Mediaeval Society* (No. 177021), funded by the Ministry of Education, Science and Technological Development of the Republic of Serbia. I would like to thank Dr Ivan Bugarski for improving the English style of the manuscript, and MA Uglješa Vojvodić for the layout of the illustrations.

NOTES

1. For the latest overview of results and literature cf. Costa 2013, 122-26.
2. Poblome 2013; 2015; 2016; Anderson 2014, 133-36.
3. Cf. Vroom, J. 2004; Grandi 2007; Whittow 2013; Ladstätter, S. 2014; Martin 2014; Zachariadis 2014.
4. Ivanišević 2016a, fig. 1.
5. Bavant 2012, 337-42.
6. Novellae 94.
7. Ivanišević, 2010b, 451.
8. Bavant et Ivanišević 2006; Ivanišević 2010a; *Idem* 2016b, 109-21.
9. Zanini 2006, 398-407.
10. Ivanišević 2010a, 4-5; Bavant 2012, 342-72.
11. Bikić, forthcoming.
12. Bjelajac 1990; Bikić, forthcoming.
13. Damjanović *et al.* 2014, 165-67.
14. Damjanović *et al.* 2014, 167-69.
15. Bjelajac 1990, 176-78, 184, Pl. XVIII-XX.
16. Bjelajac 2010, 580-84, fig. VII; Ivanišević 2010a, 19, fig. 16; Birk *et al.* 2016; I would like to thank Dr Vujadin Ivanišević for information on unpublished finds from the Upper Town's northern plateau.
17. Bikić and Ivanišević 2012, fig. 6.
18. Bikić and Ivanišević 2012, 42.
19. Bikić and Ivanišević 2012.
20. Bikić and Ivanišević 2012, fig. 3; Karagiorgou 2001, 146-49; Morrison and Sodini 2002, 206-12.
21. Stamenković 2013, 83-84; Ivanišević 2016b, 122-23.
22. Bikić and Ivanišević 2012, 43, figs. 1, 2.
23. Bikić and Ivanišević 2012, 43.
24. According to A.J. Cappel in the *Oxford Dictionary of Byzantium* (1991, 105-106), 'annona' is the financial term, referring to in-kind taxation, including both '*annona civica*'and '*annona militaris*' – the requisition and transfer of commodities from Africa and Egypt for the maintenance of Rome and Constnatinople, or for the miliarty troops. By the 6th century the term is applied almost exclusively to rations and supplies, distinct from the public tax.
25. Karagiorgou 2001, 149-56; Kingsley 2003, 129-33; Curta 2016, 308-20.
26. Cf. Costa 2013, 122-26; Whittow 2013, 135, 159-60; Cirelli and Canavicci 2014, 963-64; Dafi 2014, 738-42; Martin 2014, 761-63; Bikić and Ivanišević 2012, 42-45.
27. Bavant 2007, 340-42.
28. Cf. Sinopoli 2003; Costin 2005.
29. Duval *et al.* 2010, 75-80; Damjanović *et al.* 2014, 170-71; Ivanišević 2016b, fig. 4.
30. Murphy and Poblome 2011, 30-33; Murphy and Poblome 2016, 195-97.
31. Birk *et al.* 2016; Schreg *et al.* 2016.
32. Costin 1991, 3-10; *Idem* 1998, 4-5.
33. Sinopoli 1988, 581-82.
34. Cf. Morrisson and Sodini 2002; Gutteridge and Machado 2006; Cantino Wataghin 2006; Lopez Quiroga 2016, 82-83.
35. Sinopoli 1988, 581.
36. Zanini 2016, 123-38.
37. Arthur 2007, 178-79.
38. Bjelajac 1990, 182, Pl. XXI/8-12; Bikić, forthcoming.
39. Ivanišević *et al.* 2016, 147-55.

40 Cf. review article: Sodini 2003.
41 Ivanišević 2017, 112, fig. 11.
42 Baldenheim-type helmets were worn by either East Roman officers or Germanic leaders They were made of gold-plated bronze, while the rivets were silver, or silver and lead. One example from Iustinian Prima was quite special due to a curved bronze strip engraved with a hunting scene.
43 Ivanišević 2010a, 771, fig. 20; *Idem* 2016b, 121-22.
44 Ivanišević 2010a, 760-67.
45 Bikić forthcoming.
46 Bjelajac 2010.
47 It concerns here just 6 sherds of African Red Slip Ware and 10 fragments of imported amphorae originating from the old excavations of the Acropolis and of a small part of the *principia* in the upper town; cf. Bjelajac 1990, 171-74, Pls. XVI/12-14, 21, XVII/14.
48 Bikić and Ivanišević 2012.
49 Ivanišević 2016b, 124-26.
50 Bjelajac 2010.
51 Vroom 2003, 141-43. For a more recent critical review, cf. Curta 2010, 308-15.
52 Arthur 2007, 165-68.
53 Ivanišević 2012, 60-62, fig. 3/3-7.
54 Ivanišević 2012, 181-83. For the most illustrative examples, see Vroom 2004, 324-26; Borisov 2010, 142-68, 173-90; Martin 2014, 761-68; Zachariadis 2014, 705-707, figs. 7-12; Cirelli 2015, 17-19.
55 Laiou and Morrison 2007, 33-38.
56 Cf. Lopez Quiroga 2016; Ivanišević 2016b.
57 Lopez Quiroga 2016, 79-83.

BIBLIOGRAPHY

PRIMARY SOURCES

Novellae. In: R. Schoell and G. Kroll (eds.), *Corpus Iuris Civilis 3*, Berlin, 1895.

LITERATURE

Anderson, W. 2014. From manufactured goods to significant possessions: Theorising pottery consumption in late antique Anatolia, in: A. Bokern and C. Rowan (eds.), *Embodying Value? The Transformation of Objects in and from the Ancient World*, BAR International Series 2592, Oxford, 131-44.

Arthur, P. 2007. Form, function and technology in pottery production from Late Antiquity to the Early Middle Ages, in: L. Lavan, E. Zanini and A. Sarantis (eds.), *Technology in Transition A.D. 300-650*, Late Antique Archaeology 4, Leiden & Boston, 173-87.

Bavant, B. 2012. Caričin Grad and the changes in the nature of urbanism in the Central Balkans in the sixth century, in: A. Poulter (ed.), *The Transition to Late Antiquity, on the Danube and Beyond*, Oxford, 337-74.

Bavant B. and V. Ivanišević 2006. *Ivstiniana Prima – Caričin Grad*, Leskovac.

Bikić, V. forthcoming. The pottery of Caričin Grad in the light of finds in Early Byzantine Illyricum, in: B. Bavant and V. Ivanišević (eds.), *Caričin Grad IV: Early Byzantine City and Society, Conference Dedicated to the Centenary of Archaeological Research in Caričin Grad, October 3rd to October 7th 2012, Leskovac, Serbia*, Belgrade & Rome.

Bikić, V. and V. Ivanišević 2012. Imported pottery in the Central Illyricum – Case study: Caričin Grad/Iustiniana Prima, *Rei Cretariae Romanae Fautorum Acta* 42, 42-44.

Birk, J.J., I. Bugarski, S. Fiedler, V. Ivanišević, H. Kroll, N. Marković, A. Reuter, C. Röhl, R. Schreg, A. Stamenković, S. Stamenković and M. Steinborn 2016. An imperial town in a time of transition: Life, environment, and decline of early Byzantine Caričin Grad, in: *3rd International Landscape Archaeology Conference*, LAC 2014 proceedings, [S.l.], 11, Amsterdam, doi:http://dx.doi.org/10.5463/lac.2014.4.

Bjelajac, Lj. 1990. La céramique et les lampes, in: N. Duval and V. Popović (ed.), *Caričin Grad II: Le quartier sud-ouest de la ville haute*, Rome & Belgrade, 161-90.

Bjelajac Lj. 2010. La „maison aux pithoi" – Les trouvailles, in: B. Bavant, V. Kondić and J.M. Spieser (eds.), *Caričin Grad III: L'Acropole et ses Monuments, quartier sud-ouest de la ville haute*, Belgrade & Rome, 579-85.

Borisov, B.D. 2010. *Djadovo, Vol. 2: The Sanctuary of the Thracian Horseman and The Early Byzantine Fortress*, Varna.

Cantino Wataghin, G. 2006. Architecture and power: Churches in Northern Italy from the 4th to the 6th c., in: W. Bowden, A. Gutteridge and C. Machado (eds.), *Social and Political Life in Late Antiquity*, Late Antique Archaeology 3.1, Leiden & Boston, 287-309.

Cirelli, E. 2015. Dall'alba al tramonto: Il vasellame di uso comune a Ravenna e nel suo territorio tra la tarda Antichità e il Medioevo (III-VIII secolo), in: E. Cirelli, F. Diosono and and H. Patterson (eds.), *Le forme della crisi: Produzioni ceramiche e commerci nell'Italia centrale tra Romani e Longobardi (III-VIII sec. d.C.)*, Atti del convegno, Spoleto-Campello sul Clitunno, 5-7 ottobre 2012, Bologna, 13-19.

Cirelli, E. and A. Cannavicci 2014. A 6th-century dump from Classe (Ravenna), in: N. Poulou-Papadimitriou, E. Nodarou and V. Kilikoglou (eds.), *LRCW 4. Late Roman Coarse Wares, Cooking Wares and Amphorae in the Mediterranean, Archaeology and archaeometry, The Mediterranean: A Market Without Frontiers, Volume 1*, BAR International Series 2616 (1), Oxford, 963-74.

Costa, S. 2013. The Late Antique economy: Ceramics and trade, in: L. Lavan (ed.), *Local Economies? Production and Exchange of Inland Regions in Late Antiquity*, Late Antique Archaeology 10.1, Leiden, 91-130.

Costin, C.L. 1991. Craft specialization: Issues in defining, documenting, and explaining the organization of production, in: M. Schiffer (ed.) *Archaeological Method and Theory 3*, Tucson, 1-55.

Costin, C.L. 1998. Introduction: Craft and social identity, in: C.L. Costin and R.P.Wright (eds.), *Craft and Social Identity*, Archeological Paper, No. 8, Washington, DC, 3-16.

Costin, C.L. 2005. Pottery production, in: H.D.G. Maschner and C. Chippendale (eds.), *Handbook of Archaeological Methods*, Lanham, New York, & O, 1032-1105.

Curta, F. 2010. The early Slavs in the northern and eastern Adriatic region – A critical approach, *Archaeologia Medievale* 37, 307-29.

Curta, F. 2016. Amphorae and seals: The 'Sub-Byzantine' Avars and the *Quaestura Exercitus*, in: Á. Bollók, G. Csiky, T. Vida (eds.), *Between Byzantium and the Steppe: Archaeological and Historical Studies in Honour of Csanád Bálint on the Occasion of His 70th Birthday*, Budapest, 307-34.

Dafi, E. 2014. Amphorae and cooking wares from the coastal site of Antikyra in Boeotia, in: N. Poulou-Papadimitriou, E. Nodarou and V. Kilikoglou (eds.), *LRCW 4. Late Roman Coarse Wares, Cooking Wares and Amphorae in the Mediterranean, Archaeology and Archaeometry, The Mediterranean: A Market Without Frontiers, Vol. 1*, BAR International Series 2616 (1), Oxford, 737-48.

Damjanović, Lj., V. Bikić, K. Šarić, S. Erić and I. Holclajtner-Antunović I. 2014. Characterization of the early Byzantine pottery from Caričin Grad (South Serbia) in terms of composition and firing temperature, *Journal of Archaeological Science* 46, 156-72.

Duval, N., M. Jeremić, V. Popović and Č. Vasić 2010. Généralités, Historique des recherches, topographie et techniques des construction, in: N. Duval and V. Popović (eds.), *Caričin Grad III: l'acropole et ses monuments*, Rome & Belgrade, 1-100.

Grandi, N., 2007. Late Antique and Early Medieval (5th-7th cent. AD) fine pottery from archaeological contexts in the Lagoon of Venice, in: Böhlendorf-Arslan, A. O. Uysal, J. Witte-Orr (eds.), Çanak, Late Antique and Medieval Pottery in Mediterranean Archaeological Contexts, Byzas 7, Istanbul, 1-24.

Gutteridge, A. and C. Machado 2006. Social and political life in Late Antiquity: An introduction, in: W. Bowden, A. Gutteridge, and C. Machado (eds.), *Social and Political Life in Late Antiquity*, Late Antique Archaeology 3.1, Leiden & Boston, xv-xxx.

Haldon, J. 2005. *The Palgrave Atlas of Byzantine History*, Basingstoke.

Ivanišević, V. 2010a. Caričin Grad – the fortification and the intramural housing in the Lower Town, in: F. Daim and J. Drauschke (eds.), *Byzanz – Das Römerreich im Mittelalter*, Mainz, 747-748.

Ivanišević, V. 2010b. La monnaie paléobyzantine dans l'Illyricum du nord, Mélanges Cecile Morrisson, Travaux et Mémoires 16, Paris, 441-54.

Ivanišević, V. 2012. Barbarian settlementa in the interior of Illyricum: The case of Caričin Grad, in: V. Ivanišević and M. Kazanski (eds.), *The Pontic-Danubian Realm in the Period of the Great Migration*, Centre de Recherche d'Histoire et Civilisation de Bzyance, Monographies 36, Paris & Belgrade, 57-69.

Ivanišević, V. 2016a. Late Antique cities and their environment in Northern Illyricum, in: F. Daim and J. Drauschke (eds.), *Hinter den Mauern und auf dem offenen Land*, Mainz, 89-99.

Ivanišević, V. 2016b. Caričin Grad (Justiniana Prima): A new-discovered city for a 'new' society, in: Smilja Marjanović Dušanić (ed.), *Proceedings of the 23rd International Congress of Byzantine Studies: Plenary Papers, Belgrade, 22-27 August, 2016*, Belgrade, 107-26.

Ivanišević, V. 2017. Une capitale revisitée: Caričin Grad (*Justiniana Prima*), Comptes rendus des séances de l'Académie des Inscriptions et Belles-Lettres (CRAI) 2017, 1, 93-114.

Ivanišević, V., I. Bugarski and A. Stamenković 2016. Nova saznanja o urbanizmu Caričinog grada – Primena savremenih metoda prospekcije i detekcije, *Starinar* 67, 143-60.

Karagiorgou, O. 2001. The Late Roman 2 amphora: A container for the military *annona* on the Danubian border?, in: S. Kingsley and M. Decker (eds.), *Economy and Exchange in the East Mediterranean during Late Antiquity*, Oxford, 129-66.

Kingsley, S. A. 2003. Late Antique trade: Research methodologies & field practices, in: L. Lavan and W. Bowden (eds.), *Theory and Practice in Late Antique Archaeology*, Late Antique Archaeology 1, Leiden & Boston, 113-38.

Ladstätter, S. 2014. Keramik, in: H. Thür and E. Rathmayr (eds.), *Hanghaus 2 in Ephesos. Die Wohneinheit 6. Baubefund, Ausstattung, Funde*, FiE 8, 9, Vienna, 435-588 (with A. Waldner).

Laiou, A. And C. Morrisson 2007. *The Byzantine Economy*, Cambridge.

Lopez Quiroga, J.L. 2016. Early Byzantine urban landscapes in the southwest and southeast Mediterranean, in: S. Merjanović Dušanić (ed.), *Proceedings of the 23rd International Congress of Byzantine Studies: Plenary Papers, Belgrade, 22-27 August, 2016*, Belgrade, 69-105.

Martin, A. 2014. A sixth-century context at Olympia (SW building), in: N. Poulou-Papadimitriou, E. Nodarou and V. Kilikoglou (eds.), *LRCW 4. Late Roman Coarse Wares, Cooking Wares and Amphorae in the Mediterranean, Archaeology and Archaeometry, The Mediterranean: A Market Without Frontiers, Vol. 1*, BAR International Series 2616 (1), 761-68.

Morrison, C. and J.-P. Sodini 2002. The sixth-century economy, in: A. E. Laiou (ed.), *The Economic History of Byzantium: From the Seventh through the Fifteenth Century*, Washington, DC, 171-220.

Murphy, E.A. and J. Poblome 2011. Producing pottery vs. producing models: Interpreting workshop organization at the potters' quarter of Sagalassos, in: M. Lawall and J. Lund (eds.), *Conference Proceedings of Pottery in the Archaeological Record: A View from the Greek World, Danish School at Athens, 20-21, June, 2008*, Aarhus, 29-36.

Murphy, E. A. and Poblome, J. 2016. A late antique ceramic workshop complex: Evidence for workshop organisation at Sagalassos (southwest Turkey), *Anatolian Studies* 66, 185-99.

Poblome, J. 2013. Money makes pottery go round, in: J. Poblome (ed.), *Exempli gratia – Sagalassos, Marc Waelkens and Interdisciplinary Archaeology*, Leuven, 81-95.

Poblome, J. 2015. Life in the Late Antique countryside of Sagalassos, in: H. Metin, B. Ayça P. Becks, R. Becks and M. Fırat (eds.), *Pisidia Yazıları Hacı Ali Ekinci Armağanı / Pisidian Essays in Honour of Hacı Ali Ekinci*, İstanbul, 99-109.

Poblome, J. 2016. The potters of Ancient Sagalassos revisited, in: A. Wilson and M. Flohr (eds.), *Urban Craftsmen and Traders in the Roman World*, Oxford, 377-404.

Schreg, R., J. Birk, S. Fiedler, H. Kroll, N. Marković, A.E. Reuter, C. Röhl and M. Steinborn 2016. Wirtschaftliche Ressourcen und soziales Kapital: Gründung und Unterhalt der Kaiserstadt Iustiniana Prima, *Mitteilungen der Deutschen Gesellschaft für Archäologie des Mittelalters und der Neuzeit* 29, 9-20.

Sinopoli, C. 1988. The organization of craft production at Vijayanagara, South India, *American Anthropologist, New Series* 90.3, 580-97.

Sinopoli C.M. 2003. *The Political Economy of Craft Production: Crafting Empire in South India, c. 1350-1650*, Cambridge.

Sodini, J.-P. 2003. Archaeology and Late Antique social structures, in: L. Lavan and W. Bowden (eds.), *Theory and Practice in Late Antique Archaeology*, Late Antique Archaeology 1, Leiden & Boston, 25-56.

Stamenković, S. 2013, *Rimsko nasleđe u Leskovačkoj kotlini / Roman Legacy in the Leskovac Valley*, Belgrade.

Vroom, J. 2003. *After Antiquity. Ceramics and Society in the Aegean from the 7th to the 20th century A.C. A Case Study from Boeotia, Central Greece*, Archaeological Studies Leiden University 10, Leiden.

Vroom, J. 2004. Late Antique pottery, settlement and trade in the east Mediterranean: A preliminary comparison of ceramics from Limyra (Lycia) and Boeotia, in: W. Bowden, L. Lavan and C. Machado (eds.), *Recent Research in the Late Antique Countryside*, Late Antique Archaeology 2, Leiden & Boston, 281-331.

Whittow, M. 2013. How much trade was local, regional and inter-Regional? A comparative perspective on the Late Antique economy, in: L. Lavan (ed.), *Local Economies? Production and Exchange of Inland Regions in Late Antiquity*, Late Antique Archaeology 10, Leiden, 133-65.

Zachariadis, S. 2014. Pottery from the workshop building, in the Early Byzantine city of Philippi, Greece, in: N. Poulou-Papadimitriou, E. Nodarou and V. Kilikoglou (eds.), *LRCW 4. Late Roman Coarse Wares, Cooking Wares and Amphorae in the Mediterranean, Archaeology and Archaeometry, The Mediterranean: A Market Without Frontiers*, BAR International Series 2616 (1), 705-13.

Zanini, E. 2006. Technology and ideas: Architects and master-builders in the Early Byzantine world, in: L. Lavan, E. Zanini and A. Sarantis (eds.), *Technology in Transition A.D. 300-650*, Late Antique Archaeology 4, Leiden & Boston, 381-405.

Zanini, E. 2016. Coming to the end: Early Byzantine cities after the mid-6th century, in: S. Merjanović Dušanić (ed.), *Proceedings of the 23rd International Congress of Byzantine Studies: Plenary Papers, Belgrade, 22-27 August, 2016*, Belgrade, 127-40.

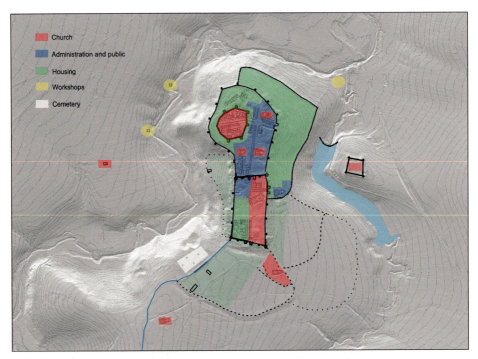

FIG. 1 – Caričin Grad and neighbouring sites (after Ivanišević 2016b, fig. 2).

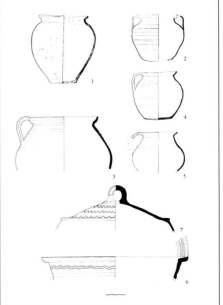

FIG. 2A-B – Caričin Grad: Cooking ware (1-6), and baking cover; (A) – photo; (B) – drawings (Institute of Archaeology, Belgrade).

FIG. 3A-B – Caričin Grad: *'Maison aux pithoi'* on the Acropolis; (A) – general overview; (B) – detail of a pithos (photo: Institute of Archaeology, Belgrade).

FIG. 4 – Caričin Grad: Pithoi (photo: Institute of Archaeology, Belgrade).

FIG. 5A-B – Caričin Grad: Tableware; (A) – photo; (B) – drawings (Institute of Archaeology, Belgrade)

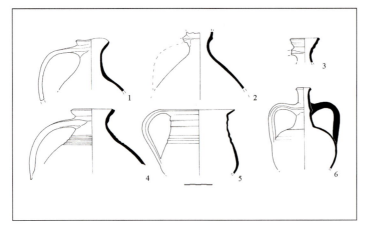

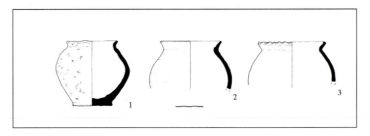

FIG. 6 – Caričin Grad: Handmade pottery; (A) – photo; (B) – drawings (Institute of Archaeology, Belgrade)

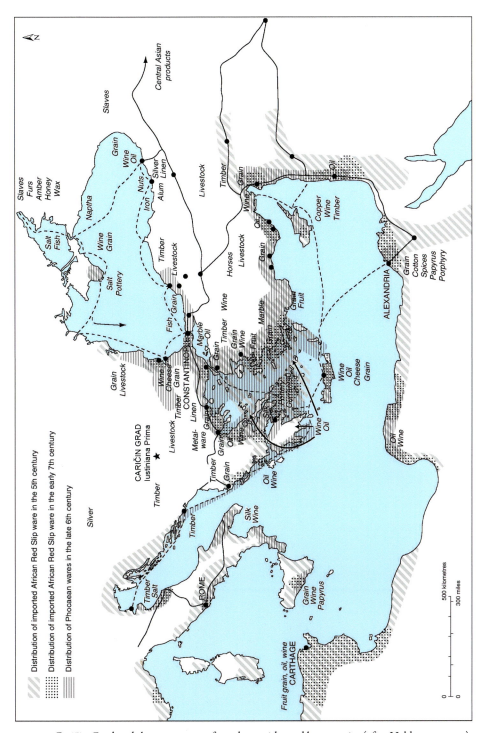

FIG. 7 – Caričin Grad and the movement of goods as evidenced by ceramics (after Haldon 2005, 45).

FIG. 8 – Caričin Grad: Imported pottery (photo: Institute of Archaeology, Belgrade).

* * *

Geographies of consumption in Byzantine Epirus: Urban space, commodification, and consumption practices from the 7th to the 12th century

Myrto Veikou

*

*« Cette perfection géométrique résume aussi, au mode présent, des efforts plus ou moins conscients mais in*n*ombrables, accumulés par l'histoire et qui visent tous le même but :atteindre un seuil, sans doute le plus profitable aux sociétés humaines, où s'instaure un juste équilibre entre leur unité et leur diversité; et qui maintient la balance égale entre la communication, favorable aux illuminations réciproques, et l'absence de communication, elle aussi salutaire, puisque les fleurs fragiles de la différence ont besoin de pénombre pour subsister. »* – CLAUDE LÉVI-STRAUSS (1973, 300).

The anthropologist Daniel Miller once told an anecdote about a tribe of transhumant camel nomads in North Africa. Their annual migration was taking place in March since time immemorial, but on one occasion, during the 1990s, their migration was several months delayed. The reason was that the tribesmen did not want to miss the final episodes of the American soap opera 'Dallas'.[1] If this break with a perhaps centuries-old tradition makes anything clear, it is that buying, using and disposing of commodities, including cultural products, connect us to other people and other places – and that this process of consumption changes our lives in ways which may be beyond our imagination. In this way commodities are more than just objects to be sold and bought; they are shifting assemblages of social relations which develop and assume form and meaning in time and space.[2]

Thus, the study of consumption offers insights not only into economic processes but also into society and culture as a whole. Geographies of consumption, in particular, look at the ways in which relationships between people, things and places are constituted through the availability, appropriation and use of goods and services. As will be explained in detail below (in Part III), the term 'geographies of consumption' comes from the field of cultural geography, a discipline seeking to investigate the interplays of geography and culture by studying everyday formations of cultural phenomena and identities.[3]

Using this perspective, the present chapter discusses the Middle Byzantine province of Epirus (in northwestern Greece). Through a comparative consideration of archaeology and textual evidence it aims to provide answers to five main questions:

(1) – How can we define the notion of consumption in Middle-Byzantine Epirus?
(2) – How fitting is the use of the modern term 'consumption' in relation to a pre-modern society?
(3) – If we can define a Byzantine notion of consumption in Epirus, is it related to 'urbanism' and urban environments, as it was in its original context during its emergence in early modern times?
(4) – When it comes to different geographic approaches to consumption, can place-, region- or province-specific consumption patterns be discerned in Middle-Byzantine Epirus?
(5) – Last but not least, what can such different geographic approaches to consumption contribute to the research of Byzantine culture at large?

In addressing these questions, I will explore the usability of interdisciplinary analytical tools from the 'postmodernist' theoretical framework (specifically the perspectives of social anthropology and cultural geography). The aim is to produce a set of diachronic located views of various Byzantine cultures of consumption, i.e. distinct and dated Byzantine consumption geographies (in Part II). The latter can be documented in material forms (as discussed in Part III.A. and visualized in Figs. 2-7), as well as in narrative forms (cf. Part III.B). The discussion of these issues inevitably involves a consideration of certain broader problems, such as the different approaches towards a definition of the notion of 'consumption', and the use of 'consumption geographies' in Medieval studies in the first place (in Part I).

I – MEANINGS OF CONSUMPTION THROUGH TIME

My intention is to begin with a historical analysis of the concept of consumption, to explore the term's origin and use. The concept and the term 'consumption' emerged within the context of urban studies in association with modern cities; it refers to the complex sphere of social relations and discourses which centre on the sale, purchase and use of commodities.[4] In this perspective it is argued that consumption and culture have been incorporated into the schemes used by cities as they promote themselves in a 'new urban order' marked by increased competitiveness from the 19th cnnncencentury to the present.[5]

Several studies have examined the way in which citizenship was and is produced through consumption practice with specific commodities and the social practices surrounding them and providing a starting place for reflections on the regulation and surveillance of public space.[6] Research examining the discourses, relationships and practices, which produce normative prescriptions of appropriate subject positions and the implications for who might be included and excluded from particular spaces, has also been prevalent in the social sciences.[7] Their main task is to frame how and whether groups of people come to be shaped as consumer citizens, across what places and spaces, as well as the sorts of orientation these subjects have towards objects of consumption.

Consumption has also become one of the grand narratives of the second half of the 20th century; rather than production it is the driving force in contemporary society, and it is almost impossible to avoid in capitalist social formations.[8] Consumption practices and preferences are also instrumental in identity formation, self-expression and the development of lifestyle cultures built around such things as diet, fashion, music and leisure tastes. Consumption is not simply about the using up of things, but also involves the production of meaning, experience, knowledge or objects – the outcome of which may or may not take the form of a commodity.[9]

The concept of commodity is thus central to understanding consumption. According to the geographer Juliana Mansvelt, commodities exchanged in capitalist societies through an economic system assume a use value (the capacity to satisfy a want or need) and an exchange value (the ability to command other commodities in exchange).[10] While production for profit will give a commodity a distinctive meaning or essence, meanings of objects also arise from their non-commodified moments; in fact, commodities are exchanged and circulated outside, alongside and even in contradiction to market exchange.[11]

'Commodification' denotes the extension of the commodity form to goods and services previously existing outside the market but commodities are also objects of cultural symbolic exchange. Anthropologists suggest that they are an important means of communication in societies and they constitute a 'non-verbal medium for the human creative faculty' both conveying and constituting cultural meaning.[12] Thus consumption is as much an act of imagination as it is the use of things, with spatial and temporal contexts making the link between an object and its meaning. Commodity meanings are constituted through a diverse range of consumption practices including rituals of exchange, possession and disinvestment.[13]

When it comes specifically to historical studies, Nigel Thrift and Peter Glennie have shown that modern consumption 'is not modern', and that the implied chronology in so many accounts of modern consumption, a chronology that ties 'modern' to the 19th century, is a mistaken one.[14] They have argued that consumption practices were significant in life prior to the industrial revolution: urbanisation from 1650 onwards. Especially from 1700, they contributed to physical and relative distance between producers and consumers and the consequent creation of consuming as a significant social and economic practice.

Thrift and Glennie suggested that new consumer practices emerged in new socialities which developed from the close associations and interactions of urban living. In urban settings, new knowledge about commodities, practices and experiences of consuming emerged. The creation of new discourses, based around 'novelty' for example, influenced how goods were consumed and interpreted and (re)produced selectively by different consumers. Consumption was actually a contributory factor to processes of industrialisation as capitalist enterprises developed to meet the rising demand of the elite for luxuries but also to provide commodities for consumption by 'other classes.' What was the effect of the industrial revolution? From the late 18th-century onward factory-produced commodities were incorporated into existing and evolving consumption discourses. Consumption was now marked by increasing access of the general population to ever more commodities and an acceptance of consumerist attitudes.[15]

Along these lines Thrift's and Glennie's new perspective was an attempt to relocate the chronological limits of 'modern' economy. But what was – was there – 'consumption' in pre-industrial societies? In particular, how exactly useful the particular term of 'consumption' is – in its specific context – for the study of Byzantine societies and cultures? In 2006, Angeliki Laiou touched upon the questions of our thinking of Byzantine economy in modern terms.[16] In her study, she discussed production and consumption of goods as an aspect of urban economy and urbanism, thus retaining the concept of consumption within the original context in which the term was invented. What seems to have actually been her main point of interest is whether one may think of Byzantine consumption (considered exclusively within cities) in the same way as one thinks of them within the context of capitalist economies.[17] She conceived consumption and production on the basis of economic theories by Moses Finley (on Antiquity) and Max Weber (on Early Modern Europe), although she expressed serious doubts on the validity of Finley's model in respect to Byzantine cities.[18]

On the other hand, consumption is not only an economic phenomenon connected with capitalist modern economies. People's (economic) acts of providing themselves with necessary goods also have complex social and cultural dimensions, as discussed above; the latter are important aspects of communities' histories, no matter what type of economy they have. A good example of this in Byzantine studies is Dionysios Stathakopoulos' work on food supply and shortage, which displays its consequences at a social and cultural level.[19] It is, therefore, fitting and meaningful, hence purposeful, to look into consumption practices as social and cultural aspects, which reveal communities' relations to either nearby or distant and imagined others.

In this direction, one needs to alter two parameters of previous research on the Byzantine concept of consumption with the help of the aforementioned research in the cultural studies, and this is my intention in this chapter. The first change involves looking into Byzantine consumption of goods by zooming out of closed contexts and specific settlements, i.e. by looking over an entire province (Epirus, in this case). The second change involves examining consumption beyond its capitalist connotations and with a focus on cultural practices.

The aim of changing these two parameters in the present context is to allow disconnecting the concept from its original frameworks (positivist economic reasoning and urban studies), and in doing so bring it more in line with current cultural theoretical approaches such as those by Nigel Thrift, Peter Glennie, and Juliana Mansvelt. Therefore, the main axis of this work is defined as the production of a set of 'geographies of consumption' in reference to Middle Byzantine Epirus. This task is pursued by means of geographic considerations of i) assorted cultures of consumption, and ii) the spatial practices related to these cultures.

II – TRACING CONSUMPTION PRACTICES IN MIDDLE BYZANTINE EPIRUS

At this point the question arises whether it is possible to define 'consumption' in relation to the region of Epirus from the 7th to the 12th century. Two sources of evidence offer some insights: archaeological finds and a limited amount of written texts. Several studies allow an overview of archaeological finds concerning commodities in Epirus during this period (a summary is presented in chronological order in Tables 1-2).[20] Among the limited number of written sources offering relevant information, one text is of particular importance to our approach. It concerns a letter by the Metropolitan of Nafpaktos, John Apokaukos (ca. 1155-1233), to the Metropolitan of Thessaloniki, Dimitrios, dated to 1225 (see Appendix).

In discussing this letter three preliminary points are important in my opinion. First of all, in Middle Byzantine Epirus consumption seems to have concerned a variety of different goods, as shown in Tables 1 and 2:

(A) – non-durable goods (foods, consumable artefacts such as coarse pottery and basic tools);
(B) – durable goods (sophisticated artefacts, mainly made of metals);
(C) – services (industry, craftmanship);
(D) – symbolic goods (works of art, inscriptions).

These commodities were either locally produced (Table 1) or imported (Table 2). The inhabitants' preferences for each of these categories of commodities are discussed in detail below (Part III.A.) in reference to four characteristic sites or site-assemblages which present the highest rates of consumption in the region: Nafpaktos, Chalkis (Ag. Triada Hill near Kato Vassiliki), Kefalos and Arta (Fig. 1).

The second point to be underlined, is that Apokaukos' letter allows us an insight into Byzantine cultural consumption practices in one of the mentioned four sites. While describing the goods in Nafpaktos (the provincial capital of the theme of Nikopolis), he specifically mentions the ones citizens enjoy the most. These are:

(A) – non-durable goods, such as fish and citrus;
(B) – durable goods, such as abundant and clean water, which was considered healthy;
(C) – services, such as the manufacture of furniture, draperies, and household equipment; the construction of paved roads and buildings (including an impregnable fort, baths, churches, and big houses).

Among the consumption of these services, we can discern the consumption of spaces as symbolic goods. These issues are discussed in length below (in part III.B).

The third preliminary point to mention, is that practices of the production and consumption of goods greatly diverged from place to place. The preferences of consumers towards either locally made or imported goods, and towards diverse symbolic goods, greatly varied depending on location. Four clear examples of such different consumption cultures are found in the areas of cities, such as Nafpaktos and Arta, and non-cities, such as Mt Varassova and Kefalos (discussed below; in Part III.A).

III – BYZANTINE CONSUMPTION GEOGRAPHIES

These remarks bring us to 'consumption geographies'. This term comes from Cultural geography, a field which works to produce 'maps of meaning' through an understanding of the interplays of geography and culture. It focuses on how cultures work in practice and in space, and how cultures are embedded in everyday situations, as locatable, specific phenomena.[21] Cultural geography has a long tradition in suggesting that spaces, places, goods and services are produced to be consumed and that they are constituted by economic, political, socio-spatial and cultural practices and processes which are geographically diverse.[22]

III.A – CONSUMING CITIES OR CONSUMING 'URBAN' ENVIRONMENTS? – I will now discuss evidence from Middle Byzantine Epirus in order to investigate whether the Byzantine notion of consumption in this Greek region is related to 'urbanism' and urban environments, as it did in its original setting of emergence in modernity and as Angeliki Laiou has previously assumed. At present, the definition of urban settlements in southern Epirus based on their form and planning has previously been unproductive.[23] Explicitly, apart from the provincial capital 'city', Nafpaktos, and a few 'town'-formations at Nikopolis (7th-11th century), Lefkada (7th-12th century), Vonitsa (9th-12th century) and Arta (12th century), settlement patterns mostly allowed for more hybrid (dispersed or multinucleate) settlement formations: a) around Arta (10th-12th century), b) in the upper delta of the Acheloos River (9th-12th century), c) around the lower delta of the Acheloos River and Varassova Mountain (7th-12th century), d) on the western coast of Acarnania (7th-12th century).[24] A comparative evaluation of consumption practices in these areas, based on several kinds of commodities, seems to confirm my previous interpretation that some of these hybrid settlement formations worked as 'urban' environments.[25] This allows concluding that the Byzantine notion of consumption clearly preserves the prototype 'urban' connotations of the term, yet it was not exclusive to towns and cities.

A mapping of the archaeological evidence of Byzantine consumption in southern Epirus helps illustrating this point. The maps in Figs. 2-7 represent consumption of different kinds of locally-produced and imported goods, according to the archaeological finds, at different sites for every century.[26] These maps do not support a dramatic concentration of consumption in the Epirote cities as opposed to the countryside. In fact, they amplify Michel Carrié's recent rejection of Moses Finley's dichotomy between 'consumer city' and 'producing hinterland'.[27] They show that high-level and low-level consumption is associated with chronological periods but not necessarily with the existence or lack of cities. Within a given period of time, consumption practices spread equally in cities, towns, and other settlements[28].

Four examples support this argument while taking us to place-, region- or province-specific consumption patterns. Around the city of Nafpaktos, the population has not only been consuming a wide range of goods, produced either in the city and its hinterland or imported from Boeotia and the Peloponnese, but also enjoyed services, artisanal production, monumental art and intellectual production. Mount Varassova and southern Aetolia are considered as part of Nafpaktos' integral hinterland, but Mount Varassova seems to have functioned as a 'dispersed urban environment' on its own. Archaeological evidence from ancient Chalkis ('Aetolian Chalcis' on the Ag. Triada hill below Mt. Varassova), for example, shows that this area supplied and consumed industrial products: ceramics, metalwork and probably silk textiles.[29] Furthermore, the area of Nafpaktos offered lines of communication with the Peloponnese towards an even wider network of commodity-chains.

Another large consumption centre was the area of the Ambracian Gulf in southwestern Epirus. Part of another such 'dispersed urban environment' after the 6th century, the site of Kefalos, consumed goods typical of a Late Antique provincial capital. The dense concentration of commodities on the islet can only be compared with those of the city of Nikopolis itself and with the later, also multinucleate, urban setting of Arta. Cultural goods in the entire region of Arta were very important; some were local products but made using systematically imported expertise or workmanship.[30] Many commodities here were locally manufactured (see Table 1), and others were imported from Corinth, Boeotia, central and western Greece, Albania and Italy (see Table 2).[31]

These four sites, Nafpaktos, Arta, Varassova and Kefalos present evidence for the highest rates of consumption: they were one city, one town, one multinucleate site of secular and monastic settlements and one off-shore island-shelter which developed perhaps into a monastery. Consequently, the answer to our original question in this part of the chapter is negative: the city is not central in the definition of the notion of consumption in Byzantium as it is in modern times.

IIIB – BYZANTINE SPATIALITIES OF CONSUMPTION – But, if not the existence of cities, what was then the vital factor for the creation of Middle Byzantine places of consumption? The answer is the proximity to land and water routes (i.e. the cause of the emergence of an urban settlement – not the settlement itself). By juxtaposing a map of settlement with communication routes used during that period and a map of consumption, one can understand why people in the region of Nafpaktos and Aetolia were mainly orientated towards the Peloponnese and Boeotia, while people living around the Ambracian Gulf were more cosmopolitan.

These practices and connections signify cultural movements and flows from one space to another depending on communication access, contact and connectedness. They confirm that spaces, places, goods and services are produced to be consumed and that they are constituted by – geographically diverse – economic, political, socio-spatial and cultural practices and processes. This is evident from the diversity of consumption practices from place to place within Middle Byzantine Epirus, which mainly depend on locality but not on the settlements' administrative status (city, town, monastery, village or otherwise), as discussed above. Space was also a commodity since it was a social and cultural product, as I have discussed extensively elsewhere.[32]

John Apokaukos' letter (see Appendix), discussed above, allows us to build up on these ideas. It is a kind of ekphrastic text[33] which seems to be well grounded on real-time, everyday spatial experience of the city, as I have discussed in length in another study.[34] His narrations about historical buildings (such as the castle, the episkopeion, and the baths) match very well their archaeologically-documented material remains.[35] Nevertheless, Apokaukos' main intention in this letter is not to provide a precise description of the city; instead he aims for a praise of his city's advantages and an expression of collective local identity. So, on the one hand, he discusses the goods available in the city by designating a large range of commodities, which citizens enjoy.

On the other hand, he writes as a metropolitan to another metropolitan of higher rank (i.e. of Thessaloniki) comparing the two bishoprics and wondering why the metropolitan of Thessaloniki did not choose Nafpaktos for himself.[36] Hence, in his narrative about his own city, this availability of goods and this specific consumption culture is not only part of the citizens' collective local identity, but also an integral part of power relations within the community and with others.[37] Apokaukos fulfils his aim by using the following arguments.

The citizens of Nafpaktos have adequate resources in order to produce and consume a variety of fish and citrus of excellent quality:

'[…] wouldn't you praise our fish and our citrus fruits profoundly? Because among the latter some are as large as jars, as beautiful in appearance as they are good to eat and pleasing to the sense of smell? And [because] the former are diverse and delicious and clean, and belonging to all kinds and races, one might say, they are of countless colours?' (Apokaukos, l. 14-19)[38]

The citizens of Nafpaktos support and enjoy a local administration which cares for providing materials as well as services (l. 19-35) for keeping the religious and secular infrastructure in good shape:

'[…] isn't our fortress hard to capture or even near impregnable? Hasn't it been built as if hanging in the air? Doesn't it rival the comedian's cloud-cuckoo-land? This city next to it not touching the ground, but [sitting] in thin air and having walls elevated to an almost breathless height and an aerial enceinte. And isn't our entire city free from mud? Indeed, I hear many deem our citizens happy because neither do their shoes get dirty and muddy during stormy weather and rain, nor do they crawl in the dirt […] even if the celestial waterfalls would again open up over my Nafpaktos.' (Apokaukos l. 22-29)[39]

In short, the inhabitants of Nafpaktos had the smartness of selecting a high, airy and beautiful location as their residence, with lovely views over the sea, and with abundance of clean, healthy water, (l. 6-12, 19-26, 35-58). Last but not least, they had the power and aesthetic education to demand and ensure services for cleanness and safety. For example, besides the impregnable fort and the paved roads, they had the pleasure of large dwellings:

'Don't reproach the marble staircases of our houses and the marble-slab floors of their terrasses, which because of their elevated foundation throws the eyes of the viewers towards the sea below and are shadowed by fragrant plants, and this circular railing, traversing the pavement, [made] by dappled marble columns supporting other transverse beams made of the same material [...]' (Apokaukos l. 6-12)[40]

And then there were the beautiful buildings, including baths and cisterns, in the town itself:

'Aren't our baths suspended? Don't they attract the spectator's look? Aren't they adorned with lively colours? Aren't they illuminated by glass windows? Don't they offer pleasure to the one who takes a bath? Aren't they entirely of marble? Aren't there bright white cisterns next to them? (Apokaukos l. 19-22)[41]

Furthermore, there were the springs with clean water, accessible to all citizens, regardless of age:

'[In our city there are many water springs] from which we drink abundant water, drawing the clean water with our hands and drinking from them, like dormice [...] this would be unfortunate, not fortunate, for a city in which an old man might die of thirst if his hands are not steady enough to draw water from the well and doesn't have someone to do it for him. But in our city, old men and women, just like the young, easily draw water, they drink as they want all the time; there is no need for a bucket that often spills the water so one has to fetch it again, no rope rubbing their palms, no chain hurting their fingers, no rope rotting from the humidity. The myth tells the story of how Pegasus stroke the ground with his foot and water immediately gushed forth and the place was named Tarsus [...]. Yet in Nafpaktos it seems that not one Pegasus, but several stroke the land and made many springs gush forth; and there are in the city springs pouring water both within and outside the walls. And, if Elim cannot be recorded for its twelve springs, Nafpaktos can rather be recorded for their great number. And perhaps a water surveyor would hesitate to deliver the number of springs in Nafpaktos [...]' (Apokaukos l. 35-56)[42]

However, life in Nafpaktos was enjoyed with respect for the soul and without provoking with extreme luxury:

'My episkopeion is not all made of marble, it is not a small palace white like milk, no jeering man should say that! [...] And my semantron for the morning call is placed by the door and it does not sound loudly through the open space of marble, nor does it confine the soul with an unpleasant sound [...] but mildly and in a moderate voice it encourages the bishop to say his blessings.' (Apokaukos l. 1-6)[43]

Thus, for the inhabitants of this town in the Middle Byzantine period space was not only a durable, but also a symbolic good.[44] In Apokaukos' narration, the consumption not only of foods and services but also of a wealthy, beautiful environment and of sophisticated personal and public spaces provided the citizens of Nafpaktos with significant prestige.

In the very same way, a recent study showed how water consumption in Australia is to be understood as part of a broader set of consumption practices, associated with suburban space, which allowed citizens accumulating cultural capital.[45] In a more general perspective, the construction and use of magnificent public and private buildings and monuments in metropolitan cities (from the Parthenon in Athens to the Eiffel tower in Paris and the Aspire Tower in Doha) is a similar diachronic phenomenon. It is no coincidence, therefore, that considering the many metaphors and symbols of an economic and cultural way of life captured in the built space of the World Trade Center in New York, the Twin Towers provided for enemies of that way of life a clear target to focus their attack on.

As far as Middle Byzantine Epirus is concerned, the mapping of the consumption of culture in this Greek region reveals a complex cultural organisation of economic transactions, social institutions and ideological constructions that continually redrew the boundaries between social classes, between public and private life, and between high-level and low-level art. However, this is not the place to discuss the details of that multifaceted and multilayered phenomenon. Still, the example of textual evidence provided by the letter of Apokaukos helps discern three reasons why archaeological research alone seems inadequate to get a full picture of the consumption of culture in Middle Byzantine Epirus.

Firstly, archaeological evidence only partly reveals what Byzantines considered as valuable goods; this knowledge can only be obtained by the contribution of textual sources. Secondly, archaeology is often unable to allow distinguishing between spatial lives of commodities and that of de-commodified objects, i.e. objects which are found in use settings posterior to their original consumption context (such as grave offerings), and whose original spatial life as commodities is now untraceable. Thirdly, archaeology somehow easily assumes consumption as a process which follows a singular and universal trajectory, to be differentiated simply in terms of rate of change, geographic extent and time. However, consumption is a quite contingent and certainly complex phenomenon which variations are highly influced by geographical location and by social, political and economic interactions among people, things and processes.[46]

CONCLUSION

As a general conclusion, it seems quite clear that only the use of the full range of textual and archaeological sources, as well as of historical, archaeological, economic and cultural approaches, will result in a better understanding of 'consumption' in the Byzantine world. In a more specific perspective, the focus on geographies of consumption in Middle Byzantine Epirus seems to allow some answers to the questions formulated at the beginning of this chapter, as well as to offer a few additional observations.

First of all, archaeological and textual evidence reveal the existence of multiform consumption patterns in Middle Byzantine Epirus. Relevant consumption practices concern a variety of different goods: (A) – non-durable (foods, consumable artefacts such as coarse pottery and basic tools); (B) – durable (sophisticated artefacts, mainly made of metals); (C) – services (industry, craftsmanship); (D) – symbolic goods (works of art, inscriptions, spaces).

Secondly, the city does not seem to have played a central role in defining Byzantine consumption in the way urbanism does for modern consumption. High levels and variable patterns of consumption are in fact evident in other kinds of settlements, which produced an effect of what has been described as 'alternative or dispersed urban environments'. In other words, the Byzantine notion of consumption in Epirus is not exclusively related to 'urbanism' and urban environments, in the way it was in the early modern context when the present-day concept of 'consumption' emerged. As opposed to a dominant role for a hierarchy of settlements, the vital factor for the creation of places of consumption in Byzantine Epirus seems to have been the proximity to communication routes.

When it comes to geographies of consumption, the place-specific, region-specific or province-specific consumption patterns, which can be discerned in Middle Byzantine Epirus, suggest a significant diversity of consumption practices from place to place. Differences seem to have dependend principally on place-specific or region-specific cultural practices and orientations, and not so much on the administrative status of settlements, such as city, town, monastery, village, etc.

The situation in Epirus indeed suggest, that, when it comes to the spatiality of cultural practices of consumption in Byzantine culture, spaces were connected and made meaningful through consumption practices. Furthermore, Middle Byzantine textual evidence from that region seems to indicate that spaces themselves functioned as produced and consumed commodities, taking the form of durable goods, services and symbolic goods.

Last but not least, every step forward in our understanding of the interconnectedness of Byzantine consumption places and practices, as well as of their complex social, political and economic interactions, calls for further theoretical advances in the integration of textual, archaeological, economic and cultural approaches. The study of geographies of consumption provides an excellent starting ground for such a multi-disciplinary perspective on a vital aspect of daily life in the Byzantine world.

APPENDIX

*

Extract from a letter by John Apokaukos, Metropolitan of Nafpaktos, to Demetrios, Metropolitan of Thessaloniki.⁴⁷

[...] Καὶ τὸ ἐπισκοπεῖον δέ τὸ ἐμόν οὐ καταμάρμαρον ὅλον, οὐ λευκὸν ᾗ γάλα,
εἴποι τις τοῦτο μὴ σκώπτης ἀνήρ, συνεπτυγμένον παλάτιον. [...]
Ὁ δέ γε ἐμὸς τοῦ ὄρθρου σημαντὴρ θυραῖος ἱστάμενος καὶ παρὰ μαρμαρίνῳ
ὑπαίθρῳ οὐκ ἀνάγει τὴν φωνὴν ἐκ τῶν σπλάχνων, οὐδέ τῇ ἐξηχήσει
5 στενοχωρεῖται τοῦ πνεύματος [...] ἀλλ᾽ ἡμέρως καὶ με μετρημένῃ φωνῇ εὐλογεῖν
προτρέπεται τὸν ἐπίσκοπον. [...] Μὴ κακίζεις καὶ τοὺς τῶν ἡμετέρων
καταλυμάτων μαρμαρίνους ἀναβαθμοὺς καὶ τὰ μαρμαρόστρωτα ὕπαιθρα, διὰ
τὴν ὑψηλότοπον ἵδρυσιν τὴν ὄψιν τῶν δρώντων πρὸς τὴν ὑποκειμένην
θάλασσαν ἀκοντίζοντα καὶ τοῖς τῶν φυτῶν εὐώδεσι σκιαζόμενα, καὶ τὸν ἐν
10 κύκλῳ τοῦτον φραγμόν, τοῦ ἐδάφους μὲν ἀνατρέχοντα, ἐκ κιονίσκων δὲ
ποικιλλομένων μαρμαρίνων ἐπὶ τὰς κεφαλὰς ἀνεχόντων ἑτέρας ἐγκαρσίας
εὐθείας, ἐξ ὁμοίας τῆς ὕλης, αἷς ἐπιστηθίζουσιν ἑαυτοὺς οἱ περὶ τὸ τῆς αὐλῆς
προκύπτοντες ἔδαφος; ταῦτα τὰ τῶν ἐλαχίστων ἡμῶν, τῶν σμικροπολιτῶν, τῶν
ἐρημοπολιτῶν, ἵνα τι καὶ τῶν σῶν φίλων εἴπω. μὴ καὶ τοὺς ἰχθύας ἡμῶν, μὴ καὶ
15 τὰ κίτρα ἡμῶν οὐκ ἐπαινέσεις εἰς ἐπαρκές; ὅτι τῶν μὲν ἔστιν ἃ κάδδοις
ἁμιλλῶνται πρὸς μέγεθος καὶ ὡς ὡραῖα μὲν ἰδεῖν, καλὰ δ[ε] φαγεῖν καὶ τὴν
ὀσφραντικὴν θηλῦναι διὰ τὴν εὔπνοιαν; οἱ δὲ διαφορογενεῖς μέν, εὔβρωτοι δέ,
καθαροὶ δέ, ποῖοι δὲ καὶ γένος παντοδαπὸν καὶ φυλαί, ὡς εἴποι τις,
μυριόχρωμοι; τὸ δὲ λουτρὸν ἡμῶν οὐ μετάρσιον; οὐ τὴν ὄψιν ἕλκει τοῦ
20 βλέποντος; οὐ γραφικοῖς ποικίλλεται χρώμασιν; οὐ φωταγωγοῖς ὑέλοις
καταπεφώτισται; οὐχ ἡδονὴν τῷ λουομένῳ ἐντίθησιν; οὐ καταμάρμαρον ὅλον;
οὐ δεξαμεναὶ διάλευκοι παρ᾽ αὐτῷ; τὸ φρούριον δὲ ἡμῶν οὐ δυσανάλωτον ἢ
μικροῦ καὶ ἀνάλωτον; οὐκ ἐπὶ μετεώρου τοῦ ἀέρος ἐπῳκοδόμηται; οὐ τῇ τοῦ
κωμικοῦ Νεφελοκοκκυγίᾳ παραμιλλᾶται; πόλις αὕτη παρ᾽ ἐκείνῳ μὴ ψαύουσα
25 γῆς, ἐν δὲ τῷ μανῷ ἀέρι καὶ τῷ μικροῦ μὴ ἀναπνευστῷ διῃρμένα ἔχουσα
τείχη καὶ τὸν περίβολον ἐνάεριον. ἡ δὲ πᾶσα πόλις ἡμῶν οὐχὶ ἄπηλος; καὶ μὴν
πολλῶ ἀκούω μακαριζόντων τοὺς ἡμετέρους πολίτας, ὅτι μηδὲ τὰ περὶ τοὺς
πόδας τούτων καττύματα ἐν χειμῶνι, ἐν ὄμβρῳ, καταμολύνονται τῷ πηλῷ,
οὐδ᾽ ἰλυσπῶνται βορβόροις, ὡς τὰ τῶν ζώων φιλόπηλα, οὐδὲ τῆς τετριμμένης
30 διὰ τὸ ἐκ τοῦ πηλοῦ πλαδαρὸν ἐκ τοῦ παραβαδίζειν ἀπομηκίζονται, οὐδὲ
ξυλίνας ἐμβάδας, ὡς ποδοκάκην, ἕκαστος ὑποδέεται, καθηλωμένας, καὶ

ταῦτα, ὡς μὴ τὸ περὶ τὴν γῆν μέρος τῶν ὑποδημάτων τούτων ἐκτρίβοιτο, οὐδ᾿
ἀλληλόκτυπον πάταγον ἐξηχοῦσι περὶ τὸ ἔδαφος τοῦ ναοῦ, οὐδὲ μολύνουσιν
ὁπωσοῦν πατοῦντες αὐτὸ, κἂν οἱ καταρράκται αὖθις τοῦ οὐρανοῦ τῇ ἐμῇ
35 Ναυπάκτῳ ἐπανοιχθῶσιν. ὅσαι τοῦ ἡμετέρου περιβόλου ἐντὸς, ὅσαι τούτου
ἐκτὸς καὶ ὅσαι ἄλλη ἐπ᾿ ἄλλη προρρέουσιν ἀργυρίζουσαι οὐδ᾿αὐταὶ σου τὴν
γλῶσσαν πρὸς ὕμνησιν ἐκκαλέσονται; ἐξ ὧν ἡμεῖς πίνομεν ἄφθονον ὕδωρ, τὸ
ποτὸν καθαρὸν καὶ χερσὶν αὐτῶν ἀπαντλοῦμεν καὶ τούτων ἀπορροφῶμεν, ὡς
οἱ ἀσπάλακες, καὶ χειρόκμητον ὕδωρ καὶ κατορωρυγμένον ἀφύσσομεν, οὐδὲ
40 ποσὶ περὶ τὸ στόμα τοῦ φρέατος ἀντιβαίνομεν καὶ δακτυλοσκοπούμεθα σχοίνῳ
διὰ τὴν ἐκ ταύτης τραχύτητα. δυστυχήματα ταῦτα, οὐκ εὐτυχήματα πόλεως,
παρ᾿ ᾗ καὶ γέρων ἴσως ἀποτελεῖται τῇ δίψῃ, αὐτὸς μὲν παρεμείνας ἔχων τὰς
χεῖρας καὶ μὴ δυναμένας ἀντλεῖν, ἑτέρου δὲ μὴ εὐτυχῶν τοῦ ἀντλήσαντος· αἱ
δὲ παρ᾿ ἡμῖν καὶ γραῖαι καὶ γέροντες, ὡς οἱ νέοι, πρόχειρον ἀντλοῦσιν ὕδωρ,
45 πίνουσιν ὡς θέλουσιν εἰς ὅλον χρόνον· οὐ κάδος αὐτοῖς ἐξεχύθη πολλάκις εἰς
δευτέραν ἄντλησιν ἠναγκασμένοις, ἡ σχοῖνος οὐκ ἔτριψεν αὐτῶν παλάμας,
ἅλυσις οὐκ ἔθλιψεν αὐτῶν δακτύλους, σκληρὸν παρακρέμασμα πρὸς τῷ
σχοινίῳ ἐξ ὑγρότητος μὴ σαπῇ τὸ σπαρτίον. ὁ μὲν οὖν μῦθος αὐτονόμων τὸν
τοῦ Πηγάσου ταρσὸν πατάξαι λέγει τὴν γῆν καὶ πηγὴν εὐθὺς ἀναροιβδῆσαι τῷ
50 παταγμῷ καὶ Ταρσὸν ὀνομασθῆναι τὸν τόπον· Κιλίκων πόλις αὕτη περιφανὴς
καὶ τοῦ Ταρσέως Παύλου πατρίς. τὴν Ναύπακτον δὲ οὐχ εἷς, ὡς ἔοικε,
Πήγασος, δυσάριθμοι δὲ πατάξαντες ἐν αὐτῇ πολλῶν πηγῶν ἀνάδοσιν
ἐποιήσαντο· καὶ ἔστι ταύτης τὰ ἔσωθεν καὶ τὰ ἔξωθεν καὶ ὕδασι
κατανλούμενα· καὶ εἰ διὰ τὰς δυοκαίδεκα πηγὰς ἀνάγραπτος ἡ Ἑλήμ,
55 ἀναγραπτ[έα] μᾶλλον ἡ Ναύπακτος διὰ τὴν τούτων διαψιλείαν, καὶ ὀκνήσειεν
τάχα ὑδατομέτρης ἀριθμῷ παραδοῦναι τὰς ἐν Ναυπάκτῳ πηγάς, ἐξ ὧν ἔπιες,
ἐξ ὧν ἐλούσω, ἐν αἷς τὸ σὸν τριβώνιον ἀπερρύπωσας, ὦ δυσάρεστε σὺ καὶ τὰς
ἀλλοτρίας περιφρονῶν ἀγαθότητας.

CENTURIES	7th	8th	9th	10th	11th	12th
I. SYMBOLIC AND DURABLE GOODS							
Lead seals	Nikopolis (Theme) – Epirus				Arta	
			Kephallenia (Theme) – Acarnania			
				Nafpaktos		
	Nikopolis (City)				
Lead egkainion				Evinochori, near Agios Georgios		
Pendant cross, simple (copper alloy)?	Kefalos				
Pendant cross, reliquary (copper alloy)?			Mavrikas, Ag. Triada			
Buckle, plain 8-shaped (iron)	Kato Vassiliki, Ag. Triada Hill				
Buckle, simple square (copper alloy)	Riza				
Jewellery (copper alloys)				Evinochori, Ag. Georgios, cemetery	Arta	
			Ag. Thomas, Rachi Bobora			
Coin hoards				Efpalio (Nafpaktos)		
				Kato Vassiliki, Ag. Triada Hill	Agrinio
Coins	Kefalos				Arta	
	Nikopolis		Nafpaktos			Ermitsas River, Taxiarchis
			Varassova S, Ag. Nikolaos	Kandila, Mytikas, Ag. Sophia		
				Aetoliko, Panagia Finikia, basilica	Neochori	
				Ag. Thomas, Rachi Bobora	Stratos	
				Macheras		

TABLE 1 (A) – Evidence of local production and supply of goods (M. Veikou).

CENTURIES	7th	8th	9th	10th	11th	12th
Inscriptions, painted				Mt Arakynthos, Ag. Nikolaos Kremastos		Mt Arakynthos, Ag. Nikolaos Kremastos
Inscriptions, carved						Efpalio, Varnakova Monastery
						Louros, Ag. Varnavas
						Nafpaktos, castle
Opus sectile and mosaics	Mytikas, Ag. Sophia			Mt Arakynthos, Panagia Trimitou		Efpalio, Varnakova Monastery
	Mastro, Episkopi					
Frescoes			Stamna, Ag. Theodoroi	Agrinio, Mavrikas, Ag. Triada	Gavrolimni, Panagia Panaxiotissa	Agrinio, Mavrikas, Ag. Triada
	Kandila, Mytikas, Ag. Sophia				Nea Kerassounda, Kastro ton Rogon	Kandila, Mytikas, Ag. Eleousa
				Varassova N-E, Ag. Pateres		Myrtia, Myrtia Monastery
				Arakynthos, Ag. Nikolaos Kremastos		Mt Arakynthos, Ag. Nikolaos Kremastos
					Lefkada, Vurnikas, Ag. Ioannis Karavias	
						Mastro, Episkopi

TABLE I (B) – Evidence of local production and supply of goods (M. Veikou).

CENTURIES	7th	8th	9th	10th	11th	12th
Sculptures	Skala, Metamorfosi Sotiros	Plissioi, Ag. Dimitrios Katsouris		Skala, Metamorfosi Sotiros	Plissioi, Ag. Dimitrios Katsouris	
	Aetoliko, Finikia, basilica	Mt Arakynthos, Panagia Trimitou			Arta, Ag. Vasileios stin Gefyra	Kandila, Mytikas, Agia Eleoussa
	Kandila, Mytikas, Ag. Sophia	Gavrolimni, Panagia Panaxiotissa			Efpalio, Varnakova Monastery	
	Kefalos				Vomvokou, Ag. Ioannis Prodromos Monastery	Kirkizates, Ag. Nikolaos Tis Rodias
			Kato Vassiliki, Ag. Triada Hill		Arta, Kato Panagia	
				Arta, town		
				Varassova S, Ag. Nikolaos	Aetoliko, Panagia Finikia	Agios Georgios (Evinochori), Agios Georgios
				Nafpaktos, city		
				Vlacherna, Vlachernai Monastery		
	Arta, Ag. Vassilios					Koronissia, Genethlio tis Theotokou
					Mt Kordovitza, Loutra Tryfou	
					Monastiraki, Metamorfosi Sotiros	
					Nea Kerassounda, Kastro ton Rogon	Nea Sampsounda, Agiolitharo, Agioi Apostoloi
						Oropos, Ag. Dimitrios
Buildings – infrastructures	Epirote settlements (see Veikou 2012, Tables 1-6; Chouliaras et ales 2014; Katsaros 2014; Kosti 2014; Koumousi 2014)					

TABLE 1 (C)   Evidence of local production and supply of goods (M. Veikou).

CENTURIES	7th	8th	9th	10th	11th	12th
	II. SERVICES						
Ceramic Tiles production	Kato Vassiliki, Ag. Triada Hill						
	Kefalos			Skala		
	Stefani, Ag. Varvara					
	Mastro, Episkopi			Mastro, Episkopi		
Pottery production	Nortwestern and Western Acarnania						
	Central and Southern Aetolia						
Textile industry	Kato Vassiliki, Ag. Triada Hill						
Metal industry	Kato Vassiliki, Ag. Triada Hill						
Glass (windowpanes?) workshop	Nikopolis					
Sculpture craftmanship				Nafpaktos		
	III. DURABLE GOODS						
Loom weights	Kato Vassiliki, Ag. Triada Hill						
	Kefalos						
Nails (iron)	Kato Vassiliki, Ag. Triada Hill						
	Kefalos						
Tools, utensils (copper alloy)?						Arta
Vessels (copper alloy)?				Macheras, Vristiana?		
Weight (iron)	Kefalos						
	IIII. NON DURABLE GOODS						
Domestic Ware, coarse (cooking-, serving-, storage-) wares, plain / glazed	Pleuron		Stamna		Stratos	
				Monastiraki		
	Koulmos						
	Kefalos						

TABLE 1 (D) – Evidence of local production and supply of goods (M. Veikou).

CENTURIES	7th	8th	9th	10th	11th	12th
Local Ware, coarse, plain / glazed	Ag. Ilias					
	Nafpaktos					
						Arta
"Slavic Ware"	Megali Chora					
Plain Glazed Wares				Varassova, Ag. Nikolaos		
				Kato Vassiliki, Ag. Triada Hill		
Glass (tesseare / vessels)	Kefalos					
	Nikopolis					

TABLE 1 (E) – Evidence of local production and supply of goods (M. Veikou).

CENTURIES	7th	8th	9th	10th	11th	12th
I. SYMBOLIC AND DURABLE GOODS						
Sculpture craftmanship (Peloponnese, central Greek mainland, western Macedonia)				Arta		
Fibula, copper alloy (Corinth)	Kato Vassiliki, Ag. Triada Hill					
Buckle, rectangular, copper alloy (Corinth)		Drymos				
II. NON DURABLE GOODS						
LR1 amphorae	Kefalos					
LR2 amphorae	Kryoneri					
	Kefalos					
	Kato Vassiliki, Ag. Triada Hill					
LR13 amphorae	Kefalos					
Stamped dish (Phocean Ware?)	Drymos					
ARS lamp	Kato Vassiliki, Ag. Triada Hill					
Red Slip Ware (lamps)	Kefalos					
Bread stamp (Patras)	Nafpaktos					
Amphorae Günsenin Type 1				Varassova, Ag. Dimitrios		
				Skala, Monastiraki		
Amphorae Günsenin Type 2 (Riley type 13)				Kefalos		
Otranto I amphora				Kefalos		
Amphorae Günsenin Type 2 or 3					Trigardo	
					Kefalos	
Coarse unglazed ware (Boeotia)				Lefkada, Koulmos		
Glazed White Ware II				Lefkada, Koulmos		

TABLE 2 (A) – Evidence of a local supply of imported goods (M. Veikou).

CENTURIES	7th	8th	9th	10th	11th	12th
Fine-sgraffito wares						Kato Vassiliki, Ag. Triada Hill
						Nafpaktos
Fine-sgraffito (central & northern Albania)					Arta	
Painted Fine-sgraffito wares						Kato Vassiliki, Ag. Triada Hill
						Nafpaktos
Slip-painted Wares					Nafpaktos	
Painted glazed wares					Kato Vassiliki, Ag. Triada Hill	
Slip painted 'dotted or Oyster/Spotted Style'					Kato Vassiliki, Ag. Triada Hill	
Fine-Sgraffito 'Spiral Style' (Corinth)						Arta
					Nafpaktos	
Green and Brown Painted Ware						Arta
						Nafpaktos
						Megali Chora
Sgraffito (Corinth)						Arta
Incised Sgraffito 'Medallion Style' (Corinth)						Arta
Monochrome Green Glazed Ware						Arta
Glazed Green Painted Red Ware						Megali Chora
						Angelokastro
Glazed & coarse wares (Italy)						Arta
Glass Vessels (Corinth?)		Kato Vassiliki, Ag. Triada Hill			Arta	
				Varassova S, Ag. Nikolaos		
Buckle, rectangular, copper alloy (Corinth)		Drymos				

TABLE 2 (B) – Evidence of a local supply of imported goods (M. Veikou).

NOTES

1. Miller 2005, 152.
2. Mansvelt 2005, 1.
3. Mansvelt 2005, 56-79; *Idem* 2008.
4. Mansvelt 2006, 1-6.
5. Jayne 2006.
6. Mansvelt 2008, 106.
7. Mansvelt 2008, 106.
8. Mort 2000.
9. Mansvelt 2005, 7.
10. Mansvelt 2005, 7.
11. Mansvelt 2005, 7.
12. Mansvelt 2005, 7.
13. Mansvelt 2005, 7.
14. Glennie and Thrift 1992; *Idem* 1996.
15. Mansvelt 2005, 34.
16. Laiou 2006.
17. See also Laiou and Morrisson 2007, 54 and 132-3.
18. Laiou 2006, 91-95, 121, esp. 94-95.
19. Stathakopoulos 2007.
20. The tables are based on the following literature: Vanderheyde 2005; Veikou 2012 (with previous literature); Chouliaras 2014; Chouliaras *et al.* 2014; Katsaros 2014; Kosti 2014; Koumousi 2014; Stavrakos 2014; Veikou 2015.
21. Mansvelt 2005, 56-79; *Idem* 2008.
22. See accounts by Mansvelt (2005, 56-57), and by Goodman *et al.* (2010, 13-40).
23. Veikou 2009; *Idem* 2010.
24. Veikou 2012, 273-303, 346-57.
25. Veikou 2010; *Idem* 2012, 273-303.
26. The maps are based on the following literature: Vanderheyde 2005; Veikou 2012 (with previous literature); Chouliaras 2014; Chouliaras *et al.* 2014; Katsaros 2014; Kosti 2014; Koumousi 2014; Stavrakos 2014; Veikou 2015.
27. Carrié 2012.
28. Veikou 2010; *Idem* 2012, 273-303.
29. See also Dunn 2006; Laiou 2012, 139-140, for the wider context of this production, further to the east.
30. See Vanderheyde 2005, *passim*; Veikou 2012, *passim*.
31. Veikou 2012, *passim* (with previous literature).
32. Veikou 2019.
33. The structure and phrasing of Apokaukos' narration recalls those used in the ekphraseis of Thessaloniki (Iohannes Kameniates, 10th century) and Nicaea (Theodore Doukas Laskaris, 1254); see Saradi 2012, 20-23, for a discussion of the structure of the text and an English translation of extracts.
34. Veikou 2018.
35. See Veikou (2012, 465-68) for the existing archaeological evidence of the Byzantine walls; Mamaloukos 2015, 15-20 for a topographic outline of the walls. See Athanassoulis and Androudis 2004, 520-23 for the existing archaeological evidence of the Byzantine *episkopeion*. See Kosti 2014 for a discussion of the existing archaeological evidence of the baths.
36. Lambropoulos 1988, 149-59.
37. Cf. Bourdieu 1993.
38. English translation by the author; see Appendix for the original text.
39. English translation by the author; see Appendix for the original text.

40 English translation by the author; see Appendix for the original Greek text of Apokaukos.
41 English translation by the author; see Appendix for the original Greek text.
42 English translation by the author; see Appendix for the original Greek text.
43 English translation by the author; see Appendix for the original Greek text
44 For the term see Bourdieu 1993.
45 Askew and McGuirk 2004.
46 Mansvelt 2005, 43; *Idem* 2008.
47 John Apokaukos, *Letters*, nr. 67, ed. Bee-Sepherle, 122-25.

BIBLIOGRAPHY

PRIMARY SOURCES

John Apokaukos, *Letter*, ed. by E. Bee-Sepherle, Unedierte Schriftstücke aus der Kanzlei des Johannes Apokaukos, des Metropoliten von Naupaktos (in Aetolien), *Byzantinisch-neugriechische Jahrbücher* 21 (1971-1974), 122-25, no. 67 (1-243). Modern Greek translation by E. Karayanni-Charalambopoulou, Η Ναύπακτος στα χρόνια του Απόκαυκου, *Naupaktiaka* 5 (1990-1991), 100-104. (New edition forthcoming by V. Katsaros.)

LITERATURE

Askew, L.E. and P.M. McGuirk 2004. Watering the suburbs: Distinction, conformity and the suburban garden, *Australian Geographer* 35, 17-37.

Athanassoulis, D. and P. Androudis 2004. Παρατηρήσεις στην οικοδομική ιστορία του βυζαντινού λουτρού του Κάστρου Ναυπάκτου, *Β΄ Διεθνές Ιστορικό και Αρχαιολογικό Συνέδριο Αιτωλοακαρνανίας (Αγρίνιο, 29-30-31 Μαρτίου 2002), Πρακτικά*, Vol. 2, Agrinion, 515-34.

Bourdieu, P. 1993. *The Field of Cultural Production. Essays on Art and Literature* (ed. Randal Johnson), New York.

Carrié, M. 2012. Were Late Roman and Byzantine economies market economies? A comparative look at historiography, in: C. Morisson (ed.), *Trade and Markets in Byzantium*, Washington DC, 13-26.

Chouliaras, I.P. 2014. Revealing of a mosaic floor in the excavation of an Early Byzantine basilica in Drymos of Vonitsa, in: I.P. Chouliaras (ed.), *The Archaeological Work of the Ephorate of Byzantine Antiquities in Aetoloakarnania and Lefkas, Conference Proceedings*, Nafpaktos, 197-212 (New Greek).

Chouliaras, I., K. Chamilaki, K. Katsika and G. Georgiou 2014. The rescue excavations of the 22nd Ephorate of Byzantine Antiquities in 2013, in: I.P. Chouliaras (ed.), *The Archaeological Work of the Ephorate of Byzantine Antiquities in Aetoloakarnania and Lefkas, Conference Proceedings*, Nafpaktos, 181-96 (New Greek).

Dunn, A. 2006. The rise and fall of towns, ports, and silk production in Western Boeotia: The problem of Thisvi-Kastorion, in: E. Jeffreys (ed.), *Byzantine Style, Religion and Civilization. In honour of Sir Steven Runciman*, Cambridge, 38-71.

Dunn, A. 2007. Rural producers and markets: Aspects of the archaeological and historiographic problem, in: M. Grünbart, E. Kislinger et al. (eds.), *Material Culture and Well-Being in Byzantium (400-1453)*, Vienna, 101-109.

Glennie, P.D. and N.J. Thrift 1992. Modernity, urbanism, and modern consumption, *Environment and Planning D: Society and Space* 10, 423-43.

Glennie, P.D. and N.J. Thrift 1996. Consumers, identities, and consumption spaces in Early Modern England, *Environment and Planning A: Economy and Space* 28, 25-45.

Goodman, M.K., D. Goodman and M. Redclift 2010. *Consuming Space. Placing Consumption in Perspective*, Farnham & Burlington.

Jayne, M. 2006. Cultural geography, consumption and the city, *Geography* 91.1, 34-42.

Katsaros V. 2014. The Early Christian and Byzantine monuments in Western Greece: survey of the research, in: I.P. Chouliaras (ed.), *The Archaeological Work of the Ephorate of Byzantine Antiquities in Aetoloakarnania and Lefkas, Conference Proceedings*, Nafpaktos, 57-78 (New Greek).

Kosti, I.Th. 2014. Byzantine baths: Aspects of daily life at Byzantine Nafpaktos, in: I.P. Chouliaras (ed.), *The Archaeological Work of the Ephorate of Byzantine Antiquities in Aetoloakarnania and Lefkas*, Nafpaktos, 91-100 (New Greek).

Koumoussi, A. 2014. Lead enkainion found in a Middle-Byzantine basilica at 'Agios Georgios' of Evinohori, Mesolongi, in: I.P. Chouliaras (ed.), *The Archaeological Work of the Ephorate of Byzantine Antiquities in Aetoloakarnania and Lefkas, Conference Proceedings*, Nafpaktos, 87-90 (New Greek).

Laiou, A. 2006. Μεταξύ παραγωγής και κατανάλωσης: είχαν οικονομία οι βυζαντινές πόλεις;, *Praktika tes Akademias Athinon* 81/B, 85-126.

Laiou, A. 2012. Regional networks in the Balkans in the Middle and Late Byzantine Period, in: C. Morisson (ed.), *Trade and Markets in Byzantium,* Washington DC, 125-46.

Laiou, A. and C. Morrisson 2007. *The Byzantine Economy*, Cambridge.

Lambropoulos, K. 1988. Ιωάννης Απόκαυκος, Συμβολή στην έρευνα του βίου καιτου συγγραφικού έργου του, Athens.

Lévi Strauss, C. 1973. *Anthropologie structurale deux,* Paris.

Mamaloukos, S. 2015. Παρατηρήσεις στην αρχιτεκτονική και την οικοδομική ιστορία των μεσαιωνικών οχυρώσεων της Ναυπάκτου, *Naupaktiaka* 18, 13-38.

Mansvelt, J. 2005. *Geographies of Consumption,* London.

Mansvelt, J. 2008. Geographies of consumption: Citizenship, space and practice, *Progress in Human Geography* 32.1, 105-17.

Miller, D. 1992. The young and the restless in Trinidad: A case of the local and the global in mass consumption, in: R. Silverstone and E. Hirsch (eds.), *Consuming Technologies*, London, 163-82.

Mort, E. 2000. Introduction. Paths to mass consumption: Historical perspectives, in: P. Jackson, M. Lowe, D. Miller and E. Mort (eds.), *Commercial Cultures, Economies, Practices and Spaces,* Oxford, 7-13.

Saradi, H. 2012. Idyllic nature and urban setting: An ideological theme with artistic style or playful self-indulgence, in: P. Odorico (ed.), *Villes de toute beauté: l'ekphrasis des cites dans les litteratures byzantine et byzantino-slaves*, Dossiers byzantins 12, Paris, 9-36.

Stathakopoulos, D. 2007. To have and to have not: Supply and shortage in the Late Antique world, in: M. Grünbart, E. Kislinger, D. Stathakopoulos and A. Muthesius (eds.), *Material Culture and Well-Being in Byzantium (400-1453)*, Vienna, 211-17.

Stavrakos, Ch. 2014. Ein Goldenes Hyperpyron des Kaisers Johannes III Vatatzes aus den Ausgrabungen des Hagios Georgios in Evinochorion von Aitoloakarnanien (Griechenland), in: I.P. Chouliaras (ed.), *The Archaeological Work of the Ephorate of Byzantine Antiquities in Aetoloakarnania and Lefkas*, Conference Proceedings, Nafpaktos, 151-58.

Vanderheyde, C. 2005. *La sculpture architecturale byzantine dans le thème de Nikopolis*, BCH Suppl. 45, Paris.

Veikou, M. 2009. 'Rural towns' and 'in-between' or 'third' spaces: Settlement patterns in Byzantine Epirus (7th-11th c.) from an interdisciplinary approach, *Archaeologia Medievale* 36, 43-54.

Veikou, M. 2010. Urban or rural? Theoretical remarks on the settlement patterns in Byzantine Epirus (7th-11th centuries), *Byzantinische Zeitschrift* 103.1, Abteilung, 118-29.

Veikou, M. 2012. *Byzantine Epirus: A Topography of Transformation. Settlements from the 7th to the 12th Centuries*, Leiden & Boston.

Veikou, M. 2014. Three buckles, two crosses, a fibula, and a coin-weight. Metalwork and some industrial features of Byzantine settlements in Western Greece from the seventh through the tenth century, in: P. Petrides and V. Foskolou (eds.), *Δασκάλα. Απόδοση τιμής στην καθηγήτρια Μ. Παναγιωτίδη-Κεσίσογλου*, Athens, 65-90.

Veikou, M. 2018. 'Telling Spaces' in Byzantium – Ekphraseis, place-making and the 'thick' description, in: Ch. Messis, M. Mullett and I. Nilsson (eds.), *Telling Stories in Byzantium: Narratological Approaches and Byzantine Narration*, Studia Byzantina Upsaliensia 19, Uppsala, 15-32.

Veikou, M. 2019. The reconstruction of Byzantine lived spaces: A challenge for survey archaeology, in: Ch. Diamanti, An. Vassiliou and Sm. Arvaniti (eds.), Ἐν Σοφίᾳ μαθητεύσαντες. Essays in Byzantine Material Culture and Society in Honour of Sophia Kalopissi-Verti, Oxford, 17-24.

FIG. 1 – Map of western Greek mainland, marking the location of the four archaeological sites discussed in this chapter (M. Veikou; the background is courtesy of Google Maps).

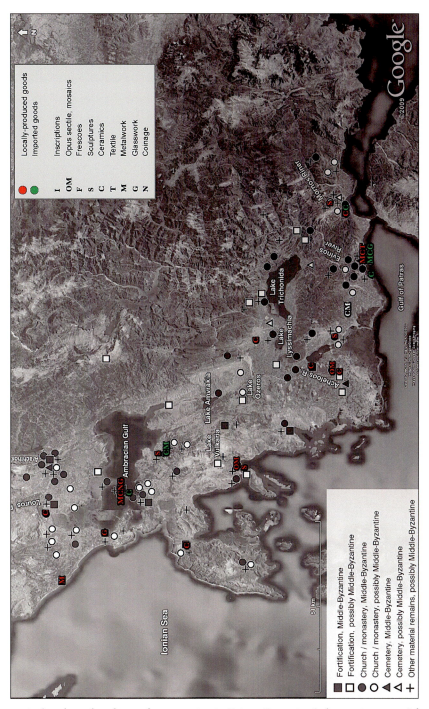

FIG. 2 – Archaeological evidence of consumption in Epirote Byzantine 'urban environments' during the 7th century (after Veikou 2012, map 16; the background is courtesy of Google Maps).

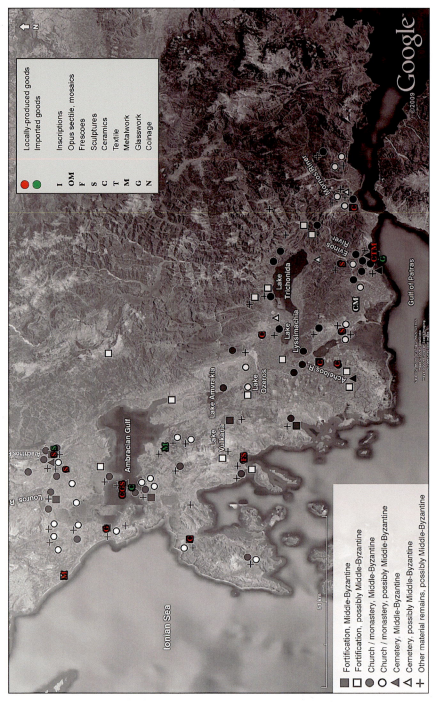

FIG. 3 – Archaeological evidence of consumption in Epirote Byzantine 'urban environments' during the 8th century (after Veikou 2012, map 16; the background is courtesy of Google Maps).

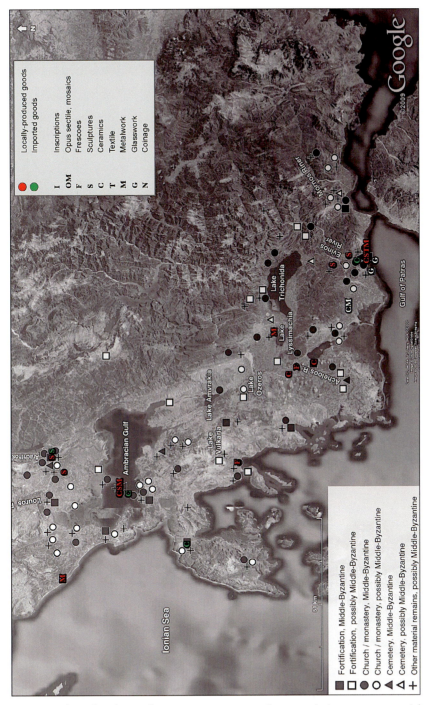

FIG. 4 – Archaeological evidence of consumption in Epirote Byzantine 'urban environments' during the 9th century (after Veikou 2012, map 16; the background is courtesy of Google Maps).

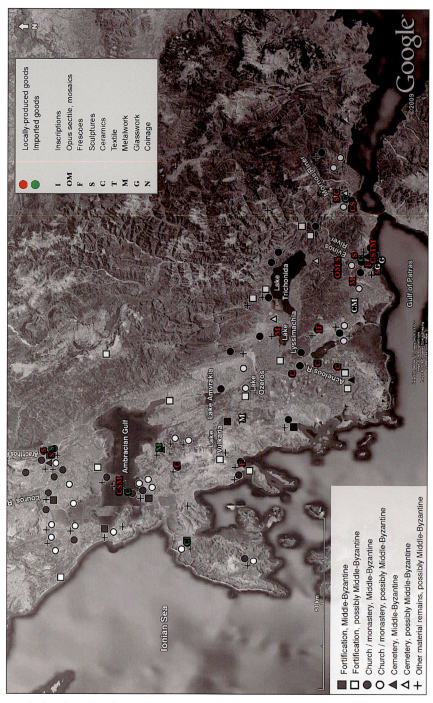

FIG. 5 – Archaeological evidence of consumption in Epirote Byzantine 'urban environments' during the 10th century (after Veikou 2012, map 16; the background is courtesy of Google Maps).

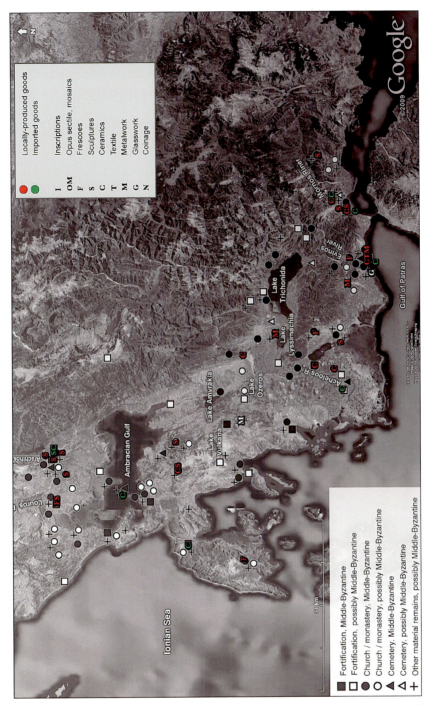

FIG. 6 – Archaeological evidence of consumption in Epirote Byzantine 'urban environments' during the 11th century (after Veikou 2012, map 16; the background is courtesy of Google Maps).

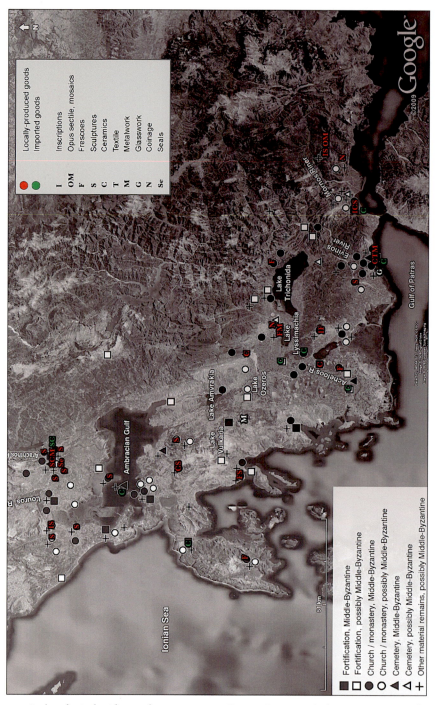

FIG. 7 – Archaeological evidence of consumption in Epirote Byzantine 'urban environments' during the 12th century (after Veikou 2012, map 16; the background is courtesy of Google Maps).

Production and consumption in Crete from the mid-7th to the 10th century AD: The archaeological evidence

Natalia Poulou

*

The Island of Crete was an important province of the Byzantine Empire, but on account of the Arab conquest in 827/828, it had turns and twists in its history which were rather different from those of the quite nearby Aegean islands.[1] This distinctive Byzantine history left its traces in a characteristic archaeological record on Crete. Of particular interest is the period from the mid-7th to the late 10th century. It concerns both the timespan which is sometimes described as the 'Transitional Period' (the era from the mid 7th to the 9th century, traditionally labelled as the early Middle Ages) and the period of the Arab occupation (9th and 10th centuries).

This chapter sets out to explore the ways in which larger and smaller cities as well as less substantial settlements in Crete participated in the trade network which was under development in the Byzantine Empire in spite of all the turbulence during this eventful period (Fig. 1). More specifically, I discuss here the trading contacts of Crete with the Aegean islands and with Constantinople from the 7th to the 10th century. Additionally, I will try to shed light on daily life activities during the Arab occupation (827/828-961).

Research has shown that throughout the centuries there always existed a functioning trade network across the Byzantine Empire, and that no matter the political and military ups and downs Byzantine cities engaged in trading activities on a local but also on an international level.[2] To explore the role of Crete in all this, we need to examine recent archaeological finds that shed light on the commercial activities and exchange of goods on the island during the time period under consideration. Developments in the material culture, more particular in ceramic objects recovered on different sites on the island may enable us to discern changes in production, fluctuations in commerce and imports, and, through those, variations over time in the consumption of goods in cities as well as in small-scale settlements on Crete.

Here, we focus on pottery and on amphorae in particular, as these provide evidence about the production and transfer of goods. At the same time, we will try not to lose sight of painted and glazed wares, as these also constitute important evidence for tracing production and consumption in Byzantine cities. In addition, I will use metal objects and examples of jewellery as well to substantiate the line of argument. The archaeological data will be presented here according to fabric and time of production, following a chronological sequence from the mid-7th to the 10th century.

CITIES, SETTLEMENTS AND ENCLOSURES FROM THE MID-7TH TO THE EARLY 9TH CENTURY

Before proceeding with the discussion of the archaeological objects recovered on Crete, it is usseful to relate briefly what is known from past archaeological research regarding human activity in cities, non urban settlements as well as coastal sites on Crete during the Byzantine period.[3] Although this is a broader topic that falls outside the scope of the present study, a brief overview will help to interpret the archaeological data that will be presented below.

Archaeological research has established that human activity in Byzantine cities and non-urban (large or small) settlements on Crete did not cease during or by the end of 7th century, but, in the majority of cases, continued uninterrupted throughout the 8th and at least the early decades of the 9th century. During the 7th century – probably around the middle of the century – existing urban fortifications were reinforced, either extensively or partially, as in the cases of Cydonia/Chania, Eleutherna, Herakleion, Chersonisos, Lyktos/Lyttos and Ierapetra.[4] In other cases, even new fortifications were constructed during this time, as was the case at Gortyn (Fig. 2).[5] Smaller fortified enclosures dating from the same 7th century have been documented at various sites in southern and eastern Crete, including the Psamidomouri hill at Lenta, as well as the hills at Tsoutsouros, Oxa/Oxia and Liopetro.[6] The archaeological record clearly shows that during this period human activity outside the fortified areas was equally maintained, as in the cases of Eleutherna and Gortyn.[7]

Finds from other cities, coastal areas or islets are equally informative: research at Knossos showed for instance apparently uninterrupted human activity up to the 9th century.[8] On the eastern coast of Crete, human activity at the site of Itanos continued at least until the early 9th century, contrary to what has been argued earlier. The pottery published from this site (ovoid amphorae and imported Glazed White Ware from Constantinople) can be dated to the 8th century,[9] while, the third phase of basilica A at Itanos must almost certainly be dated to the 9th century, and in any case after the late 8th century foundation of Saint Titus in Gortyn, the plan of which the Itanos basilica freely replicated (Fig. 3).[10]

Furthermore, the coastal settlements of Aghia Galini on the southern coast, and those of Priniatikos Pyrgos, of Mochlos (both the islet and the settlement on the northern Cretan coast) and that of Pseira island, date to the 8th century and also yielded evidence of occupation during the 9th century, a period of intense Arab advances. This seems to suggest that the Byzantine central administration, perhaps in view of that danger, had chosen to strengthen its coastal defence system on Crete in order to secure safe conditions for maritime commercial activities. The archaeological record shows that several of these coastal settlements remained commercially active during the Second Byzantine period (961-1210/11) as well.[11]

THE PERIOD FROM THE LATE 7TH TO THE 9TH CENTURY

The ceramic evidence – On Crete, the 7th, 8th and 9th centuries are characterized by a variety of centres of local pottery production. Macroscopic examination and archaeometrical research have shown that local production of ceramics continued throughout this period in several places of the island. It is worth noting that in Gortyn and in the wider Messara region there was local production of Painted Ware (see Fig. 4), of Coarse and Plain Ware (jugs, small jars, basins) and of amphorae.[12] At Eleutherna, fabric study and macroscopic examination have documented local production of everyday pottery (cups, jugs, bowls) since the 6th century. The actual workshops were possibly located in the wider area of Eleutherna or in the region of Mylopotamos, and they continued their production into the 7th, 8th and probably the 9th century. Petrographic analyses of ceramic samples from Eleutherna indicate a local production of amphorae during the same period. In these Eleutherna workshops, a first attempt was made to manufacture glazed pottery during the early 8th century (Fig. 5).[13]

Research on fabrics of ceramic finds from the Byzantine settlement of Pseira islet, provided substantial evidence on local (i.e. Cretan) pottery production from the end of the 7th to the early 9th century. Products included amphorae and vessels for daily-life use (such as basins), made by workshops which were probably located in the broader area of Mochlos (Figs. 6 and 8). During the late 8th/early 9th centuries, glazed vessels (i.e. chafing dishes) were made in the region of Kalo Chorio, in the gulf of Mirambello. Also, ovoid amphorae were locally produced on the southern Cretan coast (Figs. 7 and 9).[14]

It is interesting to note that the types of transport vessels produced on the island were identical to the ones produced in various production centres across the Empire, in particular the Byzantine globular amphorae, the ovoid amphorae and the amphorae type Hayes 45 (the so-called 'survival' type of LRA 1) (Figs. 8-10a-b). The local production of these amphorae suggests not only the existence of agricultural production in Crete, as the written sources inform us as well, but also the trade of certain products. At the same time, the archaeological record (i.e. amphorae) in many areas of the island also shows that the imports of agricultural products from a variety of Aegean regions continued in the period under study.[15]

As far as the fine pottery is concerned, we know that during the 8th to 9th centuries the first glazed wares, namely Glazed White Ware I and II, were imported from Constantinople. So far, these wares have been found at Heraklion, Gortyn, Ag. Galini, Pseira, Loutres (Mochlos) and Itanos.[16]

Metal artefacts: the belt buckles – Publications on metal objects from Crete are not numerous, but the recovery of a considerable number of bronze belt buckles and of one golden example seems of considerable importance for our discussion (Figs. 11a-b). They clearly suggest the presence of Byzantine dignitaries in Crete during the 7th, 8th and 9th centuries.[17]

THE ERA OF ARAB OCCUPATION (827/28-961)

It is well known that the Andalusian Arabs led by Abu Hafs Omar conquered Crete in 827/828, a fact which changed the status quo in the eastern Mediterranean. As far as the period of Arab occupation is concerned, there is surprisingly little material evidence documented on the island until now. The fact that this scarce material evidence comes from Heraklion corroborates the hypothesis that the Andalusian Arabs took this ciy, chose it as the capital of their emirate and named it Rabdh Al-Khandaq (or 'Fortress of the Ditch', after the dry moat surrounding the city; 'Chandax / Χάνδακας' in Greek, 'Candia' in Latin).[18]

The imported pottery – The three objects discussed here and dated to the period of the Arab occupation, have all been found at Heraklion.

The first is the upper part of an amphora which was found during an excavation at the Archaeological Museum of Heraklion in a 9th-century layer (Fig. 12). It is a fragment of the well-known amphora type known as 'Palestinian Amphora', or 'Late Roman Amphora 5/6', manufactured at an amphora production centre in Palestine, a wine exporting area.[19]

The second object from the Arab period is a jug with impressed decoration and green glaze dating to the first half of the 10th century; it was found during excavations at the Dominican monastery of St. Peter near the byzantine sea walls (Fig. 13). Comparative material is provided by finds from the Middle East: similar objects with relief decoration have been found in Mesopotamia (e.g., Raqqa, Samarra, Shiraz in modern Syria, Iraq and Iran) where they were dated to the 8th and 9th centuries.[20] It is well-kniown that caravans from the eastern Mediterranean with all kinds of products, such as wheat, oil, wine and nuts, reached these cities and other places around the Persian Gulf.[21] There, the traders from the Mediterrenean would sell their products, while supplying themselves with spices and precious silk carpets before returning home. In these areas not only food, precious materials and works of art changed hands, but it was also the end of the Silk Road, over which ideas, stylistic trends and techniques were transferred from far-away China to Persia, which from there found their way to the eastern Mediterranean area. It is not certain whether this particular jug with the impressed decoration and green glaze was manufactured in Persia. Nevertheless, I seems to me quite likely that the decoration style originated from the broader Mesopotamian area.[22]

The third object is a deep glazed dish with green and brown painted decoration, which was also found at the excavation of Saint Peter's monastery and can be dated to the 10th century (Fig. 14). It came all the way from the other side of the Mediterranean, that is to say: from one of the pottery workshops at Cordoba in modern Spain.[23]

The unglazed pottery from the period of the Arab occupation: a hypothesis – It seems that during the period of Arab occupation (827/28-961) life on Crete continued without serious changes in all cities and smaller settlement that were untouched by the conquest. The textual sources indicate that there was an abundance of agricultural products during this period.[24] These products were almost certainly transported in transport vessels such as amphorae, while common pottery for everyday use was probably to be found in every household, in cities and small settlements alike. Yet defining the distinctive features of pottery production dating to the Arab period in Crete has not been an easy task.

Any dating of objects to the Arab period on Crete seems in need to meet two criteria: 1 – There must be features that indicate a break with the prior Byzantine tradition; 2 – There must be numismatic evidence for that period which can be linked to the objects to be dated.

However, until now a lack of numismatic data from the Arab period hampers the secure dating of excavated layers to the period after 827/828. It is interesting to note that on the entire island, Arab coins have so far been found only at Heraklion and

Gortyn, while a coin of uncertain provenance is mentioned to have been retrieved from the Eleutherna region.[25] Still, the lack of numismatic evidence from the rest of the island is not necessarily a clear indication for a lack of activity. As proposed by Tsougarakis and as also argued above, a great number of settlements from the Early Byzantine period must have survived during the Arab occupation.[26] There seems to have been no serious disruption in the occupation or activities of these settlements. As a consequence, one may infer that pottery production did continue relatively uninterupted on Crete during the Arab period.

This brings us back to the first criterion: was there any detectable change in shapes, forms, features, fabrics or techniques detectable in the ceramic material which gives a clue for dating it to in the Arab period? Archaeological research and studies conducted by me during the past 25 years in various parts of the island, did *not* find any evidence or indication for changes in the production of pottery during this period. On the contrary, in several areas I have excavated or studied pottery which could be dated to the 9th century and fitted completely in the Byzantine tradition. In former days, the dating of such finds would be restricted to the first two decades of the 9th century, in other words prior to the Arab occupation of the island in 827/28. This, however, is unsatisfactorily, and I suggest a new approach.

In my view, the following is a good example. An amphora found in the Cretan Islet of Mochlos and dated to the 9th century belongs to the Gunsenin's type I, of late 9th-century production (Fig. 15).[27] One of the Yenikapı shipwrecks, dated with a coin to the end of the 9th century, carried amphorae of this same type.[28] So, when was the amphora found at Mochlos produced? Before 827/28, or rather after 961? I would propose to date this vessel to the period of Arab occupation on Crete. Not only is it an Gunsenin I amphora, indicating a late 9th-century date, but there are other arguments which lead to this conclusion. Apart from the small amount of imported pottery found on the island, bulk goods must have been transported in containers that were locally produced in Crete. This local pottery production most probably followed the previous local Byzantine pottery traditions of the the 8th and early 9th centuries. Moreover, imported goods were transported in ceramic containers from all over the Aegean and the Asia Minor which were also produced according to the Byzantine repertoire.

An interesting analogy may be offered by the situation in Syria right after the Arab conquest in the mid-7th century. In most of the regions, except for Damascus and several other large cities, archaeological research has shown that the societal structure and human activities of the Early Byzantine period remained almost intact and pottery production continued using shapes which were common before. During at least one century after the Arab conquest, there were no indications of significant changes in these aspects of daily life.[29] Taking into account all the differences between Syria and Crete, it seems seems no unreasonable to suggest that a similar situation existed in Crete during the Arab period.

In short: it now looks as if the two criteria mentioned earlier as necessary for dating objects found on Crete to the period of the Arab conquest, are after all not as indispensable as previously assumed. In fact, I believe that the first criterion cannot be sustained at all: pottery production in Crete was not different during the Arab period and seemed to have continued in all aspects along the lines of the 8th and 9th centuries.

Jewellery – Small artefacts such as jewellery securely dated to the period of Arab occupation in Crete are limited. Valuable evidence is provided however by a group of golden earrings, part of a treasure found at Messonisi (Rethymnon) along with a *solidus* of Michael II (820-829) and another one of Constantine VIII (913-959) (Fig. 16). Two of these earrings bear Kufic inscriptions with the invocation to God to bless their owners Aisa and Zaynab.[30] On the basis of the hybrid character of their decoration, closely related to both Byzantine and Fatimid traditions, it has been suggested that these earrings were manufactured in 10th-century Crete for Arab residents, probably before the Byzantine reconquest of 961.[31] In any case, since these golden earrings were found on the island, they serve as an important indication for the presence of a wealthy élite among the Arabs conquerors. Moreover, these finds seem to indicate the existence of the local production of luxury objects during this period on Crete.

THE SECOND BYZANTINE ERA (961-1210/11): THE 10TH CENTURY

In the spring of 961, after a well-organized campaign headed by the Byzantine general Nicephorus Phocas (912-969), Chandax/Heraklion was reconquered by the Byzantine Empire. Following the occupation of Cyprus in 965, the Byzantines consolidated their presence in the entire eastern Mediterranean.[32] What is most characteristic about Crete during the Second Byzantine period is its close contact with the capital Constantinople. Chandax became a city with significant commercial activity, while agricultural production was increasing all over the island. Land was a fundamental source of wealth, and a powerful aristocratic élite emerged.[33] At the same time, due to its geographical location on the intersection of various maritime routes, Crete became a very important station on the East-West trade networks.

The pottery – As far as the production of pottery is concerned, it is noteworthy that various regions with confirmed human activity during the last centuries of the Early

Byzantine (or First Byzantine) period continued their various activities throughout the Second Byzantine period as well (e.g., Heraklion, Eleutherna, Priniatikos Pyrgos, Mochlos, Pseira, Petras/Siteia).[34] The function of pottery workshops in these or nearby areas during the First Byzantine period has been the subject of various publications.[35] The same perspective may be fruitful if we set out to discuss the function of workshops of metal objects.

An assemblage of imported Polychrome White Ware – Among the glazed wares which were imported in Crete during the Second Byzantine period, an assembladge of Polychrome White Ware stands out in particular. This is a fine tableware produced at Constantinople during the second half of the 10th century.[36] Six examples of Polychrome White Ware were found in the same layer in Heraklion during an excavation in the area between the Monastery of St. Peter and the Byzantine fortification sea walls of the city, and they constitute one of the most interesting groups of painted glazed ware of the Middle Byzantine period found in Greece.[37] The find is yet another indication that besides Thessaloniki and Corinth, also Chandax/Heraklion had close contacts with Constantinople during this period. In addition, the presence of the ware in the main urban centre of Crete suggests that there existed on the island an prosperous, perhaps even aristocratic class with a clear preference for luxury items.

The finds of Polychrome Ware on Crete include plates and small cups. Here, I discuss two of them in some detail. The first is a small cup with a handle (now missing). On the inside the cup is decorated with a rosette in manganese and ochre, and covered with a glaze (Figs. 17a-c);[38] A cup with a similar shape has been excavated at Corinth.[39] Its exterior decoration is in manganese and ochre as well, and it looks similar to the decoration on painted tiles from Constantinople which are currently in the Louvre Museum.[40]

The second object is a large plate, of which only a part has been preserved (Fig. 18). Its interior is decorated in manganese and ochre with an ornamented elephant in front of a tree, while a half-acanthus leaf decorates the surface in front of the animal representation, and the rim of the plate is adorned with a tongue and dart motif. Although animal representations on plates of this category are not unknown,[41] the depiction of an elephant in a medallion on this plate is still unique, which makes this a one of a kind piece of Polychrome White Ware. Comparative decorations are only provided by objects of different materials belonging to different artistic traditions. Moreover, the elephant is clear evidence of Eastern influences, as the animal is, for instance, known to have been the symbol of royal or imperial power in Sasanian Persia, India as well as China. In this context, the decoration seems to suggest Eastern Sassanid influences.[42]

It is well known that artistic trends from the East spread westwards during various periods, following different paths each time, it is likely that also Byzantine artists of the 10th century made use of them. As Polychrome White Ware was produced in Constantinople, the artist who painted the scene may very well have copied a work which had been imported in the Byzantine capital. Designs based on Eastern influences are well documented on other luxury objects made of various materials. Byzantine silk fabrics manufactured at Constantinople may be mentioned in particular. Some of these silk textiles eventually ended up in cities of the West as gifts, like the example found in Charlemagne's tomb at Aachen (Germany), currently in the Aachen Cathedral's Treasury (Figs. 19a-b). An inscription on the textile shows that it was made in Constantinople:[43]

Ἐπί Μιχ(αήλ) πριμι(κηρίου ἐπί τοῦ) κοιτ(ῶνος) (καί) εἰδικοῦ
Πέτρου ἄρχοντ(ος) τοῦΖευξήπου ἰνδ(ικτυῶνος) [...]

The close relation between the decoration of the plate and the silk fabric even suggests that certain decorations which betray Eastern influeces used on Polychrome Ware, sculpture and minor objects were in fact introduced to the repertoire of Byzantine artists through the patterns of silk fabrics.[44] This underlines once more that not only precious artefacts, but also ideas, artistic expressions and techniques followed the Silk Road from China through Persia to Byzantium, and from there to the Medieval West.

CONCLUSION

The archaeological evidence from Crete discussed here seems to permit several conclusions. Finds in cities as well as in large and small settlements on the island suggest that human activity did not stop in the middle or by the end of the 7th century, the era of great upheaval and contraction of the Byzantine Empire, but continued, in many cases, throughout the 8th and at least the early decades of the 9th century. The finds from coastal areas and islets seem especially important in this respect. Dating the occupation of these settlements to the 8th and, occasionally, to the early 9th century, a period of increasing and acute Arab danger, may suggest an increased effort of the central administration to strengthen the defence system of the island and to create safe conditions for commercial activities and the harbouring of ships in cases of emergency. Several of these coastal settlements continued their activities during the Second Byzantine period as well.

There is significant evidence for the existence of pottery-production centres on Crete during the 8th and 9th centuries. Aside from the workshop of Painted Ware at Gortyn, I was able to document local production in the areas of Messara, Mochlos,

Kalo Chorio and Eleutherna. During the Second Byzantine period, local production has been identified at Heraklion, Eleutherna and probably the Kalo Chorio area, places where production also existed before the Arab conquest.

As far as objects datable to the Arab occupation of Crete (827/28-961) are concerned, the ongoing excavations at Heraklion and in other regions of the island are bound to furnish information on the material culture of this period, As for now, the archaeological remains of the Arab occupation period are scarce, and what is available comes mainly from Heraklion. Still, this evidence seems to corroborate the hypothesis that the Andalusian Arabs occupation was largely confined to the city of Heraklion, now called Rabdh Al-Khandaq, while at the same time, life continued without serious changes in all other Cretan cities that had survived the Arab Conquest, as it did in the smaller and rural settlements.

All in all, it now seems highly probable that pottery production on Crete did not change much during this period and continued to follow the local Byzantine tradition of the 8th and the 9th centuries. The imported pottery finds suggest contacts with production centres within the Byzantine Empire, but also with regions of the eastern and western Mediterranean. The golden earrings found on Crete which date from the period of Arab occupation were made in a Byzantine artistic tradition, but obviously produced for a wealthy Arab élite.

The Second Byzantine era on Crete (961-1210/11) was characterised by notable close contacts with Constantinople. It is interesting to see that in various Cretan regions where the archaeological record clearly indicates human activity during the last centuries of the Early Byzantine period, a continuation of these activities can be seen during the Second Byzantine period (e.g., Eleutherna, Priniatikos Pyrgos, Mochlos, Pseira, Petras/Siteia). The archaeological evidence for this phenomenon includes both pottery production centres and metal workshops.

Finally, the archaeological record and the textual sources seem to make it clear that Crete had a significant agricultural production during the First and the Second Byzantine period as well as throughout the period of Arab occupation. The agricultural products were evidently transported in locally produced amphorae. Written sources which refer to the eastern Mediterranean, such as the 8th-century *Vita* of St. Pankratios of Taormina, make mention of traders (*pragmateutai*) who sail between Sicily and Jerusalem, and comment on imports to Sicily, carpets from Asia, olive oil from Crete, incense and wine from other islands.[45] At the same time, agricultural products were imported in Crete from numerous areas throughout the Aegean region and from other eastern Mediterranean regions as well. In addition, luxury tablewares were imported from Constantinople from the 8th to 10th centuries (such as Glazed White Wares, Polychrome Ware).

Summarizing, I would like to stress that throughout the entire Byzantine era Crete had contacts with many Byzantine centres. During this period the island's most important markets were the eastern Mediterranean in general and the Aegean in particular. Only after 1210/11, when the Second Byzantine period came to an end with the beginning of the Venetian occupation (1210/11-1669), fundamental changes occurred in many sectors of everyday life and of human activity on the island: Crete became increasingly oriented to the West, while the bulk of its imports of both everyday and luxury goods now came mainly from Venice and from other Italian cities, such as Genoa and Pisa.

NOTES

1. Tsougarakis 1988, 30 ff.; see also Christides 1984.
2. Laiou 2002, 697-770; Laiou 2006, 86; *Idem* 2013, with bibliography.
3. A first overview of Late Roman and Early Byzantine cities and settlements of Crete was published by Sanders 1982.
4. Andrianakis 2012, 75-90; Tsigonaki 2007, 263-97; Sythiakaki, Kanaki and Bilmezi 2015; Sythiakaki and Mari 2017; Sanders 1982, 148-49; Mari 2010, 200-10. For examples of human activity at Eleutherna from the 7th to 9th centuries, see Poulou-Papadimitriou 2005 and 2008b, 83-86; Poulou 2020b, 225-233.
5. Perna 2012.
6. Sythiakaki and Mari 2017; Sanders 1982, 136, 141; Gigourtakis 2011, 365. In addition, based on personal observations during a visit in 2013 at the sites of Gortyn, Lyttos, Tsoutsouros and Liopetro.
7. Di Vita 2010; Tsigonaki 2007, 263-97.
8. Dunn 2004, 139-46; Sidiropoulos 2004, 651-53.
9. Xanthopoulou 2015, 585-86; Xanthopoulou *et al.* 2014, 811.
10. Tantsis and Pantelidou 2021, 122, n. 120.
11. Poulou-Papadimitriou 2011, 386-87 with bibliography.
12. Di Vita 1988, 144-48; Vitale 2001, 86; Poulou-Papadimitriou and Nodarou 2014, 876-78; Gilboa *et al.* 2017, 559-93.
13. Poulou-Papadimitriou 2004, 209-26; Poulou-Papadimitriou 2011, 288-390, with bibliography; Poulou 2020b; Poulou and Nodarou 2021.
14. Poulou-Papadimitriou and Nodarou 2007, 755-66; Poulou-Papadimitriou and Nodarou 2014.
15. Poulou-Papadimitriou 2014, 137-41; Poulou-Papadimitriou and Nodarou 2014, 873-83; Poulou 2017, 195-216.
16. Hayes 1992, 12-34; Di Vita 1993, 35-55; Poulou-Papadimitriou 2011, 393-95; Poulou 2020a, 365-375 as well as unpublished sherds from Heraklion (St. Petros excavation) and Mochlos (Loutres excavation).
17. Poulou-Papadimitriou 2005a, 687-704.
18. Tsougarakis 1988, 30-41; Sythiakaki, Kanaki and Bilmezi 2015, 1179-1194; Starida 2016, 57-76.
19. Hayes 1992, 65, fig. 48, 30, 172-73.
20. Grube 1976, 27, no. 1; Soustiel 1985, 44, fig. 23; Rosen-Ayalon 1974, 12, 34, 159, 164-66, figs. 40-41, 367; Poulou-Papadimitriou 2008a, 156-58, fig. 6.
21. Frankopan 2019.
22. Poulou-Papadimitriou 2008a, 156; Poulou 2021, 83-114.
23. Borboudakis 1968, 429; Dodds 1992, 232, no. 25, 234-35, no. 28, 236, no. 28; Poulou-Papadimitriou 2008a, 158, fig. 7.
24. Tsougarakis 1988, 278 as well as *Idem* 2011, 294.
25. Miles 1970; Warren 1972, 285; Poulou-Papadimitriou 2008b, 83-86. I would like to thank Mr. Kl. Sidiropoulos for this information.
26. Tsougarakis 2011, 292-94.
27. Soles and Davaras 1992, 443, pl. 104.a; Günsenin 2009, 145-153; Günsenin 2016,

28 399-402; Poulou-Papadimitriou and Konstantinidou 2016.
28 Denker *et al.* 2013, 205, no. 239.
29 Pićri 2005, 583-96.
30 Sidiropoulos and Vasileiadou 2011, 40-46.
31 Albani 2010, 193-202, fig. 7a-b; Sidiropoulos and Vasileiadou 2011, 43; Poulou-Papadimitriou 2011, 434-35.
32 Tsougarakis 1988, 58-74.
33 Tsougarakis 1988, 58-74.
34 Heraklion: Sythiakaki, Kanaki and Bilmezi 2015; Poulou-Papadimitriou 2008a, 149-201. Eleutherna: Poulou-Papadimitriou 2008b. Priniatikos Pyrgos: Klontza-Jaklova 2014, 135-142. Mochlos: Poulou-Papadimitriou and Konstantinidou 2016. Pseira: Poulou-Papadimitriou 1995, 1119-1131; Poulou-Papadimitriou 2005b, 7-273; Poulou-Papadimitriou and Nodarou 2007, 755. Petras/Siteia: Poulou-Papadimitriou 2012, 315-23. Cf. Poulou and Nodarou 2021.
35 Poulou-Papadimitriou and Nodarou 2014, 876-78; Kanaki and Bilmezi 2011.
36 Hayes 1992, 35-37.
37 Polychrome wares have been found in Corinth, Heraklion, Thessaloniki, Ierissos (Chalkidice), Samothrace and Philippi (unpublished), see Morgan 1942, 64-70; Sanders 2001, 89-103; Kanonidis 2003, 71-76; Tsanana forthcoming; Poulou-Papadimitriou 2011, 414-18; Poulou 2021, 83-114.
38 Peschlow 1977-1978, 363-414, no. 103, 373, 405-406, fig. 16, pl. 141, 2.
39 Morgan 1942, pl. 13b, no. 44; Sanders 2001, 10.4, 22.
40 Durand 1997, 26, fig. 6.
41 Hayes 1992, 36, pl. 8k.6; Totev 1984, 69-71, fig. 9-10, 5-6, 7-8; Papanikola-Bakirtzis et al. 1999, 21-22.
42 Anquetil 1995, 20-21. For Eastern influences on Byzantine art, see Grabar 1971, 679-707; *Idem* 1980; Alfieri 1994, 113-19.
43 De Maffei 1994, 91, fig. 3; Wilckens 1991, 52-53, pl. 49.
44 Poulou-Papadimitriou 2011, 417-18; Poulou 2021.
45 Laiou 2002, 697-770 and esp. 708, n. 50.

BIBLIOGRAPHY

Albani, J. 2010. Elegance over the borders: The evidence of Middle Byzantine earrings, in: Ch. Entwistle and N. Adams (eds.), «*Intelligible Beauty*»: *Recent Research on Byzantine Jewellery, Papers Presented at the Fifth Annual Conference on Byzantine Art, British Museum and King's College, London, May 2008*, British Museum Research Publication 178, London, 193-202.

Alfieri, M.B. 1994. Seta islamica, in: *La seta e la sua via,* Rome, 113-19.

Andrianakis, M. 2012. Η πρωτοβυζαντινή Ακρόπολη των Χανίων, in: A. Kavvadia and P. Damoulos (eds.), *Η οχυρωματική αρχιτεκτονική στο Αιγαίο και ο Μεσαιωνικός Οικισμός Αναβάτου Χίου,* Chios, 75-90.

Anquetil, J. 1995. *La soie en Occident,* Paris.

Borboudakis, E. 1968. Δοκιμαστική ανασκαφή Αγίου Πέτρου των Ενετών Ηρακλείου, *ΑΔ* 23, 429.

Christides, V. 1984. *The Conquest of Crete by the Arabs (ca. 824): A turning Point in the Struggle between Byzantium and Islam*, Athens.

Decker, A., F. Dermikök, G. Kongaz, M. Kiraz, Ö. Korkmaz Kömürcü and T. Akbaytogan, 2013. 'YK12', in: Z. Kızıltan, and G. Baran Çelik (eds), *Stories from the Hidden Harbour: Shipwrecks of Yenikapı,* Istanbul, 198-209.

Dodds, J.D. 1992. *Al – Andalus: Las Artes Islamicas en Espana*, New York.

Dunn, A. 2005. A Byzantine fiscal official's seal from Knossos excavations and the archaeology of 'Dark-Age' cities, in: A. Di Vita (ed.), *Creta romana e protobizantina. Atti del Congresso Internazionale, Vol. 1*, Athens, 139-46.

Durand, J. and Ch. Vogt 1992. Plaques de céramique décorative byzantine d'époque macédonienne, *Revue du Louvre* 4, 38-44.

Durand, J. 1997. Plaques de céramique byzantine des collections publiques françaises in: H. Maguire (ed.), *Material Analysis of Byzantine Pottery*, Washington, DC, 25-50.

Frankopan, P. 2019. *La route de la soie: L'historie du coeur du monde*, trans. Guillaume Villeneuve (Champs histoire, Flammarion), Paris.

Hayes, J.W. 1992. *Excavations at Saraçhane in Istanbul, Vol. II: The Pottery*, Princeton, NJ.

Gigourtakis, N. 2011. Οχυρώσεις στην Κρήτη κατά τη Β' Βυζαντινή περίοδο, in: E. Kapsomenos, M. Andreadaki-Vlazaki and M. Andrianakis (eds.), *Πεπραγμένα του Ι' Διεθνούς Κρητολογικού Συνεδρίου (Χανιά, 1-8 Οκτωβρίου 2006), Vol. A*, Chania, 363-80.

Gilboa, A. *et al.* 2017. Cretan pottery in the Levant in the fifth and fourth Centuries B.C.E. and its historical implications, *American Journal of Archaeology* 121.4, 559-93.

Grabar, A. 1970. Le rayonnement de l'art sassanide dans le monde chrétien, in: *La Persia nel Medioevo: Atti del Convegno Internationale, Rome, 1970,* Rome, 679-707.

Grabar, A. 1980. Le rayonnement de l'art sassanide dans le monde chrétien, in: *L'art du Moyen Age en Occident, influences byzantines et orientales,* London.

Grube, E.J. 1976. *Islamic Pottery of the Eighth to the Fifteenth Century in the Keir Collection,* London.

Günsenin, N. 2009. Ganos wine and its circulation in the 11th century, in: M. Mandell Mango (ed.), *Byzantine Trade, 4th-12th Centuries,* Farnham & Burlington, 145-53.

Günsenin, N. 2016. Ganos Limani'ndan Portus Theodosiacus'a, in: P. Magdalino and N. Necipoğlu (eds.), *Trade in Byzantium: Papers from the 3rd International Sevgi Gönül Byzantine Studies Symposium,* Istanbul, 399-402.

Kanaki E. and Ch. Bilmezi 2011. Ενδείξεις ύπαρξης βυζαντινού κεραμικού εργαστηρίου στο Ηράκλειο, *11° Διεθνές Κρητολογικό Συνέδριο,* Rethymnon (poster presented at the 11th International Cretological Congress).

Kanonidis, I. 2003. Μεσοβυζαντινή εφυαλωμένη κεραμική με λευκό πηλό από ανασκαφές οικοπέδων στη Θεσσαλονίκη, in: Ch. Barkitzis (ed.), *VIIe Congres International sur la Céramique Médiévale en Méditerranée, Thessaloniki, 11-16 Octobre 1999,* Athens, 71-76.

Klontza-Jaklova, V. 2014. The Byzantine sequences at Priniatikos Pyrgos: Preliminary observations on ceramic chronology and architectural phasing, in: B. Molloy and C. Duckworth (eds.), *A Cretan Landscape Through Time: Priniatikos Pyrgos and its Environs,* Oxford, 135-42.

Laiou, A. 2002. Exchange and trade: Seventh-twelfth centuries, in A. Laiou, (ed.), *The Economic History of Byzantium: From the Seventh through the Fifteenth Century,* Washington, DC, 697-770.

Laiou, A. 2006. Μεταξύ παραγωγής και κατανάλωσης: Είχαν οικονομία οι βυζαντινές πόλεις, Public lecture held on June 6th 2006, *Praktika tis Akadimias Athinon* 81, Vol. B, 85-126.

Laiou, A. 2013. The Byzantine city: Parasitic or productive? Paper presented at the XXIst International Congress of Byzantine Studies (London, August 2006), in: C. Morrisson and R. Dorin (eds.), *Economic Thought and Economic Life in Byzantium,* Aldershot, 1-35.

De Maffei F. 1994. La seta a Bisanzio, in: *La seta e la sua via,* Rome, 89-98.

Mari, M. 2010. Διερεύνηση του βυζαντινού τείχους στην Κάτω Μερά Ιεράπετρας, *Αρχαιολογικό Έργο Κρήτης* 1, 200-210.

Miles, G.C. 1970. *The Coinage of the Arab Amirs of Crete,* New York.

Morgan, C.H. 1942. *Corinth XI: The Byzantine Pottery,* Cambridge, MA.

Papanikola-Bakirtzis, D., F.N. Mavrikiou and Ch. Bakirtzis 1999. *Βυζαντινή κεραμική στο Μουσείο Μπενάκη*, Athens.

Perna, R. 2012. *L'acropoli di Gortina: La tavola 'A' della carta archeologica della città di Gortina*, Ichnia, Collana del Dipartimento di Studi Umanistici, Serie Seconda 6, Macerata.

Peschlow, U. 1977-1978. Byzantinische Keramik aus Istanbul, *Istanbuler Mitteilungen* 27-28, 363-414.

Piéri, D. 2005. Nouvelles productions d'amphores de Syrie du Nord aux époques protobyzantine et omeyyade, in: F. Baratte, V. Déroche, C. Jolivet-Lévy and B. Pitharakis (eds.), *Mélanges Jean-Pierre Sodini*, Travaux et Mémoires 15, Paris, 583-96.

Portale, E.C. and I. Romeo 2001. Contetitori da trasporto, in: A. Di Vita (ed.), *Gortina V, 3: Lo scavo del Pretorio (1989-1995). I materiali*, Monografie della Scuola Archaeologica Italiana di Atene e delle Missione Italiane in Oriente XII, Padova & Athens, 260-410.

Poulou-Papadimitriou, N. 1995. Le monastère byzantin à Pseira (Crète): la céramique, *Akten des Internationalen Kongresses für christliche Archäologie, Bonn, 22- 28 September 1991*, t.2, Münster, 1119-1131.

Poulou-Papadimitriou, N. 2003. Μεσοβυζαντινή κεραμική από την Κρήτη: 9^{ος}-12^{ος} αιώνας, in: Ch. Bakirtzis (ed.), *VIIe Congrès International sur la Céramique Médiévale en Méditerranée, Thessaloniki, 11-16 Octobre 1999*, Athènes, 211-226.

Poulou-Papadimitriou, N. 2004. Η εφυαλωμένη κεραμική. Νέα στοιχεία για την εμφάνιση της εφυάλωσης στο Βυζάντιο, in: P. Themelis (ed.), *Πρωτοβυζαντινή Ελεύθερνα – Τομέας ι, Vol. ι*, Rethymnon, 209-26.

Poulou-Papadimitriou, N. 2005a. Les plaques-boucles byzantines de l'île de Crète (fin VIe-IXe siècle), in: F. Baratte, V. Déroche, C. Jolivet-Lévy and B. Pitharakis (eds.), *Mélanges Jean-Pierre Sodini*, Travaux et Mémoires 15, Paris (Collège de France - CNRS Centre de Recherche d'Histoire Civilisation de Byzance), 687-704.

Poulou-Papadimitriou, N. 2005b. The site data and pottery (Byzantine pottery), in: Ph.P. Betancourt, C. Davaras and R.H. Simpson (eds.), *The Archaeological Survey of Pseira Island, Part 2: The Intensive Surface Survey*, Philadelphia, PA, 7-244.

Poulou-Papadimitriou, N. 2008a. Στιγμές από την ιστορία του Ηρακλείου, in: A. Karetsou *et al.* (eds.), Ηράκλειο. Η άγνωστη ιστορία της αρχαίας πόλης, Heraklion, 149-201.

Poulou-Papadimitriou, N. 2008b. Βυζαντινή κεραμική από την Ελεύθερνα. Η στέρνα της Αγίας Άννας, in Th. Kalpaxis *et al.* (eds.), *Ελεύθερνα. Τομέας ιι. 3. Βυζαντινό σπίτι στην Αγία Άννα*, Rethymnon, 25-187.

Poulou-Papadimitriou, N. 2011. Τεκμήρια υλικού πολιτισμού στη βυζαντινή Κρήτη: από τον 7ο έως το τέλος του 12ου αιώνα, in: E. Kapsomenos, M. Andreadaki-Vlazaki and M. Andrianakis (eds.), *Πεπραγμένα του Ι' Διεθνούς Κρητολογικού Συνεδρίου (Χανιά, 1-8 Οκτωβρίου 2006)*, A, Chania, 381-447.

Poulou-Papadimitriou, N. 2012. Pottery of the Middle Byzantine period and the first centuries of the Venetian occupation from Petras, Siteia, in: M. Tsipopoulou (ed.), *Petras, Siteia – 25 Years of Excavations and Studies,* Monographs of the Danish Institute at Athens 16, Athens, 315-23.

Poulou-Papadimitriou, N. and E. Nodarou 2007. La céramique protobyzantine de Pseira: la production locale et les importations. Etude typologique et pétrographique, in: M. Bonifay, J.-C. Tréglia (eds.), *LRCW 2. Late Roman Coarse Wares, Cooking Wares and Amphorae in the Mediterranean: Archaeology and Archaeometry,* BAR International Series 1662 (II), Oxford 2007, 755-66.

Poulou-Papadimitriou, N. and E. Nodarou 2014. Transport vessels and maritime routes in the Aegean from the 5th to the 9th c. AD. Preliminary results of the EU funded 'Pythagoras II' project: The Cretan case study, in: N. Poulou-Papadimitriou, E. Nodarou, V. Kilikoglou (eds.), *LRCW 4. Late Roman Coarse Wares, Cooking Wares and Amphorae in the Mediterranean: Archaeology and Archaeometry, The Mediterranean, A Market Without Frontiers,* BAR Int. Series 2616 (II), Oxford, 873-83.

Poulou-Papadimitriou, N. and S. Konstantinidou 2016. Μεσαιωνική κεραμική από τον Μόχλο, *4η Συνάντηση για το Αρχαιολογικό Έργο Κρήτης, Ρέθυμνο 24-27 Νοεμβρίου 2016* (oral presentation).

Poulou, N. 2017. Transport Amphorae and Trade in the Aegean from the 7th to the 9th, Century AD: Containers of Wine or Olive Oil?, *Byzantina* 35, 195-216.

Poulou, N. 2020a. Εφυαλωμένη κεραμική με λευκό πηλό από την Κωνσταντινούπολη (GWW I-II/7ος-9ος αιώνας): Η διάδοση στον αιγαιακό χώρο, in P. Kalogerakou et al. (eds), *Κυδάλιμος. Τιμητικός Τόμος για τον Καθηγητή Γεώργιο Στυλ. Κορρέ.* AURA SUPPLEMENT 4, vol. 3, 365-375.

Poulou, N. 2020b. Η Ελεύθερνα και η Κρήτη στα θαλάσσια δίκτυα της ανατολικής Μεσογείου κατά την Βυζαντινή περίοδο, in N.Chr. Stambolidis and M. Giannopoulou (eds.), *Η Ελεύθερνα, η Κρήτη και ο Έξω Κόσμος, Πρακτικά Διεθνούς Αρχαιολογικού Συνεδρίου*, Athens-Rethymnon, 225-233.

Poulou, N. 2021. 'Polychrome Ware: The Long Journey of Decorative Motifs', in N.D. Kontogiannis, B. Böhlendorf-Arslan and F. Yenişehirlioğlu (eds.), *Glazed Wares as Cultural Agents in the Byzantine, Seljuk and Ottoman Lands. 13th International ANAMED Annual Symposium*, Istanbul, 83-114.

Poulou, N. and Nodarou, E. 2021. The 12th century under the microscope: Middle-Late Byzantine pottery from the cistern of Agia Anna in Eleutherna, Crete, in P. Petridis, A. Yandaki et al. (eds.), *12th Congress AIECM3. On Medieval and Modern Period Mediterranean Ceramics. Proceedings*, Athens, 285-293.

Rosen-Ayalon, M. 1974. *La poterie islamique, ville royale de Suse IV: Mémoires de la délégation archéologique en Iran,* Paris.

Sanders, G.D.R. 2000. New relative and absolute chronologies for 9th to 13th century glazed wares at Corinth: Methodology and social conclusions, in K. Belke, F. Hild, J. Koder and P. Soustal (eds.), *Byzanz als Raum: Zu Methoden und Inhalten der historischen Geographie des östlichen Mittelmeerraumes,* Tabula Imperii Byzantini Band 7, Österreichische Akademie der Wissenschaften, Philosophische-Historische Klasse, Denkschriften, 283. Band, Vienna, 153-73.

Sanders, I.F. 1982. *Roman Crete: An Archaeological Survey and Gazeteer of Late Hellenistic, Roman and Early Byzantine Crete,* Warminster.

Sidiropoulos, Kl. 2004. Κνωσός, Colonia Iulia Nobilis Cnosus, Μακρυτοίχος: Τα νομισματικά ίχνη της ιστορίας, in: *Το Ηράκλειο και η περιοχή του. Διαδρομή στο χρόνο,* Heraklion, 651-53.

Sidiropoulos, Kl. and M. Vasileiadou 2011. Ο θησαυρός Μεσονησίου Ρεθύμνου της Συλλογής Σταθάτου, in: *Βυζάντιο και Άραβες, Κατάλογος Έκθεσης,* Thessaloniki, 40-46.

Sidiropoulos, Kl. 2012. Numismatic Finds from Priniatikos Pyrgos: Major gains from minor capital, in: *Fieldwork and Research at Priniatikos Pyrgos and Environs 1912-2012, A Conference, Athens, 1-2 June 2012,* Athens, 13.

Soles, J. and C. Davaras 1992. Excavations at Mochlos, 1989, *Hesperia* 61.4, 413-45.

Soustiel, J. 1985. *La céramique islamique: Le guide du connaisseur* (avec la collaboration de Charles Kiefer), Freiburg.

Starida, L. 2016. Αρχιτεκτονικά κατάλοιπα στο Ηράκλειο από την περίοδο της αραβοκρατίας, in: M. Patedakis and K. Giapitzoglou (eds.), *Μαργαρίται. Μελέτες στη Μνήμη του Μανόλη Μπορμπουδάκη,* Sitia, 57-76.

Sythiakaki, V., E. Kanaki and Ch. Bilmezi 2015. Οι παλαιότερες οχυρώσεις του Ηρακλείου: μια διαφορετική προσέγγιση με βάση τα νεότερα ανασκαφικά δεδομένα, *Αρχαιολογικό Έργο Κρήτης 3, Vol. Α΄,* 395-410.

Sythiakaki, V. and M. Mari 2017. Συνέχειες, ασυνέχειες και μεταβολές στην κατοίκηση των πόλεων της κεντρικής Κρήτης κατά την περίοδο μετάβασης από την ύστερη αρχαιότητα στους μέσους βυζαντινούς χρόνους. Τα τεκμήρια της νεότερης αρχαιολογικής έρευνας, *12th International Congress of Cretan Studies (12th ICCS) Heraklion 21-25 September 2016.* http://www.12iccs.proceedings.gr/

Tantsis, A. and Ch. Pantelidou. Μια ενδιαφέρουσα ομάδα ναών: Βασιλική με εγκάρσιο τμήμα και πλευρικές κόγχες, *Byzantina* 38, 2021, 91-134.

Tsanana, A. forthcoming. Middle Byzantine Hierissos: Archaeological research at the entrance of Mount Athos, in: A. Dunn (ed.), *Byzantine Greece: Microcosm of Empire?,* London.

Tsigonaki, C. 2007. Les villes crétoises aux VIIe et VIIIe siècles: l'apport des recherches archéologiques à Eleutherna, *Annuario della Scuola Archeologica Italiana di Atene* 85, serie III, 7, 263-97.

Tsigonaki, C. 2009. Ίτανος. Ιστορία και τοπογραφία μιας παράκτιας θέσης της ανατολικής Κρήτης κατά την πρωτοβυζαντινή περίοδο, in: O. Gratziou and Chr. Loukos (eds.), Ψηφίδες. Μελέτες Ιστορίας, Αρχαιολογίας και Τέχνης στη Μνήμη της Στέλλας Παπαδάκη-Oekland, Herakleion, 159-74.

Tsougarakis, D. 1988. *Byzantine Crete: From the 5th Century to the Venetian Occupation*, Athens.

Tsougarakis, D. 2011. Βυζαντινοί οικισμοί στην Κρήτη, in: E. Kapsomenos, M. Andreadaki-Vlazaki and M. Andrianakis (eds.), Πεπραγμένα του Ι' Διεθνούς Κρητολογικού Συνεδρίου (Χανιά, 1-8 Οκτωβρίου 2006), *Vol. A*, Chania, 294.

Vitale, E. 2001. Ceramica sovradipinta bizantina, in: A. Di Vita (ed.), *Gortina V.3: Lo scavo del Pretorio (1989-1995), Vol. 3*, t. I, *I Materiali*, Padova, 86-113.

Warren, P. 1972. An Arab building from Knossos, *Annual of the British School at Athens* 67, 285-96.

Wilckens, L. von. 1991. *Die textilen Künste: Von der Spätantike bis um 1500*, Munich.

Xanthopoulou, M., E. Nodarou and N. Poulou-Papadimitriou 2014. Local coarse wares from late roman Itanos (East Crete), in: N. Poulou-Papadimitriou, E. Nodarou and V. Kilikoglou (eds.), *LRCW 4. Late Roman Coarse Wares, Cooking Wares and Amphorae in the Mediterranean: Archaeology and Archaeometry, The Mediterranean: A Market Without Frontiers*, BAR International Series 2616 (II), Oxford, 811-17.

Xanthopoulou, M. 2015. Ένας αμφορέας της όψιμης πρωτοβυζαντινής περιόδου από την Ίτανο, in: P. Karanastasi, A. Tzigkounaki, and X. Tsigonaki (eds.), Αρχαιολογικό Έργο Κρήτης, Πρακτικά 3ης Συνάντησης, Ρέθυμνο 5-8 Δεκεμβρίου 2013, Vol. β', Rethymnon, 585-93.

Zanini E., S. Costa and E. Triolo 2015. The excavation of the Early Byzantine district near the Pythion in Gortyn (field seasons 2011-2013): An image of the end of the Mediterranean city, *Αρχαιολογικό Έργο Κρήτης* 3, 565-74.

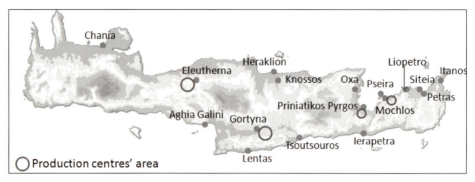

FIG. 1 – Map of Crete (N. Poulou).

FIG. 2 – Gortyn fortification, polygonal tower (photo: N. Poulou).

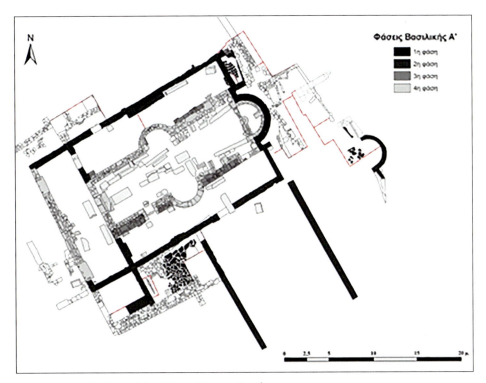

FIG. 3 – Itanos, Basilica A (after Tsigonaki 2009, fig. 7).

FIG. 4 – Painted bowl produced in Gortyn. Excavation of Pseira (PS 3623, after Poulou-Papadimitriou 2011, fig. 3).

FIG. 5 – Jug with slip painted decoration and traces of glaze. Eleutherna, Sector I (after Poulou-Papadimitriou 2004, fig. 7).

FIG. 6 – Basin. Fabric from Mochlos area. Excavation of Pseira (PS 4180, after Poulou-Papadimitriou 2011, fig. 6).

FIG. 7 – Chafing dish. Fabric from Kalo Chorio area. Excavation of Pseira (PS 493, after Poulou-Papadimitriou 2011, fig. 8).

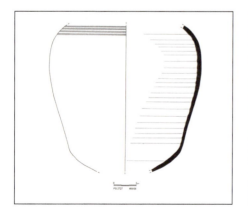

FIG. 8 – Byzantine globular amphora. Fabric from Mochlos area. Excavation of Pseira (PS 2727, after Poulou-Papadimitriou 2011, fig. 25).

FIG. 9 – Ovoid amphora. Fabric from South Coast. Excavation of Pseira (PS 2646, after Poulou-Papadimitriou 2011, fig. 18).

FIG. 10 – Amphora survival of LRA 1 type. Excavation of Pseira (PS 1407, after Poulou-Papadimitriou 2011, fig. 30).

FIG. 11A-B – (A) – Bronze belt buckle. Heraklion Archaeological Museum (after Poulou-Papadimitriou 2011, fig. 61); (B) – Golden belt buckle from Crete. Ashmolean Museum (after Poulou-Papadimitriou 2005, fig. 11).

FIG. 12 – Palestinian amphora. Heraklion Archaeological Museum (after Poulou-Papadimitriou 2003, fig. 3).

FIG. 13 – Jug with impressed decoration and green glaze. Heraklion (after Poulou-Papadimitriou 2008, fig. 6).

FIG. 14 – Glazed dish with green and brown painted decoration. Heraklion, excavation at the Dominican monastery of St. Peter (after Poulou-Papadimitriou 2008, fig. 7).

FIG. 15 – Amphora from Mochlos (after Poulou-Papadimitriou and Konstantinidou 2016).

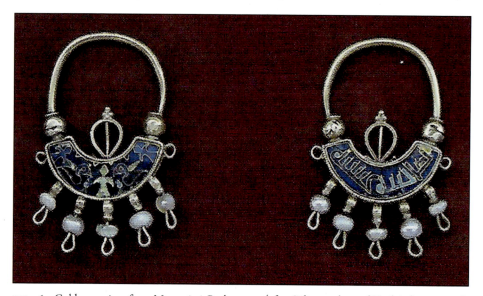

FIG. 16 – Golden earrings from Messonissi, Rethymnon (after Sidiropoulos and Vasileiadou 2011, 43).

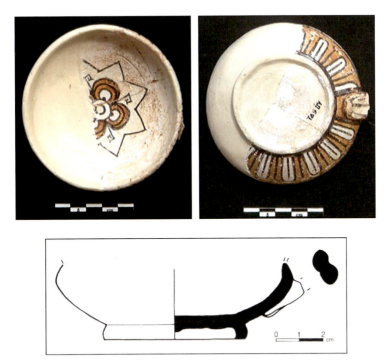

FIG. 17A-B-C – Cup, Polychrome Ware. Heraklion (after Poulou-Papadimitriou 2003, fig. 11, 12).

FIG. 18 – Dish, Polychrome Ware. Heraklion (after Poulou-Papadimitriou 2003, fig. 13).

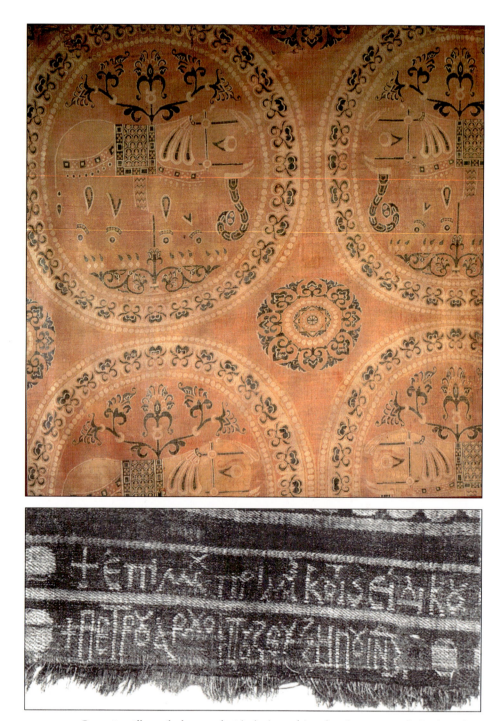

FIG. 19A-B – Byzantine silk textile decorated with elephants (above) and inscription (below). Aachen Cathedral's Treasury (after Wilckens 1991, pl. 49).

Mapping Byzantine amphorae: Outlining patterns of consumption in present-day Bulgaria and the Black Sea Region (7th-14th century)

Evelina Todorova

*

INTRODUCTION

Just as in classical antiquity amphorae were in Byzantine times the standard containers used for storage and the long-distance transport of agricultural goods (both liquid and dry, but mostly wine and oil). Although these large ceramic vessels have often been neglected by archaeologists as an unappealing (and difficult to date) type of ware, it has in recent years become clear that they in fact can offer much information. When studied with due care, amphorae may enable the archaeologist: (1) – to establish typological diversity and chronological span; (2) – to establish distribution patterns and trade networks; (3) – to outline primary and secondary trade routes; (4) – to better understand seafaring and ship construction; (5) – to reconstruct amphora content, volume, and capacities, both of single types and of entire cargoes; (6) – to deduce mechanisms for taxation, production, and control; and finally, (7) – to draw conclusions on consumption patterns of agricultural goods.

After realizing that these transport jars have been underestimated as a source of information, I set out in 2006 to launch a study on 7th- to 14th-century amphorae in existence in present-day Bulgaria.[1] This was easier said than done. The amphorae I was able to publish or revise the typochronology of constituted only a fraction of the quite unexpected large amount of unpublished container vessels that remained in storage at various Bulgarian museums. In addition, a noticeable discrepancy existed between the number of publications as well as the state and level of research in Bulgaria on the one hand and in other countries on the other. In fact, Bulgarian scholars had published so far less than ten works on Byzantine amphorae and related subjects.[2] In addition, there existed some 20 publications in which amphorae appeared or were mentioned without commentary.[3] At that point in time, scholars in other countries had published more than 150 works, some of them probing deeply into the details of specific topics related to Byzantine amphorae.[4]

Consequently, it seemed inescapable in the Bulgagain context to create a new, more extensive and exhaustive research. The study not only had to go beyond an ordinary formal typology and chronology of the vessels in the Bulgarian storage rooms, but also had to include drawing attention to the full potential of amphorae as carriers of archaeological information by the analysis of aspects such as capacity, content, etc.

In this chapter, I will limit myself to one aspect. It is my intention to discuss how plotting the find spots of amphorae as well as the quantities in which they are found may be used to outline patterns of trade and distribution, and to pinpoint consumption centres in the networks.

BENEFITS AND PITFALLS OF MAPPING

Mapping pottery is a method which is quite widely applied in archaeology. It allows for visualising the distribution of objects, making their geographical spread in a generalised way immediately perceptible and comprehensible in easy overviews. Also in the case of the 7th- to 14th-century amphorae from Bulgaria, the mapping of the vessels, of course after they were duly classified and their chronology determined, helped to analyse the geographic distribution of types during different periods of Byzantine history. The plotting of every single find enabled the outlining of distribution patterns, trade routes and networks, as well as the indentification of contact zones between various areas. Mapping amphora quantities found at certain locations enabled the identification of primary and secondary consumption and/or distribution centres, while it also offered an idea about the volume of the imported agricultural products and the scale of the commercial transactions. Combining all this information with the characteristics of the sites in Bulgaria where amphorae had been found (urban, rural, monastic, etc.), enabled the formulation of general theories about the production and distribution of Byzantine amphorae in the Bulgarian region.

Even though mapping the amphorae ultimately proved successful, certain shortcomings must be noted and taken into account when interpreting the results. The first and primary problem encountered was data collection itself. Of course, it is never possible to have a perfect and complete dataset due to the inherent bias in all forms of data collection. In this case, published amphorae had to be traced through library research, while all published and unpublished containers had to be located in the respective museum where they were stored. Despite all perseverance, the library research could never be absolutely exhaustive and certain publications may have been missed.

Although present-day Bulgaria is a relatively small country (only 111 km²), it was virtually impossible to visit all museums and work through every single amphora fragment ever found. The territory of the country is divided into 28 districts with 28 Regional museums of History with their respective archaeological departments. In addition, there are also more than 30 historical or archaeological museums in smaller towns or at archaeological preserves and sites of significance. In addition, some modest archaeological collections are kept in community centres and libraries. Consequently physical, time, financial, and subjective constrains required the use of an efficient strategy.[5]

At first, it was my aim to create an initial picture of amphora distribution by mapping all the published finds. This gave an idea in which museums they may have been stored. The presence or absence of amphorae at every possible museum had to be found out and the information added to the map. Analysing the characteristics of the locations of the finds allowed for distinguishing certain patterns. They helped in locating other areas or sites with high probability of containing transport jars and in discounting areas with less or no potential, thus saving time, efforts, and money.

The initial mapping showed that amphorae clustered in five areas: along the western Black Sea coast; along the River Danube; in north-eastern Bulgaria, along the middle and upper reaches of the Maritsa River and its tributaries; along the Struma River (Fig. 1). The fact that amphorae were often produced to be transported by ship made it natural that all sites which had yielded amphorae were located either at the sea coast or along navigable rivers. Also, except for the amphorae from the Struma River valley, all other finds came from areas that are accessible by water, and relatively flat. Consequently, regions with high mountain ranges (this is almost half of the Bulgarian territory – Stara planina, Rhodopa, Rila, and Pirin mountains), although they may contain large rivers, were judged to be with less or no potential for finding amphorase and were ruled out.

Even after applying this selection, it was not possible to visit all the selected sites and museums. The museums that were contacted, granted or denied access to amphorae, or stated there were none in their possession. They also provided different levels of access. Some museums (Silistra, Sozopol) gave complete access to all finds and materials, while others (Varna) restricted access to some based on the personal judgment of the curator or director. Access was denied due to personal (Plovdiv, Nessebar) or objective reasons (such as being busy making an inventory – Shumen, Veliko Tarnovo, Haskovo), but most did not provide information if transport jars were available.

The varying degree of reliability of the obtained information from the museums claiming no amphorae in their possession also influenced the research by allowing entire areas to be ruled out of the survey. The museums in Sofia were never contacted, because, according to the initial distribution pattern, the area showed no potential at all. Later, it became clear that both the National Museum of History and the National Institute of Archaeology with Museum did possess amphorae. Fortunately, this additional information did not distort the observed distribution patterns. The jars did not reach Sofia during the Middle Ages, but were later collected from different sites and exhibited in the capital for political reasons.

When museum staff declared no transport containers were available at their institution this could indeed mean there were none, but sometimes they were unaware of how Medieval amphorae looked like or mistook them for containers from another period. According to one article, there was a so-called Günsenin I amphora[6] (which can generally be dated to the 10th-11th centuries) in Svishtov's museum.[7] When asked about this example, the director convincingly denied. It was much later, when I visited personally the museum, that the container was identified. It was stored together with some other amphorae (such as LRA 1) and was wrongly dated in the 6th century.

Finally, after dealing with the problems and applying the respective corrections, the initial picture of amphora distribution did not change much, despite the fact that some find spots were overlooked.

DIFFICULTIES AND DRAWBACKS OF VISUALISATION

Visualizing both the location and the quantity of amphorae allowed achieving quite informative results about the role of present-day Bulgarian lands in the Byzantine economy and politics. However, several difficulties and drawbacks became apparent in the process of using the data.

Comparing the quantity of vessels from successive periods from the entire research territory or from only one site offered information about the ebbs and flows of the volume of imported agricultural products, and the scale of commercial transactions (Fig. 2). There turned out to be, for instance, a sharp contrast between the less than 200 7th- to 9th/10th-century amphorae identified so far, the tens of thousands 10th- to early 12th-century ones, and the hundreds of 12th- to 14th-century containers. The result was confirmed when applied to case studies of material from the 2007 excavations in Silistra[8] and from the museum in Sozopol.[9]

During the 2007 campaign in Silistra, a plot of ca. 3700 m² was excavated in the heart of the Medieval fortified area. Although the exact calculation of the number of amphora shards is still forthcoming, it can be stated that the late 10th- to early 12th-century ones were more than 5000, while the 12th- to 14th-century ones were about 200. More than 500 10th- to early 12th-century entirely or partially preserved vessels, rims, handles, walls with stamps, *dipinti*, or *graffiti*, and only three 12th- to 14th-century pieces from other excavation plots in Silistra were kept in the museum. To date, no 7th- to 9th-century jars were identified at all.

In the Sozopol Archaeological Museum more than 300 diagnostic shards and large parts from the bodies of 10th- to early 12th-century amphorae were kept. They were brought to light during the excavations of a cistern at 48-50, Milet str. Another twenty two entirely preserved amphorae from the same period originated from the sea bed. There were only two 8th- to 9th-century and twelve 12th- to 14th-century containers, also found at sea.

Comparing the quantity of contemporaneous amphora types such as the multiple finding spots of the tens of thousands Günsenin I and II shards and the only four examples of my type XV (Fig. 3, mentioned as 'Todorova type XV', see also Fig. 6) established the share of each type in the overall import and led to the conclusion that some products were more sought after and better marketed than others.

Similar proportions were valid in case studies of jars from Silistra, Pliska, and Preslav. As already mentioned, the biggest share of amphorae from Silistra, almost 99 percent, consisted of the Günsenin I and II type vessels. Four more, still unidentified, 10th- to early 12th-century jars were each represented by only a few fragments.

A recent research on the amphorae found during the excavations of a plot meant for the building of the new archaeological base at Pliska concluded that the entirely or partially preserved examples of Günsenin I and II jars added up to a tortal of 1497 and 1479 respectively, while there were only two unidentified amphora types, each represented by four fragments.[10] As far as the amphorae kept in the Preslav Archaeological Museum were accessible, the Günsenin I type was represented by 150 items, the Günsenin II only by 13 items, while another six different amphora types were represented by eight entirely or partially preserved vessels.

PROBLEMS OF MAPPING QUANTATIVE DATA

Comparing the quantities of only one amphora type (be it either the Günsenin I, or the Günsenin II) found at different locations enabled the identification of primary and secondary centres of consumption and/or distribution (Fig. 3). When combined with typological diversity, centres of prominent importance and outstanding position emerged, notably Sozopol, Varna, Preslav, Pliska, and Silistra (Fig. 8).

However, one of the problems of adding quantitative data to mapping is that comparison and conclusions should be based on data of equivalent nature and value. Any bias in data collection alone can put the results under question. This proved certainly true for my research. On the one hand the Sozopol museum provided full access to twenty-five entirely or partially preserved Günsenin I amphorae and a few hundreds fragments. On the other hand the Varna museum restricted the access to only four completely preserved Günsenin I jars, but not to any of the fragments. Did this mean that Sozopol was the bigger and more important centre on the Black Sea coast?

Comparing entirely preserved vessels with fragments can also induce bias. If only mere quantities are visualized, the four Günsenin I amphorae from the Varna museum appear insignificant next to the thirty-one small shards from the Medieval settlement near Zlatna livada. Thus, this small village may appear as larger consumption centre than Varna, a big sea port.

It has to be emphasized that when comparing material from excavations of two or more sites, all fragments should be taken into account. Even today many archaeologists tend to neglect body fragments and register, if at all, only the most diagnostic pieces of a vessel, such as rims, handles or bottoms, while on other sites all shards are dully recorded and counted. For example the Günsenin I amphorae found during the 2007 campaign at Silistra and at the Medieval settlement near Zlatna livada, where all fragments were recorded, numbered in total more than 5000 and 31 respectively. This is in contrast to the only one preserved upper part of an amphora sampled at the fortified settlement near Kladentsi, which was stored in the Dobrich museum.

Comparisons in quantity also depend on the scale and state of the exploration of the site. While large areas of Silistra have been excavated for decades (just the 2007 campaign explored an area of about 3700 m²) yielding great amount of pottery, it is only in recent years that amphora fragments came to light at Plovdiv after a few small plots of some 75 to 200 m² each were excavated.[11]

Combining the geographic distribution of amphorae, their quantities, and the characteristics of the archaeological sites where they were found (capital of an administrative unit, city, large coastal town, large inland town, village, hamlet, etc.) gave hints about the nature of amphora distribution. While in some areas, such as the Maritsa River valley, a limited quantity of amphorae from the same type and time period was documented at villages and randomly at large towns; in other geographic areas, such as north-eastern Bulgaria, containers of different types and varying quantity appeared simultaneously on sites of different nature (large cities, towns, and villages at the coast or inland) (Figs. 7-9). All this means that a demand with varying intensity was satisfied through an intentionally created, well-organized, relatively large-scale supply system, even though random occasional small-scale supplies cannot be excluded. Bias in the data collection is again a shortcoming.

As already stated, the main goal of the study of the transport containers from present-day Bulgaria was to show the potential of using the various aspects of Byzantine amphorae to shed light on developments in the wider Mediterranean economy. Signs and marks on amphorae such as amphora stamps, painted *dipinti* and incised *graffiti*, form one of these aspects and can also be used for this purpose. These signs and marks mainly relate to the control of amphora production, amphora capacities, taxation, and reuse. The mapping of identical signs and marks can help to identify of the distribution patterns, to outline the trade routes, to establish the nature of commercial transactions (state organized or private, large-scale or small-scale), and to get some idea of volumes and of the share of certain producers within the overall trade.

AMPHORA STAMPS AND 'GRAFFITI'

This is not the place to discuss in detail the variety and interpretations of amphora marks and signs. Since there were less than ten painted *dipinti* on amphorae in Bulgaria, I will focus here on amphora stamps. At the present moment, more than 70 amphora stamps and two metal matrices for stamping amphorae are known in Bulgaria. The vast majority of the stamps (62) were put on Günsenin I amphorae. They can be divided in two groups, the first dating respectively to the second half and end of the 10th century to the first half of the 11th century, and the second dating to the late 10th/early 11th century to the early 12th century. There were two more stamps from the late 10th to 11th century, which were put on amphorae from my types XII and XV (see Fig. 6). Only two 12th- to 14th-century amphora stamps on Günsenin IV jars were documented.[12]

When mapped, the amphora stamps appeared to cluster mainly along the western Black Sea coast, in north-eastern Bulgaria, and along the upper reaches of the Danube River. Preslav (27), Silistra (22), and Varna (ca. 10) were the sites where the majority of the stamps were found (Fig. 4). Except for two amphorae (from Svishtov[13] and Preslav[14]) that were each stamped with two identical stamps, and two amphora handles from Preslav with the same type of stamp,[15] there were no two stamps that were exactly alike, although some may have contained a similar letter, a combination of letters, a monogram, or a symbol. The stamps differed one from another in outline (round, rectangular, etc.) or the way the letters/monograms were shaped/spaced. Assuming that amphora stamps were used as signs of the workshop that produced the container vessels, they gave information about the content of the jar and the location of the agricultural estate it belonged to.

The amphora stamps found in Bulgaria suggest that quite a large number of producers supplied rather few significant consumption centres. The fact that most of the stamps were set on Günsenin I amphorae indicates that a measure of unification existed across the Byzantine Empire and many workshops were conforming to it by using standardized containers. Consequently, they were part of a large economic system that was to a certain degree responsible to market their production. The few stamps on other transport vessels from the same period suggests that there was also a small-scale supply from other, most probably independent or private merchants. They may not have conformed to the standards of the central government for staple goods, and catered to a more exquisite demand that existed only in the larger consumption centres, as is indicated by the number of these amphorae found there.

The small number of matching amphora stamps found in Bulgaria and their concentration in only a few findspots did not offer enough evidence to outline distribution patterns or discuss the share of particular producers. A more fruitful way would be to take a more general look at the distribution of amphora stamps, since some of the stamps from Bulgaria do find parallels across the Mediterranean and the Black Sea.

Here, four different types of amphora stamps will be dicussed. They are all dated roughly to the 11th century and are set on Günsenin I amphorae.[16] The stamps bearing the monogram ΚΩΣ/ΚΩΣΤ are the most numerous (19 stamps and three metal matrices), followed by the indented circular stamps (12), the ones with the monogram ΕΙ (9), and the stamps with the monogram ΘΕΣΝ (5). Supposing that stamps with the same monogram or symbol were produced in the same workshop, an outline of main and secondary paths can be tentatively reconstructed on a distribution map (Fig. 5).

Taking Constantinople as a focal point for amphora circulation, there were two major directions going South – along the western coast of Asia Minor and along the northern Aegean coast to Athens via Thessaloniki. Two secondary bifurcations went up the Maritsa River to Edirne and from Thessaloniki inland. Traffic on these routes seemed to be not as intense as the one along the lanes going north of Constantinople. The busiest artery was apparently the one following the western Black Sea coast, heading to Kiev via the Dniepr River. It had three forks along the road. The first one going up the river Don to Sarkel-Belaya Vezha via Chersonesus and the southern shore of the Crimea; the second one entering the Danube River; and the third one penetrating inland via Varna. The commercial traffic on the river Danube was also quite intense. The last route followed the southern shore of the Black Sea to Sinope.

Graffiti are often connected to the reuse of amphorae. They are considered to denote ownership, since most of them are abbreviations of the name of the owner or the recipient, but some may also refer to amphora content or capacity. The use of *graffiti* seems to have been related especially to amphorae used in privately organized trade ventures. When two or more merchants shared the load of one ship, they had to mark their containers in order not to confuse them with the merchandise of others.[17] Thus, each merchant chose a distinct mark – either writing his name or putting a sign.

Tracing back similar signs through the Mediterranean world would enable us to have a glimpse at the area of operation of certain traders, the itineraries they used (did they follow the main stream or used alternative routes), the scale and other aspects of their trade (how many amphorae marked were known so far, how many of them came from the same site, were these amphorae distributed in bigger or smaller sites, were merchants operating and distributing foods locally, regionally or more globally, etc.). For example, the same sign was incised on the upper parts of three of the Günsenin III amphorae found in Balchik, thus indicating that the jars belonged to one owner/merchant. Who was he? Where was his home town? What did he trade?

The answers may now beyond our reach, but that may change when we succeed in tracing similar *graffiti* from all over the Mediterranean area. In fact, some of the *graffiti* found in Bulgaria do seem to have close similarities with others from the eastern Mediterranean, the northern Black Sea coast, and the Lower Danube area. However, this topic is clarly a subject of a separate, larger study, and will not be discussed here.

INTERPRETING THE RESULTS

Fully recognizing its benefits and pitfalls of mapping the 7th to 14th century amphorae found in Bulgaria, the results can only be interpreted with due caution. Supporting information from sphragistic evidence and from other sources will be added.

All amphorae that were collected and documented during the study were classified according to their formal characteristics. Thus, types and chronology of the vessels were defined. As far as possible production centres were identified and could be assigned to some amphorae. This enabled dividing the amphorae in three larger chronological time spans; (1) – the 7th to 9th/10th century; (2) – the 9th/10th to 11th/12th century; (3) – the 11th/12th to 14th century (Fig. 6). Some amphorae could not be typologically defined due to their fragmentary state. Still, their find spots were mapped according to their chronology.

The 7th- to 9th/10th-century amphorae – Of the group of 7th- to 9th/10th-century amphorae 25 entirely or partially preserved examples could be typochronologically classified and divided into two distinct groups with subgroups. Some 150 rim and body fragments could be dated to this period, but could not be typologically identified. An origin within the northern Black Sea region was supposed for some of the containers, while the rest were most likely of Aegean or eastern Mediterranean origin. A potential southern Italian provenance was eventually suggested for only one amphora.[18]

The 7th- to 9th/10th-century amphorae clustered at two major areas: the larger part was found along the western Black Sea coast and the Bay of Burgas, while only few were documented on the middle reaches of the Maritsa River. There were clearly two major lanes of distribution: one along the western Black Sea coast linking Constantinople to the Crimea and the North, while the other went from the Aegean up the Maritsa River (Fig. 7).

All amphorae were found at sites located within the Byzantine Empire and no amphorae were identified in territories belonging to the Medieval Bulgarian state. The majority of the sites where amphorae were recorded were major towns and/or ports (Ropotamo River, Sozopol, Debelt, Nessebar, Plovdiv), or fortresses (Sredets), while only two sites were unfortified settlements (Kapitan Andreevo and Georgi Dobrevo). The combination of typological diversity, quantity and settlement characteristics of the find spots at the western Black Sea coast seems to indicate that there was a higher demand here on a relatively regular basis from several production centres, while the Maritsa River area seemed to have had rather occasional contacts with only a few production centres.

Byzantine military and administrative offices resided in Sozopol.[19] Debelt and Nessebar were seats of *kommerkiarioi*, or Byzantine customs officers, responsible for controlling exported goods and taxation.[20] Here Bulgarians would come to trade with the Byzantines. The sources indicate that the Bulgarians were primarily interested in luxury goods,[21] making it less likely that wine and oil, the regular content of amphorae, were exchanged. It seems therefore likely that the amphorae carried supplies (wine, oil, food) for the military and officials quartered at Debelt and Nessebar.

The same is valid for the Sredets fortress, some 10 km away from Debelt. Presumably a military garrison was housed here that guarded the border between the two states. The supplies would have been officially organized by the Byzantine state in the framework of what was known during the Late Antiquity as *annona militaris*.[22] No evidence for military presence south of the Stara Planina Mountain is known, consequently the scattered amphorae along the Maritsa River either resulted from small-scale occasional trade, or from organized state supplies (*annona civica*) for the residents of the larger town in the area and the civic population in its hinterland.

The 9th/10th- to 11th/12th-century amphorae – The period from the 9th/10th to the 11th/12th century is marked by a sudden increase in amphora diversity and quantity at multiple sites (Fig. 8). Apart from the well-known Günsenin I and II containers, there was a small number of other transport jars that could be identified as seven different types. A dozen fragments could not be classified due to their fragmentary state and the lack of diagnostic features. The Günsenin I and II amphorae were clearly the most common and most numerous, with a couple of thousand fragments. It has to be noted that the Günsenin II jars were always found together with the Günsenin I vessels. At least at several key sites (Silistra,[23] Pliska,[24] Skala,[25] etc.) the two types were found in more or less equal quantities. Although no chemical and petrographic analyses of the fabric of the Günsenin I and II amphorae have been conducted so far, it is not unlikely that some of them were produced in well-known pottery workshops for these types, such as Ganos[26] and Chalcis.[27] The rest of the amphorae were represented with no more than four specimens per type and had a quite limited distribution. One can only suppose that their origin was Aegean or eastern Mediterranean.

Most of the 9th/10th- to 11th/12th-century transport containers found in Bulgaria can be seen to cluster in the eastern part of the country. Still, as a result of the mapping, five distinct areas of distribution can be outlined: (1) – the ports and towns along the western Black Sea coast; (2) – the cities, towns, fortified settlements, and villages in north-eastern Bulgaria; (3) – the towns and ports on the River Danube; (4) – two towns and the unfortified villages (mainly) along the Maritsa River and its tributaries; and (5) – one fortified town along the Struma River valley.

As stated before, it is obvious that contacts and trade with the Mediterranean basin were conducted via the route along the western Black Sea coast. During the Byzantine period, more ports emerged in this region, with Sozopol and Varna standing out as far as typological diversity of the amphorae is concerned. The Bay of Burgas and the area around Varna offered the easiest way for transport inland.

The second most important artery for the transfer of goods was the River Danube. the last port on the river that could be reached by large ships, was Silistra, a substantial port city, and an important redistribution centre. Quite some Günsenin I and II amphorae were found here. In a wider perspective more amphorae were recorded closer to the Danube delta in the east, while further westwards ever fewer container vessels have been found.

Judging from the archaeological record, a secondary, but no less important, distribution lane was the route linking the ports at the Bay of Burgas through the eastern Stara Planina passes to Preslav and Pliska, and eventually via a couple of small fortified settlements to Silistra and the Danube River. The significance of this route is underlined by the remarkable number of amphora finds and amphora diversity recorded in Preslav and Pliska. The Maritsa River and its tributaries appeared of lesser importance for amphora distribution, while there were only stray contacts with the Struma River valley via Thessaloniki.

It should be noted, that, like in the previous period, all amphorae were found in territories under Byzantine control, while only a few container vessels were, rightly or not, labelled as having been discovered in lands belonging to the Medieval Bulgarian state. This territorial distribution of the finds underlines the fact that amphorae suddenly appeared in large numbers in north-eastern Bulgaria and the Lower Danube since the end of the third quarter of the 10th century, the period in which the Byzantines started to reconquer the area. The earliest documented amphorae from this time (Pliska, Preslav, Odartsi, Huma, Skala, Kladentsi), as well as Byzantine coins,[28] seem to outline quite neatly the route used by the imperial troops to reach the Danube in the fastest possible way, and thus to be able to reconnect with the imperial fleet that was to enter the Delta.

The reconquista of these areas was a result of the change in Byzantine politics towards the Crimea, which became severly threatened by barbarian attacks and the emergence of the Kievan Rus'. In order to safeguard Byzantine economic interests in the area, imperial troops were stationed in smaller and larger fortified towns along the Lower Danube. These settlements were also used as market places where barbarians and Rus' came to trade.[29] As suggested above, the large number of amphorae found in the region apparently transported supplies (wine, oil, food) for the military and for civil servants, as well as merchandise to be sold at the numerous *emporia*.[30]

The diversity within the recovered group of Günsenin I and II amphorae seems to suggest that several large production centres were organized in a well-functioning supply network along which wine and oil were collected and distributed for the *annona militaris* or were marketed under state control.[31] The small number of other amphora types and the signs of multiple reuse of these amphorae seems to suggest that although centrally organized state supplies held the biggest share of the transports of goods, private trade also existed.

Based on amphora diversity and concentration of amphora stamps, the largest consumption centres in territories under Byzantine control were Preslav, Pliska, and Silistra. They received supplies from many production centres. It is no coincidence that all three cities were headquarters of the Byzantine military and administrative governors, while Silistra (Dristra) had also a customs office and was a bishopric seat.[32]

Similarly, on the western Black Sea coast amphorae were attested at sites with strong Byzantine military and administrative presence. Although not much is known for Sozopol, the diversity of amphorae emphasizes its importance as both a port and a city. In the second half of the 11th century Pomorie (Anchialo) and Nessebar (Messembria) were important military, religious and administrative centres used to station naval forces participating in the Byzantine expeditions to the Danube against the nomadic tribes.[33] A military governor was dispatched in Varna.[34] The three amphorae from Vidin can probably be linked to the presence of the Byzantine army in the town in the early 11th century.[35]

According to the amphorae evidence, the southern and south-western part of present-day Bulgaria were left to self-sufficiency. No evidence is available for strong military presence in the region except for a military unit dispatched in Stara Zagora at the end of the 11th/early 12th century.[36] It is unclear if a Byzantine governor was present in Plovdiv (Philippopolis), but there was certainly a bishop.[37] The small number of amphorae that arrived at the unfortified villages of the Maritsa River reaches can probably be linked to the *annona civica*.

The 11th/12th- to 14th-century amphorae – The variety and circulation of amphorae diminished considerably during the 11th/12th to 14th century (Fig. 9). The several hundred of Günsenin III and IV amphorae represented almost 100 percent of all ceramic containers from this period. There were only three other jars that differed typologically. Some of the Günsenin III amphorae were probably produced in Chalcis,[38] while the production centre of the Günsenin IV ones remains unknown. A southern Italian origin has been proposed for the amphora from Pernik.[39]

The majority of the ceramic containers from this period cluster along the western Black Sea coast, while the inland finds are scarce and isolated. These amphorae found in the inland areas were also of quite varying dates, such as 11th-12th century (Pernik),[40] late 12th century (Djadovo),[41] 12th-first half of the 13th century (Silistra),[42] early 13th century (Preslav),[43] 12th-14th century (Melnik and Perperikon)[44], and 13th-14th century (Cherven[45] and Veliko Tarnovo[46]). This suggests that traffic with container vessels along the Lower Danube and its tributaries, the Kamchia River, the Maritsa River and its tributaries, as well as the Struma River was very weak, thus hinting at rather occasional contacts with the Black Sea, the Aegean, and eventually the Adriatic Sea.

Again, almost all the amphorae of this period were found in territories under Byzantine control or with strong Byzantine presence, mainly large towns and/or ports (the ones along the western Black Sea, Silistra, Preslav, Melnik), a fortress (Pernik), and one unfortified settlement (Djadovo). There were only few examples found in the parts of the mainland that were under control of the Medieval Bulgarian state (Veliko Tarnovo – a capital city, Cherven – a fortified town) or of independent local rulers (Perperikon). Obviously, the amphora distribution, especially that of the 13th-14th centuries, did not result from the well-organized state supplying system, as before. Contacts were probably limited to a handful production centres, and trade was likely to be much more than before local, small-scale, and private.

During the 12th century both Pomorie and Nessebar most probably kept their important position as naval and religious centres.[47] However, from the end of the 11th century onward the Byzantines changed their politics towards the Lower Danube region. They retreated to the south, establishing a new frontier at the Stara Planina Mountain. This resulted in abrupt decrease in the circulation of amphorae and Byzantine coins.[48] The only military and civic units which were left to oversee the activity of the enemy were located at Preslav and Silistra. The amphorae found at these locations transported most probably food supplies for the Byzantines, as well as merchandise for the few fortresses-emporia close to the Danube delta where Cumans and Rus' came to trade.

The situation in territories south of the Stara planina was similar. Except for the single amphora from Djadovo that can possibly be connected to food supplies for the participants of the Third Crusade,[49] the Maritsa River was no longer used for the transport of goods. It is known from the sources that in the late 11th century Byzantine military units from southern Italy resided in Krakra fortress (Pernik),[50] which may explain the presence of amphora there. However, a single piece is certainly no indication for regular shipments of Italian wine, but perhaps rather of a 'nostalgic' gift for the commander. The other single find from the Struma River valley (at Melnik) also suggest that the exchange up the river of goods known to have been trasported by amphorae was not very active. This may be because the area is known, even today, as a wine-producing region.

After the end of the 12th century, most of the present-day Bulgarian lands were included in the Second Bulgarian Kingdom, that existed between 1185 and 1396. Tarnovo was now the capital of Bulgaria, while Cherven was an important fortified town and bishop's seat. It is highly probable that small quantities of selected wines were delivered through the Danube River and its reaches as occasional purchases or gifts to the Bulgarian ruler and the aristocracy. According to written sources, commercial traffic up and down the Danube River in the 14th century was quite active and was controlled by the Bulgarian rulers. The merchants were mostly Italians using small vessels to transport wine.[51] In this perspective, the only – and somewhat unexpected – amphora find at the fortified town of Perperikon[52] should probably been intrepreted as an occasional gift of wine to a local ruler. It is certainly not an indication of intentional and long-term commercial contacts, or food supplies organised by the state.

The sharply decreasing number of amphorae from this period found in Bulgaria should also be understood in the context of the general tendency in which wooden barrels, used by Italian merchants, were gradually replacing the much less profitable ceramic containers.[53] By this time Italians dominated all Byzantine markets, pushing aside local merchants who could not withstand the competition.

The Italians traded in raw materials and agricultural products, including wine and oil.[54] Government control over trade was by now much weaker and private commerce flourished. Aristocratic families, the owners of large estates and ships, held the largest share, although clerics and small holders such as soldiers, craftsmen and peasants, were also involved in transactions. Byzantine producers did not sell their products directly to the market, but used Italians as middlemen. Trade ventures between Italians and Greeks did exist, but Greeks were kept away from long-distance trade and sailed mainly to Black Sea ports,[55] as underlined by the amphora finds.

CONCLUSION

Mapping amphorae proved to be a highly successful method for analyzing the patterns of distribution and consumption over time of these container vessels. Notwithstanding methodological pitfalls, this approach makes it crystal clear that amphorae have been found almost exclusively in territories under Byzantine control. The finds cluster along important trade arteries or outline secondary distribution lanes. The quantity of the amphorae and geographical distribution of their find spots suggest that the jars circulated essentially in two ways: via free trade and via the Byzantine system of government control over the food supplies, the so-called *annona*. The relative importance of the two systems throughout the 7th to the 14th century varied according to political and economic circumstances.

The archaeological record of amphorae found in present-day Bulagria highlights the important role played by this region in the wider Byzantine economy. The trends in the circulation and distribution visualised by the mapping, while suggesting some local specifics, quite neatly fit the general framework of the Mediterranean trade and patterns of communication during Byzantine times. Although the results may have been to some degree distorted by the nature of the collected data, they certainly seem well suited as a starting point for future studies in the field of Medieval amphora and trade relations.

NOTES

1. Todorova 2012.
2. Changova 1959; Doncheva-Petkova 1977, 98-103; Aladzhov 1993; Doncheva-Petkova 1993; Yotov and Atanassov 1998, 74-75; Balbolova-Ivanova 2000a; *Idem* 2000b; Borisov 2002, 26-28; Grozdanova 2009.
3. Mihaylov 1955, 92, fig. 36; Changova 1957, 253-54, 264, tabl. VII, 1-3; Stanchev 1960, cat. no. 331, fig. 10B; AM Varna 1965, 145, fig. 78; Vazharova and Zlatarski 1969, 49-50, fig. 3b; Dimova 1979, 99, taf. 42d; Hensel 1980, 131, 164, tabl. V, fig. 6/IV$_2$; Georgieva 1985, 137, figs. 20-21; Ovcharov 1985, 151, fig. 36, 3-4; Radeva 1986, 72, 77, tabl. IV$_3$; Valov 1987, 29, fig. 12; Borisov 1989, 193-94, figs. 225-26; Changova 1992, 110-11, fig. 107, 1; Doncheva-Petkova 1992, fig. 22a,b; Doncheva-Petkova *et al.* 1999, 74, 149, cat. nos. 172-73, tabl. XXVI, 172-173; Henning and Doncheva-Petkova 1999, 50, cat. nos. 141-42, table XII, 141-42; Tsvetkov 2002, fig. 54P; Dimitrov and Dimitrov 2003; Daskalov and Trendafilova 2008, fig. 3.
4. Only the most consistant works are listed here, since it is impossible to mention all publications. Demangel and Mamboury 1939, 2-3, 44-46, 148-52, fig. 49, fig. 197-200; Yacobson 1951; Barnea 1954; Antonova *et al.* 1971; Barnea and Ştefanescu 1971, 261-69; Brusić 1976; Yacobson 1979; Bass and Doorninck, Jr. van 1982, 155-65; Bakirtzis 1989, 70-88; Déroche and Spieser 1989; Günsenin 1990; Arthur 1992; Hayes 1992, 61-78; Arthur 1993; Doorninck, Jr. van 1993; Garver 1993; Günsenin 1993; Hocker 1995; Günsenin 1995; Romanchuk *et al.* 1995; Hocker and Scafuri 1996; Sazanov 1997; Günsenin 1998; Hocker 1998a; *Idem* 1998b; Günsenin 2001; *Sea trade* 2001; Günsenin 2003; *Idem* 2009.
5. The study was to be completed within a 4-year period.
6. Günsenin I amphorae may vary in size and the way different parts were shaped. The one under consideration here is a relatively large, round-bellied jar, with wide sloping shoulders and shallow rounded bottom covered with horizontal ribs. The arched heavy handles flank the rim and the short neck, and rise at rim level. The fabric is relatively fine, clean-breaking; the color after firing is light red. The entire outer surface is covered with dense creamish slip. A representative example can be seen in Fig. 6, the first amphora from the second group.
7. Changova 1959, fig. 7, 5-6.
8. I would like to thank the director of the Silistra 2007 excavations, Dr. Rumyana Koleva (Sofia University), for allowing me to publish the amphorae and all information related to them.
9. I would like to thank Dimitar Nedev, director of Sozopol Archaeological Museum, for allowing me to use the unpublished amphorae kept in the museum.
10. Todorova 2022.
11. Stanev 2015.

12　Todorova 2012, 90-93. Some 10 amphora stamps from Günsenin IV jars were kept in the Regional Museum of History – Varna, but were not accessed.
13　Changova 1959, fig. 7, 5-6.
14　Manolova-Voykova 2015, fig. 3, 5.
15　Aladzhov 1993, fig. 1, 2a-b.
16　Todorova 2012, 91-93, T. XLVII, S36-S47, S49.
17　Hocker and Scafuri 1996, fig. 7f; Hocker 1998a, 14; *Idem* 1998b, 4-5, fig. 4; *Idem* 2005, 104; Doorninck, Jr. van 1989, 253-56; Günsenin and Hatcher 1997, footnote 14; Bass 2005, 117.
18　Todorova 2018.
19　Jordanov 2003, 159-60, no. 74.1.
20　Jordanov 1992b; *Idem* 2003, 58-61, nos. 22.1-22.5, 118-19.
21　Laiou 2002, 704; Oikonomides 1993, 641-42; *Idem* 2002, 86.
22　The *annona militaris* is a tax payable in kind (usually grain but also other foodstuffs) by the population of certain provinces for the maintenance of troops and government officials. The *annona civica* is the supply of food for Constantinople and the larger cities in the Byzantine Empire.
23　As already stated, all amphora shards from the 2007 excavations in Silistra were collected and studied. The author is responsible for their future publication.
24　Todorova 2022.
25　Yotov and Atanassov 1998, 74-75.
26　Günsenin 1990, 47-56; *Idem* 1993; *Idem* 1995, 165-77; *Idem* 1999, 127, fig. 1; *Idem* 2002, 127, 132-33.
27　Waksman *et al.* 2018.
28　Kirilov 2009, 328-33, fig. 3, fig. 7-8, fig. 10-11.
29　Stephenson 1999; *Idem* 2004, 51-105.
30　These are the fortresses and fortified settlements along the Lower Danube, which were used as market places for trade with the barbarians.
31　For more comments on the topic of the diversity of Günsenin I and II amphorae see Todorova 2022.
32　Jordanov 1992a; *Idem* 1993b; *Idem* 2000; *Idem* 2003; 62-69, nos. 23.1-23.10, 143, no. 62.1, 106, no. 38A.3, 144-54, nos. 63.1-63.9; *Idem* 2011; *Idem* 2015.
33　Jordanov 1993a, 36-39, 46; *Idem* 2003, 25-29, nos. 2.1, 2.2, 121-24, nos. 47.5-47.8.
34　Jordanov 2003, 45, no. 15.1.
35　Valov 1987, 25.
36　Kirilov 2009, 333.
37　Jordanov 2003, 162, no. 77.1, 165-66, nos. 77.3-5.
38　Waksman *et al.* 2018.
39　Todorova 2012, 72-73.
40　Changova 1992, 110-11, fig. 107, 1.
41　Borisov 1989, 59, 193-94, figs. 225-26.
42　Todorova 2012, 75, 81.
43　Manolova-Voykova 2015, 380, fig. 2, 16.
44　No chronology was available for the amphorae found at Melnik and Perperikon, but according to the general chronology of the Günsenin III and IV containers they should fall within the 12th-14th century.
45　Georgieva 1985, 137, figs. 20-21.
46　Rabovyanov 2015, 273-75.
47　Jordanov 1993a, 47; *Idem* 2003, 26, 28-29, no. 2.3.
48　Kirilov 2009, 328-33, fig. 3, fig. 7-8, figs. 10-11.

49 Stephenson 2004, 296-97.
50 Yurukova 1983, 107, 117-20, Tabl. II, 3-4; Changova 1992, 169-70, fig. 152, 2.
51 Matschke 2002, 792; Todorova 1984, 43, 49; *Idem* 1988, 340-41.
52 Perperikon is located at a steep hilltop surrounded by mountains. The town is not that close to the river Arda. There are no hints that Arda was navigable during the Middle Ages.
53 Μπακιρτζής 1989, 84-86.
54 Todorova 1988, 333-35, 339-40; Laiou 1988, 185; *Idem* 1993, 84-85, 87; Matschke 2002, 786-88.
55 Laiou 1988, 167; Matschke 2002, 773-76, 786-88, 800-801; Karpov 2011, 422-23.

BIBLIOGRAPHY

Aladzhov, Zh. 1993. *Novi amforni pechati ot Veliki Preslav* (Нови амфорни печати от Велики Преслав), *Godishnik na natsionalnia arheologicheski muzei* (Годишник на националния археологически музей) 9, 101-105.

AM Varna 1965. *Arheologicheski muzei Varna. Album* (Археологически музей Варна. Албум), Sofia.

Antonova, I., V.N. Danilenko, L.P. Ivashuta, V.I. Kadeev and A.I. Romanchuk 1971. Srednevekovye amfory Hersonesa (Средневековые амфоры Херсонеса), *Antichnaya drevnost' I srednie veka* (Античная древность и средние века) 7, 81-101.

Arthur, P. 1992. Amphorae for bulk transport, in: F. D'Andria and D. Whitehouse (eds.), *Excavations at Otranto, Vol. II: The Finds*, Lecce, 199-217.

Arthur, P. 1993. Early Medieval amphorae, the Duchy of Naples and the food supply of Rome, *Papers of the British School at Rome* 61, 231-44.

Bakirtzis, Ch. 1989. *Βυζαντινά τσουκαλολάγηνα*, Athens.

Balbolova-Ivanova, M. 2000a. A contribution to the research of the Early Medieval ceramics in Bulgaria, *Archaeologia Bulgarica* IV.1, 73-85.

Balbolova-Ivanova, M. 2000b. Keramika ot krepostta v grad Sredets kato dokazatelstvo za targovskite I vrazki s Chernomorskoto kraibrezhie prez VII–IX vek (Керамика от крепостта в град Средец като доказателство за търговските й връзки с Черноморското крайбрежие през VII–IX век), *Izvestiya na narodnia muzei Burgas* (Известия на народния музей Бургас) 3, 145-48.

Barnea, I. 1954. Amforele feudale de la Dinogetia, *Studii și cercetări de istorie veche* V.3-4, 513-30.

Barnea, I. and S. Ştefanescu 1971. *Bizantini, Romani şi Bulgari La Dunarea de Jos*, in: *Din Istoria Dobrugei, Vol. III*, Bucharest.

Bass, G.F. 2005. Solving a million-piece jigsaw puzzle: Serçe Limanı, Turkey, in: G.F. Bass (ed.) *Beneath the Seven Seas*, London, 106-17.

Bass, G.F. and F.H. van Doorninck, Jr. 1982. *Yassı Ada. A Seventh Century Byzantine Shipwreck, Vol. I*, College Station.

Borisov, B. 1989. *Djadovo. Mediaeval Settlement and Necropolis (11th-12th Century)*, Tokyo 1989.

Borisov, B. 2002. *Keramika I keramichno proizvodstvo prez XI–XII v.* (Керамика и керамично производство през XI–XII в.), in: Maritsa–Iztok, vol. 6, Radnevo.

Brusić, Z. 1976. Byzantine amphorae (9th to 12th century) from Eastern Adriatic underwater sites, *Archaeologia Iugoslavica* 17, 37-49.

Changova, Y. 1957. Targovski pomeshtenia krai yuzhnata krepostna stena v Preslav

(Търговски помещения край южната крепостна стена в Преслав), *Izvestiya na arheologicheskia institut (Известия на археологическия институт)* 21, 233-90.

Changova, Y. 1959. Srednovekovni amfori v Balgaria (Средновековни амфори в България), *Izvestiya na arheologicheskia institut (Известия на археологическия институт)* 22, 243-61.

Changova, Y. 1992. *Pernik, Vol. III: Krepostta Pernik VIII–XIV v. (Перник, т. III: Крепостта Перник VIII–XIV в.)*, Sofia.

Daskalov M. and K. Trendafilova 2008. Prouchvane na krastokupolen hram do Sozopol (Проучване на кръстокуполен храм до Созопол), *Arheologicheski otkritia I razkopki prez 2007 g. (Археологически открития и разкопки през 2007 г.)*, Sofia, 648-51.

Demangel, R. and E. Mamboury 1939. *Le quartier des Manganes et la première région de Constantinople*, Paris.

Déroche, V. and J.-M. Spieser (eds.) 1989. *Recherches sur la céramique byzantine*, Bulletin de Correspondance Hellénique Supplément 18, Athens.

Dimitrov, M. and B. Dimitrov 2003. *Baltschik – Die Perle des Schwarzen Meeres*, Varna.

Dimova, V. 1979. Die mittelalterliche Siedlung über den Ruinen des Kastells Iatrus, in: *Iatrus-Krivina, Vol. I: Spätantike Befestigung und frühmittelalterliche Siedlung an der Unteren Donau, Ergebnisse der Ausgrabungen 1966-1973*, Berlin.

Doncheva-Petkova, L. 1977. *Balgarska bitova keramika prez rannoto srednovekovie (vtora polovina na VI–kraia na X v.) (Българска битова керамика през ранното средновековие (втората половина на VI–края на X в.))*, Sofia.

Doncheva-Petkova, L. 1992. Sgradi pri yuzhnia sektor na Zapadnata krepostna stena na Pliska (Сгради при южния сектор на Западната крепостна стена на Плиска), *Pliska-Preslav (Плиска-Преслав)* 5, 124-45.

Doncheva-Petkova, L. 1993. Glineni sadove ot XI v. ot Pliska (Глинени съдове от XI в. от Плиска), *Preslav (Преслав)* 4, 250-62.

Doncheva-Petkova, L., L. Ninov and V. Parushev 1999. *Odartsi, Vol. I: Selishte ot Parvoto balgarsko tsarstvo (Одърци, т.I: Селище от Първото българско царство)*, Sofia.

Doorninck, Jr. F.H. van 1989. The cargo amphoras on the 7th century Yassı Ada and 11th century Serçe Limanı shipwrecks: Two examples of a reuse of Byzantine amphoras as transport jars, in: V. Déroche and J.-M. Spieser (eds.), *Recherches sur la céramique byzantine*, Bulletin de Correspondance Hellénique Supplément 18, Athens, 247-57.

Doorninck, Jr. F.H. van 1993. Giving good weight in eleventh-century Byzantium: The metrology of the glass wreck amphoras, *The Institute of Nautical Archaeology Quarterly*, 20.2, 8-12.

Garver, E.L. 1993. Byzantine Amphoras of the Ninth Through Thirteenth Centuries in the Bodrum Museum of Underwater Archaeology, *unpublished* master thesis, Texas A&M University.

Georgieva, S. 1985. Grancharstvo (Грънчарство), in: *Srednovekovniat Cherven (Средновековният Червен), Vol. I*, Sofia, 133-65.

Grozdanova, G. 2009. Amforniat material ot rannosrednovekovnoto selishte pri s. Kapitan Andreevo, obshtina Svilengrad (Амфорният материал от ранносредновековното селище при с. Капитан Андреево, община Свиленград), in: V. Grigorov, M. Daskalov and E. Komatarova-Balinova (eds.), *Eurika. In honorem Ljudmilae Doncevae-Petkovae,* Sofia, 213-21.

Günsenin, N. 1990. Les amphores byzantines (xe-xiiie siècles). Typologie, production, circulation d'après les collections turques, *unpublished* doctoral dissertation, Université de Paris I (Panthéon-Sorbonne).

Günsenin, N. 1993. Ganos – centre de production d'amphores à l'époque byzantine, *Anatolia antiqua* 2, 193-201.

Günsenin, N. 1995. Ganos: resultats des campagnes de 1992 et 1993, *Anatolia antiqua* 3, 165-78.

Günsenin, N. 1998. Récentes découvertes sul l'île de Marmara (Proconnèse) à l'époque byzantine. Épaves et lieux de chargement, *Archaeonautica* 14, 309-316.

Günsenin, N. 1999. Les ateliers amphoriques de Ganos à l'époque byzantine, in: *Production et commerce des amphores anciennes en mer Noir,* Provence, 125-28.

Günsenin, N. 2001. L'épave de Çamaltı Burnu I (l'île de Marmara, Proconnèse): resultats des campagnes 1998-2000, *Anatolia Antiqua* 9, 117-33.

Günsenin, N. 2002. Medieval trade in the Sea of Marmara: the evidence of shipwrecks, in: R.J. Macrides (ed.), *Travel in the Byzantine world. Papers from the 34th Spring Symposium of Byzantine Studies, Birmingham, April 2000*, Birmingham, 125-35.

Günsenin, N. 2003. L'épave de Çamaltı Burnu I (l'île de Marmara, Proconnèse): resultats des campagnes 2001-2002, *Anatolia Antiqua* 11, 361-76.

Günsenin, N. 2009. Ganos wine and its circulation in the 11th century, in: M. Mundell Mango (ed.), *Byzantine Trade, 4th-12th Centuries. The Archaeology of Local, Regional and International Exchange. Papers of the Thirty-eighth Spring Symposium of Byzantine Studies, St John's College, University of Oxford, March 2004,* Society for the Promotion of Byzantine Studies Publications 14, Farnham & Burlington, 145-53.

Günsenin, N. and H. Hatcher 1997. Analyses chimiques comparatives des amphores de Ganos, de l'île de Marmara et de l'épave de Serçe Limanı (Glass-wreck), *Anatolia Antiqua* 5, 249-60.

Hayes, J.W. 1992. *Excavations at Saraçhane in Istanbul, II: The Pottery*, Princeton, NJ.

Henning, J. and L. Doncheva-Petkova (eds.) 1999. *Parvoprestolna Pliska. 100 godini arheologicheski prouchvania (Първопрестолна Плиска. 100 години археологически проучвания)*, Frankfurt am Main.

Hensel, W. 1980. *Styrmen nad Jantra (Bułgaria). Badania archeologiczne w Latach 1961-1964 I 1967-1968, Praca wykonana w ramach problemu resortowego*, 37.

Hocker, F.M. 1995. The Byzantine shipwreck at Bozburun, Turkey: The 1995 field season, *The Institute of Nautical Archaeology Quarterly* 22.4, 3-8.

Hocker, F.M. 1998a. The Byzantine shipwreck at Bozburun, Turkey: The 1997 field season, *The Institute of Nautical Archaeology Quarterly* 25.2, 12-19.

Hocker, F.M. 1998b. Bozburun Byzantine shipwreck excavation: The final campaign 1998, *The Institute of Nautical Archaeology Quarterly* 25.4, 3-12.

Hocker, F.M. 2005. Sampling a Byzantine vintage: Bozburun, Turkey, in: G.F. Bass (ed.) *Beneath the Seven Seas*, London, 100-105.

Hocker, F.M. and M.P. Scafuri 1996. The Bozburun Byzantine shipwreck excavation: 1996 campaign, *The Institute of Nautical Archaeology Quarterly* 23.4, 3-9.

Jordanov, I. 1992a. Vizantijski olovni pechati ot Pliska (Византийски оловни печати от Плиска), *Pliska-Preslav (Плиска-Преслав)* 5, 281-301.

Jordanov, I. 1992b. *Pechatite na komerkiariata Develt (Печатите на комеркиарията Девелт)*, in: *Poselishtni prouchvania (Поселищни проучвания), Vol. 2*, Sofia.

Jordanov, I. 1993a. Anhialo – spored dannite ot sfragistikata (Анхиало – според данните от сфрагистиката), *Arheologia (Археология)* XXXV.3, 36-50.

Jordanov, I. 1993b. Pechatite ot strategiata Preslav (971-1088) (Печатите от стратегията Преслав (971-1088)), in: *Monumenta Slavico-Byzantina et Mediaevalia Europensia, Vol. II*, Sofia.

Jordanov, I. 2000. Moneti i pechati ot Pliska 1899-1999 g. (Монети и печати от Плиска 1899-1999 г.), *Pliska-Preslav (Плиска-Преслав)* 8, 135-67.

Jordanov, I. 2003. *Corpus of Byzantine Seals from Bulgaria, Vol. 1: Byzantine Seals with Geographical Names*, Sofia.

Jordanov, I. 2011. Srednovekovniat Drastar spored dannite na sfragistikata (VI-XII v.) (Средновековният Дръстър според данните на сфрагистиката (VI–XII в.), *Antichnaya drevnost' i srednie veka (Античная древность и средние века)* 40, 79-120.

Jordanov, I. 2015. Pliska (IX–XI v.), spored dannite na sfragistikata (Плиска (IX–XI в.), според данните на сфрагистиката), *Pliska-Preslav (Плиска-Преслав)* 11, 261-74.

Karpov, S. 2011. Main Changes in the Black Sea Trade and Navigation, 12th-15th Centuries, in: *Proceedings of the 22nd International Congress of Byzantine Studies, Sofia 22-27 August 2011, Vol. 1*, Sofia, 417-29.

Kirilov, Ch. 2009. Mnimoto izselvane na balgari ot Paristrion. Niakoi belezhki po vaprosa za demografskite protsesi mezhdu Dunav I Stara planina prez XI–XII v. (Мнимото изселване на българи от Паристрион. Някои бележки по въпроса за демографските процеси между Дунав и Стара планина през XI–XII в.), in: V. Grigorov, M. Daskalov and E. Komatarova-Balinova (eds.), *Eurika. In honorem Ljudmilae Doncevae-Petkovae*, Sofia, 321-40.

Laiou, A. 1988. Byzantium and the Black Sea, 13th-15th centuries: Trade and the native populations of the Black Sea areas, *Bulgaria Pontica Medii Aevi* 2, 164-201.

Laiou, A. 1993. Byzantine traders and seafarers, in: S. Vryonis, Jr. (ed.), *The Greeks and the Sea*, New Rochelle, New York, 79-96.

Laiou, A. 2002. Exchange and trade, seventh-twelfth centuries, in: A. Laiou (ed.), *The Economic History of Byzantium: From the Seventh through the Fifteenth Century, Vol. II*, Dumbarton Oaks Studies 39, Washington, DC, 697-770.

Manolova-Voykova, M. 2015. Amfori ot obekt 'Vladetelska tsarkva' vav Veliki Preslav (Амфори от обект 'Владетелска църква' във Велики Преслав), *Pliska-Preslav (Плиска-Преслав)* 11, 377-88.

Matschke, K.-P. 2002. Commerce, trade, markets, and money – Thirteenth-fifteenth centuries, in: A. Laiou (ed.), *The Economic History of Byzantium: From the Seventh through the Fifteenth Century, Vol. II*, Dumbarton Oaks Studies 39, Washington, DC, 771-806.

Mihaylov, St. 1955. Arheologicheski materiali ot Pliska (1948-1951 g.) (Археологически материали от Плиска (1948-1951 г.)), *Izvestiya na arheologicheskia institut (Известия на археологическия институт)* 20, 49-182.

Oikonomides, N. 1993. Le marchand byzantin des provinces (IXe-XIe s.), in: *Mercati e mercanti nell'alto medioevo: l'area euroasiatica e l'area mediterranea*, Settimane di studio del centro italiano di studi sull'alto medioevo 40, Spoleto, 633-60.

Oikonomides, N. 2002. The role of the Byzantine state in the economy, in: A. Laiou (ed.), *The Economic History of Byzantium: From the Seventh through the Fifteenth Century, Vol. II*, Dumbarton Oaks Studies 39, Washington, DC, 973-1058.

Ovcharov, D. 1985. Razkopki I prouchvania na iztochnata stena na Vatreshnia grad v Preslav (1970-1976) (Разкопки и проучвания на източната стена на Вътрешния град в Преслав (1970-1976)), *Pliska-Preslav (Плиска-Преслав)* 4, 132-60.

Rabovyanov, D. 2015. *Archaeological Studies in the Southern Section of Trapezitsa, Vol. I: The Medieval Town (Археологически проучвания в Южния сектор на Трапезица, Т. 1: Средновековният град)*, Veliko Tarnovo.

Radeva, M. 1986. Rannosrednovekovna keramika ot Sliven (Раннсредновековна керамика от Сливен), *Izvestiya na muzeite v yugoiztochna Balgaria (Известия на музеите в югоизточна България)* 9, 67-78.

Romanchuk, A.I., A.V. Sazanov and L. Sedikova 1995. *Amfory iz kompleksov vizantijskogo Hersona (Амфоры из комплексов византийского Херсона)*, Ekaterinburg.

Sazanov, A. 1997. Les amphores de l'Antiquité tardive et du Moyen Âge: Continuité ou rupture? Le cas de la Mer Noire, in: G.D. d'Archimbaud (ed.), *La céramique médiévale en Méditerrannée. Actes du VIe congrès de l'AIECM2*, Aix-en-Provence, 87-102.

Sea Trade in North Black Sea Region. The collection of scientific articles. (Морская торговля в Северном Причерноморье. Сборник научных статей), Kiev 2001.

Stanev, K. 2015. Rannosrednovekoven plast ot obekt 'Ivan Karadzhov' No. 4, grad Plovdiv (Ранносредновековен пласт от обект „Иван Караджов" № 4, град Пловдив), in: *Balgaria v evropeiskata kultura, nauka, obrazovanie, religia, Part 1* (България в европейската култура, наука, образование, религия, част 1), Materiali ot chetvartata natsionalna konferentsia po istoria, arheologia i kulturen turizam 'Patuvane kam Balgaria' – Shumen, 14-16.05.2014 godina (Материали от четвъртата национална конференция по история, археология и културен туризъм 'Пътуване към България' – Шумен, 14-16.05.2014 година), Shumen, 432-46.

Stanchev, St. 1960. Materiali ot dvortsovia tsentar v Pliska (Материали от дворцовия център в Плиска), *Izvestiya na arheologicheskia institut (Известия на археологическия институт)* 23, 23-66.

Stephenson, P. 1999. Byzantine policy toward Paristrion in the mid-eleventh century: Another interpretation, *Byzantine and Modern Greek Studies* 23, 43-66.

Stephenson, P. 2004. *Byzantium's Balkan Frontier. A Political Study of the Northern Balkans, 900-1204*, Cambridge.

Todorova, E. 1984. River trade in the Balkans during the Middle Ages, *Études balcaniques* 4, 38-50.

Todorova, E. 1988. The Genoese and the Danube River, *Bulgaria Pontica Medii Aevi* 2, 333-49.

Todorova, E. 2012. Byzantine Amphorae from Present-day Bulgaria (7th-14th century AD) (Амфорите от територията на България (VII–XIV в.)), *unpublished* doctoral thesis, Sofia University, 2012.

Todorova, E. 2018. 'Dark Age' Amphorae from present-day Bulgaria – State of research, typology, problems and future perspectives, *Archeologia Medievale* 45, 65-76.

Todorova, E. 2022. Amphorae found during excavations for construction of the NAIM-BAS base in Pliska, Bulgaria, *Contributions to Bulgarian Archaeology (Приноси към българската археология)* 12

Tsvetkov, B. 2002. *Selishtna mrezha v dolinata na sredna Struma prez Srednovekovieto (IX–XVII v.)* (Селищната мрежа в долината на средна Струма през Средновековието IX–XVII в.), Sofia.

Valov, V. 1987. Sedalishteto I teritorialniat obhvat na Bdinskata oblast ot sredata na IX do nachaloto na XI vek (Седалището и териториалният обхват на Бдинската област от средата на IX до началото на XI век), *Izvestiya na muzeite v severozapadna Balgaria (Известия на музеите в северозападна България)* 13, 21-47.

Vazharova, Zh. and D. Zlatarski 1969. Srednovekovnoto selishte I nekropol v gr. Dalgopol, Varnenski okrag (Средновековното селище и некропол в гр. Дългопол, Варненски окръг), *Arheologia (Археология)* XI.3, 49-58.

Waksman, S.Y., N.D. Kontogiannis, S. Skartsis, E.P. Todorova and G. Vaxevanis 2018. Investigating the origins of two main types of Middle and Late Byzantine Amphorae, *Journal of Archaeological Science: Reports* 21, 1111-1121.

Yakobson, A.L. 1951. Srednevekovye amfory Severnogo Prichernomor'ya (Средневековые амфоры Северного Причерноморья), *Sovetskaya arheologia (Советская археология)* 15, 325-344.

Yakobson, A.L. 1979. *Keramika I keramicheskoe proizvodstva srednevekovoi Tavriki (Керамика и керамическое производства средневековой Таврики)*, Leningrad.

Yotov, V. and G. Atanassov 1998. *Skala. Krepost ot X-XI v. do s. Kladentsi, Tervelsko (Скала. Крепост от X–XI в. до село Кладенци, Тервелско)*, Sofia.

Yurukova, Yo. 1983. Nimizmatichni I sfragistichni pametnitsi (867-1195/1203) (Нумизматични и сфрагистични паметници (867-1195/1203)), in: D. Ovcharov (ed.), *Pernik, Vol. II: Krepostta Pernik VIII-XIV v. (Перник, т. II: Крепостта Перник VIII-XIV в.)*, Sofia, 120-71.

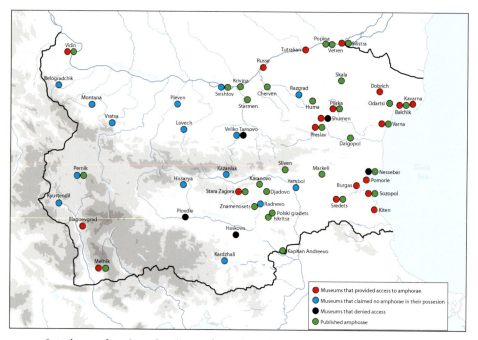

FIG. 1 – Initial map of amphora distribution (E. Todorova).

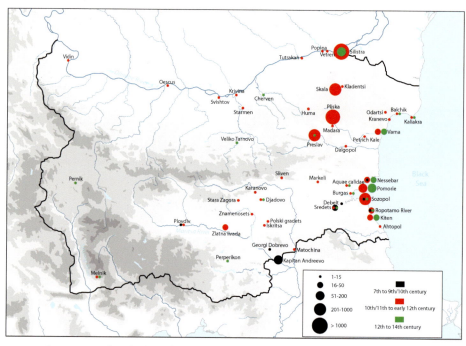

FIG. 2 – Quantitative distribution of the 7th- to 14th-century amphorae from present-day Bulgaria (E. Todorova).

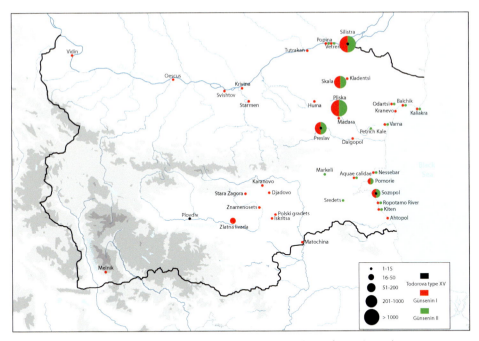

FIG. 3 – The quantitative distribution of contemporaneous amphorae (E. Todorova).

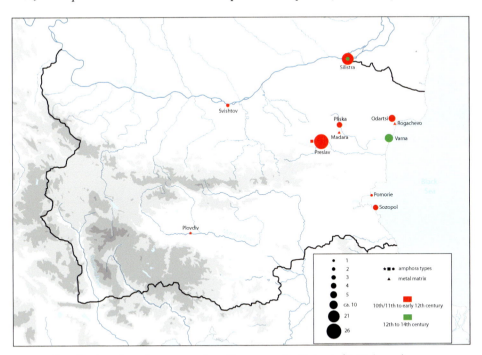

FIG. 4 – Distribution of amphora stamps found in present-day Bulgaria (E. Todorova).

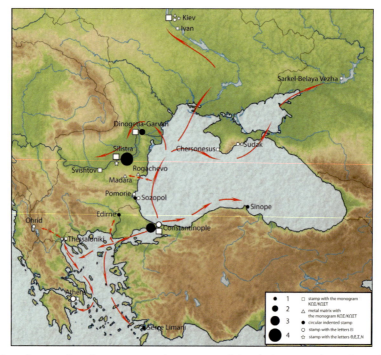

FIG. 5 – Distribution of amphora stamps in the Aegean and the Black Sea area (E. Todorova).

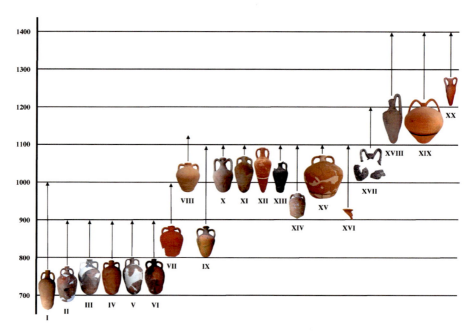

FIG. 6 – Chronology of amphorae found in present-day Bulgaria: (1) – 7th to 9th/10th century; (2) – 9th/10th to 11th/12th century; (3) – 11th/12th to 14th century (E. Todorova).

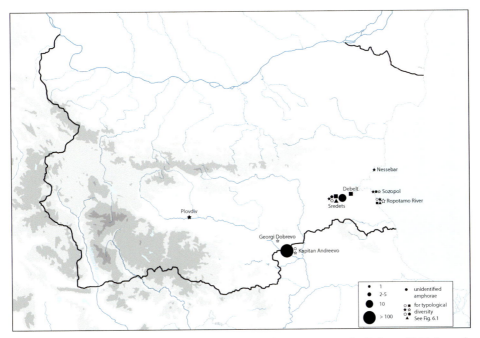

FIG. 7 – Distribution of the 7th- to 9th/10th-century amphorae in present-day Bulgaria (E. Todorova).

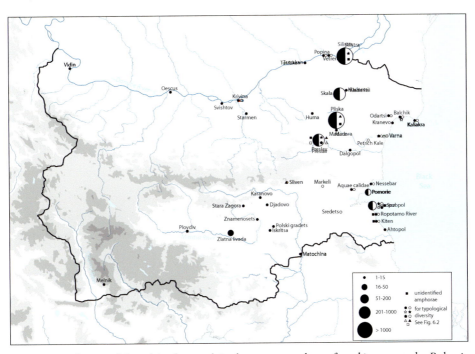

FIG. 8 – Distribution of the 9th/10th- to 11th/12th-century amphorae found in present-day Bulgaria (E. Todorova).

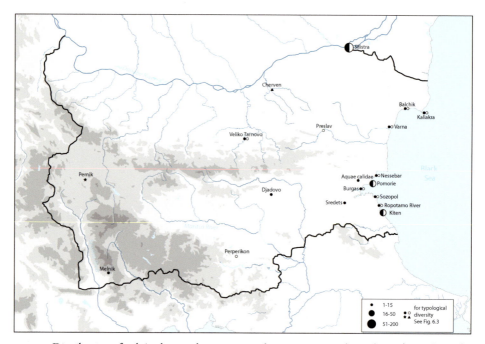

FIG. 9 – Distribution of 11th/12th-to 14th-century amphorae in present-day Bulgaria (E. Todorova).

* * *

MIDDLE BYZANTINE &

LATE BYZANTINE PERIODS

* * *

Elaborate Incised Ware bowl of Late Byzantine times (after D. Talbot Rice 1930, *Byzantine Glazed Pottery*, Oxford, pl. 1 and J. Vroom 2014², *Byzantine to Modern Pottery in the Aegean – An Introduction and Field Guide, Second & Revised Edition*, Turnhout, 122, fig. LBYZ/FR 8.2).

* * *

Not a consumption crisis: Diversity in marble carving, ruralisation, and the collapse of urban demand in Middle Byzantine Asia Minor

Philipp Niewöhner

*

INTRODUCTION

The 23rd International Congress of Byzantine Studies' round table on *New Perspectives on the Byzantine City as Consumption Centre* appeared to address an obvious truism.[1] In so far as Byzantine cities concentrated population, they must also have been centres of consumption, if only because the inhabitants had to feed, dress, and keep busy.[2] Similarly, the converse argument has also often been taken for granted: consumption above subsistence level has been understood to indicate urbanisation, for example in the case of Middle Byzantine Asia Minor: after a slump during the Invasion Period, when between the 7th and the 9th centuries Persians and Arabs devastated the region for more than two hundred years, economic recovery in the Middle Byzantine period was taken to signify urban revival.[3]

However, when marble carvings are considered, the assumption of urban revival in Middle Byzantine Asia Minor appears less straightforward. In fact, seen from this perspective, the picture is quite complicated. Marble carvings for churches and other buildings were employed throughout the entire Byzantine period, and their production and distribution in city and countryside seems to reflect not only the state of the economy but also the structure of the settlement pattern, as well as the way in which these changed over time.[4] Thus, a great many Middle Byzantine carvings do attest to economic revival,[5] but assigning this revival to cities as consumption centres is rather problematic, for Middle Byzantine production does not seem to have been centred, or focused, on cities, as becomes apparent through its greater diversity in comparison with the more standardized output of the Early Byzantine period.

This paper sets out by describing Middle Byzantine diversity in marble carving and comparing it to Early Byzantine standardisation. Trying to understand the mechanism behind the changed mode of production then leads to considerations of settlement history, i.e. ruralisation and a Middle Byzantine collapse of urban consumption centres. In conclusion, Middle Byzantine diversity in marble carving may be explained through, and be indicative of, a largely ruralised settlement pattern that, whilst still economically prosperous, was not dominated by cities any more.

MIDDLE BYZANTINE DIVERSITY IN MARBLE CARVING

To start with, much Middle Byzantine marble carving was repair work,[6] for example templon epistyles, i.e. the architraves of high sanctuary screens (that later developed into iconostases). Marble templon epistyles appear to have replaced predecessors made of wood, with metal and other precious sheathing, all of which would have been robbed, burned, or otherwise lost since the Early Byzantine period.[7] Even in the exceptional case that a Middle Byzantine church was fitted out in total with newly carved marbles, their number would have been lower than in the Early Byzantine period, because the later churches were smaller and included fewer columns.[8]

The lesser demand can explain the absence of large scale production centres that, in the Early Byzantine period, used to provide great amounts of standardized marble carvings for countless new churches – typically columnar basilicas – and for secular buildings, for example for porticoes along streets.[9] Thus, the quarry and workshop of Proconnesus/Marmara Adası in the Sea of Marmara, close to the capital city of Constantinople, used to provide many minor cities around the Mediterranean with the same marble carvings.[10] On the central Anatolian high plateau, where Proconnesian marble was not available due to the prohibitively high cost of overland transport, the same standard carvings were instead produced by the quarry and workshop of Docimium in Phrygia.[11]

In contrast, the Middle Byzantine period appears to have known no such standard, as no two carvings are alike, and it is hardly ever possible to assign more than one monument to the same workshop.[12] Middle Byzantine marble carving seems to have been organized locally, with countless different workshops in various parts of Asia Minor and beyond. Some of these otherwise obscure workshops achieved remarkably high quality and produced unique showpieces, for example two exceptional marbles at Konya on the central Anatolian plateau (Figs. 1 and 2).

However, notwithstanding diversity in detail and execution, most Middle Byzantine marble carvings employed the same formal repertoire, and that is how they are recognized and dated.[13] One example for this are knotted columns that were not yet customary in the Early Byzantine period, but became ubiquitous later, with no two sets alike, but all representing the same general idea, e.g. at Afyon in Phrygia (Fig. 3) and at Edirne in Thrace (Fig. 4).[14] Another example are slabs with a concentric decoration of interlaced rectangles, lozenges, and circles, a central rose or cross, as well as additional smaller circles and roses in the four corners, e.g. at Akşehir (Figs. 5-6) and Afyon (Fig. 7) in central Anatolia, at Myra/Demre (Fig. 8) and Antalya (Fig. 9) in southern Asia Minor, and at Denizli (Fig. 10) as well as Edirne (Fig. 11) in western Turkey.[15] Or column capitals with eagles at the corners and human heads under the abacus bosses or knobs, e.g. at Istanbul (Fig. 12) and at Konya (Fig. 13).[16] Or pairs of animals that drink from a central fountain or chalice or flank a central plant, e.g. on column capitals at Konya (Fig. 14) and at Edirne (Fig. 15 to 18) and on slabs at Kütahya in central Anatolia (Figs. 19-20) and at Anatalya (Fig. 21).[17] Or templon epistyles that are decorated with arcades, e.g. at Afyon (Figs. 22-23).[18]

The application of the same formal repertoire throughout Asia Minor and beyond[19] shows that the various Middle Byzantine workshops must have been in touch, either with each other or with some centre or centres, which led to the proliferation of the same fashion or period style across the whole region. In comparison with the Early Byzantine period, the Middle Byzantine repertoire in all its diversity is conspicuously homogeneous, without apparent provincial or sub-regional traits of the kind that are characteristic of the earlier times.

LOCAL STYLES

In the Early Byzantine period, local workshops in Caria,[20] Lycia,[21] and Cilicia[22] each adhered to a distinct style in marble or lime stone carving that can be told apart from other provinces as well as from the leading regional and supra-regional workshops of Proconnesus and Docimium. Similarly, Proconnesus/Constantinople,[23] Docimium as well as other local workshops on the central Anatolian high plateau,[24] and local workshops in south-western Asia Minor each constructed and decorated a distinct kind of *ambo* or pulpit.[25]

Comparable provincial styles can also be made out in the Early Byzantine church architectures of Constantinople, of Lycia and Cilicia along the south coast of Asia Minor, and of Galatia and Lycaonia on the central Anatolian high plateau. Characteristic metropolitan and, respectively, provincial features included free-standing apses and eastern exits at Constantinople,[26] annexed chapels and triconch sanctuaries in Lycia,[27] inscribed apses with flanking side rooms in Cilicia,[28] and arcaded as well as barrel vaulted churches, often with wide narthexes and with galleries, in Galatia and Lycaonia.[29]

For the Middle Byzantine period, comparable provincial traits are not in evidence, and church architecture is as diverse throughout all of Asia Minor as has above been observed for marble carving.[30]

Why, then, was the provincial structure evident in Early Byzantine art not also reflected in Middle Byzantine architecture and marble carving? What had changed since the earlier period that prevented provincial centres to exert a similar influence as before? The answer may be found in the rural contexts of most Middle Byzantine churches and marble carvings and in the lack of contemporary provincial centres, as shall be argued in the following sections.

RURALISATION

Middle Byzantine churches and marble carvings are as often found in remote rural locations as at ancient city sites. The same was the case already in the Early Byzantine period and distinguishes these later centuries from Roman times, when marble architecture used to be an urban prerogative.[31] In fact, Early Byzantine churches known from the rural hinterland of Aezani, an ancient city in Phrygia, hugely outnumber the urban ones, and the inhabitants of the Early Byzantine countryside collectively seem to have employed more marble and stonemasonry than their urban counterparts.[32]

The extensive use of marble for rural churches was a new development of the 5th and 6th centuries. Until the last urban building boom around AD 400, architectural sculpture had been employed almost exclusively for the monumental embellishment of cities. The new ascendance of the countryside was enhanced by an increase in rural settlements and apparently also in rural population. In the territory of Aezani, the number of settlements doubled during the 5th and 6th centuries.[33] A similar expansion in conjunction with an enlargement of the pre-existing Roman settlements can be observed in various parts of Asia Minor and points to a general increase of rural population during the Early Byzantine period.[34]

Simultaneously, urbanism went into decline from the later 5th century onwards: large bath buildings or *thermae* stopped functioning, porticoes and peristyle houses were downgraded, subdivided, and given up, and city walls were pulled down and/or rendered indefensible by lean-to structures.[35] At Aezani, the last *thermae* and the city's *macellum* or delicatessen were converted into churches.[36] The colonnaded porticoes of a street that had been built during the Theodosian period, around AD 400, were subdivided and turned into workshops and a smithy by the second half of the 5th century.[37] By the 6th century, when the colonnade finally collapsed due to an earthquake, a thick layer of accumulated earth already covered the pavement. The street had apparently been given up altogether by this time, and the earthquake debris was never subsequently cleared away, although it completely blocked the passage along the street. A similar encroachment of formerly public urban spaces by workshops and even by agricultural installations occurred in numerous cities during the 5th and 6th centuries, including the largest and most important metropoleis like Ephesus.[38]

However, urban churches continued to be erected in great numbers throughout the Early Byzantine period and appear to have been the only major exception to urban decline.[39] Although urban churches were outnumbered by rural ones, the urban buildings were typically bigger, their architecture more sophisticated, and their marble carvings more numerous and sumptuous, for example the 6th-century church inside the former bath building at Aezani that had one of the finest Early Byzantine ambos made of marble from Docimium.[40] Major urban churches undoubtedly constituted the most important single building projects in Early Byzantine architecture and marble carving; as such they will have set the trends that were followed in the surrounding countryside and in minor cities, which can explain how the various provincial styles of the Early Byzantine period came about.

Most of this came to an end during the Invasion Period, when from the 7th to the 9th centuries the unfortified rural sites would have had no defences against the Persian army and Arab raids and settlement activity concentrated on heavily fortified cities.[41] Rural church building lapsed, and urban building was also reduced, but some two dozen major cathedrals throughout the region continued to be built or repaired on a lavish scale and count among the largest and most innovative buildings of the age.[42]

Ruralisation appears to have set in again with the return of peace in the later 9th century. As in the Early Byzantine period, this is attested by numerous rural church buildings and countless marble carvings. However, other than before, the cities did not retain pre-eminence any more. Middle Byzantine churches at ancient city sites are hardly larger or otherwise superior to buildings in the countryside.[43] To the contrary, some of the most noteworthy Middle Byzantine churches in Asia Minor have rural locations, for example Üçayak in Cappadocia,[44] and the same is true for some of the finest regional ensembles of Middle Byzantine marble carvings, for example at Kümbet in Phrygia.[45]

This is not to say that rural Asia Minor had reached urban standards in the Middle Byzantine period, but that the ancient city sites stopped to achieve above average. Major innovative church building, for which Anatolian cities had last been known during the Invasion Period,[46] now took place in other regions of the recovering empire, for example in Greece.[47] Most Anatolian cities had probably come down to the level of villages or were altogether deserted in the Middle Byzantine period, as the following section shall argue.

COLLAPSE OF URBAN CONSUMPTION CENTRES

In the course of the 9th century, the Byzantines regained full control over Asia Minor and pushed back the Arab frontier far to the south-east. Thereafter fortification stopped to be an issue in western and central Anatolia, and urbanism seems to have lost any attraction. By the 11th century, well before the onset of the Turkish conquest, most cities seem to have been neglected, apparently largely deserted and reduced to little more than villages.[48]

A clear example of this development is provided by Miletus in Caria. While a large part of the city centre has been excavated down to ancient levels,[49] including two Early Byzantine churches,[50] there is as yet no evidence at all for Middle Byzantine occupation, which contrasts sharply with an abundance of finds from this period in rural areas.[51] The city's downfall seems to be underlined by the excavation of the two only landward gates of Byzantine Miletus. The excavators found the remains of these gates as they had collapsed in an earthquake, burying the streets and blocking any access to the city.[52] The debris was never cleared away, indicating that the city was already abandoned when the earthquake occurred. Circumstantial evidence dates the collaps of the gates to the Middle Byzantine period.[53] When the Turks started to arrive in the region from the later 11th century onwards, and the Byzantine population returned to the cities in search of safety behind urban fortifications, Miletus was re-founded at a different location and under a new name.

Elsewhere in Asia Minor, clear evidence for urban abandonment is not (yet) available, but the Middle Byzantine period often forms a conspicuous gap in the archaeological record. This may be accepted as an argument from silence, pointing to decline and temporary abandonment, for example at Side in Pamphylia, at Patara in Lycia, at Nicaea in Bithynia, and at Ancyra in Galatia.[54] Likewise, the ancient city centre of Priene in Asia was largely deserted and only came to life again from the later 11th century onwards, when it was re-fortified against the Turks. Pergamon in Asia and Sagalassos in Pisidia are comparable to Miletus in so far as the Middle Byzantine period is poorly attested and new, later-11th or 12th-century fortifications against the Turks were built on defensive sites outside the Early Byzantine cities. At Sagalassos, the dearth of urban evidence is again paired with a relative abundance of Middle Byzantine finds in the surrounding countryside.

CONCLUSION

The archaeological evidence in Asia Minor indicates that the Middle Byzantine period was charactrised by a dual process of urban decline and rural revival. This suggests a shift in the social and economic centre of gravity from cities towards villages and landholdings of the aristocracy.[55] It would thus seem to be no coincidence that the central administration had long since started to levy taxes directly from rural settlements.[56] Landed magnates are thought to have greatly increased their power in the Middle Byzantine period,[57] and were by now living in the countryside rather than in cities.[58] Apparently, they also preferred to build small churches on their estates rather than contribute to larger urban building projects.[59] A proliferation of rural monasteries in this period may have resulted from the pull of the landed aristocracy, in particular as some of these religious foundations were established to take care of the aristocratic dead.[60]

Palynological evidence points to a general recovery and intensification of agriculture, in the hinterland of Miletus,[61] in Cappadocia,[62] and elsewhere in Asia Minor,[63] confirming that the countryside flourished in the 10th and 11th centuries.[64] This means Middle Byzantine Asia Minor was not short of human activity and agricultural resources, and it confirms that the downscaling of urbanism does not reflect general decline, but rather ruralisation. It is also not surprising that, with the shift from city to country, material culture tended to become simpler and more utilitarian, as is in evidence for example at Cadır Höyük[65] or in the territory of Sagalassos.[66]

As to urban consumption centres, there is no evidence for any such thing on the provincial level in Middle Byzantine Asia Minor, and the region may have looked for guidance to the capital Constantinople instead. This would explain the lack of provincial styles in church building and marble carving, and why for these genres the same formal repertoire was applied throughout the region and beyond. It would also mirror a political system that was dominated by landed magnates who were oriented directly to Constantinople rather than to any nearby provincial city.[67] Thus, Middle Byzantine Asia Minor appears to have been an example for prosperity and consumption above subsistence level that did not depend on, or generate, urban centres.[68]

NOTES

1. I would like to thank the convenor Joanita Vroom for inviting me to contribute to her session and for editing this volume.
2. Hawkins 2016.
3. Foss 1977; Harvey 1989. For a recent bibliography, see Zavagno 2021.
4. Niewöhner 2006; *Idem* 2007a.
5. For example the hinterland of Miletus in Caria: Niewöhner 2016d.
6. Sodini 1995; Melvani 2018.
7. Niewöhner 2008, 297-305.
8. Ćurčić 2010; Buchwald and Savage 2017; Ousterhout 2019, 431-54.
9. Betsch 1977, 204; Niewöhner 2021a.
10. Barsanti, Guiglia Guidobaldi, and Sodini 1998.
11. Niewöhner 2007a; *Idem* 2013.
12. For some notable exceptions, see Peschlow 1990, 237-39; Niewöhner 2007b, 6, 16, 27, fig. 40, cat. 40; *Idem* 2008, 292-95, 331-36, cat. 40-48, fig. 2, 44-52.
13. Grabar 1963; Ulbert 1969; Barsanti 1988; Dennert 1997; Pennas and Vanderheyde 2008; Vanderheyde 2020; Niewöhner 2021a.
14. Kalavrezou-Maxeiner 1985; Altripp 2006, 11-13; Mert and Niewöhner 2010, 381-84.
15. Ulbert 1969. For some more examples, see Niewöhner 2008, 321 f., cat. 18-20, fig. 22-24; Büyükkolanci and Öztaşkin 2010, 44 f., cat. 7, fig. 7; Niewöhner 2021a, 158.
16. Dennert 1997, 149 f. For more such capitals, see also Karabacak 2019.
17. Niewöhner 2008, 290, fig.1; 313, cat. 6, fig. 10; 316, cat. 11, fig. 15, 335 f., cat. 47 f., fig. 51 f. For other interesting and informative examples, see Sodini 2012; Vanderheyde 2020, 198-201.
18. Buchwald 1995; Niewöhner 2008, 331-40, cat. 40-54, fig. 44-58; Niewöhner 2021a, 160.
19. Vanderheyde 2007, 84 (templon epistyles with arcades).
20. Niewöhner 2016a, 114-18.
21. Peschlow 1998; Grossmann and Severin 2003.
22. Geyer 1984/85; Mietke and Westphalen 2006.
23. Mathews 1971, *passim*. For more marble ambos with some additional recent bibliography, see Iaţcu 2013; Niewöhner 2021a, 140.
24. Niewöhner 2007a, 129 f.; *Idem* 2013, 242-45; Niewöhner 2021a, 145-46.
25. Acconci 2005; Niewöhner 2016a, 116 f.; Militsi-Kechagia 2017; Peirano 2017; Baldini and Lamanna 2021.
26. Mathews 1971; Ousterhout 2019, 101-9.
27. Aydın 2006; Altripp 2010; Niewöhner 2021c.
28. Hill 1996; Mietke and Ristow 2004, c. 842-62; Westphalen 2015.
29. Bell and Ramsay 1909; Eyice 1971; Peschlow 2015; Niewöhner 2021b.
30. Buchwald and Savage 2017, 142-45; Ousterhout 2019, 431-44; Niewöhner 2020a, 99-115.
31. Vandeput 1997; Halfmann 2001; Heller 2006; Raeck 2017.
32. Niewöhner 2006, 246; *Idem* 2007a, 76-79.
33. Niewöhner 2006, 242-45; *Idem* 2007a, 80 f.

34 Dappner *et al.* 1998, 132, fig. 10; Blanton 2000, 60; Baird 2004; Rose 2011, 164; Coulton 2012, 175-81.
35 Zaccaria Ruggiu 2007; Rose 2011, 161 f.; Niewöhner 2017, *passim*.
36 Niewöhner 2007a, 143-45 (*thermae*); 145-58 (*macellum*).
37 Rheidt 1995, 699-712.
38 Ladstätter 2017.
39 Niewöhner 2017, *passim*.
40 Naumann 1987, 311-13; Niewöhner 2007a, 143-45.
41 Niewöhner 2017, *passim*. For some notable exceptions and qualifications, see Armstrong 2006; Izdebski 2013, 145-215; Niewöhner 2016d.
42 Mango 1974, 161-80; Ruggieri 1991; Buchwald 1994; Ruggieri 1995; Buchwald and Savage 2017, 138-42; Ousterhout 2019, 245-65.
43 Niewöhner 2020a, 99-115.
44 Strzygowski 1903, 32-41; Eyice 1968 (earlier bibliography); Eyice 2004 (corrected drawings); Mihaljević 2014.
45 Niewöhner 2008, 292-94, 309, 329 f., 333-35 cat. 36 f., 42-47, fig. 2, 40 f., 46-50.
46 See above note 46.
47 Buchwald 1984, 227 f.; Ćurčić 2010; Ousterhout 2019, 405-29.
48 Niewöhner 2017, *passim*.
49 Kleiner 1968; Niewöhner 2016b.
50 Niewöhner 2016a.
51 Niewöhner 2016d.
52 Knackfuß 1924, 69-73 (Market Gate). 185-87 (Serapeion Gate).
53 Niewöhner 2016c.
54 See the respective chapters in Niewöhner 2017 for all the sites mentioned here.
55 Whittow 2008, 473 f.; Sarris 2017.
56 Brandes and Haldon 2000; Brandes 2002.
57 Vryonis 1986, 70-80; Haldon 2009, 182-92; Stephenson 2010. For a caution, see Whittow 1995; Cheynet 2000; Whittow 2008, 487-91.
58 Whittow 1995, 62-65; Schreiner 1997; Niewöhner 2020a.
59 Niewöhner 2020a, 99-115.
60 Ousterhout 2017, chapter 4.
61 Niewöhner 2016d; Niewöhner 2020b, 248-51.
62 Eastwood *et al.* 2009.
63 Izdebski 2012.
64 Lefort 2002; Cassis et al. 2018.
65 Cassis 2009.
66 Poblome *et al.* 2009.
67 See above note 62.
68 This seems to have been different in Middle Byzantine Greece, see Bouras 2002; Sanders 2002; Bouras 2010; Albani and Chalkia 2013.

BIBLIOGRAPHY

Acconci, A. 2005. Gli amboni Cari: Coordinate storico-artistiche, in: V. Ruggieri (ed.), *La Caria bizantina. Topografia, archeologia ed arte. Mylasa, Stratonikeia, Bargylia, Myndus, Halicarnassus*, Soveria Mannelli, 232-41.

Albani, J. and E. Chalkia (eds.) 2013. *Heaven and Earth: Cities and Countryside in Byzantine Greece*, Athens.

Altripp, M. 2006. Geknotete Säulen in der byzantinischen und romanischen Architektur, *Mediaevistik* 19, 9-19.

Altripp, M. 2010. Kirchen und Kapellen, in: F. Kolb (ed.), *Die Siedlung von Kyaneai in Zentrallykien*, Lykische Studien 9, Bonn, 277-363.

Armstrong, P. 2006. Rural settlement in Lycia in the eighth century: New evidence, in: K. Dörtlük (ed.), *The 3rd Symposium on Lycia, Vol. 1*, Antalya, 19-29.

Aydın, A. 2006. Die Trikonchosbauten in Lykien, in: K. Dörtlük *et al.* (eds.), *The 3rd Symposium on Lycia, Vol. 1*, Antalya, 31-47.

Baird, D. 2004. Settlement expansion on the Konya Plain, Anatolia: 5th-7th centuries AD, in: W. Bowden, L. Lavan, and C. Machado (eds.), *Recent Research on the Late Antique Countryside*, Late Antique Archaeology 2, Leiden, 219-46.

Baldini I. and C. Lamanna 2021. The early Byzantine architecture in Kos and the interactions with the nearby regions of Asia Minor, in: B. Poulson, P. Pedersen and J. Lund (eds.), *Karia and the Dodekanes. Cultural Interrelations in the Southeast Aegean, vol. 2*, Oxford, 229-46.

Barsanti, C. 1988. Scultura anatolica di epoca mediobizantina, in: C. Barsanti, A. Guiglia Guidobaldi, and A. Jacobini (eds.), *Milion*, Rome, 275-95.

Barsanti, C. 2003. The Iznik-Nicea's archaeological museum: In search of a catalogue, in: I. Akbaygil, O. Aslanapa and H. Inalcık (eds.), *Iznik Throughout History*, Istanbul, 267-300.

Barsanti, C., A. Guiglia Guidobaldi, and J.-P. Sodini 1998. La sculpture architecturale en marbre au 6e siècle à Constantinople et dans les régions sous influence constantinopolitaine, in: N. Cambi and E. Marín (eds.), *Acta 13 Congressus internationalis archaeologiae christianae*, Studi di antichità cristiana 54 = Vjesnik za arheologiju i historiju dalmatinsku supplement 87-89, Rome, 301-76.

Bell, G.L. and W.M. Ramsay 1909. *The Thousand and One Churches*, London (Reprint: Philadelphia, 2008).

Betsch, E. 1977. The History, Production, and Distribution of the Late Antique Capital in Constantinople, *unpublished* Diss. University of Pennsylvania, USA.

Blanton, R.E. 2000. *Hellenistic, Roman, and Byzantine Settlement Patterns of the Coastal Lands of Western Rough Cilicia*, BAR International Series 879, Oxford.

Bouras, C. 2002. Aspects of the Byzantine city, eighth-fifteenth centuries, in: A.E. Laiou (ed.), *The Economic History of Byzantium from the Seventh Through the Fifteenth Century, Vol. 2*, Dumbarton Oaks Studies 39, Washington, DC, 497-528.

Bouras, C. 2010. *Byzantine Athens, 10th-12th Cent.*, Mouseio Benaki supplement 6, Athens.

Brandes, W. and J. Haldon 2000. Towns, tax, and transformation: State, cities, and their hinterlands in the East Roman world. C. 500-800, in: G.P. Brogiolo, N. Gauthier, and N. Christie (eds.), *Towns and Their Territories Between Late Antiquity and the Early Middle Ages*, The Transformation of the Roman World 9, Leiden, 141-72.

Brandes, W. 2002. *Finanzverwaltung in Krisenzeiten. Untersuchungen zur byzantinischen Administration im 6.–8. Jahrhundert*, Forschungen zur byzantinischen Rechtsgeschichte 25, Frankfurt.

Buchwald, H. 1984. Western Asia Minor as a generator of architectural forms in the Byzantine period: Provincial back-wash or dynamic center of production?, *Jahrbuch der Österreichischen Byzantinistik* 34, 199-234.

Buchwald, H. 1994. Criteria for the evaluation of transitional Byzantine architecture, *Jahrbuch der Österreichischen Byzantinistik* 44, 21-31.

Buchwald, H. 1995. Chancel barrier lintels decorated with carved arcades, *Jahrbuch der Österreichischen Byzantinistik* 45, 233-76.

Buchwald H. and M. Savage 2017. Churches, in: P. Niewöhner (ed.), *The Archaeology of Byzantine Anatolia. From the End of Late Antiquity unitl the Coming of the Turks*, Oxford, 129-147.

Büyükkolanci M. and G.K. Öztaşkin 2010. Selçuk-Efes Müzesi'nde Sergilenen St. Jean Kilisesi'ne ait Korkuluk Levhaları ve Templon Arşitravları, *Pamukkale Üniversitesi Sosyal Bilimler Enstitüsü Dergisi* 7, 39-49.

Cassis, M. 2009. Çadır Höyük: A rural settlement in Byzantine Anatolia, in: T. Vorderstrasse and J.J. Roodenberg (eds.), *Archaeology of the Countryside in Medieval Anatolia*, Uitgaven van het Nederlands Instituut voor het Nabije Oosten te Leiden 113, Leiden, 1-24.

Cassis, M. et al. 2018. Not the End of the World? Post-Classical Decline and Recovery in Rural Anatolia, *Human Ecology* 46/3, 305-322.

Cheynet, J.-C. 2000. L'aristocratie byzantine (8e-13e siècle), *Journal de Savants*, 281-322. Translated as The Byzantine aristocracy (8th-13th centuries), in: J.-C. Cheynet, *The Byzantine Aristocracy and Its Military Function*, Aldershot 2006, 19-38.

Coulton, J. 2012. Late Roman and Byzantine Balboura, in: J. Coulton (ed.), *The Balboura Survey and Settlement in Highland Southwest Anatolia 1*, British Institute of Archaeology at Ankara Monograph 43, London, 163-84.

Ćurčić, S. 2010. *Architecture in the Balkans*, New Haven, CT.

Dappner, M. de, F. Vermeulen, and T. Wiedemann 1998. Vers un approche géo-archéologique intégrée: le territoire antique de Pessinonte (Turquie), in: M. Clavel-Lévêque and A. Vignot (eds.), *Cité et territoire 2*, Paris, 123-39.

Dennert, M. 1997. *Mittelbyzantinische Kapitelle. Studien zur Typologie und Chronologie*, Asia Minor Studien 25, Bonn.

Eastwood, W., O. Gümüşçü, H. Yiğitbaştoğlu, J. Haldon, and A. England 2009. Integrating palaeoecological and archaeo-historical records: Land use and landscape change in Cappadocia (central Turkey) since Late Antiquity, in: T. Vorderstrasse and J. Roodenberg (eds.), *Archaeology of the Countryside in Medieval Anatolia*, Uitgaven van het Nederlands Instituut voor het Nabije Oosten te Leiden 113, Leiden, 45-69.

Eyice, S. 1968. La ruine byzantine dite 'Üçayak' près de Kırşehir en Anatolie centrale: un monument architectural de la fin du 10e ou du 11e siècle, *Cahiers Archéologiques* 18, 137-55.

Eyice, S. 1971. *Recherches archéologiques à Karadağ (Binbirkilise) et dans la région de Karaman*, Istanbul Üniversitesi Edebiyat Fakültesi Yayınlarından 1587 = Türkiye'de Ortaçağ Sanatı Araştırmaları 2, Istanbul.

Eyice, S. 2004. Untersuchungen in der Üc-Ayak genannten Ruinenstätte bei Kırşehir, *Anadolu Araştırmaları* 17/2, 141-67.

Foss, C. 1977. Archaeology and the ‚twenty cities‛ of Byzantine Asia Minor, *American Journal of Archaeology* 81, 469-86. Reprint in: C. Foss, *History and Archaeology of Byzantine Asia Minor*, London, chapter 2.

Geyer, A. 1984/85. Aspekte der Bauornamentik von Alahan Monastir, *Jahrbuch für Antike und Christentum* 27/28, 151-70.

Grabar, A. 1963. *Sculptures byzantines de Constantinople (4e-10e siècle)*, Bibliothèque archéologique et historique de l'Institut français d'archéologie d'Istanbul 17, Paris.

Grossmann, P. and H.-G. Severin 2003. *Frühchristliche und byzantinische Bauten im südöstlichen Lykien*, Istanbuler Forschungen 46, Tübingen.

Haldon, J. 2009. Social élites, wealth, and power, in: J. Haldon (ed.), *A Social History of Byzantium*, Oxford, 168-211.

Halfmann, H. 2001. *Städtebau und Bauherren im römischen Kleinasien*, Istanbuler Mitteilungen suppl. 43, Tübingen.

Harvey, A. 1989. *Economic Expansion in the Byzantine Empire 900-1200*, Cambridge.

Hawkins, C. 2016. *Roman Artisans and the Urban Economy*, Cambridge.

Heller, A. 2006. *Les bêtises des Grecs: conflits et rivalités entre cités d'Asie et de Bithynie à l'époque romaine (128 a.C. – 235 p.C.)*, Bordeaux.

Hill, S. 1996. *The Early Byzantine Churches of Cilicia and Isauria*, Birmingham Byzantine & Ottoman Monographs 1, Aldershot.

Iațcu, I. 2013. The ambos of the Christian basilicas within the province of Scythia, *Studia Antiqua et Archaeologica* 19, 49-78.

Izdebski, A. 2012. The changing landscapes of Byzantine northern Anatolia, *Archaeologia Bulgarica* 16/1, 47-66.

Izdebski, A. 2013. *Rural Economy in Transition. Asia Minor from Late Antiquity into the Early Middle Ages*, Journal of Juristic Papyrology supplement 18, Warsaw.

Kalavrezou-Maxeiner, I. 1985. The Byzantine knotted column, in: S. Vryonis Jr. (ed.), *Byzantine Studies in Honor of Milton V. Anastos*, Malibu, 95-103.

Karabacak, E. 2019. *Bir Orta Bizans Dönemi Sütun Başlığı ve Kullanim Yeri Üzerine Tartişmalar, TÜBA-KED* 20, 29-40.

Kleiner, G. 1968. *Die Ruinen von Milet*, Berlin.

Knackfuß, H. 1924. *Der Südmarkt und die benachbarten Bauten*, Milet I, 7, Berlin.

Ladstätter, S. 2017. Ephesus, in: P. Niewöhner (ed.), *The Archaeology of Byzantine Anatolia: From the End of Late Antiquity until the Coming of the Turks*, Oxford, 238-48.

Lefort, J. 2002. The Rural economy, seventh-twelfth centuries, in: A.E. Laiou (ed.), *The Economic History of Byzantium, Vol. 1*, Dumbarton Oaks Studies 39, Washington, DC, 231-310.

Mango, C. 1974. *Architettura bizantina*, Venice.

Mathews, T.F. 1971. *The Early Churches of Constantinople. Architecture and Liturgy*, University Park.

Melvani, N. 2018. Late, middle, and early Byzantine sculpture in Palaiologan Constantinople, in: I. Jevtić and S. Yalman (eds.), *Spolia Reincarnated*. Istanbul, 149-69.

Mert, I.H. and P. Niewöhner 2010. Blattkapitelle in Konya, *Istanbuler Mitteilungen* 60, 373-410.

Mietke, G., S. Ristow, *et al.* 2004. Kilikien, in: *Reallexikon für Antike und Christentum* 20, Stuttgart, c. 803-64.

Mietke, G. and S. Westphalen 2006. Studien zur frühbyzantinischen Bauornamentik im Rauhen Kilikien, *Istanbuler Mitteilungen* 56, 371-405.

Mihaljević, M. 2014. Üçayak: A forgotten Byzantine church, *Byzantinische Zeitschrift* 107, 725-54.

Militsi-Kechagia, E. 2017. Οι Μαρμάρινοι Ἄμβωνες των Παλαιοχριστιανικών Βασιλικών της Κω, in: Το Αρχαιολογικό Έργο στα Νησιά του Αιγαίου, Vol. 3, Mytilini, 295-305.

Naumann, R. 1987. Aizanoi. Bericht über die Ausgrabungen und Untersuchungen 1983 und 1984, *Archäologischer Anzeiger* 1987, 301-40.

Niewöhner, P. 2006. Aizanoi and Anatolia: Town and countryside in late Late Antiquity, *Millennium* 3, 239-53.

Niewöhner, P. 2007a. *Aizanoi, Dokimion und Anatolien. Stadt und Land, Siedlungs- und Steinmetzwesen vom späteren 4. bis ins 6. Jh. n. Chr.*, Aizanoi 1 = Archäologische Forschungen 23, Wiesbaden.

Niewöhner, P. 2007b. Byzantinische Steinmetzarbeiten aus dem Umland von Milet, *Anadolu ve Çevresinde Ortaçağ* 1, 1-28.

Niewöhner, P. 2008. Mittelbyzantinische Templonanlagen aus Anatolien. Die Sammlung des archäologischen Museums Kütahya und ihr Kontext, *Istanbuler Mitteilungen* 58, 285-345.

Niewöhner, P. 2013. Phrygian marble and stonemasonry as markers of regional distinctiveness in Late Antiquity, in: P. Thonemann (ed.), *Roman Phrygia*, Cambridge, 215-48.

Niewöhner, P. 2016a. *Die byzantinischen Basiliken von Milet*, Milet 1, 11, Berlin.

Niewöhner, P. (ed.) 2016b. *Miletus/Balat. Urbanism and Monuments from the Archaic through the Turkish Period*, Istanbul.

Niewöhner, P. 2016c. The end of the Byzantine city in Anatolia: The case of Miletus, in: E. Gruber, M. Popovic, M. Scheutz, and H. Weigl (eds.), *Städte im lateinischen Westen und im griechischen Osten. Topographie – Recht – Religion (9.-19. Jahrhundert)*, Veröffentlichungen des Instituts für Österreichische Geschichtsforschung 66, Vienna, 63-77.

Niewöhner, P. 2016d. The Byzantine settlement history of Miletus and its hinterland – quantitative aspects: Stratigraphy, pottery, anthropology, coins, and palynology, *Archäologischer Anzeiger* 2016/2, 225-90.

Niewöhner, P. (ed.) 2017. *The Archaeology of Byzantine Anatolia. From the End of Late Antiquity Until the Coming of the Turks*, Oxford.

Niewöhner, P. 2020a. What went wrong? Decline and ruralisation in eleventh century Anatolia: The archaeological record, in: J. Howard-Johnston (ed.), *Eleventh-Century Byzantium. Social Change in Town and Country*, Oxford, 98-132.

Niewöhner, P. 2020b. Die Arbeiten in Milet in den Jahren 2012 bis 2016. Chronik, neue Befunde aus antiker, byzantinischer und türkischer Zeit sowie Denkmalpflege, *Archäologischer Anzeiger* 2020/1, 224-67.

Niewöhner, P. 2021a. *Byzantine Ornaments in Stone. Architectural Sculpture and Liturgical Furnishings*. Berlin.

Niewöhner, P. 2021b. The regional paradigm in early Christian art and architecture. The case of Anatolia, in: N.D. Kontogiannis and T.B. Uyar (eds.), *Space and Communities in Byzantine Anatolia*, International Sevgi Gönül Byzantine Studies Symposium 5, Istanbul, 275-300,

Niewöhner, P. 2021c. The tomb of St Nicholas, in: E. Akyürek (ed.), *Byzantine Anatolia*, Anatolian Civilisations 8, Istanbul, 187-203.

Ousterhout, R. 2017. *Visualizing Community. Art, Material Culture, and Settlement in Byzantine Cappadocia*, Dumbarton Oaks Studies 46, Washington, DC.

Ousterhout, R.G. 2019. *Eastern Medieval Architecture,* Oxford.

Peschlow, U. 1990. Materialien zur Kirche des H. Nikolaos in Myra im Mittelalter, *Istanbuler Mitteilungen* 40, 207-58.

Peschlow, U. 1998. Tradition und Innovation. Kapitellskulptur in Lykien, in: S. Möllers and U. Peschlow (eds.), *Spätantike und byzantinische Bauskulptur*, Forschungen zur Kunstgeschichte und Christlichen Archäologie 19, Stuttgart, 67-76.

Peschlow, U. 2015. *Ankara. Die bauarchäologischen Hinterlassenschaften aus römischer und byzantinischer Zeit*, Vienna.

Peirano, D. 2017. Alcune osservazioni sul decoro musivo e sull'ambone delle chiese di Sinuri, *Bollettino dell'Associazione Iasos di Caria* 23, 24-30.

Pennas, C. and C. Vanderheyde (eds.) 2008, *La sculture byzantine, 7e-12e siècles*, Bulletin de Correspondance Hellénique suppl. 49, Athens.

Poblome, J., H. Vanhaverbeke, N. Vionis, and M. Waelkens 2009. What happened after the 7th century AD? A different perspective on Post-Roman rural Anatolia, in: J. Roodenberg and T. Vorderstrasse (eds.), *Archaeology of the Countryside in Medieval Anatolia*, Uitgaven van het Nederlands Instituut voor het Nabije Oosten te Leiden 113, Leiden, 177-90.

Raeck, W. 2017. Zeichen der Machtteilhabe: zur Architektursprache der kleinasiatischen Städtekonkurrenz im 2. Jahrhundert n. Chr., in: A.W. Busch, J. Griesbach, and J. Lipps (eds.), *Urbanitas – Urbane Qualitäten. Die antike Stadt als kulturelle Selbstverwirklichung*, Mainz, 167-181.

Rheidt, K. 1995. Aizanoi. Bericht über die Ausgrabungen und Untersuchungen 1992 und 1993, *Archäologischer Anzeiger* 1995, 693-718.

Rose, B. 2011. Troy and the Granicus river valley in Late Antiquity, in: O. Dally and C. Ratté (eds.), *Archaeology and the Cities of Asia Minor in Late Antiquity*, Kelsey Museum Publication 6, Ann Arbor MI, 151-71.

Ruggieri, V. 1991. *Byzantine Religious Architecture (582-867): Its History and Structural Elements*, Orientalia Christiana Analecta 237, Rome.

Ruggieri, V. 1995. *L'architettura religiosa nell'Impero Bizantino (fine 6-9 secolo)*, Saggi, studi, testi 2, Soveria Mannelli.

Russo, E. 2002. Considérations sur la sculpture architecturale et décorative à Nicée à l'époque paléochrétienne, *Bizantinistica. Rivista di studi bizantini e slavi*, 2, 4, 1-11.

Sanders, G.D.R. 2002. Corinth, in: A.E. Laiou (ed.), *The Economic History of Byzantium from the Seventh Through the Fifteenth Century, Vol. 2*, Dumbarton Oaks Studies 39, Washington, DC, 647-54.

Sarris, P. 2017. Beyond the great plains and the barren hills. Rural landscapes and social structures in eleventh-century Byzantium, in: M. Lauxtermann and M. Whittow (eds,), *Being In Between: Byzantium in the Eleventh Century*, London, 77-87.

Schneider, A.M. 1943. *Die römischen und byzantinischen Denkmäler von Iznik-Nicaea*, Istanbuler Forschungen 16, Tübingen.

Schreiner, P. 1997. Das Haus in Byzanz nach den schriftlichen Quellen, in: H. Beck and H. Steuer (eds.), *Haus und Hof in ur- und frühgeschichtlicher Zeit. Gedenkschrift für Herbert Jankuhn*, Kolloquium der Kommission für die Altertumskunde Mittel- und Nordeuropas 34-35 = Abhandlungen der Akademie der Wissenschaften in Göttingen. Philologisch-Historische Klasse. Folge 3, Nr. 218, Göttingen, 277-320.

Sodini, J.-P. 1995. La sculpture médio-byzantine. Le marbre en ersatz et tel qu'en lui-même, in: G. Dagron and C. Mango (eds.), *Constantinople and its Hinterland*, Society for the Promotion of Byzantine Studies Publications 3, 289-311.

Sodini. J.-P. 2012. A Slab with opposed peacocks in the Xanthos Eastern Basilica, in: N. Asutay-Effenberger and F. Daim (eds.), Φιλοπάτιον. Festschrift für A. Effenberger, RGZM Monographien 106, Mainz, 135-45.

Stephenson, P. 2010. The rise of the Middle Byzantine aristocracy and the decline of the imperial state, in: P. Stephenson (ed.), *The Byzantine World*, London, 22-33.

Strzygowski, J. 1903. *Kleinasien, ein Neuland der Kunstgeschichte*, Leipzig.

Ulbert, T. 1969. *Studien zur dekorativen Reliefplastik des östlichen Mittelmeerraums. Schrankenplatten des 4. bis 10. Jhs.*, Miscellanea byzantina monacensia 10, Munich.

Vandeput, L. 1997. *The Architectural Decoration in Roman Asia Minor*, Studies in Eastern Mediterranean Archaeology 1, Turnhout.

Vanderheyde, C. 2007. The Carved decoration of Middle and Late Byzantine templa, *Mitteilungen zur spätantiken Archäologie und byzantinischen Kunstgeschichte* 5, 77-111.

Vanderheyde, C. 2020, *La sculpture byzantine du IXe au XVe siècle*, Paris.Vryonis Jr., S. 1986. *The Decline of Medieval Hellenism in Asia Minor and the Process of Islamization from the Eleventh through the Fifteenth Century*, Publications of the Center for Medieval and Renaissance Studies 4, Berkeley.

Westphalen, S. 2015. Die Kirche von Işıkkale, *Olba* 23, 535-52.

Whittow, M. 1995. Rural fortifications in Western Europe and Byzantium, 10th-12th century, in: S. Efthymiadis, C. Rapp, and D. Tsougarakis (eds.), *Bosphorus. Essays in Honour of Cyril Mango = Byzantinische Forschungen* 21, 57-74.

Whittow, M. 2008. The Middle Byzantine economy (600-1204), in: J. Shepard (ed.), *The Cambridge History of the Byzantine Empire c. 500-1492*, Cambridge, 465-92.

Zaccaria Ruggiu, A. 2007. Regio VIII, insula 104. Le strutture abitative: Fasi e trasformazioni, in: F. D'Andria and M. Piera Caggia (eds.), *Hierapolis di Frigia I. Le attività delle campagne di scavo e restauro 2000-2003*, Istanbul, 211-56.

Zavagno, L. 2021. *The Byzantine City from Heraclius to the Fourth Crusade, 610-1204*, Cham.

FIG. 1 – Ciborium arch that depicts a ciborium and numerous roses, Archaeological Museum Konya in Lycaonia, inv. 201 (Niewöhner 2020).

FIG. 2 – Closure slab with a base profile, interlace that encloses a griffon, an eagle, a lion, as well as a deer, and a handrail with a scroll, Archaeological Museum Konya (J. Kramer).

FIG. 3 – Small impost capital of a knotted column with four shafts, lion heads and bird protomes at the corners, as well as a rose and a palmette in the middle, from Kidyessos/Çayhisar in Phrygia, Archaeological Museum Afyon inv. E1589-3930 (J. Kramer).

FIG. 4 – Knotted column with two shafts and vine capitals, Archaeological Museum Edirne in Thrace, inv. 17 (Niewöhner 2016).

FIG. 5 – Flanking ambo slab with interlace, lozenge, roses, and post, Güdük Minare Camii at Akşehir in Pisidia (Niewöhner 2020).

FIG. 6 – Closure slab with interlace, lozenge, roses, and handrail with astragal, an arcade, four palmettes, and a central cross (erased), Ulu Camii at Akşehir (Niewöhner 2020).

FIG. 7 – Closure slab with interlace, lozenge, roses, and handrail with an arcade, two palmettes, and a central cross (erased), Archaeological Museum Afyon (Niewöhner 2020).

FIG. 8 – Closure slab with cross, interlace, lozenge, and handrail with a scroll, Church of St Nicholas at Myra/Demre in Lycia (Niewöhner 2020).

FIG. 9 – Closure slab with cross, interlace, lozenge, and roses, Archaeological Museum Antalya, inv. 185 (J. Kramer).

FIG. 10 – Closure slab with interlace, lozenge, and roses, Denizli in western Asia Minor (J. Kramer).

FIG. 11 – Closure slab with interlace, lozenge, and roses, Archaeological Museum Edirne (Niewöhner 2016).

FIG. 12 – Eagle and head capital, Archaeological Museum Istanbul, inv. 4722 (J. Kramer).

FIG. 13 – Eagle and head capital, bearded, Archaeological Museum Konya, inv. 1980.12.1 (Niewöhner 2008).

FIG. 14 – Same as FIG. 13, other side with a fountain and a pair of drinking birds (Niewöhner 2008).

FIG. 15 – Impost capital with a pair of bearded goats (?) that drink from a central chalice or fountain, Archaeological Museum Edirne (Niewöhner 2016).

FIG. 16 – Same as FIG. 15, other side with a pair of doves and a central plant (Niewöhner 2016).

FIG. 17 – Same as FIG. 15, other side with a dog (?) and an ivy leaf (Niewöhner 2016).

FIG. 18 – Same as FIG. 15, other side with a pair of birds and a central plant (Niewöhner 2016).

FIG. 19 – Closure slab with fountain (node?) and flanking peacocks, Archaeological Museum Kütahya in Phrygia (Niewöhner 2010).

FIG. 20 – Closure slab with a pair of hunting lions and a pair of peacocks that drink from a central fountain with node, Archaeological Museum Kütahya, inv. 698 (Niewöhner 2002).

FIG. 21 – Closure slab with a pair of griffons and a central plant, Archaeological Museum Antalya (J. Kramer 1970-1971).

FIG. 22 – Left fragment of a templon epistyle with a central (?) cross, interlace, roses, arcade on twin columns, palmettes, and lozenges, Archaeological Museum Afyon (Niewöhner 2020).

FIG. 23 – Fragment of a templon epistyle with interlace, roses, arcade, palmettes, lozenge, and donor inscription, Archaeological Museum Afyon (Niewöhner 2020).

* * *

Central Greece in the Middle Byzantine and Late Byzantine periods: Changing patterns of consumption in Thebes and Chalcis

Stefania S. Skartsis & Nikos D. Kontogiannis

*

INTRODUCTION

During the Middle Byzantine period Thebes and Chalcis were among the principal cities of central Greece (see map in Fig. 1). Thebes, being the administrative and military capital of the *Theme* of Hellas from the 9th century onwards, developed into the largest population centre of the area. Its prosperity and the increase of its population were partly due to the exploitation of its rich agricultural hinterland, combined with a large output of manufactured products. This is reflected in the notable building activity, not only in the city centre but also in various suburbs that developed on the foothills around the city walls by the 11th century.[1] The population of Thebes comprised civilian, military and ecclesiastic administrators, members of the local land aristocracy, various merchants and craftsmen, including those involved in the production of silk textiles and architectural sculpture, as well as a considerable Jewish community.[2]

Chalcis, on the other hand, is much less documented during the Middle Byzantine period. It seems that the city (also known as *Euripos* or *Egripos* in medieval times) was relocated in the 9th century from its ancient position to the area next to the Euripos Channel, in order to better serve the strategic interests of the Byzantine Empire. It therefore acquired a certain importance, and became the main harbour in the Aegean for Thebes.[3] From the late 11th century onwards the historical and archaeological evidence points to an increasing economic and demographic growth, based mainly on its flourishing commercial activity.[4] The image provided by rescue excavations is that of a dense fortified Middle Byzantine settlement, with houses, streets and churches, the earliest of which have been dated to the 9th-11th century.[5]

After the Fourth Crusade (1204) and the political fragmentation of the Aegean during the 13th century, Thebes and Chalcis became the centres of two distinct Latin states. Thebes became the capital of the Duchy of Athens and seat of a Latin archbishop. The city remained prosperous throughout the 13th century, with a flourishing industry, including the manufacture of silk and metal products.[6] However, the 14th century was a period of political upheavals and crisis, due to the Catalan (1311) and later Florentine (1380) conquest of Boeotia. Despite plagues, raids and wars, the area seems to have recovered during the late 15th century, when it passed to the Ottomans and a more stable period set in.[7]

The history of Chalcis was equally eventful: from serving as seat of a lesser feudal lordship in the early 13th century, it gradually became under Venetian influence until 1390, when the Republic of Venice assumed direct control of the entire island. Being ideally located for the Serenissima's maritime interests, the city (by then called *Negroponte*) became a major commercial and naval hub of the Venetian Empire, located on the routes connecting the Black Sea and Constantinople with southern Greece, the Adriatic and Venice.[8]

Within this general historical framework, this chapter will first examine the ceramic evidence retrieved in Thebes and Chalcis. In the second part, the focus will shift to another aspect of material culture: that of the luxury products which were either produced or consumed by the inhabitants of the two cities, namely silk textiles, jewellery and accessories, and precious objects. The intention of this twofold approach is that it results in conclusions that may lead to a better understanding of the social and economic circumstances, production models as well as consumption patterns in central Greece in general.

CERAMICS[9]

9th-11th centuries – In the period between the 9th and the 11th century, the excavated deposits from Thebes and Chalcis provide a uniform picture of ceramic use. In both cities a considerable amount of high-quality 'Polychrome Ware' and 'Glazed White Ware'-variants was imported from the area of Constantinople.[10] The number and wide variety of the latter category of wares clearly indicate that it did not concern here isolated pieces that had somehow found their way to local households; the pottery finds represent the ceramic reflection of a steady flow of commodities sold for local consumption. They circulated alongside various locally made wares, among which a distinct class of unglazed incised ceramics (Figs. 2a-b).[11]

With regard to Byzantine amphorae for the storage and transport of agricultural products, such as oil and wine, there is a similar picture of both local and imported wares. As far as the local amphorae are concerned, substantial quantities of these containers vessels have been identified in 10th-11th-century contexts, most probably meant for the local produce from the countryside.[12] Agricultural products must have been transported to the two cities and were destined either for local consumption or for more distant markets.

In short, the archaeological record clearly suggests that Thebes and Chalcis functioned as hubs in a pattern of production and consumption, which is propably comparable with patterns in other important agricultural regions of the Byzantine Empire, such as the Ganos region which rises from the western shore of the Sea of Marmara. In these areas an agricultural surplus was combined with the availability of good clay deposits for local pottery production (in the case of Chalcis, these were situated in the nearby Lelantine Plain), and also with the accessibility of markets through maritime networks.[13]

As for the two cities under study here, the presence and quantity of imports, both of amphorae (related to agricultural products such as wine and oil) and of glazed ceramics (industrially produced luxury wares), clearly indicate there must have existed a substantial degree of socio-economic development. In other words, the archaeological records provided material evidence for the existence of a financially independent class, as well as for the availability of maritime networks that supplied city residents.

The 12th century – The 12th century emerges as a period of great prosperity for both Thebes and Chalcis. At the same time, there seems to have existed a remarkable uniformity in the pottery used throughout the Byzantine Empire, which was now mainly confined to areas around the Aegean and adjacent coastal sites.

As far as tablewares are concerned, Glazed White Ware disappeared during this period. All over the Byzantine lands tablewares are now characterised by the same repertoire of decorative styles and forms, particularly in harbours and urban centres. This uniformity seems to reflect a closely integrated cultural and economic sphere with identical consuming needs and dining habits.[14]

In recent years Chalcis has been identified as one of the main manufacturers of what we have called 'Middle Byzantine Production' (shortened to MBP).[15] MBP included a variety of 12th-13th century glazed decorative types, such as 'Slip-Painted Ware', 'Green and Brown Painted Ware', 'Fine Sgraffito Ware', 'Painted Sgraffito Ware', 'Champlevé Ware', 'Aegean Ware' and 'Incised Sgraffito Ware' (Figs. 3, 4, 5). Although it is possible that other cities, such as Corinth, manufactured similar wares as well, Chalcis appears to have been a major provider of MBP ceramics. This almost mass-produced pottery was mainly intended for the markets of the Byzantine Empire and beyond.

The MBP ceramics have been found in abundance in Thebes and Chalcis, but also in rural sites of Boeotia and Euboea. This may reflect the availability and accessibility of these wares to a large part of the local population beyond the urban centres.[16]

As far as amphorae are concerned, all samples which have been analysed until now, including those belonging to the amphora type known as 'Günsenin III' (Fig. 6), clearly belong to the Chalcis production.[17] The large amount of amphorae seems a probable indication for a substantial agricultural surplus that covered not only local needs, but also provided enough for export through the same maritime network as the tablewares. All evidence suggests that this maritime route departed from Chalcis towards the southern Euboean Gulf, from there reaching the open Aegean Sea, and ultimately extending around the entire eastern Mediterranean, where it can be traced through finds at various coastal sites and in shipwrecks.[18]

All in all, it seems quite plausible to assume that during the 12th century a dense network of economic activity existed in the area of Thebes and Chalcis, led by a dynamic class of local magnates, who exploited all the resources available to them in the wider region of Boeotia and Euboea. Their products (agricultural or industrial), when not consumed locally, were distributed to the rest of the Byzantine Empire, through the flourishing port of Chalcis.

The early 13th century – The archaeological evidence indicates that the new political conditions following the Latin conquest of central Greece in the early 13th century did not immediately affect production and distribution patterns. Excavations at both Chalcis and Thebes support the findings to this effect of excavations of other production sites, such as Corinth. The production and distribution of MBP ceramics continued on a substantial scale up to at least the middle of the century.[19] This indicates that the political upheaval did not result in sudden and radical socio-economic changes, in any case not in everyday life and in food consumption.[20]

More specifically, the use of 'Günsenin III' amphorae during the early 13th century suggests continuity in the transportation and trade of local agricultural products.[21] This is underlined by textual sources which, for example, mention that in 1214 Nikolaos Mesarites, being on a diplomatic mission in the Latin Patriarchate of Constantinople, was offered a pungent wine from Euboea.[22] An intriguing hint of reciprocal relations with the area of Constantinople can be found in the presence of a few examples of 'Zeuxippus Ware' in both Chalcis and Thebes.

It seems, therefore, that during the first half of the 13th century the pre-existing organized system of production and distribution of goods continued to function, at least to a certain degree, with the port of Chalcis remaining a focal point of supraregional commerce.

The second half of the 13th century – The second half of the 13th century marked the beginning of significant and wider changes in pottery production and consumption in the eastern Mediterranean. New pottery types and new forms appeared, which were produced uniformly around the Aegean by a multitude of (often newly-founded) local workshops.[23] This development can be understood as the result of the territorial fragmentation of the Aegean to various political entities, and the increasing commercial supremacy of the Italians, predominantly the Venetians, in the trade of ceramics.

Chalcis remained a vital producer of ceramics, but by now also Thebes had its own workshops.[24] They both followed the trend of the period, producing wares similar in form and decoration to those manufactured all over the eastern Mediterranean. These included mainly deep and small glazed bowls, which replaced the large wide-open dishes of the Middle Byzantine period and have been considered as indicators of changes in diet and dining habits under Western influence.[25]

At the same time, the production of Thebes and Chalcis included decorated bowls of the distinctive 'Sgraffito with Concentric Circles' type (also known as 'Zeuxippus Ware family, imitations, derivatives or subtypes') (Fig. 7). This type was manufactured in many places, among which Constantinople, various centres in northern Greece and Asia Minor, as well as in Sparta and even in northern Italy.[26] In this context, the production of Thebes and Chalcis seemed to have been destined mainly for local demand, rather than for export.

In the second half of the 13th century the two cities also witnessed the first imports of southern and northern Italian wares, such as 'Protomaiolica' from the Salento region in Apulia, and 'Roulette Ware' from the Veneto region.

The 14th – 15th centuries – From the beginning of the 14th century until they were conquered by the Ottomans in the second half of the 15th century, Thebes and Chalcis followed very different paths through history. On the one hand, local production in Thebes may have been temporarily affected by the upheavals caused during the Catalan rule of Boeotia in the 14th century. Chalcis, on the other hand, became an international trading post and a hub of the Venetian maritime network. Local manufacturers in the city continued to produce a variety of ceramic types following contemporary Byzantine styles. Tableware consisted mainly of small deep bowls decorated with simple geometric or floral designs and animal figures (Figs. 7, 8).

At the same time, both cities witnessed a multitude of imports originating from centres in the northern Aegean (such as Thessaloniki and Serres), as well as from North and South Italy (RMR Ware, 'Archaic Maiolica', 'Sgraffito Ware' of the Po Valley), Spain, and the Mamluk eastern Mediterranean. At the end of this period, Venetian 'Renaissance Sgraffito' Wares made their appearance in the local markets (Fig. 9).

Apart from the high quality decorated wares, either local or imported, we also witnessed a variety of plainer items produced in Chalcis, such as 'Simple Painted', 'Plain Glazed', 'Partially Glazed' (Fig. 10) and 'Unglazed' wares of various shapes.[27]

As far as amphorae are concerned, the evidence for their use from the 14th century onwards is somewhat unclear. Still, it is evident that Chalcis not only exported local or regional products (such as wine, honey and grain), but also acted as a warehouse for the storage, distribution, and transhipment of various commodities traded between the eastern Mediterranean and Italy.[28]

The image emanating from the study of the ceramics in Thebes and Chalcis suggests that, despite being under Latin rule, the use of Western pottery remained limited throughout the 13th-15th centuries, as opposed to what happened in the Frankish Peloponnese.[29] Particularly for this period, a question which often arises is whether it is possible to assign ceramic wares to particular ethnic groups; for example, were Italian products consumed only by Westerners?[30] Our evidence, which originates from excavations in all parts of both cities (including the recent excavations of the Venetian 'House of Bailo' in Chalcis and the Tower of Saint Omer in Thebes), seems to show a uniform pattern of ceramic use: in all contexts imports (especially from Italy) exist next to wares of traditional Byzantine style.[31] It may therefore be assumed, that all ethnic groups (including Greeks, Westerners and Jews) used more or less the same ceramics.

Perhaps it is this common usage of pottery by a mixed population that is at the root of two interesting features in the wares of this period. The first is that of common shapes, which may reflect common foodways and dining habits, a subject matter which has been addressed adequately elsewhere.[32] The second has to do with the decoration: quite similar decorative patterns (such as concentric circles, birds, geometric and floral designs etc.) are encountered in both local and imported wares, a feature that needs to be further investigated in the future.[33]

Although cultural or ethnic identity cannot be traced in the ceramic evidence, pottery may serve as indirect evidence for exploring social and economic differences within the urban population. The wide range of available pottery products in this period (local or imported high quality decorated wares and plainer items) may point to the emergence of an advanced and diversified consumer market. In this market, the multiple qualities of the ceramics may reflect a varied socio-economic structure, heterogeneous cultural values, and perhaps clients from all different groups of society.

SILK TEXTILES

The 11th-12th centuries – Discussion on the silk industry relies greatly on the work of the historian David Jacoby.[34] During the 11th and 12th centuries, Thebes was the major silk weaving centre of the western part of the Byzantine Empire, closely followed by Chalcis. The local silk production was destined for the imperial court, the domestic free market (the elites of the various centres of the Byzantine Empire), but also for foreign customers both in the West and the Islamic Asia Minor. Production and circulation of high quality silks were closely controlled by imperial authorities, as was the case in Constantinople.[35]

Especially those dyed with *murex purpurea* (purple dye), were included by imperial administration in the *kekolymena* group, that is they were prohibited from private use, sale or export.[36] The production of shellfish purple, the most expensive colorant, was restricted to the colouring of the silks destined for the imperial court. Large concentrations of shellfish remains were located on the outskirts of the village of Thisvi, which is identified with Middle Byzantine Kastorion.[37] They originated from the nearby harbour of Aghios Ioannis and were obviously destined for the silk textile industry of Thebes (see map in Fig. 1). *A terminus ante quem* for this find is 1204, since their use in silk production ceased in Byzantium at that time due to a lack of funds.

This lucrative production prompted King Roger II of Sicily in the mid-12th century to capture Thebes and to deport its silk workers to his capital Palermo, where they were ordered to teach their crafts to local workers. Jacoby has even suggested that the famous Coronation Mantle of Roger II is in fact a Theban product, ornamented later on by local embroiders.[38]

The production of silk textiles in Thebes and in the island of Euboea continued after the Latin conquest. However, they now faced a fierce competition by silk textiles imported from the Italian city of Lucca and from the Islamic world. Because local manufacture did no adapt to new fashions, it gradually declined and was restricted to the export of raw material for Italian silk manufacturers.[39]

In the area of Thebes, a rescue excavation uncovered a workshop installation which has been interpreted as a dye shop (for textiles or leathers?). The finds suggested that it operated roughly during the period of silk production, in other words from the late 11th to the early 14th century.[40]

JEWELLERY AND ACCESSORIES

The second category of luxury objects discussed here includes minor artefacts mainly for personal adornment. They were made of materials that were obviously valuable; yet they were not excessively expensive, and therefore there is a distinction with the next category (precious objects).[41] Important is that there existed both in the Byzantine and in the Latin period a noticeable uniformity in the forms and decorations of the objects that were found in Thebes and Chalcis. Furthermore, it is quite striking that finds from rural sites (e.g., the village cemeteries in Xeronomi, Afrati, and Eretria, see map in Fig. 1) clearly indicate that similar objects were used as grave goods for the deceased in the countryside.

The Middle Byzantine period – The archaeological record shows that during the Middle Byzantine period (9th-12th centuries) there existed a variety of luxury objects, destined mainly for personal use. Rings were made of bronze, brass, base silver or glass (Fig. 11). Many of them were inscribed with linear motifs, invocations or schematic figures that could have had an apotropaic and magical function. Some examples were decorated with glass paste and granules.

Earrings come in a number of different shapes, including types which were popular throughout Byzantine Greece. Circular earrings are often decorated with glass beads, spiral wire, metal beads or pending crosses (Figs. 12, 16c). Lunate-type earrings are usually hollow with an opening thought to be destined for perfumed tissues (Fig. 13). Some are decorated with enamel motifs; most of them have, however, simple inscribed decorations.

Pendants are usually religious in character. Crosses are made of bronze, silver alloys, lead or iron. They are either solid, or hollow, functioning as reliquaries. They can be plain or engraved with crucifixion motives (Fig. 14). We also encountered a small steatite icon with a mounted warrior saint (Fig. 15a), as well as a circular bronze pendant with a lion (Fig. 15b).[42] Furthermore, a number of bracelets were made of glass or bronze, while glass beads were commonly used for necklaces.

Dress accessories included straps for garments and bronze buckles. The buckles were obviously coming from belts, though it is impossible to discern whether they were destined for male or female costumes. Finally, we can mention a number of incised bone plaques, obviously coming from the casing of small jewellery boxes.

Similar objects come, as mentioned above, from a number of excavated village cemeteries, in the countryside of both Boeotia and Euboea. In the case of Xeronomi in Boeotia we encountered steatite and iron pendant crosses; a glass bracelet; bronze and silver rings, some with glass paste; bronze earrings, of the circular and basket type; glass or faience beads probably from necklaces (Figs. 11d, 16).[43] In Afrati and Eretria (Euboea) excavation revealed bronze circular (either plain or with beads and spirals) and lunette earrings, bronze rings, and pendant crosses.[44]

The period of Latin rule – For the period of Latin rule (13th-early 14th century), the evidence suggests that the same categories of luxury objects persisted in both cities. The excavation sequences indicate that there was no clear discontinuity between this period and the preceeding Byzantine era. Personal jewellery still included bronze rings, and earrings, although the latter were now smaller and were mainly versions of the earlier 'lunette' type.

A number of features, however, point to changes which were the result either of garment changes or of the arrival of Latin settlers. A new feature of the period is the use of tight fit garments, a feature that gradually emerged during the 13th century. Linked to it, we witness the appearance of buttons and clasps (Fig. 17), which we find both in urban communities and in the countryside. All buttons are made of bronze, half sphere blanks, which were soldered together to a globular form.

In Thebes, a number of minor objects were found which are related to the function of the city as the administrative centre of the Burgundian dominion (until 1311) and the Latin Church hierarchy, as well as the home of a large number of Western settlers. Being the seat of a rather active mint, the city apparently drew together a number of specialized craftsmen.

A metal workshop, excavated in the city centre of Thebes, produced dress accessories and other accoutrements, and had the ability to manufacture precious objects, as indicated by the discovery of Lydian stones used for checking metal alloys.[45] A number of artefacts from the workshop are obviously connected to the Latin rite, such as a pair of tongs for stamping Eucharist wafers, its tweezers bearing relief decoration, and a stamp bearing a Latin inscription around a cross.[46] In addition, there were also other finds related to the Latin newcomers, such as a bronze object (box cover?) with a repousse scene of the Annunciation (Fig. 18), and a kit-shaped disc destined for the decoration of horse bridles, and obviously connected with the presence of the Western mounted knights in the city.[47]

PRECIOUS OBJECTS

Objects of exceptional value were found both in Thebes and Chalcis. Their presence in the cities suggest the existence of a well-to-do upper class, whose members would have owned and cherished these precious posessions. Some of these precious objects can be dated to the Middle Byzantine period, while a large hoard can be attributed to the final centuries of Latin rule.

A silver bowl or plate of the late 8th century is the only –so far- known stamped object dated after the middle of the 7th century, when it is believed that the whole Byzantine system of metal control had collapsed (Fig. 19).[48] It was found in 2004 at a rescue excavation in Thebes within a complex which was apparently in continuous use up to the Frankish period. The shallow bowl or plate is hammered and chased with high-quality linear and vegetal motifs on its inner side. On the underside it preserved two control stamps: one bearing the bust and the monogram of Empress Irene the

Athenian (780-802) and the second containing a four-line inscription of a certain imperial administrator, called Ioannes.[49]

A few personal accessories, made of precious materials, indicate the level of luxury enjoyed by upper class members in this region of the Byzantine Empire. These include a gold earring of the 'lunate' type, as well as a gold ring with a gem, both originating from Thebes (Fig. 20).[50] An ivory comb dated to the 10th-11th century is an exceptional find from Chalcis.[51] It is decorated with relief representations of lions on the one side, and peacocks drinking from a fountain on the other. Its material and art suggest that this was a highly valuable object.

The most impressive assemblage in this category is a large treasure of jewellery, concealed in the foundations of an old city house of Chalcis, on the eve of the Ottoman conquest in 1470.[52] Some 630 items have been documented until now. Of these, the rings have attracted much scholarly attention. They were adorned with precious stones and pearls; personal rings were engraved with Western coat-of-arms and Latin inscriptions, obviously belonging to noblemen; others were inscribed with verses of the famous 14th century poet, Manuel Philes, and their origin has been traced to the imperial workshops of Constantinople. Apart from these rings, a number of earrings have been found (Fig. 21), as well as silver gilt parts from belts. The decoration and techniques of these objects suggest various influences and provenances.

Finally, the treasure contained also a group of 340 silver gilt buttons in various forms and sizes together with two cloak fasteners decorated with the symbol of Venice, the Lion of St. Mark, and a precious silver plate which can be dated to the early 1400s.

CONCLUSION

During the period from the 9th to the 15th century, the two main urban centres of central Greece, Thebes and Chalcis, witnessed changing patterns of consumption and production. The changes can be understood as the result of wider developments in the Byzantine world in general and of regional political events.

During the Middle Byzantine period the two cities were clearly connected and functioned complementary to one another. Thebes was the administrative capital and major urban centre, housing also the highly specialized and lucrative silk industry. Chalcis served as the port for the export of local agricultural and industrial products and as the connection to other urban centres within the Byzantine Empire, while it housed ceramic workshops for both the local and the wider markets. Large quantities of ceramics made in Chalcis were destined for export, either as commodities or as product containers.

Under Latin rule, the connection between the cities was gradually lost due to historical reasons. Thebes was restricted to its local role, while Chalcis turned into an international maritime hub. Both cities, acting as epicentres of respective hinterlands, had their own agricultural, ceramic and industrial production, which was now destined for local or regional use. In their markets one could find also a variety of imported objects from other regions which were provided thanks to the international commercial network of Venice.

Within this general historic and economic context, the artefacts from the two cities discussed in this chapter provide information about the preferences, habits and financial capacity of the consumers that used them. Each category of objects also offers glimpses of social groups that were involved in the production and distribution of these objects to markets and fairs. Through further study of this archaeological record we may gain a better understanding of the socio-economic conditions of urban societies in central Greece during Middle Byzantine and Late Byzantine times.

The silk production, which flourished particularly in the 11th-12th century at Thebes, was studied earlier by David Jacoby. His invalubale analysis of the specifics of this production, has shed light on how multiple groups of the local population were involved and were closely intertwined in this economic activity.[53] Jacoby eventually proposed a model that included a series of interconnected networks. First came the rural circuit of raw material production by peasants and fishermen, then a series of urban workshops with silk weavers and craftsmen; third came the circuit of distribution with merchants, ship owners and commissioners. Members of the local elite, the Archontes, functioned as moderators and main leaders of these networks, but were later replaced by Venetian wholesale dealers. All these groups were obviously acting in the local market both as producers and as consumers.

On the basis of archaeological evidence, we were to a certain extent able to conjecture multiple similar networks, which were active both for minor objects (jewellery and accessories) and for pottery. For the minor objects, we may envisage a first network of metal extraction and commercial supply of raw materials; then, a group of various workshops and professionals producing affordable jewellery for local consumption.

For the pottery, one should underline the domination of the market by mainly local products, alongside lesser quantities of imports. The network of workshops manufacturing pottery vessels was producing on the one hand amphorae for storage and transport (local and long distance) of agricultural products (obviously produced by respective networks), and on the other hand tableware. The latter was destined as an export commodity in the 12th-13th centuries, and dominated the internal market both in the Middle Byzantine and in the Latin periods. In particular from the time following the Latin occupation onwards, one should have an open eye for the widening functions of pottery, beyond its utilitarian purpose, and recognize that luxury ceramics may also reflect economic capacities, and perhaps even fashions and aesthetics, at least in urban centres.

Furthermore, the precious objects discovered in both Thebes and Chalcis were obviously destined for elite members, probably the leading agents of the aforementioned networks. Whether they had been purchased in the local market or brought as ownerships from afar, is as yet impossible to tell.

The study of the material evidence available from the cities of Thebes and Chalcis over a period of six centuries seems to permit the following conclusions: (1) – there existed an interconnected and highly active socio-economic environment; (2) – multiple products reached both local and overseas markets; (3) – there was a degree of material culture commonly and continuously available to and shared by cities and countryside alike.

This complexity, vigor and fluidity of the local market and of local socio-economic patterns in general is both in the Middle Byzantine and in the Late Byzantine period distinctly apparent through the artefacts available to the Medieval consumer.

ACKNOWLEDGEMENTS

The authors were fortunate to study the objects discussed in this article during their years of service in the region. We would like, therefore, to thank the successive directors, Dr. Pari Kalamara (Chalcis) and Dr. Alexandra Charami (Thebes), as well as all our colleagues, with a special mention to our long term collaborator Giannis Vaxevanis, for their valuable help and constant support.

NOTES

1. Louvi-Kizi 2002.
2. Gerolymatou 1987; Jacoby 1991-92; Koilakou 2004; *Idem* 2013, 183-86.
3. Koder and Hild 1976, 156; Triantafyllopoulos 1990, 170.
4. Savvidis 1981-2; Waksman *et al.* 2014.
5. Kontogiannis 2012, 30-35.
6. Koilakou 2004; *Idem* 2013, 187-90.
7. Bintliff 1996.
8. Papadia-Lala 2006; Kontogiannis 2012, 35-46.
9. The pottery discussed here is coming from rescue excavations in Thebes, Chalcis and their countryside, including published examples in Armstrong 1993; Vroom 2003; *Idem* 2006; Koilakou 2012; Arvaniti 2013; Waksman *et al.* 2014; Dafi and Skartsis 2015; Waksman *et al.* 2018; Kontogiannis *et al.*, 2020; Skartsis and Vaxevanis 2017, many of which are either currently on display or meant to be so, in the new archaeological museums of Thebes (*Guide to Archaeological Museum of Thebes*, 44-49) and Chalcis. For further details on the main characteristics and the chronology of the pottery types of the 9th to 15th centuries included in the discussion, see especially: Hayes 1992; Papanikola-Bakirtzis 1999; Vroom 2003; *Idem* 2014[2]; Skartsis 2012; Yangaki 2012 (with the respective bibliography).
10. The abundance of these wares in Constantinople indicates their Constantinopolitan origin, but workshops have not been located so far; see especially Hayes 1992; Waksman 2012.
11. For the identification of the local unglazed incised ware (Chalcis production), see Kontogiannis *et al.* 2020 and Vroom *et al.* in this volume.
12. For the identification of local (Chalcis production) and imported amphorae of this period. see Waksman *et al.* 2018, 8-10, cat. nos. 8-17, 18-25, 40-41 ('Gunsenin II' and 'transitional type').
13. For Ganos see Gunsenin 1993; For the clay deposits of the Lelantine plain near Chalcis see Waksman *et al.* 2014, 414-15.
14. Waksman *et al.* 2014, 379-80 (with respective bibliography)
15. Waksman *et al.* 2014.
16. E.g., Vroom 2003, 145-64 (Boeotia); Armstrong 1993 (Eastern Phokis); Papanikola-Bakirtzis 1999, 32, 42, cat. nos. 11, 26 (Afrati); Dafi and Skartsis 2015, 711 (Aliveri); Gani 2012 (Fylla).
17. Waksman *et al.* 2018, 6, cat. nos. 1-7, 26-39, 42-45.
18. Waksman *et al.* 2014, 380; Koutsouflakis 2020.
19. Waksman *et al.* 2014, 416.
20. For similar conditions in other sites, see Vroom 2011, 413-17.
21. Waksman *et al.* 2018, 6.
22. Jacoby 2010b, 137.
23. Papanikola-Bakirtzis 2003, 64; *Idem* 2012.
24. For the table wares produced in Thebes and Chalcis between the second half of the 13th c. and the 15th c. see Waksman *et al.* 2014, 414-15.
25. Vroom 2003, 331-32; Papanikola-Bakirtzis 2005.

26 See especially Waksman and François 2004-2005; Waksman and Girgin 2008.
27 See above, note 24.
28 Jacoby 2010a, 192.
29 Vroom 2011; Skartsis 2012, 87-96.
30 For example Francois 1997; Vroom 2011; Stern 2015.
31 The excavations of the 'House of Bailo' and the Tower of Saint Omer are currently studied by the authors.
32 For example Vroom 2003, 233-34, 329-31; *Idem* 2011, 419-21; *Idem* 2015; Papanikola-Bakirtzis 2005; Vionis 2005, 295-99; *Idem* 2014.
33 On this issue see also Skartsis 2012, 89-90. For example, birds similar to that of a 14th-century bowl from Chalcis (fig. 7): Papanikola-Bakirtzis 1999, 191-98, cat. nos. 216-224 (Thessaloniki or Constantinople production); Papanikola-Bakirtzis 1996, pl. x (Cypriot production); Athanasoulis 2005, picture in page 45, bottom (southern Italian production). 'Grid-iron' patterns similar to that of a bowl of the late 13th-early 14th century from Chalcis (Waksman *et al.* 2014, 401, fig. 12f, cat. no. 43): Papanikola-Bakirtzis 1999, 215-16, cat. nos. 246-249 (Thessaloniki or Constantinople production); Papanikola-Bakirtzis et al. 1999, 167, no. 167 (Cypriot production); Williams and Zervos 1995, pl. 4, nos. 1-2 (southern Italian production); Facial representations similar to that of 13th-century bowls from Chalcis (fig. 3, two incised bowls on top right; see also Waksman et al 2014, 406, fig. 10h, cat. no. 77): Papanikola-Bakirtzis 1996, pl. XI, no. 60 (Cypriot production); a southern Italian example ('RMR' Ware) displayed in Chlemoutsi castle, Peloponnese (personal observation).
34 See Jacoby 2008 with previous bibliography.
35 Jacoby 1991-1992, esp. 462-70.
36 Jacoby 1991-1992, esp. 456-58 and 488-91.
37 Dunn 2006, 46-47, 53-55; Koilakou 2013, 185.
38 Jacoby 1991-1992, 464.
39 Jacoby 2008, 426-27.
40 Koilakou 2004, 225-29.
41 The objects used for compiling this section derive – as in the case of the ceramics- from multiple rescue excavations of the Archaeological Service, and were all published in the relevant yearly reports for Boeotia and Euboea (*Archaiologikon Deltion* - hence *AD*). They will not be referenced individually here, except when specific items are concerned. As with the pottery, many of them are currently exhibited in the Archaeological Museum of Thebes (*Guide to the Archaeological Museum of Thebes*, 44-49), while others will hopefully find their place in the new Archaeological Museum of Chalcis.
42 For the steatite pendant, see *AD* 48 (1993), 78, pl. 33α (entry: Ch. Koilakou). For the bronze pendant, see *AD* 49 (1994), 117, pl. 48β (entry: Ch. Koilakou); Tsivikis 2012, 74.
43 For the finds of Xeronomi, see Voltyraki 2006, 1149-63.
44 *AD* 62 (2007), 604-606 (Aik. Tsaka).
45 For the metal workshop, see Koilakou 2004, 231-33.

46   For the tongs, Koilakou 2004, 235-37.
47   For the Annunciation artifact, see *AD* 42 (1997), 118 (entry: Ch. Koilakou). For the bridle decoration, see *AD* 55 (2000), 152-53 (entry: Ch. Koilakou).
48   Voltyraki 2014, 349-60.
49   Voltyraki 2015, 355 and 358.
50   For the gold earring, Andreadaki-Vlazaki 2012, 38, figs. 23-25 (Ergodomiki Plot). The gold ring was found during works by the municipality of Thebes on Epameinonda Street.
51   *AD* 29 (1973-74), 508, pl. 330α-β (entry: M. Georgopoulou-Meladini); currently in the collection of the Byzantine and Christian Museum, Athens (catl. nr. ΒΧΜ01185).
52   Dalton 1911, 391-404; McLeod 2010, 233-36; Kontogiannis and Orfanou 2019, 115-25.
53   Jacoby 1991-1992, 470-88.

BIBLIOGRAPHY

Andreadaki-Vlazaki, M. (ed.) 2012. *2000-2010 Από το Ανασκαφικό Έργο των Εφορειών Αρχαιοτήτων*, Athens.

Armstrong, P. 1993. Byzantine Thebes: Excavations on the Kadmeia, 1980, *Annual of the British School at Athens* 88, 295-335.

Arvaniti, S. 2013. Η εφυαλωμένη κεραμική από την πόλη των Θηβών' 13ος αιώνας έως και όψιμη Οθωμανική περίοδος (1204-1829). Η μαρτυρία των ανασκαφικών ευρημάτων από την περιοχή της Καδμείας, *unpublished* doctoral thesis, University of Athens.

Athanasoulis, D. (ed.) 2005. *Glarentza-Clarence*, Athens.

Bintliff, J. 1996. Frankish countryside in central Greece: The evidence from archaeological find survey, in: P. Lock and G.D.R. Sanders (eds.), *The Archaeology of Medieval Greece*, Oxford, 1-18.

Dalton, O.M. 1911. Medieval personal ornaments from Chalcis in the British and Ashmolean Museums, *Archaeologia* 62, 391-404

Dunn, A. 2006. The rise and fall of towns, loci of maritime traffic, and silk-production: The problem of Thisvi-Kastorion, in: E. Jeffreys (ed.), *Byzantine Style, Religion and Civilization: In Honour of Sir Steven Runciman*, Cambridge (Reprint edition 2012), 38-71.

François, V. 1997. Céramiques importés à Byzance: une quasi-absence, *Byzantinoslavica* LVIII, 2, 387-404.

Gani, P. 2012. Ανασκάπτοντας μια αγροτική εγκατάσταση στον οικισμό των Φύλλων Εύβοιας, *40 Αρχαιολογικό Έργο Θεσσαλίας και Στερεάς Ελλάδας, Επιστημονική συνάντηση (Βόλος 15-18.3.2012)*, Abstracts of papers, 3.

Gerolymatou, G. 1987. Η Θήβα κέντρο εμπορίου και επικοινωνιών τον 12ο αι., *Σύμμεικτα* 11, 102-105.

Guide to the Archaeological Museum of Thebes, 2016. Athens

Günsenin, N. 1993. Ganos: Centre de production d'amphores à l'époque byzantine. *Anatolia Antiqua* 2, 193-201.

Hayes, J. 1992. *Excavations at Saraçhane in Istanbul, Vol. 2: The Pottery*, Princeton, NJ.

Jacoby, D. 2008. Silk production, in: E. Jeffreys, J. Haldon and R. Cormack (eds.), *The Oxford Handbook of Byzantine Studies,* Oxford, 421-28.

Jacoby, D. 1991-2. Silk in Western Byzantium before the Fourth Crusade, *Byzantinische Zeitschrift* 84-5, 452-500.

Jacoby, D. 2010a. Thirteenth-century commercial exchange in the Aegean: Continuity and change, in: Vehbi Koç Vakfı (ed.), *Change in the Byzantine World in the Twelfth and Thirteenth Centuries, First International Sevgi Gonul Byzantine Studies Symposium*, Istanbul, 187-94.

Jacoby, D. 2010b. Mediterranean food and wine for Constantinople: The long-distance trade, eleventh to mid-fifteenth century, in: E. Kislinger, J. Koder and A. Külzer (eds.), *Handelsgüter und Verkehrswege. Aspekte der Warenversorgung im östlichen Mittelmeerraum, Akten des internationalen Symposions (Wien, 19-22 Oktober 2005)*, Wien, 127-47.

Koder, J. and F. Hild 1976. *Hellas und Thessalia*, Tabula Imperii Byzantini 1, Vienna.

Koilakou, Ch. 2004. Βιοτεχνικές εγκαταστάσεις βυζαντινής εποχής στη Θήβα, in: *Αρχαιολογικά τεκμήρια βιοτεχνικών εγκαταστάσεων κατά τη βυζαντινή εποχή, 5ος-15ος αι. Ειδικό θέμα του 22ου Συμποσίου Βυζαντινής και Μεταβυζαντινής Αρχαιολογίας και Τέχνης, Αθήνα 17-19 Μαΐου 2002*, Athens, 221-41.

Koilakou, Ch. 2012. Κεραμική με λευκό πηλό από ανασκαφές στη Θήβα, *Δελτίον Χριστιανικής Αρχαιολογικής Εταιρείας* 33, 305-12.

Koilakou, Ch. 2013. Thebes, in: J. Albani and Eu. Chalkia (eds.), *Heaven and Earth, Cities and Countryside in Byzantine Greece*, Athens, 180-90.

Kontogiannis, N.D. 2012. Euripos – Negroponte – Eğriboz: Material culture and historical topography of Chalcis from Byzantium to the End of the Ottoman Rule, *Jahrbuch der Österreichischen Byzantinistik* 62, 29-56.

Kontogiannis, N.D. and V. Orfanou 2019. The Chalcis treasure: A 14th-15th century hoard from Euboea, Greece – first thoughts and preliminary results, in: in A. Bosselmann-Ruickbie (ed.), *New Research on Late Byzantine Goldsmiths' Works (13th-15th Centuries) / Neue Forschungen zur spätbyzantinischen Goldschmiedekunst (13.-15. Jahrhundert)* (Byzanz zwischen Orient und Okzident 13, Veröffentlichungen des Leibniz-WissenschaftsCampus Mainz), Mainz, 115-25.

Kontogiannis, N.D. and S.S. Skartsis (with contributions by G. Vaxevanis and S.Y. Waksman) 2020. Ceramic vessels and food consumption: Chalcis as major production and distribution center in the Byzantine and Frankish periods, in: S.Y. Waksman (ed.), *Multidisciplinary Approaches to Food and Foodways in the Medieval Eastern Mediterranean*, Archéologie(s) 4, Lyon, 239-54.

Koutsouflakis, G. 2020. The transportation of amphorae, tableware and foodstuffs in the Middle and Late Byzantine period: The evidence from Aegean shipwrecks, in: S.Y. Waksman (ed.), *Multidisciplinary Approaches to Food and Foodways in the Medieval Eastern Mediterranean*, Archéologie(s) 4, Lyon, 447-81.

Louvi-Kizi, A. 2002. Thebes, in: A.E. Laiou (ed.), *The Economic History of Byzantium: From the Seventh through the Fifteenth Century*, Dumbarton Oaks Studies 39, Washington, DC, 631-38.

Mcleod, B. 2010. Some aspects of the finger-rings in the Chalcis Treasure at the British Museum, in: Ch. Entwistle and N. Adams (eds.), *Intelligible Beauty: Recent Research on Byzantine Jewellery*, British Museum Research Publ. 178, London, 233-36.

Dafi, E. and S.S. Skartsis 2015. Βυζαντινή κεραμική από τις ανασκαφές στις εγκαταστάσεις του ατμοηλεκτρικού σταθμού (αησ) της δεη Αλιβερίου, στην Εύβοια (4ος-18ος αι.), in: *4ο Αρχαιολογικό Έργο Θεσσαλίας και Στερεάς Ελλάδας, Πρακτικά Επιστημονικής Συνάντησης II (Βόλος, 15-18 Μαρτίου 2012)*, Volos, 709-18.

Papadia-Lala, A. 2006. Κοινωνική οργάνωση και αστική κοινότητα στην Εύβοια κατά τη Βενετική περίοδο (1390-1470), in: Ch. Maltezou and Ch. Papakosta (eds.), *Πρακτικά Διεθνούς Συνεδρίου, Βενετία – Εύβοια, από τον Έγριπο στο Νεγροπόντε, Χαλκίδα, 12-14 Νοεμβρίου 2004*, Athens, 27-40.

Papanikola-Bakirtzis, D. 1996. *Μεσαιωνική εφυαλωμένη κεραμική της Κύπρου. Τα εργαστήρια Πάφου και Λαπήθου*, Thessaloniki.

Papanikola-Bakirtzis, D. (ed.) 1999. *Byzantine Glazed Ceramics: The Art of Sgraffito*, Athens.

Papanikola-Bakirtzis, D. 2003. Εργαστήρια εφυαλωμένης κεραμικής στο βυζαντινό κόσμο, in: Ch. Bakirtzis (ed.), *Actes du VIIe Congrès International sur la Céramique Médiévale en Méditerranée, Thessalonica, 11-16 Octobre 1999*, Athens, 45-66.

Papanikola-Bakirtzis, D. 2005. Βυζαντινά επιτραπέζια σκεύη – σχήμα, χρήση και διακόσμηση, in: D. Papanikola-Bakirtzis (ed.), *Βυζαντινών Διατροφή και Μαγειρείαι*, Athens, 117-32.

Papanikola-Bakirtzis, D. 2012. Byzantine glazed ceramics on the market: An approach, in: C. Morrisson (ed.), *Trade and Markets in Byzantium*, Washington, DC, 193-216.

Papanikola-Bakirtzis, D., F.N. Mavrikiou and Ch. Bakirtzis 1999. *Βυζαντινή κεραμική στο Μουσείο Μπενάκη*, Athens.

Savvidis, A.G.K 1981-2. Η Εύβοια κατά τα τέλη του ιβ' – αρχές του ιγ' αι. μ.Χ.», *Αρχείο Ευβοϊκών Μελετών* 24, 313-23.

Skartsis, S.S. 2012. *Chlemoutsi Castle (Clermont, Castel Tornese). Its Pottery and its Relations with the West (13th – early 19th centuries)*, BAR Int. Series 2391, London.

Skartsis, S.S. and G. Vaxevanis 2017. Η Χαλκίδα κατά τους μεσοβυζαντινούς χρόνους και την εποχή της Λατινοκρατίας: η μαρτυρία της κεραμικής (9ος-15ος αι.), in: Ž., Tankosić, F. Mavridis and M. Kosma (eds.), *An Island Between Two Worlds, The Archaeology of Euboea from Prehistoric to Byzantine Times, Proceedings of an international Scientific Conference, Eretria, July 12-14, 2013*, Athens, 593-612.

Stern, E.J. 2015. Pottery and identity in the Latin Kingdom of Jerusalem: A case study of Acre and Western Galilee, in: J. Vroom (ed.), *Medieval and Post-Medieval Ceramics in the Eastern Mediterranean. Fact and Fiction. Proceedings of the First International Conference on Byzantine and Ottoman Archaeology, Amsterdam, 21-23 October 2011*, Medieval and Post-Medieval Mediterranean Archaeology 1, Turnhout, 287-315.

Triantafyllopoulos, D.D. 1990. Χριστιανική και μεσαιωνική Χαλκίδα: ανασκόπηση της νεώτερης αρχαιολογικής έρευνας, in: *Διεθνές Επιστημονικό Συνέδριο «Η πόλη της Χαλκίδας»*, Athens, 165-170.

Tsivikis, N. 2012. Considerations on some bronze buckles from Byzantine Messene, in: B. Böhlendorf-Arslan and A. Ricci (eds.), *Byzantine Small Finds in Archaeological Contexts*, Byzas 15, Istanbul, 61-80.

Voltyraki, E. 2014. «...αγεται... γαμετην εκ της ελλαδος...» (Νικηφόρου Πατριάρχου, Ιστορία Σύντομος, 77.9-10), *Δελτίον Χριστιανικής Αρχαιολογικής Εταιρείας* 35, 349-60.

Voltyraki, E. 2006. Παρατηρήσεις στις ταφικές συνήθειες μικρών κοιμητηριακών συνόλων κατά τη Βυζαντινή Περίοδο, in: *Αρχαιολογικό Έργο Θεσσαλίας και Στερεάς Ελλάδας, πρακτικά επιστημονικής συνάντησης (Βόλος 27.2-2.3.2003)*, Volos, 1149-1163.

Vionis, A.K. 2005. *Crusader and Ottoman Material Life: The Archaeology of Built Environment and Domestic Material Culture in the Medieval and Post-Medieval Cyclades, Greece (c.13th-20th AD)*, Leiden.

Vionis, A.K. 2014. The archaeology of landscape and material culture in Late Byzantine – Frankish Greece, *Pharos* 20.1, 313-46

Vroom, J. 2003. *After Antiquity: Ceramics and Society in the Aegean from the 7th to the 20th centuries A.C. A Case Study from Boeotia, Central Greece*, (Archaelogical Studies Leiden University 10), Leiden.

Vroom, J. 2006. Byzantine garbage and Ottoman waste, in: E. Andrikou, V.L. Aravantinos, L. Godard, A. Sacconi and J. Vroom, *Thèbes. Fouilles de la Cadmée, Vol. II.2: Les tablettes en linéaire B de la 'Odos Pelopidou'. La céramique de la Odos Pelopidou et la chronologie du Linéaire B*, Pisa & Rome, 181-233.

Vroom, J. 2011. The Morea and its links with Southern Italy after AD 1204: Ceramics and identity, *Archeologia Medievale* 38, 409-30.

Vroom, J. 2014². *Byzantine to Modern Pottery in the Aegean: An Introduction and Field Guide, Second Revised Edition*, Turnhout (2nd and revised ed.; 1rst ed. Utrecht, 2005).

Vroom, J. 2015. The archaeology of consumption in the Eastern Mediterranean: A ceramic perspective, in: M.J. Gonçalves and S. Gómez-Martínez (eds.) *Proceedings of the 10th International Congress on Medieval Pottery in the Mediterranean*, Silves, 359-67.

Waksman, S.Y. 2012. The first workshop of Byzantine ceramics discovered in Constantinople / Istanbul: Chemical characterization and preliminary typological study, in: S. Gelichi (ed.), *Atti del IX Convegno internazionale sulla ceramica medievale nel Mediterraneo*, Florence, 147-51.

Waksman, S.Y. and V. François 2004-2005. Vers une redéfinition typologique et analytique des céramiques byzantines du type Zeuxippus Ware, *Bulletin de Correspondance Hellénique* 128-29, 629-724.

Waksman, S.Y. and Ç. Girgin 2008. Les vestiges de production de céramiques des fouilles de Sirkeci (Istanbul). Premiers éléments de caractérisation, *Anatolia Antiqua* 16, 443-69.

Waksman, S.Y., N.D. Kontogiannis, S.S. Skartsis and G. Vaxevanis 2014. The main 'Middle Byzantine Production' and pottery manufacture in Thebes and Chalcis, *Annual of the British School at Athens* 109, 379-422.

Waksman, S.Y., S.S. Skartsis, N.D. Kontogiannis, E.P. Todorova and G. Vaxevanis 2018. Investigating the origins of two main types of Byzantine amphorae, *Journal of Archaeological Science: Reports* 21, 1111-1121 [http://dx.doi.org/10.1016/j.jasrep.2016.12.00]

Williams II, C.K. and O.H. Zervos 1995. Frankish Corinth: 1994, *Hesperia* 64, 1-60.

Yangaki, A. 2012. *Εφυαλωμένη κεραμική από τη θέση «Άγιοι Θεόδωροι» στην Ακροναυπλία (11ος-17ος αι.)*, Athens.

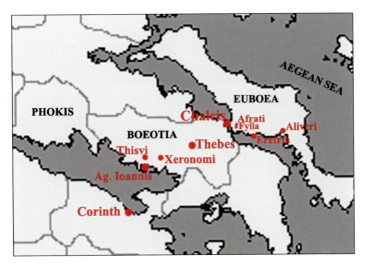

FIG. 1 – Map of central Greece showing the main sites mentioned in the text (drawing by the authors).

FIG. 2A-B – Unglazed Incised Ware: (A) – from Thebes; (B) – from Chalcis (Chalcis production) (photo by the authors).

FIG. 3 – Champlevé plate from Thebes (photo by the authors).

FIG. 4 – Green and Brown Painted, Slip Painted, Champlevé and Incised Ware from Chalcis (photo by the authors).

FIG. 5 – Green and Brown Painted, Champlevé and Aegean Ware from Chalcis (photo by the authors).

FIG. 6 – Amphora from Dokos (Euboea) (photo by the authors).

FIG. 7 – Sgraffito with Concentric Circles from Chalcis (photo by the authors).

FIG. 8 – Sgraffito bowl from Chalcis (photo by the authors).

FIG. 9 – Venetian Renaissance Sgraffito from Thebes (Archive EFA Boeotia).

FIG. 10 – Partially glazed bowls from Chalcis (photo by S.S. Skartsis).

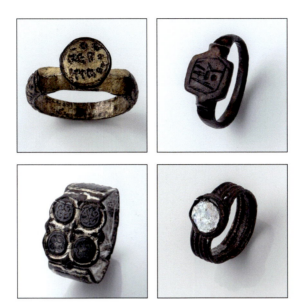

FIG. 11A-D – Rings: (A-C) – from Thebes; (D) – from Xeronomi (Boeotia) (Archive EFA Boeotia).

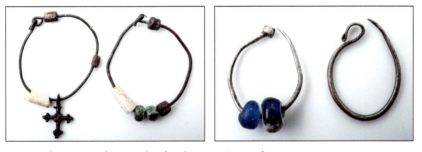

FIG. 12 – Circular earrings from Thebes (Archive EFA Boeotia).

FIGS. 13A-B – Lunate-type earrings from Thebes (Archive EFA Boeotia).

FIG. 14 – Pendant crosses from Thebes (Archive EFA Boeotia).

FIG. 15A-B – Pendants from Thebes: (A) – steatite icon with a mounted warrior saint; (B) – circular bronze pendant with a lion (Archive EFA Boeotia).

FIG. 16A-D – Jewelry from Xeronomi (Boeotia): (A) – steatite cross; (B) – bronze ring; (C) – bronze circular earrings; (D) – basket type earring (Archive EFA Boeotia).

FIG. 17A-B – Bronze buttons (A) and buckle (B) from Thebes (Archive EFA Boeotia).

FIG. 18 – Bronze box cover (?) from Thebes with repousse scene of the Annunciation (Archive EFA Boeotia).

FIG. 19 – Silver bowl from Thebes (ext., int.) (Archive EFA Boeotia).

FIG. 20 – Gold earring (lunate type) and ring from Thebes (Archive EFA Boeotia).

FIG. 21A-B – Gold earrings from the treasure of Chalcis (British Museum London, © Trustees of the British Museum).

* * *

Life, work and consumption in Byzantine Chalcis: Ceramic finds from an industrial hub in central Greece, ca. 10-13th c.

Joanita Vroom, Elli Tzavella & Giannis Vaxevanis

*

INTRODUCTION

Between May and September 2007 a rescue excavation was carried out in a plot at Orionos Street (located at number 10) in the centre of modern Chalkida (central Greece) by the former 23rd Ephorate of Byzantine Antiquities, the current Ephorate of Antiquities of Euboea (Hellenic Ministry of Culture).[1] The results of the dig were quite remarkable, and perhaps that is an understatement. In fact, the ecavation revealed finds of extraordinary and wide-ranging importance for the understanding of the history of Byzantine Chalcis (or 'Euripos/Evripos', as it was mentioned in the Byzantine written sources).[2]

Indeed, the Orionos Street excavation took not only place in a yet unidentified industrial zone of this Byzantine city, but also yielded enormous quantities of finds which provided new insights on production and consumer demands within the Byzantine Empire between the 10th and (mid) 13th centuries. These finds included evidence of pottery production (for instance, of glazed tablewares, amphorae, cooking pots and numerous unglazed plain wares), as well as proof of other industrial activities (among which the manufacture of metal, glass and bone objects). So, from a consumptive view it would be worthwhile to find out how ceramic production for various markets (including Chalcis' immediate hinterland) was organized, what the range of available products was, and why Chalcis was chosen as one of the main production centres in the Aegean?

It is our intention to introduce in this chapter the first results of our research on this large body of excavated material, with an emphasis on pottery finds from the Orionos Street excavation. In particular, we will present here a selection of the most significant locally made glazed tablewares and amphora types of the Middle Byzantine and Late Byzantine/Frankish periods which can be dated between circa the 10th/11th and 13th centuries.[3] The discovery of these local products in combination with architectural remains of the Byzantine period is, despite their fragmentary preservation, important for this specific industrial location, but also for the wider topography of medieval Chalcis, which so far remained largely unknown.

A SHORT HISTORY OF THE CITY

It is beyond dispute that Chalcis was an important harbour city and commercial hub throughout many historical periods (Fig. 1). As the chief town on the Island of Euboea, it is situated on a small peninsula next to the Euripus Strait at its narrowest point where it is connected to the mainland by a bridge. As such, Chalcis is located in a strategic position, as it could easily control the Euripus Channel and the major sea routes between Italy, Crete and Constantinople (the capital of the Byzantine Empire).[4] The city was continuously inhabited since Prehistoric times. From this period until the end of Late Antiquity, the city was located on the foothills of Mount Vathrovounia, near the Arethousa Spring and the bay of Agios Stephanos, with its size fluctuating according to changing political and economic circumstances.

In post-Classical times Chalcis was one of the main ports for transit trade in the Aegean, and had by then a considerable Jewish community. Over time the town had different names: the name 'Chalcis' is mostly preserved from Antiquity and derives from the Greek word *'chalkis'* (copper, bronze), while in Byzantine times it was known as 'Euripos'. Since the 6th century AD it served as a fortress for the protection of central Greece. Following the dismantlement of the Byzantine Empire in 1204, the city known as 'Negroponte' (Italian for 'black bridge') in the testimonies of the period became a major fortified and naval hub within the Venetian maritime network until it became a Venetian colony in 1390 (see Fig. 2 showing an engraved map of Negroponte). In 1470, after a long siege, it passed to the Ottomans, who made it the seat of the Admiral of the Archipelago (Aegean islands). During the Ottoman occupation, it was known as 'Egriboz', when it served as one of the administration and economic centres of the southern Balkans and the Aegean until the Greek War of Independence in 1821. Nowadays, the city is known as 'Chalkida'.

At some point towards the end of Late Antiquity or shortly afterwards, the ancient city of Chalcis (or Euripos) was relocated from the Arethousa area to the northwest, to the crossing point of the Euripus Strait, in order to better serve the strategic and maritime interests of the Byzantine Empire (Fig. 3).[5] Since then, the fortified walls of Euripos constituted the centre of the Medieval town. This new location was highly strategic, since it controlled the major sea routes leading from Italy and Crete to Constantinople, while it was also starting point and beginning of a major landroute into central Greece. At the same time, from the end of the 9th century, when nearby Thebes of Boeotia was declared the capital of the Theme of Hellas, the large administrative and military province of the Byzantine Empire, which encompassed Attica, Euboea and other areas of central Greece, Euripos became the station for the Theme's fleet and its port authorities.[6] Thus, it thrived as one of the most important regional and inter-regional harbours that connected its hinterland (Boeotia, Euboea) via land and sea routes with central and southern Greece, and finally with Thessaloniki and Constantinople.

So far, the archaeological evidence is fragmentary for the topography of Medieval Chalcis. The old walled town east of the Euripus bridge (also known as the 'Kastro' or 'castle') was surrounded by a full circuit of defence walls, until these were completely razed for modern urban development in the late 19th and early 20th century (Fig. 4).[7] The Kastro had the shape of a long, irregular pentagon (of ca. 400 x 700 m.) with three gates: one on the Euripus bridge and two on the land wall – these last ones surely connected the city with its direct hinterland (Euboea, Boeotia).[8] The timber-roofed Dominican church of Agia Paraskevi and the secular building known as 'House of the Bailo' (which both can be dated to the period of Venetian rule), are considered the most important and best preserved Medieval monuments of the fortified town.[9] Furthermore, travellers mentioned prominent water mills upon the fortification walls near the Euripus Strait in the 13th and 14th centuries.[10]

Various rescue excavations, which took place since the 1970s due to the construction of modern buildings, have revealed small snapshots of daily life in the Medieval city.[11] However, in most of these cases, only parts of unrelated buildings have been uncovered while their identification is problematic. Some of these structures showed extraordinary masonry built in cloisonné style, with ashlar porous blocks and brick ornaments imitating Kufic lettering at the joint. The finds from these excavations, especially the pottery, were remarkable and provided additional information on the assemblage recovered in Orionos Street.[12]

The so-called '*Proasteion*' or '*Borgo*', sometimes '*Vourgo*' ('suburb'), as it was named in the written sources, was situated outside the urban enclosure, and it extended over a wide area east of the fortification walls.[13] In this area (of the probably extended Jewish quarter, known as '*Giudecca*'), archaeological research has been limited until now.[14] Some excavated burials confirmed the view that the town's cemeteries were located outside the Medieval city.[15] Recently, rescue excavations such as the one in Orionos Street revealed more evidence of habitation outside the ramparts.[16] These recent salvages made clear that Chalcis experienced an increase in economic and demographic growth at least from the 10th century onwards.

THE EXCAVATION

The rescue excavation at Orionos Street was conducted by the archaeologist of the former 23rd Ephorate of Byzantine Antiquities Giannis Vaxevanis in May 2007 at the owner's request to construct a modern building on this plot, and was completed in September of the same year.[17] The excavation plot was located in the so-called *Proasteion* or *Vourgo/Borgo* area ca. 120 m. east of Frizi Street, where the northern section of the Medieval fortification wall was recovered, and therefore lay outside the city walls (Fig. 5).[18]

The size of the excavated area was ca. 100 square meters. Architectural remains of the Byzantine period were recovered here, as well as large quantities of various finds in a very fragmentary condition. Built remains of earlier periods are noticeably absent, since the borders of the ancient and Early Byzantine city were different than the ones of the Medieval city.[19] Noteworthy is also the fact that Ottoman remains were scarce, although the extramural area was largely inhabited during this period.[20]

The most prominent architectural remains are situated in the southern half of the plot, where the dig revealed part of a building which was identified as the *hypokauston* of a bath (Fig. 6). This consisted of a large rectangular hall, measuring 7,90 x 3,00 m, formed by three walls (Walls 1, 1a and 2). The walls have a maximum width of 0,73 m, are founded on bedrock, and show an exceptionally good masonry of roughly hewn stones, rubble, and bricks which are placed both on horizontal and vertical joints. A strong lime mortar has been used as bonding material. Wall 2 has been preserved in greater length than the others; it measures 9.05 meters in length and 2.05 in height, and extends across the whole length of the plot.

The interior of this hall has undergone considerable destruction; however, a few archaeological remains allow its identification with the *hypokauston* of a bath. In particular, the interior (south) surface of Wall 2 bears two vertical recesses of rectangular section, measuring 0,28 x 0,30 m, along its height. The two recesses are situated 3.60 m apart from each other. They may be identified with air pipes which were often constructed in the walls of a *hypokauston*. Thanks to these constructions, the hot air produced by the fire furnace (*praefurnium*) in the basement could circulate into the hot bath hall (*caldarium*) and the warm bath hall (*tepidarium*), both of which were built over the *hypokauston*, and heat them.

The identification of the excavated hall with a *hypokauston* is supported by the recovery of three large blocks of hard limestone, found in its eastern part (close to Wall 2). Of these, two were found *in situ* situated vertically on the bedrock, while the third one was uncovered leaning obliquely against the first block. The first block measures

0,87 x 0,44 x 0,43 m, while the third (lying) block measures 0,93 x 0,39 x 0,42 m. The second block, 0.87 m long, appeared only at the face of the trench; it was revealed only on one side, which was 0,40 m wide, while the rest is covered by the dumped soil. The three stone blocks may be identified with columns (*pilae*) of the *hypokauston*, which sustained the floor of the overlying hall of the bath. Their height, shorter than 1.0 m, strengthens this identification, since *pilae* are normally between 0.65 and 1.04 m high.[21] The absence of other stone columns from the remaining area may be due to the extended destruction of the building. Moreover, it is not impossible that the other *pilae* were made of clay, and were thus not preserved.

Finally, the lower parts of the walls of the hall bear traces of burning, and thus offer an additional element which supports the identification of the building as a bath. The natural greenish bedrock was used as the floor of the underground rooms of the bath house, a phenomenon observed in other examples of baths.[22]

The above-mentioned hall is connected with at least two further underground halls, as attested by an arched opening in Wall 1 and a rectangular opening in Wall 1a. The arch of the opening of Wall 1 is constructed exclusively by bricks and strong lime mortar. Investigation of the two further halls was unfortunately impossible, as these extend beyond the limits of the excavation, in the open courtyard of the proposed building and in the immediate vicinity of the modern building adjacent to the south. However, one of the trial trenches opened south of Wall 1a revealed a vertically set cylindrical pillar made of hard limestone, measuring 0,99 x 0,51 m. This was probably a further column (*pila*) of the bath. The hall south of Wall 1a may have been a second hall with a *hypokauston*.

The interior of the hall (defined by Walls 1, 1a and 2) was found full of soil dumped in a single phase, which contained many sherds of glazed tablewares, unglazed coarse wares, storage and transport vessels (amphorae), tile and brick fragments, vitrified masses of clay, copper and iron slag, as well as animal bones, sea shells and even a few human bones (although the latter were found in much lesser quantities than the animal remains).[23] The dumped soil also contained sections of demolished walls, made of rubble and hewn stones, bricks and mortar. Moreover, the soil often showed traces of burning.

It seems, therefore, that the interior of the *hypokauston* was filled with soil during a period, in which it had ceased to be in function. The majority of pottery finds from its interior date between the mid-12th and the early 13th centuries. One coin, which was found in the dump, was identified as a half *tetarteron* of Emperor Manuel I Comnenus (1143-1180).[24] The abandonment of the re-use of the building should be therefore dated to the early or mid 13th century.

The construction of the bath should probably be dated to the 10th century, based on the excavated finds and especially the pottery found in the foundation trench of the northern (exterior) face of Wall 2, which dates from the 10th to the 11th century. This chronology is supported by the masonry used for the three walls of the bath. Furthermore, most of the Byzantine coins from the Orionos Street excavation which have been cleaned so far, seem to date between the mid 10th and the late 12th centuries.[25]

A long ceramic pipe was uncovered along the northern part of the excavation plot. The pipe runs along the whole length of the plot with an east-west direction and may be connected with the function of the bath. The revealed part of the pipe measures 5.25 m in length, and it clearly continues beyond the limits of the excavation plot. The pipe is constructed on the bedrock surface in its greatest part. A small section continues through the bedrock, which has been hewn and hollowed for this purpose. The pipe is constructed with small cylindrical shafts made of clay, which are cemented into each other with strong lime mortar. The mortar has been set into a ditch in a shape with a trapezoid section, and is wider at the upper part (max. width of upper surface 0.35 m) and narrower at the lower part. The height of the pipe ranges from 0.07 to 0.20 cm.

Further architectural remains were uncovered in the remaining northern part of the plot. These belonged to many construction phases, thus indicating the continuous function and use of the site. At least thirteen walls and seven floor sections were found; however their fragmentary and often bad preservation did not permit a clear definition of their function. Walls 4 and 5 show particular interest: they define a large rectangular room oriented east-west, which lies parallel with the long axis of the *hypokauston*. Its use could be connected with the bath, since Wall 4 is perpendicular to Wall 2 of the *hypokauston*, even though it belongs to a slightly later chronological phase.

The northern half of the excavated area was probably occupied by constructions which belonged to workshops, as indicated by two circular pits and a floor made of beaten earth with traces of burning. The recovery of exceptionally large quantities of vitrified clay, masses of iron and copper, copper folios, tripod stilts and ceramic wasters supported the view that the area was used for craftsmanship. Based on the ceramic finds, the constructions of the northern excavated part could be dated between the 10th and early 13th centuries.

SUMMER SCHOOLS: PROCESSING THE FINDS

As mentioned before, the Orionos Street-excavation yielded huge quantities of pottery sherds. In some parts, these fragments exceeded the amount of soil at the excavated plot, which ultimately resulted in hundreds of large plastic bags filled with ceramics ending up in the depot of the Ephorate. In order to process all these enormous amounts, the former director of the Ephorate Dr. Kalamara and her staff invited J. Vroom and her team in 2011 to study this material from Orionos Street. In order to do this, we came with the idea to organize summer schools for groups of maximum ten students in collaboration with the Ephorate and the Netherlands Institute at Athens.[26]

After three study seasons (of about three weeks, or about 18 working days each year) in the summers of 2013, 2014 and 2015, all the finds were sorted out, recorded, documented, entered in a database, drawn and photographed. The students were able to record more bags and more sherds every year (Table 1).[27] In the end, circa 66.390 diagnostic pottery fragments were documented (Fig. 7). Apart from counting, all the ceramic fragments of various types were also weighed for quantification purposes.[28] In Fig. 8 it is possible to distinguish the total weight of ceramics per pottery type (2,414.78 kg), and interestingly enough amphorae account for the largest group (with 37 percent) in this pie chart.

Considering the ratio between glazed and unglazed pottery, it is clear from the first pie chart in Fig. 7 that there is more unglazed plain pottery counted (ca. 75 percent). This is expected, because unglazed pottery is more common, easier to produce and thus cheaper than glazed ceramics. Furthermore, it is noteworthy that approximately 759 fragments of over-fired pottery types and wasters were counted by the team (Fig. 5). Wasters of numerous pottery types were recorded, ranging from unglazed products to vitrified fragments or even completely distorted pieces. In addition, kiln furniture, tripod stilts, kiln separators and a potter's wheel were identified among the finds as further proof of local production here during Byzantine times. Due to its location, this pottery workshop undoubtedly depended on the clay beds in the Lelantine Plain for the procurement of its raw material (Fig. 9). These finds made it very clear that we had a substantial pottery production site at our hands.

The recovery of large quantities of copper and iron slag, of masses of iron and copper, of copper folios (laminas), of semi-worked fragments, of a part of a tuyère and of a small crucible supported the idea that the excavated area at Orionos Street was also used for metal production. The metal finds are usually made of copper (among which two large fragments of copper plates), while sporadically iron wasters of production are found. Based on copper stains or small masses stuck on some pottery fragments, this metal workshop could be dated to the 12th to mid 13th century.

In addition, finds of glass slag and glass waste, fragments of glass masses of small cullet fragments and of small glass blocks suggested that secondary glass production took place as well. In addition, examples of small finds included objects made of clay (animal figurines and small square boxes of an unknown purpose), of stone (grinding stones) and of bone (loom weights, buttons and a belt buckle). Finally, a variety of remains of land and sea animals from the excavated plot indicated a rich Medieval diet – or even industrial processing (as was the case with the shellfish *murex purpurea* that was used for the colouring of imperial silk textiles).[29]

The documentation of the pottery finds from Orionos Street revealed that the dating of the ceramics belonged to two main chronological phases of activity. The upper excavation layers yielded pottery which belonged to the later phase of use (ca. 12th-13th centuries), while the lower excavation layers contained finds which belonged to an earlier phase (ca. 10th-11th centuries). The earliest phase (10th-11th c.) was more present in trenches 2b, 2c and 4, whereas the sherds of the second later phase (12th-13th c.) were more common in trenches 1, 2 and 3 (Figs. 6 and 11).

After finalising the last internship (the Master Class of 2016), huge quantities of material from the 2007 Orionos street excavation had been processed. This result proved a successful method of summer schools incorporating a number of students in archaeological post-excavation processing of large amounts of finds (both pottery as metal, glass and other materials). This approach can be deemed successful in twofold: firstly, it involved BA and MA students in archaeological research to an academic level, which is unparalleled in most internships in Greece; and secondly, it has enabled a relatively small group of scholars to study significant quantities of excavated material in a relatively short period of time, by efficiently utilising a labour force generated by students. This innovative and stimulating format of investigation is certainly applicable to other post-excavation projects throughout Greece and other parts in the Mediterranean.[30]

CERAMIC FINDS FROM THE UPPER PHASE

The majority of the pottery finds in the excavated plot at Orionos Street belonged to the upper excavation layers, and thus to the later phase of industrial activity. This is characterized by the recovery of huge amounts of numerous decorated glazed tablewares (covered with a lead glaze) and amphora fragments, the last ones mostly belonging to the so-called 'Günsenin 3 amphora' and its variants (among which transitional types).[31] Locally made glazed ceramics frequently contained pieces of Incised Sgraffito Ware, Champlevé Ware and Monochrome Glazed Ware, although considerably lesser quantities and smaller fragments of Slip-Painted Ware, Green and Brown Painted Ware, (Painted) Fine Sgraffito Ware and Splashed Ware were also recognized in the Orionos Street assemblage.[32] Furthermore, through trade contacts with other parts of the Mediterranean imported glazed pottery in this phase included fragments of Glazed White Ware II from Constantinople, Zeuxippus Ware and Painted Ware from western Turkey, Islamic Glazed Fritware from Syria, and Maiolica (plus imitations of Roulette/Veneto Ware) from Italy.

Günsenin 3 amphorae – The Günsenin 3 amphora type was first identified by Nergis Günsenin followed by John Hayes, coined by the last one as number 61 in his Saraçhane series.[33] These vessels are between 53 and 70 cm tall, and their walls ca. 1.0-1.3 cm thick. Their body is carrot-shaped. In addition, they have a high conical narrow neck, an outwardly thickened rim, and two ovals handles which rise high up above the rim level. The shoulder and upper body are treated with a fine comb, which leaves characteristic thin parallel incisions on the exterior surface (Fig. 10).

A distribution map demonstrates the proportion of the Günsenin 3 amphora finds (shown in green in the pie charts) in relation to other amphorae (shown in blue in the pie charts) at the excavated trenches of the Orionos Street excavation (Fig. 11). Interesting to see is that of a total of 4 trenches, trench 4 is the only trench where other amphorae are more common than Günsenin 3 amphorae. These last ones are, on the other hand, clearly more present in trenches 1 and 3, which are considered to be the dump places of the Chalcis workshop.

Transport jars of the Günsenin 3 type have been recovered at many coastal sites in Greece, Turkey, Cyprus and Italy, whereas a large number of finds can also be discerned in the Black Sea region.[34] They have regularly been found in contexts of the (mid) 12th and (early) 13th centuries, so they were certainly the most commonly used amphorae during this period: not only in Byzantium but also in areas economically and politically connected to the Empire. During the Saraçhane excavations in Constantinople/Istanbul, for example, they occur in contexts which have been dated from the mid-12th to the early 13th century.[35] In addition, a cargo of 54 amphorae of this type was recovered at the Alonissos-Pelagonissos shipwreck, which has been dated to the mid-12th century (Fig. 12, no. 1).[36] These jars were transported in this ship's cargo together with glazed tablewares, among which examples of Fine Sgraffito Ware, Slip-painted Ware and a few 'hybrid' dishes where Fine Sgraffito designs were combined with Champlevé motifs (see Fig. 12 for shipwrecks transporting Günsenin 3 amphorae in combination with Fine Sgraffito Ware).[37]

Scholars initially formulated the hypothesis that this amphora type was produced in the Aegean, perhaps in Attica or Boeotia.[38] After 30 years of study, it now appears to have had multiple production sites. Study of the pottery finds of the Orionos Street plot shows that one key production site of the Günsenin 3 amphorae was in this extramural locality of Chalcis. This conclusion is based on three facts: firstly, the recovery of many over-fired, vitrified and deformed fragments of Günsenin 3 amphorae; secondly, the vast quantities of Günsenin 3 amphora fragments recovered during the excavation;

and thirdly, the fact that the fabric of the Günsenin 3 amphorae is identical with the fabric used for the local production of glazed tablewares, unglazed coarse wares and tiles – as has been confirmed by petrographical and archaeometrical analyses.[39]

It needs to be stressed, though, that this amphora type was also manufactured at other sites on Euboea and in Greece. At Mylopotamos (Rethymno area, Crete), for instance, Günsenin 3 amphorae have been recovered, made of a fabric which was characterized as local.[40] Furthermore, Günsenin 3 amphora fragments were identified at Eleutherna (Rethymno area, Crete), which appear to have made of a fabric variety very similar to Günsenin 1 amphorae imported from Ganos. This led to the hypothesis by Natalia Poulou that Günsenin 3 amphorae may have been produced at Ganos as well.[41] At Kythera (Agios Georgios sto Vouno), at least three different fabric varieties of Günsenin 3 amphorae were identified so far.[42]

There are strong indications that Günsenin 3 amphorae were produced in large quantities at Chalcis.[43] The local 'Chalcis type' has indeed been found at numerous sites in and around Euboea: not only during several rescue excavations at Chalcis, but also at Aliveri, Anthedon (Boeotia), the Boeotia Survey, the Marathon Bay, as well as at the shipwrecks of Portolafia, Peristera, the Pagasetic Gulf and the northern Sporades (among which the ones recovered at Pelagonnisos-Alonnisos).[44] This suggests that it was produced in considerable amounts for export: that is to say, not only for regional demand in the city's surroundings but also for wider inter-regional distribution in the Aegean. Written sources state that Euboean wine was renowned and exported to Constantinople.[45] It may therefore be assumed that Günsenin 3 amphorae, which have been found in the Byzantine capital, possibly carried wine from vineyards in the vicinity of Chalcis.[46] In fact, a wine press was discovered at Mytikas in the fertile Lelantine Plain (east of Chalcis) which had functioned in the 12th-13th centuries.

A locally made variant of the standard Günsenin 3 amphora was also recognized within the Orionos Street assemblage. It has a broad vertical rim, cylindrical neck, and handles rising high up above the rim level (Fig. 13 above). Its surface is covered with a creamish slip (5 YR 7/3), but its handles are often thinner than the handles of the classical Günsenin 3 amphora type. Furthermore, it has an orange-red fabric (7.5 YR 7/4 to 7/6) with many fine to medium quartz, some fine limestone, very many small voids and grass inclusions in the handles (Fig. 13 below). Due to the fragmentary nature of our material, we have not yet been able to establish the complete shape of this local imitation. Due to its thinner walls and smaller proportions, this Günsenin 3 amphora variant may have been a carrot-shaped Günsenin 20 / Todorova 20 amphora.[47] More examples of this smaller variant have been recovered during the Boeotia Survey on rural sites in Chalcis' hinterland.[48]

Glazed tablewares – Large quantities of decorated glazed tablewares were recovered at the Orionos Street plot, especially in its southern half (Trenches 1 and 3). In fact, the excavations at Orionos Street in Chalcis revealed a workshop area with cross-craft interaction, among which the manufacture of unglazed and glazed ceramics. These last ones included various types of the so-called 'Middle Byzantine Production Group' (shortened to 'MBP'), such as Slip-painted Ware, Green and Brown Painted Ware, (Painted) Fine Sgraffito Ware, Incised Sgraffito Ware and Champlevé Ware (Figs. 14a-b and 17).[49] This is a group of glazed tablewares with similar characteristics (such as fabric, vessel form, surface treatment, use of lead glazes), but with different decoration techniques, which co-existed or followed each other in the period from circa the late 11th/early 12th to the mid 13th century.[50] Most shapes are shallow dishes and bowls for the serving and consumption of food on the table, although two small joined cups with a small handle in the centre also existed for holding condiments (such as spices).[51]

The majority of this MBP group found during the Orionos Street excavation consisted of Incised Sgraffito Ware and Champlevé Ware.[52] These pottery types have mostly been dated to the late 12th and early 13th centuries. In both pottery types, the whitish slip of the surface (7.5 YR 8/1) is cut away with a broad blunt tool so that the decorative motifs appear in a low relief, while details are rendered with fine incisions.[53] The motifs are often placed in a central medallion, which is usually surrounded by a decorative band. The most common motif of the Champlevé dishes from Orionos Street is a rabbit or hare in a gouged medallion or tondo, although other animals and even human figures also occur.[54]

The fabric of the dishes and bowls with Champlevé decoration is reddish-brown (2.5 YR 7/6 to 5 YR 7/4), fine to medium, with a few limestone, mica and some tiny to medium white quartz inclusions. Macroscopically it appears very similar to the fabric of the Günsenin 3 amphorae, and it is assumed that it is a finer version of the same fabric. This would suggest that Champlevé Ware dishes, which were produced at some production centres of the Byzantine world, were certainly manufactured at Chalcis (see Fig. 15 for its distribution on shipwrecks). This hypothesis is supported by the recovery at the Orionos Street plot of an unfinished Champlevé Ware dish with the depiction of a rabbit or hare. The vessel has been slipped, decorated and fired in a kiln, but the glaze is totally missing from the surface (Fig. 16).

Incised Sgraffito Ware is the next most common category of glazed decorated pottery found in the Orionos Street plot. The decoration is thickly gouged through the white slip (7.5 YR 8/1) with a broad-bladed tool. The vessel is afterwards covered with a transparent yellow, green or colourless glaze.[55] The production of this pottery type has been dated to the late 12th and early 13th centuries, but this can now be extended to the 13th century.⁵⁶ These dishes were made of the same local fabric which characterizes Champléve Ware vessels, and therefore seemed to have been locally made, although we need to keep in mind that other production centres surely also existed in the (western) Aegean (such as at Corinth and Athens).⁵⁷

The decoration of Incised Sgraffito Ware dishes found at Orionos Street includes geometric, floral and faunal motifs (e.g., birds, fishes), as well as depictions of human beings (among which at least 35 sherds with representations of warriors). The figure of a warrior with armour, spear and shield can for instance be seen on a dish that we were able to reconstruct of fragments from various contexts within the Orionos Street plot (Fig. 17).⁵⁸ Glazed dishes and bowls with comparable incised designs published from Thebes, Athens, Argos, Nauplio and Corinth show a representative sample of the shapes, motifs and glaze colours which occur in the vessels from the Orionos Street plot, even though it is not certain if they were manufactured in the same workshop.⁵⁹

A cargo with similar looking Incised Sgraffito Ware has been found at the Kavalliani shipwreck, 35 km south-east of Chalcis (Fig. 18, no. 3).⁶⁰ In addition, more wrecks yielded cargoes with this type of glazed tableware, not only on both sides of the Aegean but also in the Black Sea region and along the coast of south-western Turkey (see Fig. 18). Apparently, Incised Sgraffito Ware was travelling together with Günsenin 3 amphorae during maritime transports, as is shown by finds from some recovered shipwrecks in the Aegean (Fig. 19).

Monochrome Glazed Wares comprise another large part of glazed tablewares from the Orionos Street excavation. Apart from dishes, bowls and jugs, they include standing lamps with spouted cups for holding oil and a wick. Slip-painted Ware, Green and Brown Painted Ware and Fine Sgraffito Ware were recovered as well, albeit in lesser quantities than Incised Sgraffito Ware and Champléve Ware. Glazed tablewares of the aforementioned types have been found during excavations in- and outside the urban enclosure of Chalcis as well as on many rural sites in Boeotia, showing thus not only the extent of supply to this city but also to provincial markets and/or communities in its hinterland.⁶¹ The glazed tablewares from the Orionos Street plot suggest that the later phase of use of the excavated buildings should be dated between the second half of the 12th and the middle of the 13th centuries.

Unglazed plain wares and coarse wares – The pottery workshop excavated in Orionos Street at Chalcis further produced a wide range of unglazed plain wares and coarse wares in substantial quantities. These last ones included cooking jars, spouted jugs, large storage jars (*pithoi*) and many varieties of wide-rimmed basins.⁶² The most common type of late 12th- to early 13th-century cooking pot in this assemblage has a tall folded rim, and is slightly concave on the exterior with a pronounced horizontal ridge on the upper body and a rounded base (Fig. 20). Such vessels were definitely connected to the preparation and consumption of heated food during Byzantine times.[63]

Large quantities of unglazed utilitarian vessels of a plain character were recovered as well. These included jugs, flasks, basins, lids (with a handle on top), money boxes, storage vessels and tiles, which were used for various daily life activities such as the serving and pouring of liquids, the preparation and storage of food or of other commodities. They are mostly made in the same local fabric as the Günsenin 3 amphorae and the glazed tablewares manufactured at the Orionos Street workshop. Many fragments were found over-fired or vitrified, which suggests that their place of production must surely have been near the excavated plot.

CERAMIC FINDS FROM THE LOWER PHASE

Pottery of an earlier phase was mostly found in the lower excavation layers of the northern part of the Orionos Street plot (in particular, in Trench 4 and Sub-trenches 2B and 2C). This phase included many fragments of decorated but unglazed wares, among which Unglazed Incised Ware[64] and Unglazed Gouged Ware.[65] The main shapes were jugs and jars which sometimes had burnished surfaces.

Apart from unglazed decorated wares, these layers also yielded relatively early categories of imported glazed tablewares, in particular Glazed White Ware II and Polychrome Ware from Constantinople which were both made of a kaolin clay.[66] These imports cover the period of the 10th and 11th centuries, and thus set a chronological date for the period of use of some walls and structures excavated at Orionos Street.[67]

Amphorae – Besides the above mentioned wares, the lower layers also included fragments of three distinctive amphora types. The majority of these containers could be diagnosed as belonging to the types 'Günsenin 2 amphora' and 'Otranto 1 amphora', as well as to a so-far unknown local type.[68]

Günsenin 2 amphorae are well-known, in particular from sites in the Aegean, Turkey and the Black Sea.[69] They can generally be dated between the late 10th and early 12th centuries. The exact chronology of some Günsenin 2 rim fragments recovered at Orionos Street has not been established yet, but they clearly belong to the early phase of occupation.[70]

In addition, pieces of Otranto 1 amphorae occurred in considerably less numbers; only body and handle fragments were preserved in the Orionos Street plot. Otranto 1 amphorae were mainly produced in Apulia and probably also at Corinth during the

10th and the first half of the 11th centuries.[71] They circulated in western Greece, the Adriatic and the Aegean.[72] Fragments of Otranto 1 amphorae were for example recovered at nearby Thebes, as well as on eight Boeotian sites in this city's surroundings.[73]

The third amphora type is as yet not well-known, and seems to be a local product. It has a tall conical rim with a flat upper surface, a narrow cylindrical neck, and two handles with an oval section attached to the upper part of the rim. Its ovoid body often bears a gouged wavy line on the shoulder. Macroscopic examination of its well-fired orange-red fabric (2.5 YR 7/4) suggests that this amphora type is made of a fine, very well-levigated and hard version of the local clay with some fine to large limestone (sometimes with spalling) and voids.

The same fabric was used for the manufacture of later ceramic products at Chalcis, among which Günsenin 3 amphorae and glazed tablewares of the 12th and 13th centuries. Some fragments of the third amphora type found at the Orionos Street excavations were vitrified and completely deformed due to over-firing in a kiln, so these wasters offer further evidence for its local production. To date, a variant of the third amphora type has possibly been found outside Chalcis, during a rescue excavation at Dokos (Aggelou plot; see fig. 21).[74]

Unglazed Plain Wares – Noteworthy among the finds in the Orionos plot excavation are unglazed plain jugs and jars of a finer fabric with an incised and/or gouged decoration on the exterior surface within the assemblage of the lower excavation layers at Orionos street. Similar looking vessels with a gouged body were first distinguished by John Hayes in his Saraçhane typology as 'Fine Orange-Red Burnished Ware', although we now define them rather as 'Unglazed Gouged (and Burnished) Ware'.[75]

The fabric of the fragments with a gouged decoration is soft, fine and has a pale reddish orange (2.5 YR 7/4) to orange colour (5 YR 7/6). The soapy clay contains some medium to big lumps of limestone, a few fine micaceous particles and mudstone. The surface bears no slip. The exterior surface of sherds can be decorated with light vertical burnishing and vertical gouged grooves.

The shape of the fragments indicates that they once belonged to a closed vessel. Forms included jugs with a flat base, a vertical shoulder and a short neck. These jugs are often decorated with (vertical) gouged stripes on the outside (Figs. 22a-b). It is clear that an important production centre of this unglazed, red-bodied ware was located at the Orionos Street plot outside the fortified walls of Chalcis, because we recorded over-fired wasters of this pottery type in this excavated plot. In addition, this ware was recognized at nine rural sites in Boeotia across the Euripus Strait, which strongly suggests that it was regionally distributed in the immediate hinterland of the Orionos Street workshop.[76]

During excavations at Pelopidou Street in the old city centre of Thebes, more sherds of this red-bodied gouged ware (this time also decorated with shallow incised/gouged crosses) were found in a rubbish pit of the Middle Byzantine period.[77] These Theban fragments displayed the same fabric colour (red-orange), the same decoration-technique (light vertical grooving/gouging and burnishing) and the same shape (a flat-based, round-bodied jug) as Hayes 'Fine Orange-Red Burnished Ware'.[78]

Indeed, this pottery type has been recovered during the St. Polyeuktos Church excavations in the Saraçhane excavations at Constantinople/modern Istanbul, where it was dated to the late 10th and 11th centuries.[79] Apart from finds in the Byzantine capital, similar grooved vessels were found in 9th to late 11th century deposits at excavations of Corinth and of Otranto (southern Italy) – although the Otranto fragments have a different yellowish, calcareous fabric.[80] Furthermore, they were recognized in 10th- and 11th-century contexts on several sites in Russia (Cherson; Novgorod), western Turkey (Ephesus), southern Albania (Butrint) and western Kosovo up to now.[81] Burnishing of the surface of unglazed jugs seems to have started at Corinth in the second half of the 11th century.[82]

Additionally, the Orionos Street excavations yielded fragments and wasters of unglazed closed vessels of the Middle Byzantine period with a simple linear incised decoration on the exterior body (Fig. 23). They belonged to the type 'Unglazed Incised Ware', a term that was earlier introduced by Vroom as a purely technical description of this ceramic group.[83] The fabric is soft, orange-red in colour (2.5 YR 6/8) with some coarse limestone, a few fine mica and has a soapy feel. Most of the fragments found at Chalcis and at seventeen rural sites in Boeotia have an incised, wavy decoration of 'scribbles' on the exterior body.[84] The shape is mostly of a closed vessel (a jar or jug) combined with a grooved neck, although other forms (such as small boxes) exist as well within the Orionos Street assemblage.[85]

Some fragments are identical to incised jars found at Constantinople (in the Mangana Palace excavations) and at Thessaloniki.[86] In this last city, an analogous vessel (*lagenio*) was discovered together with some Günsenin 3 amphorae during the restoration of the St. Sophia church, where it has been dated to the end of the 11th and the beginning of the 12th century.[87] This small-sized jar was surely used for the transport, storage and pouring of liquids.[88]

A similar looking fragment was also excavated at Nichoria on the south-western Peloponnese, where it was found in a late 9th-11th century context with Glazed White Ware from Constantinople.[89] More sherds (without a clear dating context) were not only recovered at rural settlements on the island of Keos,[90] but also at rural sites in eastern Phocis, closer to Chalcis.[91]

Lastly, more examples of this ware were found during excavations at nearby Thebes.[92] This happened in a period (especially from the 11th century onwards) when this city became more densely inhabited and its environs witnessed a period of prosperity.[93] In fact, the city attracted as a vibrant provincial market many foreigners (among which Italian merchants from Venice and Genoa) because of its agricultural and pastoral products as well as of its high-quality silk industry.[94]

CONCLUSION

In this chapter we have presented a first selection of ceramic finds from a hitherto unknown industrial zone in a suburb (known as *'Borgo'*) outside the fortified walls of Medieval Chalcis. Rescue excavations at Orionos Street revealed here part of a building which was initially (on the 10th-11th centuries) used as the *hypokauston* of a bath and later (in the 12th-13th centuries) re-used for the dumping of industrial waste. The choice for this extramural location (a bath complex) was not unusual in Byzantine times. Next to this bath, other architectural remains and circular pits were recovered which could be identified as workspaces of craftsmen due to the large quantities of vitrified clay, iron and copper masses, as well as the existence of potter's tools and misfired ceramic products.

So far, evidence for mixed long-period production of a range of glazed tablewares adorned with innovative decoration techniques, of unglazed transport vessels (amphorae) and of unglazed coarse wares and plain wares (with gouged and incised decoration techniques) has been established at the Orionos street plot, specifically with the help of kiln equipment and many over- and misfired wasters. In addition, slags of metal and glass suggest local activities of other contemporary industries in the excavated area.

The workshops at Orionos Street had thus a miscellaneous capacity of cross-craft production (not only pottery, but also metal ware, glass, bone etc.), and were part of a multi-layered commercial system with local, regional, interregional and long-distance distribution of locally made glazed tablewares and amphorae within and beyond the Byzantine Empire. These last containers (among which Günsenin 2 and 3 amphorae and their variants) certainly transported bulk goods (like wine) from Chalcis' rich hinterland. Undoubtedly, the neighbouring fertile Lelantine Plain functioned as a vital source for the export of agricultural products in such ceramic transport jars (conveniently made of high-quality clays from the same plain).

This can be determined from mixed ship cargoes with locally made ceramic products (both amphorae and glazed tablewares), which were recovered on shipwrecks near Euboea, in the Pagasetic Gulf and in the northern Sporades – although their spread is still under study.[95] In addition, there was a regional consumer demand for the ceramic merchandises from the Chalcis workshop, because its products were not only widely distributed to other urban markets (ranging from Thebes to Constantinople) but also to provincial rural settlements in the nearby countryside in Boeotia and on Euboea.[96]

It is our hope that the preliminary discussion of the Orionos Street finds in this paper will contribute to a better understanding of the history of Medieval Chalcis as a vital commercial and industrial hub functioning within an intricate distribution system, as well as to a better understanding of the complex nature of production, transit trade and consumption in the wider Aegean area during Middle Byzantine and Late Byzantine/Frankish times.

ACKNOWLEDGEMENTS

First of all, we would like to thank the current Ephor, Dr. A. Simosi, and the previous Ephor, Dr. Pari Kalamara, and the complete staff of the Ephorate of Antiquities of Euboea in Chalkida for their collaboration, help and assistance. Many thanks also go to the Byzantine archaeologists Dr Nikos Kontogiannis, Dr Stefania Skartsis, Dr Evi Dafi and Mrs Alexandra Kostarelli for their wonderful assistance and help during the years 2013-2016. Mrs Adamantia Panagopoulou and Mr Dimitris Karamouzas are much thanked for the conservation and restoration of some dishes and vesssels from the Orionos Street excavation. Furthermore, the previous directors Dr Winfred van der Put and Dr Chris Tytgat of the Netherlands Institute at Athens and the NIA staff are greatly thanked for all their efforts for the summer schools in 2013-2015 and the master class in 2016.

Furthermore, we would like to thank all the students who were part of the summer schools and workshops. This project was unique in the sense that this was the first time that international students were allowed to work extensively with archaeological materials from a Greek Ephorate, a partnership which proved to be very successful for all parties involved. Consequently, it our sincere hope that the fruitful approach of the project will have its successors in the future at other places throughout Greece.

Finally, we would like to honour two great scholars. The first one is Cees Bakhuizen, who wrote already in the 1970s groundbreaking books on Chalcis with titles as *'Studies in the Topography of Chalcis on Euboea'*, and *'Chalcis-in-Euboea: Iron and the Chalcidians Abroad'*. The second one is David Jacoby, who wrote extensively about the Medieval history of Chalcis and the island of Euboea. This chapter is therefore dedicated to their memory.

Year	2013	2014	2015	Total
Number of bags	47	153	210	410
Number of sherds	11.781	20.848	33.761	66.390

TABLE 1 – Chalcis, Orionos plot: quantities of the bags and sherds processed during the summer schools of 2013-2015 (J. Vroom).

Year	2013	2014	2015	Total
Weight of sherds	345.391	682.537	1.386.822	2.414.750

TABLE 2 – Total weight of sherds of the pottery finds from the 2007 Orionos street excavation processed during the Chalcis summer schools (J. Vroom).

NOTES

1. This excavation was carried out for the Ephorate by G. Vaxevanis under the auspices of the previous Ephor, Dr. Pari Kalamara; see also Vroom *et al.* 2021, and for more Byzantine finds in Chalcis the contribution by Kontogiannis and Skartsis in this volume.
2. We prefer to continue using the name of 'Chalcis' in the rest of this chapter.
3. See for the use of the term 'Late Byzantine/Frankish', Vroom 2011, 409-10.
4. This strait is subject to strong tidal currents, which reverse direction approximately four times a day lasting for about six hours each.
5. Triantaphyllopoulos 1990, 174-84; cf. Kontogiannis 2012, 30-35; Kalamara 2015, 59, stating that the building of the walls should be dated before the mid 9th century.
6. This is for example shown by the seal of an anonymous *kommerkiarios* of Euripus, dated to ca. 750-850; cf. Kalamara 2015, 58, fig. 64.
7. Only a small part of the fortification walls is still preserved at Chalcis, in which a small ethnographic museum is nowadays housed; see Kalamara 2015, fig. 63.
8. Mamaloukos 2020, 631-36.
9. The latter is recently restored under the auspices of the 23rd Ephorate of Byzantine Antiquities; cf. Kontogiannis 2012; Kalamara 2015, figs. 68-69; Kontogiannis and Skartsis 2020.
10. Kontogiannis 2012, 42-43.
11. Triantaphyllos 1990; Gerousi *et al.* 2007; 2009.
12. Kontogiannis 2012; Skartsis and Vaxevanis 2017; see also the contribution of Kontogiannis and Skartsis in this volume.
13. Koder 1973, 86-88; Triantaphyllopoulos 1990, 197-200; Kontogiannis 2012, 33-34 and 42-45.
14. Koder 1973, 71.
15. Kalamara 2015, 60.
16. Gerousi *et al.* 2007; 2009; Skartsis and Vaxevanis 2017.
17. Vaxevanis 2007, 601-603, figs. 26-29.
18. Papadakis 1975, 277-317.
19. The ancient and Early Byzantine city of Chalcis lay at the foot of Mount Vathrovouni, from the Arethousa Spring and Agios Stephanos to the outskirts of Liani Ammos and Velibaba. This is the area of the modern bus station (KTEL). During the Byzantine period, the city moved to the Euripus Strait, within the borders of the modern city centre; cf. Triantaphyllopoulos 1990, 174-84; Kontogiannis 2012, 30-35, Kalamara 2015, 57-60.
20. A bath and a fountain of the Ottoman era are preserved in excellent condition in Tzavella street 5 / Anatoliou street, in an area previously inhabited by officials of the Ottoman army, and in close proximity to the Orionos Street plot; see also Kanetaki and Stylianou 2008, 88-89.
21. Yegül 1992, 357; Eleutheratou 2000, 302, 307.
22. Eleutheratou 2000, 302, 303; Chatzidimitriou 2000, 21- 22; see for more general information on Middle Byzantine

23 baths and their daily life function, Bouras 2002, 525-26; Ousterhout 2013; Revthiadou and Raptis 2014, 5-6 and 13.

23 Large quantities of a diverse composition of land and sea animal species and various types of sea shells (among which the *murex purpurea*) were recovered at Orionos Street, of which the last ones are referring to the use of purple dye in the Byzantine silk industry; cf. Jacoby 1991-1992, 481.

24 The coins of the excavation are currently at the stage of conservation and will be studied in more detail by the archaeologist Eirini Konstantou.

25 Among the 107 coins recovered from the Orionos Street plot, 57 have not been examined yet, since they are at the stage of conservation.

26 Apart from getting lectures, the students specifically learned during the summer schools how to deal with processing techniques.

27 After these summer schools we were able to pack all the finds in boxes, so that we could resume our research in more detail starting with a master class in 2016.

28 See also Costa 2018.

29 During the 2016 Masterclass one RMA student from Leiden, Janine van Noorden, started to work on this material, under the supervision of Professor Thijs van Kolfschoten, and this archaeozoological research will continue.

30 During the summer schools, masterclass and workshop since 2013, the students visited several sites, museums and churches in Greece: not only in Athens but also on the island of Euboea. We believe that it is important and even essential to train a next generation of young students and scholars how to deal with pottery finds, and to do this in an attractive way so that we have new faces with novel ideas showing up at upcoming conferences.

31 Günsenin 1989, 271-74; Vroom 2014², 94-95.

32 Vroom 2014², 80-85, 90-93; Vroom and IJzendoorn 2018. See also for other finds of these wares at Chalcis, Skartis and Vaxevanis 2017, figs. 3-4; Kontogiannis and Skartsis 2020, fig. 1d-1; Skartsis 2020, figs. 3-9 (Bailo House).

33 Günsenin 1989, 271-274, fig. 1, 8-9; Hayes 1992, 76, fig. 26.10-11 (Type 61).

34 See in general, Hayes 1992, 76; Vroom 2014², 99. Athens: Unpublished, see Sanders 1993, 283, n. 47, no. P10735; Marathon Bay: Braemer and Marcadé 1953, 142, fig. 66b; Keos: Cherry *et al.* 1991, 354, fig. 18.2; Melos: Unpublished, see Sanders 1993, 283, n. 47; Corinth: Unpublished, see Sanders 1993, 283, n. 47, no. C-37-2007; Sparta: Sanders 1993, 283, fig. 15.1; Shipwreck off Peristera, northern Sporades: Dellaporta 1999, figs. 1, 3; Crete: Poulou-Papadimitriou 2006, 83-84, figs. 14-16; Poulou-Papadimitriou 2008, 55-58, 100-101; Shipwreck of Çamalti Burnu, near Marmaris: Günsenin 2001, 118; Bulgaria: see for an overview, Todorova 2016, 640, fig. 4 (Type 18); Rumania, northern Black Sea, Turkey (Samsun, Sinop, Tekirdag, Izmir): Günsenin 1989, 271-74 and fig. 1; Otranto: Arthur 1992, 207, no. 832, fig. 7:3; Cyprus: Megaw 1972, 334, fig. 27. The type has also been found in Gytheion,

35 Anthedon (Boeotia), Corfu, Kythera (for references see Hayes 1992, 76); finds from Kythera also in Poulou-Papadimitriou 2013, 125-26.
35 Constantinople: Hayes 1992, 76. At coastal sites of Bulgaria it has also been reported from later contexts (up to the 14th century), but this evidence remains to be published: Todorova 2016, 637, fig. 1 (Type 18) and 640.
36 Kritzas 1971, 178-79.
37 Papanikola-Bakritzis 1999, 122-142, nos. 143-163.
38 Hayes 1992, 76; Cherry *et al.* 1991, 354-55.
39 Waksman *et al.* 2018a; 2018b; Panagopoulou *et al.* 2021.
40 Poulou-Papadimitriou 2006, 83-84, fig. 16.
41 Poulou-Papadimitriou 2008, 56.
42 Poulou-Papadimitriou 2013, 125-26.
43 Waksman *et al.* 2018.
44 See for a distribution of these shipwrecks, Vroom in this volume, as well as *Idem* 2016, fig. 4 and table 2; 2021, 62-64, fig. 2.14; Koutsouflakis 2020, fig. 1. For the recovery of Günsenin 3 amphorae from rescue excavations at Chalcis, see Skartsis and Vaxevanis 2017 (Frizi street, KTEL plot; junction of Erotokritou and Olynthou streets); Aliveri: Daphi and Skartsis 2015, 641; Anthedon: Schläger *et al.* 1968, 88, fig. 90; Boeotia Survey: Vroom 2003, 153-55; Marathon: Braemer and Marcadé 1953, 142, fig. 66b; Pelagonnisos-Alonnisos shipwreck: Kritzas 1971, 178-79; Portolafia shipwreck: Koutsouflakis *et al.* 2012, 53-54, fig. 20; Peristera shipwreck, northern Sporades: Dellaporta 1999, figs. 1, 3; Kikynthos islet: Spondylis 2012, 31-34, fig.

42; Novy Svet shipwreck: Morozova *et al.* 2020.
45 Anagnostakis 2002, 65. In addition, vineyards were mentioned in the famous Cadaster of Thebes; cf. Vroom 2003,
46 Pecci *et al.* 2020 show the transport of fermented substances such as wine in these ceramic containers.
47 Günsenin 2018, 116, fig. 31; Todorova 2016, fig. 1 (type 20); see also Vroom 2022. The quantities of this type were comparable to the counts and weight of the standard Günsenin 3 amphora in the Orionos Street assemblage.
48 Vroom 2003, 154, fig. 6.7, w.12.1 and w.12.3.
49 Some early 13th-century vessels of Incised Sgraffito Ware and Champlevé Ware were previously described by A.H.S. Megaw (1975) as 'Aegean Ware' (referring to an Aegean provenance), although this term is currently no longer in use; cf. François 2018.
50 The term Middle Byzantine Pottery group was first suggested by Guy Sanders, and later taken over by other scholars: cf. Waksman *et al.* 2014, 380, note 6.
51 See also Kontongiannis and Skartsis 2020, fig 1d. Several dishes of these decorated glazed tablewares from the Orionos Street workshop were recorded in 3-D by Vroom's project assistant Vasiliki Lagari.
52 Vroom and IJzendoorn 2016.
53 Morgan 1942, 162-66 ('Incised Wares'); Papanikola-Bakirtzis 1999, 20; Papanikola-Bakirtzis *et al.* 1999, 51-112; Vroom 2014[2], 90-93.
54 Cf. Georgopoulou-Meladini 1973-1974, pl. 322; Armstrong 1991.

55 Morgan 1942, 146-51 ('Incised-Sgraffito'); Papanikola-Bakirtzis 1999, 20.

56 Morgan 1942, 146, 156-57; Sanders 1993, 260 extended their chronology to the early 13th century. At Corinth, glazed dishes and bowls with incised decoration were found in various contexts dated between ca. 1160 and ca. 1260: see Sanders 2003, 388-89, nos. 17, 19 and 392-93, table 23.3, 'As Fig. 23.2.17' and 'As Fig. 23.2.19'. See for a bowl with incised decoration found in Corinth in a context which also contains coins of Guillaume Villehardouin (1245-1278), Williams *et al.* 1998, 258-59, no. 21, pl. 46c.

57 Vroom 2022.

58 For close parallels see Morgan 1942, 153, fig. 129; T. Tsanana in Papanikola-Bakirtzis 1999, 48, no. 34 (dated to the second half of the 12th c.); Vroom 2014², 90.

59 Frantz 1941; see also the entries by Ch. Koilakou in Papanikola-Bakirtzis 1999, 49-51, nos. 36-40; 54-55, nos. 44-45.

60 Koutsouflakis *et al.* 2012, 57-58, fig. 24; Koutsouflakis and Tsompanidis 2018, figs. 2-9; Waksman *et al.* 2018a; see for more locations of shipwrecks transporting 12th- to 13th-century glazed tablewares, Vroom 2016, fig. 5 and table 3; 2021, 64-65, fig. 2.15; Koutsouflakis 2020, fig. 2.

61 E.g., Georgopoulou-Meladini 1973, 314, pl. 270 (Venizelou st.); *Idem* 1973-1974, 503-504, pls. 322d-e, 324-27 and 328a (Agia Varvara sq.); Papadakis 1975, 295-96, figs. 4-10, 13 (M. Frizi st.); Waksman *et al.* 2014, figs. 5-12; Skartsis and Vaxevanis 2017, figs. 3-4; see for finds on Boeotian sites, Vroom 2000; *Idem* 2003; *Idem* 2022.

62 Using experimental archaeology, we tried to reconstruct some of these cooking pots at Leiden University (NL). It was the intention to look also into cooking techniques, cooking practices and eating habits in Medieval Chalcis. These consumption patterns were of course dependent on the availability of local foodstuffs.

63 Vroom 2011, 421-423.

64 Vroom 2014², 70-71; Skartsis and Vaxevanis 2017, fig. 2.

65 Vroom 2014², 68-69. Gouged Ware has been found at Thebes, Corinth, Aegina, Heraklion (Crete), Azoros (Thessaly), Butrint, and in a different fabric at numerous sites of Apulia; see for a map of these last ones, Imperiale 2011, 44, fig. 25.

66 Papanikola-Bakirtzis *et al.* 1999, 15-50; Vroom 2014², 74-79.

67 See for more finds of imported Glazed White Ware and/or Polychrome Ware from Constantinople at Chalcis, Georgopoulou-Meladini 1973-1974, pl. 322f; Skartsis and Vaxevanis 2017, fig. 1; Kontogiannis and Skartsis 2020, fig. 1a-c; Skartsis 2020, fig. 1 (Bailo House).

68 Vroom 2014², 96-97; Günsenin 2018, fig. 8; Waksman *et al.* 2018b.

69 Günsenin 1989, 271; Hayes 1992, 75-76 (his type 60): Vroom 2014², 96-97.

70 See for more examples of Günsenin 2 amphorae found at Chalcis, Waksman *et al.* 2018b, fig. 1 (BZY807, BZY811, BZN310-312, BZN315-316); Kontogiannis and Skartsis 2020, fig. 2d-e.

71 See Valente 2018, fig. 3.

72 Arthur 1992, 206; Arthur and Auriemma 1996, 16-17; Vroom 2014², 102-103.

73 Koilakou 1994, 118, pl. 49c; Vroom 2003, 155-157, figs. 6.8 and 6.42, W13.1-5; *Idem* 2014, fig. 2; see also Armstrong 1993, figs. 3 and 4.
74 Waksman *et al.* 2018b, figs. 1 (BZY802) and 2 (BZY801).
75 Hayes 1992, 50; Vroom 2014², 68-69.
76 Vroom 2003, 145, fig. 6.3, W5.1-2; see also for more finds of this ware at Chalcis, Kontogiannis and Skartsis 2020, fig. 2a-b.
77 Vroom 2006, 183, fig. 2 (from pit Alpha-1).
78 See also Vroom 2003, fig. 6.40, W5.Ex; *Idem* 2014, 461, fig. 4.
79 Hayes 1992, 50, fig. 18, nos. 1-6.
80 Patterson and Whitehouse 1992, fig. 6:15, nos. 552-555 (Otranto); Sanders 1999, 159 (Corinth).
81 Vroom 2006, 183; *Idem* Vroom 2014², 68-69.
82 MacKay 1967, 274.
83 Vroom 2003, 145, fig. 6.4, W6.1-7, fig. 6.40, W6.Ex; 2014², 70-71.
84 E.g., Vroom 2003, 145, fig. 6.4, W6.1-7 (Boeotia); Skartsis and Vaxevanis 2017, fig. 2; Kontogiannis and Skartsis 2020, figs. 2c and 3a-h; Skartsis 2020, fig. 2 (Bailo House).
85 See also Kontogiannis and Skartsis 2020, fig. 3h.
86 Demangel and Mamboury 1939, fig. 185, nos. 7-8 and fig. 194; Papanikola-Bakirtzis 1999, 17, fig.1.
87 D. Papanikola-Bakirtzis, pers. comm.
88 Vroom 2022.
89 Cf. McDonald and Howell 1971 [1975], pl. 115b.
90 Cherry *et al.* 1991, fig. 18.3, nos. 63-12, 48-10, 48-9.
91 Armstrong 1989, no. 24, fig. 14, pl. 9; 1996, 357, pl. 83, nos. 10-11, 65-66, pl. 84, no. 97 under the heading 'incised coarse ware'; Vroom 2003, 145-47.
92 Vroom 2003, 145 with further literature.
93 Vroom 2003, 242; *Idem* 2014, 461.
94 Jacoby 1991-92; Vroom 2014, 461.
95 Vroom 2016, figs. 3-4, tables 1-2; see Vroom's contribution in this volume and for various Chalcis networks, *Idem* 2022.
96 Vroom 2003; *Idem* 2022.

BIBLIOGRAPHY

Anagnostakis, I. 2002. Μέγαρα και Βυζάντιο. Αμπελοοινική ιστορία της Μεγαρίδας στους Μέσους Χρόνους (4ος-13ος αι.), *Οἶνον Ἱστορῶ* 2, 55-71.

Armstrong, P. 1989. Some Byzantine and later settlements in eastern Phokis, *The Annual of the British School at Athens* 84, 1-47.

Armstrong, P. 1991. A group of Byzantine bowls from Skopelos, *Oxford Journal of Archaeology* 10, 335-47.

Armstrong, P. 1993. Byzantine Thebes: Excavations on the Kadmeia, *The Annual of the British School at Athens* 88, 295-335.

Armstrong, P. 1996. The Byzantine and later pottery, in: R.C.S. Felsch (ed.), *Kalapodi. Ergebnisse der Ausgrabungen im Heiligtum der Artemis und des Apollon von Hyampolis in der antiken Phokis*, Mainz, 336-71.

Arthur, P. 1992. 'Amphorae for bulk transport', in: F. d'Andria and D. Whitehouse (eds.), *Excavations at Otranto, Vol. II: The finds*, Lecce, 197-218.

Arthur, P. and R. Auriemma 1996. A search for Italian wine. Middle Byzantine and later amphoras from Southern Puglia, *The INA Quarterly* 23, 14-17.

Braemer, F. and J. Marcadé 1953. Céramique antique et pièces d'ancres trouvées en mer à la pointe de la Kynosoura (baie de Marathon), *BCH* 77, 139-54.

Bouras, Ch. 2002. Aspects of the Byzantine city, eighth-fifteenth centuries, in: A.E. Laiou (ed.), *The Economic History of Byzantium: From the Seventh through the Fifteenth Century, Vol. II*, Washington, DC, 497-528.

Camocio, G.-F. 1570-1573 [imprint ca. 1757]. *Isole famose porti, fortezze, e terre maritime sottoposte alla Ser.ma Sig.ria di Venetia ad altri principi Christiani* [etc.], Venice.

Chatzidimitriou, A. 2000. *Αλιβέρι. Συμβολή στην αρχαιολογική έρευνα της περιοχής*, Athens.

Cherry, J.F., J.L. Davis, E. Manzourani and J.W. Hayes 1991. Introduction to the archaeology of post-Roman Keos, in: J.F. Cherry *et al.*, *Landscape Archaeology as Long-Term History. Northern Keos in the Cycladic islands*, Los Angeles, 351-64.

Costa, St. 2018. Shard weight: A new look at the numbers, in: D. Dixneuf (ed.), *Late Roman Coarse Wares 5, Vol. I*, Cairo, 15-24.

Daphi, E. and S. Skartsis 2015. Βυζαντινή κεραμική από τις ανασκαφές στις εγκαταστάσεις του ατμοηλεκτρικού σταθμού (ΑΗΣ) της ΔΕΗ Αλιβερίου, στην Εύβοια (4ος-18ος αι.), in: *4ο Αρχαιολογικό Έργο Θεσσαλίας και Στερεάς Ελλάδας, Βόλος, 15-18 Μαρτίου 2012*, Vol. ιι, *Πρακτικά*, Volos, 709-18.

Dellaporta, A. 1999. Byzantine shipwrecks and underwater evidence for Byzantine pottery, in: D. Papanikola-Bakirtzis (ed.), *Byzantine Glazed Ceramics. The Art of Sgraffito*, Athens, 118-121.

Demangel, R. and E. Mamboury 1939. *Le quartier des Manganes et la première region de Constantinople*, Paris.

Eleutheratou, S. 2000. *Το Ανατολικό λουτρό στο οικόπεδο Μακρυγιάννη, Αρχαιολογικόν Δελτίον 55* (2000), Vol. Α', Μελέτες, 285-328.

François, V. 2018. Aegean Ware: How a typology became inoperative, in: *XIth Congress AIECM3 on Medieval and Modern Period Mediterranean Ceramics, Proceedings, 19-24 October 2015 Antalya, Vol. I*, Ankara, 197-202.

Frantz, A. 1941. Akritas and the dragons, *Hesperia* 10, 9-13.

Georgopoulou-Meladini, M. 1973. Μεσαιωνικά Μνημεία Ευβοίας, *Αρχαιολογικόν Δελτίον* 28, Vol. Β'1, *Χρονικά*, 311-17.

Georgopoulou-Meladini, M. 1973-1974. Μεσαιωνικά Μνημεία Ευβοίας, *Αρχαιολογικόν Δελτίον* 29, Vol. Β'1, *Χρονικά*, 499-512.

Gerousi, E. et al. 2007. 23η Εφορεία Βυζαντινών Αρχαιοτήτων, *Αρχαιολογικόν Δελτίον* 62, Vol. Β'1, *Χρονικά*, 590-620.

Gerousi, E. et al. 2009. 23η Εφορεία Βυζαντινών Αρχαιοτήτων, *Αρχαιολογικόν Δελτίον* 64, Vol. Β'1, *Χρονικά*, 477-512.

Günsenin, N. 1989. Recherches sur les amphores Byzantines dans les musées Turcs, in: V. Déroche and J.-M. Spieser (eds.), *Recherches sur la céramiques byzantines*, BCH Suppl. 18, Athens, 267-76.

Günsenin, N. 2001. L'épave de Çamalti Burnu I (Ile de Marmara, Proconnese): Resultats de campagnes 1998-2000, *Anatolia Antiqua / Eski Anadolu* 9, 117-33.

Günsenin, N. 2018. La typologie des amphores Günsenin. Une mise au point nouvelle, *Anatolia Antiqua* 26, 89-124.

Hayes, J.W. 1992. *Excavations at Saraçhane in Istanbul, Vol. II: The Pottery*, Princeton, NJ

Imperiale, M.L. 2011. La pietra ollare, in: P. Arthur, M.L. Imperiale and M. Tinelli (eds.), *Apigliano. Un villaggio bizantino e medieval in terra d'Otranto*, Lecce, 43-46.

Jacoby, D. 1991-92. Silk in Western Byzantium before the Fourth Crusade: A reconsideration, *Byzantinische Zeitschrift* 84-85, 452-500.

Kalamara, P. 2015. Εύριπος – Negroponte – Eğriboz: μια πόλη-κάστρο, σημαντικό λιμάνι, in: P. Kalamara, M. Kosma, K. Boukaras and G. Chairetakis (eds), *Χαλκίς – Εύριπος – Negroponte – Eğriboz. Η πόλη της Χαλκίδας*, Athens, 56-70.

Kanetaki, E. and E. Stylianou 2008. Λουτρό και κρήνη της Χαλκίδας, in: E. Brouskari (ed.), *Η Οθωμανική αρχιτεκτονική στην Ελλάδα*, Athens, 88-89.

Koder, J. 1973. *Negroponte: Untersuchungen zur Topografie und Siedlungsgeschichte der Insel Euboia während der Zeit der Venezianerherrschaft*, Vienna.

Koilakou, Ch. 1994. Θήβα. Οδός Βρυζάκη, πάροδος Δίρκης, *Αρχαιολογικόν Δελτίον* 49, Vol. Β'1, *Χρονικά*, 117-20.

Kontogiannis, N. 2012. Euripos – Negroponte – Eğriboz: Material culture and historical topography of Chalcis from Byzantium to the end of the Ottoman rule, *Jahrbuch der Österreichischen Byzantinistik* 62, 29-56.

Kontogiannis, N.D. and S.S. Skartsis (with contributions by G. Vaxevanis and S.Y. Waksman) 2020. Ceramic vessels and food consumption: Chalcis as major production and distribution center in the Byzantine and Frankish periods, in: S.Y. Waksman (ed.), *Multidisciplinary Approaches to Food and Foodways in the Medieval Eastern Mediterranean*, Archéologie(s) 4, Lyon, 239-54.

Koutsouflakis, G. 2020. The transportation of amphorae, tableware and foodstuffs in the Middle and Late Byzantine period: The evidence from Aegean shipwrecks, in: S.Y. Waksman (ed.), *Multidisciplinary Approaches to Food and Foodways in the Medieval Eastern Mediterranean*, Archéologie(s) 4, Lyon, 447-81.

Koutsouflakis, G., X. Argyri, Ch. Papadopoulou and G. Sapountzis 2012. Υποβρύχια αναγνωριστική έρευνα στο Νότιο Ευβοϊκό (2006-2008), *Enalia: The Journal of the Hellenic Institute of Marine Archaelogy* 11, 40-69.

Koutsouflakis, G.and A. Tsompanidis 2018. The Kavalliani shipwreck: A new cargo of Byzantine glazed tableware from the south Euboean Gulf, Aegean, in: *XIth Congress AIECM3 on Medieval and Modern Period Mediterranean Ceramics, Proceedings, 19-24 October 2015 Antalya, Vol. I*, Ankara, 39-48.

Kritzas, Ch. 1971. Το βυζαντινόν ναυάγιον Πελαγοννήσου Αρχαιολογικόν Δελτίον *Analekta ex Athenon* 4, 176-182.

Mamaloukos, S. 2020. The fortifications of Chalcis (Evripos/Negreponte/Egriboz), Greece, in: J. Navarro Palazón and L.J. García-Pulido (eds), *Defensive Architecture of the Mediterranean, Vol. II*, Granada, 631-38.

Megaw, A.H.S. 1972. Supplementary excavations on a castle site at Paphos, Cyprus (1970-1971), *Dumbarton Oaks Papers* 26, 322-43.

Megaw, A.H.S. 1975. An early thirteenth century Aegean glazed ware, in: G. Robertson and G. Henderson (eds), *Studies in Memory of David Talbot Rice*, Edinburgh, 34-45.

Morgan, C.H. 1942. *Corinth Vol. XI: The Byzantine Pottery*, Cambridge, MA.

Morozova, Y., Waksman, S.Y. and S. Zelenko 2020. Byzantine amphorae of the 10th-13th centuries from the Novy Svet shipwrecks, Crimea, the Black Sea: Preliminary typology and archaeometric studies, in: S.Y. Waksman (ed.), *Multidisciplinary Approaches to Food and Foodways in the Medieval Eastern Mediterranean*, Archéologie(s) 4, Lyon, 429-45.

Ousterhout, R. 2013. Houses, Markets, and Baths: Secular architecture in Byzantium, in: A. Drandaki, D. Papanikola-Bakirtzis and A. Tourta (eds), *Heaven and Earth: Art of Byzantium from Greek Collections*, Athens, 211-13.

Panagopoulou, A., J. Vroom, A. Hein and V. Kilikoglou 2021. Production technology of glazed pottery in Chalcis, Euboea, during the Middle Byzantine period, *Heritage* 4, 4473-94.

Papadakis, N. 1975. *Το μεσαιωνικό τείχος της Χαλκίδας, Αρχείο Ευβοϊκών Μελετών* 20, 277-317.

Papanikola-Bakirtzis D., F.N. Mavrikiou and Ch. Bakirtzis 1999. *Βυζαντινή κεραμική στο Μουσείο Μπενάκη*, Athens.

Papanikola-Bakitzis, D. (ed.) 1999. *Byzantine Glazed Ceramics: The Art of Sgraffito*, (in Greek and English) Athens.

Pecci, A., N. Garnier and S.Y. Waksman 2020. Residue analysis of medieval amphorae from the eastern Mediterranean, in: S.Y. Waksman (ed.), *Multidisciplinary Approaches to Food and Foodways in the Medieval Eastern Mediterranean*, Archéologie(s) 4, Lyon, 417-28.

Poulou-Papadimitriou, N. 2006. Middle Byzantine pottery from Eleutherna: The local wares, in: E. Gavrilaki and G. Tziphopoulos (eds), *Ο Μυλοπόταμος από την Αρχαιότητα ως σήμερα, Vol. V: Βυζαντινά χρόνια*, Rethymno, 77-92.

Poulou-Papadimitriou, N. 2008. Βυζαντινή κεραμική από την Ελεύθερνα: *Η στέρνα της Αγίας Άννας*, in: Th. Kalpaxis, N. Poulou, A. Yangaki, M. Xanthopoulou, L. Mantalara and D. Mylona, *Ελεύθερνα Τομέας ΙΙ. 3. Βυζαντινό σπίτι στην Αγία Άννα*, Rethymno, 25-188.

Poulou-Papadimitriou, N. 2013. Η βυζαντινή και η πρώιμη ενετική περίοδος, in: Y. Sakellarakis (ed.), *Κύθηρα. Το μινωικό ιερό κορυφής στον Άγιο Γεώργιο στο Βουνό. Vol. 3: Τα ευρήματα*, Athens, 25-266.

Revithiadou, F. and K.T. Raptis 2014. *Αποκατάσταση – Στερέωση του βυζαντινού λουτρού στη Θεσσαλονίκη / Restoration – Consolidation of the Byzantine Bath in Thessaloniki*, Thessaloniki.

Sanders, G.D.R. 1993. Excavations at Sparta: The Roman Stoa, 1988-91. Preliminary report, part 1. (c) Medieval pottery, *The Annual of the British School at Athens* 88, 251-86.

Sanders, G.D.R. 2003. Recent developments in the chronology of Byzantine Corinth, in: C.K. Williams II and N. Bookidis (eds), *Corinth Vol. XX: The Centenary, 1896-1996*, Princeton, NJ, 385-99.

Schläger, H., D.J. Blackman and J. Schäfer 1968. Der Hafen von Anthedon mit Beiträgen zur Topographie und Geschichte der Stadt, *Archäologischer Anzeiger* 1968, 21-98.

Skartsis, S.S. (with contributions by P. Taxiarchi) 2020. Catalogue of finds, in: N.D. Kontogiannis and S.S. Skartsis (eds), *Venetian and Ottoman Heritage in the Aegean. The Bailo House in Chalcis, Greece*, Turnhout, 45-93.

Skartsis, S.S. and G. Vaxevanis 2017. Η Χαλκίδα κατά τους μεσοβυζαντινούς χρόνους και την εποχή της Λατινοκρατίας: η μαρτυρία της κεραμικής (9ος-15ος αι.), [= Chalcis during the Middle Byzantine times and the Frankish era: The testimony of the ceramics (9th-15th c.)], in: Ž. Tankosić, F. Mavridis and M. Kosma (eds), *An Island Between Two Worlds: The Archaeology of Euboea from Prehistoric to Byzantine Times, Proceedings of an International Scientific Conference, Eretria, July 12-14, 2013,* Athens, 593-612.

Spondylis, N. 2012. Υποβρύχια έρευνα I.EN.A.E. στον Παγασητικό Κόλπο. Ερευνητική περίοδος 2005, *Enalia* 11, 16-39.

Todorova, E. 2016. Policy and trade in the northern periphery of the Eastern Mediterranean: amphorae evidence from present-day Bulgaria (7th-14th centuries), in: M.J. Gonçalves and S. Gómez-Martínez (eds), *Actas do X. Congresso Internacional a ceramica medieval no Mediterrâneo, Silves 22 a 27. outubro 2012,* Silves, 637-48.

Triantaphyllopoulos, D. 1990. Χριστιανική και μεσαιωνική Χαλκίδα: ανασκόπηση της νεώτερης αρχαιολογικής έρευνας, in: *Διεθνές Επιστημονικό Συνέδριο «Η πόλη της Χαλκίδας», Χαλκίδα,* 24-27 Σεπτεμβρίου 1987, Athens, 163-228.

Valente, R. 2018. Amphorae in Early and Middle Byzantine Corinth: Continuity and change, *Annuario della Scuola di Archeologica Italiana di Atene e delle missioni italiane in Oriente* 96, 355-68.

Vaxevanis, G. 2007. Χαλκίδα, Οδός Ωρίωνος 10 (οικόπεδο ιδιοκτησίας Χ. Δημαρέλου-Δεληβοριά), *Αρχαιολογικόν Δελτίον* 62, *Vol. Β΄1, Χρονικά,* 601-603.

Vroom, J. 2000. Piecing together the past: Survey pottery and deserted settlements in Medieval Boeotia (Greece), in: K. Belke, F. Hild, J. Koder and P. Soustal (eds), *Byzanz als Raum. Zu Methoden und Inhalten der historischen Geographie des östlichen Mittelmeerraumes im Mittelalter,* Österreichische Akademie der Wissenschaften, Philosophisch-Historische Klasse, Denkschriften, 283. Band, Vienna, 245-59.

Vroom, J. 2003. *After Antiquity. Ceramics and Society in the Aegean from the 7th to the 20th c. A.C. A Case Study from Boeotia, Greece,* ASLU 10, Leiden.

Vroom, J. 2006. Byzantine garbage and Ottoman waste, in: E. Andrikou, V.L. Aravantinos, L. Godard, A. Sacconi and J. Vroom (eds), *Thèbes. Fouilles de la Cadmée II.2: Les tablettes en linéaire B de la 'Odos Pelopidou'. La céramique de la Odos Pelopidou et la chronologie du Linéaire B,* Pisa & Rome, 181-233.

Vroom, J. 2011. The Morea and its links with Southern Italy after AD 1204: Ceramics and identity, *Archeologia Medievale* 38, 409-30.

Vroom, J. 2014². *Byzantine to Modern Pottery in the Aegean: An Introduction and Field Guide. Second Revised Edition,* Turnhout (1rst ed. Utrecht, 2005).

Vroom, J. 2014. Turkish rubbish in Greek soil: Byzantine, Medieval and Post-Medieval pottery from Thebes, in: V. Aravantinos and E. Kountouri (eds), *100 Χρόνια*

Αρχαιολογικού Έργου στη Θήβα: Οι πρωτεργάτες των ερευνών και οι συνεχιστές τους / A Century of Archaeological Work in Thebes: Pioneers and Continuing Research, Athens, 455-71.

Vroom, J. 2016. Byzantine sea trade in ceramics: Some case studies in the eastern Mediterranean (ca. seventh - fourteenth centuries), in: P. Magdalino and N. Necipoğlu (eds), *Trade in Byzantium: Papers from the Third International Sevgi Gönül Byzantine Studies Symposium*, Istanbul, 157-77.

Vroom, J. 2021. Thinking of Linking: Pottery connections, Southern Adriatic, Butrint and beyond, in: M. Skoblar (ed.), *Byzantium, Venice and the Medieval Adriatic. Spheres of Maritime Power and Influence, c. 700-1543*, Cambridge, 45-82.

Vroom, J. 2022. Shifting Byzantine networks: New light on Chalcis (Euripos/Negroponte) as a centre of production and trade in Greece (ca. 10th-13th c.), in: E. Fiori and M. Trizio (eds), *The 24th International Congress of Byzantine Studies, Vol. 1: Proceedings of the Plenary Sessions*, Venice, 453-87.

Vroom, J., E. Tzavella and G. Vaxevanis 2021. Exploring daily life in the Byzantine Empire: Pottery from Chalkis (Euboea, Greece), ca. 10th/11th-13th c., in: P. Petridis, A.G. Yangaki, N. Liaros and E.-E. Bia (eds), *12th Congress AIECM3 on Medieval & Modern Period Mediterranean Ceramics, Proceedings Vol. 1*, Athens, 449-58.

Vroom, J. and M. van IJzendoorn 2016. Mapping the ceramics: Production and distribution of Champlevé Ware in the Aegean (12th-13th c. AD), in: M. Ferri, C. Moine and L. Sabbionesi (eds.), *In and Around. Ceramiche e comunita. Secondo convegno tematico dell' AIECM3, Faenza, Museo Internazionale delle Ceramiche, 17-19 aprile 2015, Sesto Fiorentino*, Florence, 197-201.

Vroom, J. and M.W. van IJzendoorn 2018. Splashed Ware: A little-known Byzantine glazed ware from the Aegean (12th-13th c AD), in: *XIth Congress AIECM3 on Medieval and Modern Period Mediterranean Ceramics, Proceedings, 19-24 October 2015 Antalya, Vol. I*, Ankara, 197-201.

Waksman, S.Y., N.D. Kontogiannis, S. Skartsis and G. Vaxevanis 2014. The main 'Middle Byzantine production' and pottery manufacture in Thebes and Chalkis, *The Annual of the British School at Athens* 109, 379-422.

Waksman, S.Y., S. Skartsis, N.D. Kontogiannis, E.P. Todorova and G. Vaxevanis 2018a. Investigating the origins of two main types of Middle and Late Byzantine amphorae, *Journal of Archaeological Science: Reports* 21, 1111-21.

Waksman, S.Y., G. Koutsouflakis, J. Burlot and L. Courbe 2018b. Archaeometric investigations of the tableware cargo of the Kavalliani shipwreck (Greece) and into the role of the harbour of Chalkis in the Byzantine and Frankish periods, *Journal of Archaeological Science: Reports* 21, 1122-29.

Williams, C.K. II, L.M. Snyder, E. Barnes and O. Zervos 1998. Frankish Corinth: 1997, *Hesperia* 67, 223-81.

Yegül, F. 1992, *Baths and Bathing in Classical Antiquity*, New York, Cambridge, MA & London.

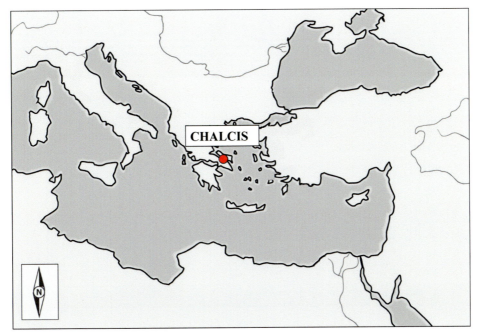

FIG. 1 – Map of the eastern Mediterranean with the location of Chalcis (J. Vroom).

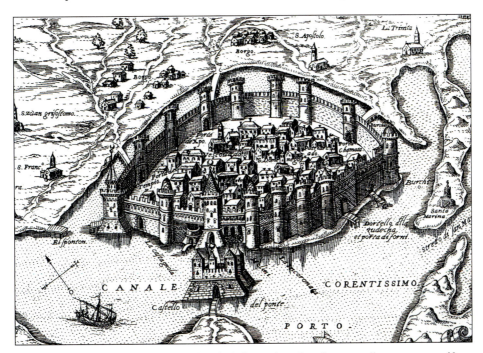

FIG. 2 – Detail of engraved map of Medieval Chalcis with its fortification walls, *ca.* 1566-1574 (from the atlas of Camocio 1570-1573, Citta di Negroponte, 16,5 x 22,5 cm).

FIG. 3 – Map of modern Chalkida with relocation of the ancient city to a more western part, next to the Euripus Strait (G. Vaxevanis; J. Vroom; the background is courtesy by Google Maps).

FIG. 4 – Old photograph of the *Kastro* of Chalcis with its original fortifications, general view from the north-east, between 1884 and 1890 (see http://square.gr/newlight-on-Negropont/4396); Remaining section of fortification walls with ethnographic museum (photo: J. Vroom).

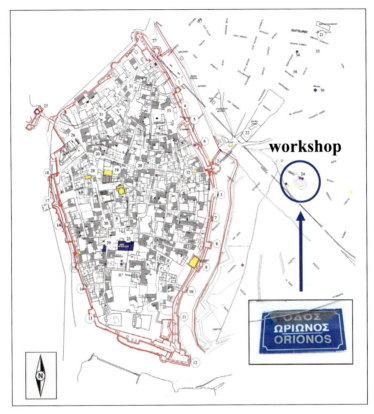

FIG. 5 – Plan of Medieval Chalcis: location of excavation at Orionos Street (map after Kontogiannis 2012, FIG. 1).

FIG. 6 – The excavated plot at Orionos Street in Chalcis (photo: G. Vaxevanis).

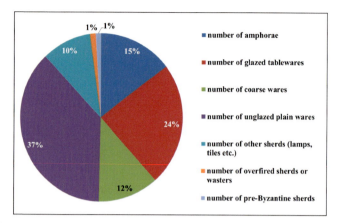

FIG. 7 – Chalcis, Orionos Street plot: total numbers of various wares. Total = 66.390 sherds (J. Vroom).

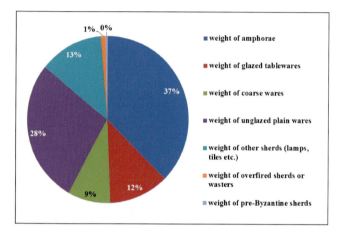

FIG. 8 – Chalcis, Orionos Street plot: total weights of various wares. Total = 2.414,75 kg (J. Vroom).

FIG. 9 – Photograph of Lelantine Plain with dug out clay bed (J. Vroom).

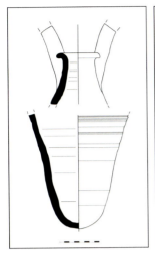

FIG. 10 – Chalcis, Orionos Street plot: Günsenin 3 amphora (J. Vroom).

FIG. 11 – Chalcis, Orionos Street plot with trenches 1-4: distribution of Günsenin 3 amphorae shown in green in pie charts (J. Vroom; I. Biezeveld).

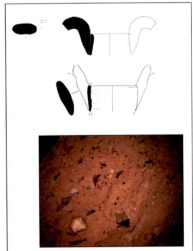

FIG. 12 – Map showing shipwrecks with mixed cargoes of Günsenin 3 amphorae and Fine Sgraffito Ware: 1 = Alonissos-Pelagonissos; 2 = Glafki (J. Vroom).

FIG. 13A-B – Chalcis, Orionos Street plot: Günsenin 3 amphora variants and picture of their fabric (J. Vroom).

FIG. 14A-B – Chalcis, Orionos Street plot: Champlévé Ware dishes with incised depictions of various animals (J. Vroom).

FIG. 15 – Map showing shipwrecks with Champlevé Ware: 1 = Alonissos-Pelagonissos; 2 = Near Izmir; 3 = Kastellorizo; 4 = Silifke (J. Vroom).

FIG. 16 – Chalcis, Orionos Street plot: unfinished fragment of Champlévé Ware showing a rabbit or hare in a tondo (J. Vroom).

FIG. 17 – Chalcis, Orionos Street plot: reconstructed Incised Sgraffito Ware dish with warrior (J. Vroom).

FIG. 18 – Map showing shipwrecks with Incised Sgraffito Ware: 1 = Novy Svet; 2 = Çamaltı Burnu 1; 3 = Kavalliani; 4 = Thorikos; 5 = Near Izmir; 6 = Tavşan Adası; 7 = Kastellorizo (J. Vroom).

FIG. 19 – Map showing shipwrecks with mixed cargoes of Günsenin 3 amphorae and Incised Sgraffito Ware: 1 = Novy Svet; 2 = Çamaltı Burnu 1; 3 = Alonissos-Pelagonissos (J. Vroom).

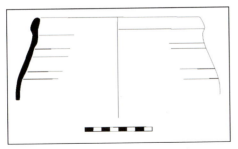

FIG. 20 – Chalcis, Orionos Street plot: rim fragment of a cooking pot (J. Vroom).

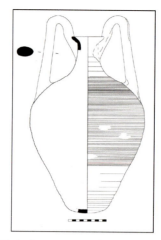

FIG. 21 – Euboea, Dokos (near Chalcis): transitional (Günsenin 2-3) amphora type (after Waksman *et al.* 2016, fig. 2, BZY801).

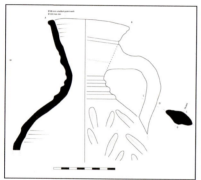

FIG. 22A-B – Chalcis, Orionos Street plot: upper part of an Unglazed Gouged jug (J. Vroom).

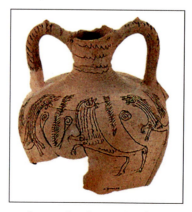

FIG. 23 – Almost complete shape of an Unglazed Incised jar (after Papanikola-Bakirtzis 1999, 17 and Vroom 2014³, fig. MBYZ 2.3).

Consumption patterns of ceramics in town and countryside: Case-studies from Corinth and Athens in central Greece

Elli Tzavella

*

INTRODUCTION

This paper sets out to test the hypothesis that Byzantine affluent households, or at least people who could consume above subsistence level, did not reside only in cities and towns, but also in various types of settlements in the countryside. This hypothesis is supported by numerous archaeological reports, which show that decorated glazed ceramics and imported wares, obviously used by households of certain means, are found both in urban and rural centres. In addition, many of the Byzantine churches with professional architectural design and craftsmanship (shown in sculptural and painted decoration) which were scattered in the countryside, were probably sponsored by prosperous members of Byzantine society, and may therefore be taken as strong indications of the presence of well-to-do households in the countryside. Comparison of consumption trends in urban and rural areas can further be made on the basis of other kinds of evidence, among which coins.

Scholars of Byzantine archaeology have not reached a consensus about the financial status of people who used glazed tableware in the Middle Byzantine and Late Byzantine periods: some share the view that the presence of these tablewares is evidence of consumers having a considerable wealth, while others argue that it was rather used by people of intermediate economic means.[1] In my opinion the arguments as well as the archaeological evidence support the former view. In any case, glazed tableware indicates consumption patterns above subsistence level. The fact that these consumers were in the economic position to select between local and imported ceramics as well as between different kinds of decorated glazed tableware suggests that were able to choose between other consumption goods, such as food and food-related objects.

Here, I will present a comparative study of consumption trends in Byzantine central Greece based on ceramic evidence of the 12th and 13th centuries. The first case study concerns pottery finds from two locations in the city of Corinth, while the second case study tries to compare ceramics found in a Byzantine monastery in rural Attica with published parallels from the Athenian Agora excavations. The overall aim of this article is to test if the ceramic repertoire of these three sites indicates similar trends in the use and function of pottery in relation to food consumption.

'CONSUMPTION' IN ARCHAEOLOGY

The use of the term 'consumption' with its current economic focus derives from industrial and post-industrial societies, therefore its use with regard to Byzantine society needs a theoretical consideration of what is meant under this term.

With regard to material culture studies, consumption is defined broadly as a material social practice involving the utilisation of objects (or services), as opposed to their production or distribution.[2] Beginning in the 1970s, but especially in the mid-1980s, consumption began to receive increasing recognition as a crucial focus of analysis especially in anthropology and sociology, but also in history. More than the economic connotation of consumption, it is the emphasis on the social and symbolic significance of commodities that has provoked an interest in material culture more broadly. Consumption was recognized as the social process by which people construct the symbolically laden material worlds they inhabit.[3]

Archaeology, of course, has always focused on evidence generated directly by consumption. Objects studied by archaeologists are remains of consumption in its broadest sense, and food habits have always played a prominent role in that respect. Amphora studies, for example, focus primarily on the identification of their production centres, their food content, and their distribution.[4] But, while until recently consumption was seen as just the result of production and distribution, now there is a tendency to see it as a domain of agentive social action which has a substantial analytical significance.[5] If we look into the example of amphora studies, purchase of this or that amphora type with its content does not depend only on the financial ability of the buyer. It also depends on his or her choice to be included into a group of people who share similar consumption habits.

'CONSUMPTION' IN BYZANTINE STUDIES

Byzantine economic historians have long been concerned with consumption, and to be more precise, with consumption features related to cities. They studied in particular the primary role of the town as a 'consumption centre'.[6] Most of these studies observe the phenomenon of consumption in combination with production, and especially with secondary production: that is to say, artisanship and industry. Actually, it is more production, than consumption, that Byzantine historians are concerned with; and especially the degree of artisanal and industrial production, and its role as a catalyst in transforming Byzantine towns and societies, as it did in the European West. In the words of Angeliki Laiou:

'[We study] whether the Byzantine cities had economic functions that contributed to the increase of national product and therefore to the growth of the Byzantine economy, or whether, on the other hand, they were agglomerations that were primarily centres of consumption, living off the agricultural surplus, and contributing little to the process of economic growth that is now generally accepted to have started sometime in the second half of the 8th century, reaching its zenith in the 12th. Of course, the question is not, or ought not to be, simply whether there was secondary production in the cities, but rather whether that production created added value.'[7]

It becomes evident from this excerpt that interest was so far often focused towards production rather than consumption. In other words, scholars have often looked at consumption trends from the perspective of drawing conclusions about production. The title of the article to which this excerpt belongs, 'The Byzantine city: parasitic or productive?', is quite significant in that regard. The excerpt is also indicative for the fact that scholars of Byzantine history have generally been more interested in the economic aspect of consumption rather than in its aspect as a social agency.[8]

Taking this short research history into account, the present paper attempts to look both at the economic significance and at the social significance of the consumption patterns in Corinth and Athens (the two case studies) as represented by ceramic finds.

A COMPARATIVE CASE STUDY FROM CORINTH

The discussion of ceramics in Byzantine and Frankish Corinth was initiated by Charles Morgan, Henry S. Robinson and Charles K. Williams, and was systematized by Guy D.R. Sanders.[9] Excavations and studies of the American School focussed on the Roman Forum at Corinth, which offered new insights regarding the form and function of the Byzantine and Frankish city. Noteworthy is that the Roman Forum had a special character throughout the Medieval period, because it has not been regarded as a 'representative' area of the city. The Forum is located outside the Early Byzantine city wall[10] (Fig. 1), and did not accommodate systematic building or domestic activity between the 6th and the mid-11th centuries.[11] During the 11th and 12th centuries, when building activity re-started and gradually expanded, its character appears to have been more commercial than domestic.[12]

In recent years, rescue excavations have revealed quarters of the Byzantine town of Corinth beyond the Forum, which appear to have had a more domestic character.[13] These quarters are located within and outside the Early Byzantine city wall (Fig. 1). Ceramics from rescue excavations undertaken between 2006 and 2012 were catalogued and entered into a database, as part of my duties at the Ephorate of the Corinthia (2011-2013). The pottery recovered during one of these excavations, in the plot of G. Koutsougeras, was studied in more detail and offered material of the 12th and 13th centuries which could be compared with ceramic finds from the Forum.[14]

These comparative data can be used to test the hypothesis that consumption patterns between the Forum and neighbouring areas were similar. 'Consumption' is here not equated only with food consumption, to which pottery studies allude, but also with consumption in the sense of purchase and use of the ceramic objects themselves, as indicators of economic and social status.[15]

The Koutsougera plot is located in the northern part of the walled area of Byzantine Corinth, in the district called 'Kraneion', where considerable evidence was found for continuity in habitation (Fig. 1).[16] The excavation revealed parts of two distinct buildings of domestic use, separated by an open corridor or narrow street (Fig. 2). The excavated part of the northern building is a single rectangular room with a square cistern. The southern building is separated in three rooms. A sewage pipe, covered with stone slabs, runs along the open corridor or narrow street which separates the two buildings. The upper excavation layers contained pottery of the 12th and 13th centuries, dated by two bronze half-tetartera coins of the Emperor Manuel I Comnenus (1143-1180), while the lower layers produced pottery of the 4th to 7th centuries.

The excavation yielded large quantities of glazed tableware of the 'Byzantine' tradition, such as Fine Sgraffito Ware, Champlévé Ware, Incised Sgraffito Ware, Late Sgraffito Ware, as well as lesser quantities of Slip-Painted Ware and Green and Brown Painted Ware. Some of these shapes and decoration styles appear in identical dishes published earlier from the Forum excavations. For instance, a shallow-shaped Fine Sgraffito Ware dish with incised grid pattern finds its exact parallel in the Forum (Fig. 3).[17] Two dish fragments with scraped away Champlévé Ware decoration are very similar with a plate found in the Forum (Fig. 4).[18] A same similarity exists between a base fragment of a large bowl from the Koutsougera plot and a fully preserved deep plate from the Forum, both with Late Sgraffito Ware-style decoration (Fig. 5a)[19], and between two bowls with Incised Sgraffito Ware decoration from either area (Fig. 5b).[20] The inhabitants in the Kraneion area also used an Islamic dish, which appears to be of

Mamluk Sgraffito Ware tradition based on its decoration, but has a pink fabric which is very different from the usual bright red fabric of Mamluk wares (Fig. 6).[21]

Regarding amphorae and storage vessels known as *lagenia*, the inhabitants of the Kraneion and the Forum used products from workshops of similar, local character (Fig. 7a-b)[22]. Those living in the Forum used more decorated wares, among which the Matt Painted category of *lagenia*, which were probably more expensive or represented different aesthetics.[23] The residents in the Kraneion used imported Unglazed White Wares from Constantinople (Fig. 7c). This type of Unglazed White Ware from the Kraneion has not been published at the Forum, although it is possible that it has been found there as well.

R. Scranton, C.K. Williams and G. Sanders have suggested that the Forum was mostly used as a commercial area, thus potentially with a higher presence of Italian traders than rural areas.[24] If this is indeed the case, it is quite intriguing to observe that the Forum residents and the Kraneion residents made similar choices. The strong similarities between these choices suggest that inhabitants of these two areas bought their ceramic tablewares from the same workshops or traders, and perhaps paid equal amounts of money to acquire them.

It is also interesting to compare ceramic evidence of the same period, namely the 12th and 13th centuries, with other sites in the Corinthia, which lie outside the urban centre of Corinth, such as *emporia*, smaller towns, and rural sites. Excavations at the harbour of Kenchreai, the eastern *emporion* of Corinth, revealed Byzantine glazed ceramics which belong to Slip-Painted Ware, Green and Brown Painted Ware, and Incised Sgraffito Ware types, to judge only from the few published examples.[25]

In the minor town of Sikyon, attested as *Vasilika* from the 14th century onwards, rescue excavations yielded Byzantine glazed wares of the same types as those at Corinth (Fine Sgraffito Ware, Incised Sgraffito Ware, Champlévé Ware) which, however, remain unpublished.[26] The systematic urban field survey at Sikyon / Vasilika generated only a few ceramics of the 12th and 13th centuries, since the Medieval town is mostly covered by the modern village and can be accessed only through excavation. These fragments include Glazed White Ware, Slip-Painted Ware, Fine Sgraffito Ware, Incised Sgraffito Ware, Champlévé Ware, the so-called 'Zeuxippus Ware subtypes' and RMR Ware.[27] Outside Sikyon / Vasilika, in the countryside, an extensive field survey indicates that at least the Byzantine ceramic types mentioned above were used at rural sites as well, although the survey did not include a systematic catalogue of the Medieval pottery finds.[28]

Excavations in the Justinianic fortress of the Hexamilion Wall, which was reused in the late Medieval period, yielded not only similar looking ceramics of the same types mentioned above with decoration of high quality (dishes with Incised Sgraffito

Ware decoration), but also an unglazed stewpot of 'Frankish' type. Apart from these published examples, a Champlévé Ware dish, a Protomaiolica dish, and RMR Ware cups from the fortress are nowadays exhibited in the Museum of Isthmia.[29] Finally, excavations at the Koutsongila Ridge, northeast of the harbour of Kenchreai, produced ceramics of Green and Brown Painted Ware, Slip-Painted Ware, Fine Sgraffito Ware and Incised Sgraffito Ware.[30]

The execution of the decoration on these examples from these rural sites is equivalent to the decoration of the ceramics found in the urban context of Corinth. The fabrics and production techniques (firing, slip, finish, glaze quality) are very similar, if not the same. It appears, therefore, that the workshops which produced these ceramic types sold their products to consumers who resided not only in the main urban centre of Corinth, but also in the minor urban centre of Sikyon/Vasilika, in the *emporion* of Kenchreai, as well as in rural sites in the territories of Sikyon, Kenchreai and Isthmia.

A RURAL MONASTERY IN ATTICA

Rural Attica has been explored archaeologically to a much higher degree than the Corinthia, although published reports of Middle Byzantine and Frankish pottery are still rare. Here I will discuss ceramics found during the excavation of a rural monastery located in the district called Kantza, situated ca. 20 kilometers east of Athens, in the Mesogeia plain (Fig. 8).

The excavation uncovered remains of a Byzantine church below the surviving basilica of Agios Nikolaos, which was built as a *metochion*, or dependent church, of the Agios Ioannis Kynegos monastery in 1592.[31] The standing basilica has a semi-hexagonal apse, underneath which the remains of a large semi-circular apse are clearly visible (Fig. 9). The foundations of the west wall of the earlier church, made of large blocks,[32] were recovered, while scanty remains of its lateral walls can still be seen on the ground surface to the north and to the south of the 16th-century basilica. The excavation took place in the area to the southwest of the standing basilica and also revealed architectural remains of a small monastery attached to the older, Byzantine church.[33] Three rooms of the monastery were excavated (Fig. 10). One of them was used as a kitchen, while another was unroofed, with a water-proof cistern in its floor.

The ceramic finds date from the 12th to the 14th centuries and show the domestic character of use of these rooms. They include a variety of glazed tablewares, such as Monochrome Glazed Ware, Slip-Painted Ware, Green and Brown Painted Ware, Fine Sgraffito Ware, and Incised Sgraffito Ware. Moreover, amphorae of the Gűnsenin 3 type (Fig. 11), imported from central Greece, were found at the monastery, and so were unglazed stew pots of local production (Figs. 12-13).

These finds can be compared with pottery from 12th- and 13th-century contexts of the Athenian Agora. For example, Slip-Painted Wares (Figs. 14-15) found at the monastery have the exact same fabric, decoration and production technique (firing, wheelmarks, etc.) as Slip-Painted Wares found in 13th-century contexts of the Agora.[34] These Slip-Painted Wares might have been obtained at ceramic workshops near the Athenian Agora, and transported to the monastery. The same degree of similarity in decoration is observed between vessels of the monastery and the Agora, among which Green and Brown Painted Ware (Fig. 16) and Incised Sgraffito Ware (Fig. 17).

Apart from glazed tableware, also unglazed tableware appears to have circulated both in the Athenian Agora and in the rural monastery: typical is a kind of unglazed jug with bulbous neck made of a cooking fabric (Fig. 18). These jugs often have a strainer in the interior of the neck. Such jugs were found in the Kantza monastery but also in Section PP' of the Agora, where they were thrown away in a well along with other debris of the 13th and 14th centuries.[35] Jugs of other categories were also found in the monastery (Fig. 19).

In short, the evidence clearly suggests that the residents of the Agios Nikolaos rural monastery made very similar choices as consumers compared to their contemporaries living in the Athenian Agora (at least as far as the pottery finds show). It seems that both the monks or nuns of Kantza and the Agora residents belonged to the same type of consumers. Evidently, the economic and social status of the monastery allowed its inhabitants to make choices which were quite similar compared to those taken by the inhabitants of the Athenian Agora regarding tablewares for meals and utilitarian utensils for cooking, storage and serving.

SOME CONCLUDING REMARKS

Byzantine towns were surely consumption centres, but it should not be forgotten that smaller hubs of consumption existed also in the countryside as well.[36] Especially rural monasteries of a certain size and status played a dominant role in this pattern of rural consumption. The archaeological evidence seems to be corroborated by written sources. For example, textual information to this effect has survived for the rural monastery of Osios Meletios, which was founded on Mount Kithairon (at the border between Attica and Boeotia) at the end of the 11th century. Soon after its foundation, the monastery acquired as many as twenty subordinate monasteries.[37] Alan Harvey noted that the early years of a monastic foundation, when the number of monks might sharply increased, created more consumption requirements in the countryside.[38]

The presence of wealthy consumers in rural areas outside urban influences is also attested by countryside churches with high quality architecture and wall-paintings.

These were probably commissioned by a rural prosperous aristocracy. In the cases of Attica and Boeotia, these rural churches were very numerous in the Byzantine period.

To sum up, I have discussed in this paper ceramic evidence retrieved outside or in the periphery of the Byzantine towns of Corinth and Athens. In the case of Corinth, this pottery was not only found in neighbourhoods outside the Roman Forum, but also in rural areas outside the urban area itself. When comparing this ceramic evidence with pottery found in the heart of the Byzantine city, the overal typochronological similarity is striking. This suggests that all examples of rural find spots discussed here can be seen as evidence for hubs of consumption in the Byzantine countryside.

This conclusion may serve as a starting point for further research. Undoubtedly, this research will not be easy, as social and cultural factors define consumption patterns as well as economic factors. Still, in that regard, the publication of this volume, dedicated to the archaeology of consumption in Byzantium, appears to be highly relevant to broader research trends within Byzantine Studies.

NOTES

1. The earlier view has been expressed by Sanders 2014, 2016 and 2018. The latter view is discussed by Bintliff 2013, but his examples are taken only from the Post-Medieval period.
2. For a comprehensive introduction of the term 'consumption' in material studies see Dietler 2010, esp. 209-10.
3. As an example, see the anthropological / archaeological study on alcohol by Dietler 2006. Equivalent anthropological studies on the Byzantine world are not common, but a broad range of archaeological studies, including studies on ceramics imported to Byzantine lands, form the basis of a discussion about how consumed products offer a certain kind of identity to the consumer: see as examples Lev-Tov 1999; Gerstel 2001; Joyner 2007; Vroom 2011.
4. See as an example Pieri 2005 for a study on amphorae of the Late Roman period.
5. E.g., Joyner 2007; Vroom 2011; various papers in Vroom, Waksman and Van Oosten (eds.) 2017.
6. Angold 1985, 8-9; Harvey 1989, 200-25; Laiou 2006, 86. The aforementioned scholars regard the Byzantine town as a 'consumer city', meaning that consumption in cities played a more prominent role than production. Dagron 2002, 392-96, 402-403, on the contrary, believes that important artisanal and commercial activities took place in Byzantine towns, and therefore does not follow the model of the 'consumer city'. See for an overview of these approaches, Laiou 2013.
7. Laiou 2013, 1.
8. Cf. publications cited in note 6 above; see also Wickham 2005.
9. Morgan 1942; Sanders 1987; *Idem* 2000; *Idem* 2003; Williams 2003. H.S. Robinson, director of the Corinth Excavations in the 1960s, contributed greatly to the organisation and future study of the voluminous Medieval ceramic material of the excavations of the American School of Classical Studies.
10. Sanders 2002, 647.
11. Scranton 1957, 49.
12. Scranton 1957, 54-83; Williams 2003, 426-27.
13. See for an overview, Athanasoulis *et al.* 2010, 173-79; Athanasoulis 2013, 194-95, figs. 171-72, and 204-206.
14. For a presentation of the Byzantine pottery excavated in the Koutsougera plot, see Tzavella 2018. Some conclusions of this study, especially concerning use of ceramics, social implications, and settlement patterns, are included in Tzavella 2020.
15. For earlier examples of this kind of approach see notes 3 and 5 above.
16. This excavation is represented by no. 14 in Athanasoulis 2013, 195, fig. 172.
17. Parallel: Williams and Zervos 1990, pl. 63b, upper left (Lot 1989-8).
18. Sanders 2003, 389, fig. 23.18 (C-34-1386).
19. Sanders 2003, 389, fig. 23.16 (C-37-1179).
20. Williams *et al.* 1998, 258-59, No. 21, pl. 46c: found in a context which contains coins of Guillaume Villehardouin (1245-1278).

21 Cf. Watson 2004, 395, 408-14, esp. 410, no. R.17; Avissar and Stern 2005, 38-39, fig. 14.7; Vezzoli 2011, 125-28, pl. 1-6. I would like to thank Valentina Vezzoli and Edna Stern for their valuable advice regarding the identification of this sherd.

22 Amphora parallels from the Forum: Williams and Zervos 1990, pl. 66b (Lot 189-63); *Idem* 1995, 30, fig. 6, C-1987-86.

23 Williams and Zervos 1990, 344; *Idem* 1992, 146 (where the *lagenia* are mentioned as 'amphoras').

24 Scranton 1957, 54-83; Williams 2003, 426-27.

25 Adamscheck 1979, pl. 25, Nos. LRB42-44, LRB49-50.

26 See as example the pottery found in the plot of Leonardos in 1969, now stored in the Archaeological Museum of Sikyon.

27 Tzavella forthcoming.

28 Lolos 2011, 345, fig. 5.57. One distinguishes Glazed White Ware from Constantinople, Fine Sgraffito, Measles Ware, Champlévé Ware, Incised Ware, as well as the upper part of a *lageni* and a stewpot rim which both belong to types well known from Corinth and from the northeastern Peloponnese. More documentation of pottery found in rural sites is needed in order to proceed with more detailed comparisons between ceramics used in urban and rural contexts.

29 Gregory 1993a, pls. 35c-d, 41e-g and 46d. See also Gregory 1989; *Idem* 1993b.

30 Gregory forthcoming.

31 Chatzesoteriou 1973, 212.

32 This way of construction was used in the 12th century (Bouras 2002, 386 and fig. 406), but was used as a technique through most part of the Middle Byzantine and Late Byzantine periods.

33 See for this excavation, Arapoyanni 1986. I would like to thank Ms Arapoyanni, as well as the Ephorate of Antiquities of East Attica, for granting the study permit for the pottery of the excavation.

34 Close parallels are Slip-Painted Ware dishes from Sector MM of the Athenian Agora, which are currently under study for publication by Dr J. Vroom.

35 On this context see Vroom and Tzavella 2017; a jug of this category is presented on fig. 7, upper left.

36 The contributions in this volume by Dr Myrto Veikou, and Dr Natalia Poulou corroborate this conclusion.

37 *Nikolaos Methones, Life of Meletios*, 53.

38 Harvey 1989, 258.

BIBLIOGRAPHY

Adamscheck, B. 1979. *Kenchreai IV: The Pottery: Eastern Port of Corinth*, Leiden.

Angold, M. 1985. The shaping of the Medieval Byzantine city, *Byzantinische Forschungen* 10, 1-38.

Arapoyanni, X. 1986. Ανασκαφή στην Κάντζα Αττικής, *Β' Επιστημονική Συνάντηση ΝΑ Αττικής, Καλύβια Αττικής*, 25-28/10/1985, Kalyvia, 255-67.

Athanasoulis, D. 2013. Corinth, in: J. Albani and E. Chalkia (eds.), *Heaven and Earth. Cities and Countryside in Byzantine Greece*, Athens, 192-209.

Athanasoulis, D., M. Athanasoula, et al. 2010. Σύντομη επισκόπηση της αρχαιολογικής έρευνας μεσαιωνικών καταλοίπων Κορίνθου, in: *Πρακτικά του Η' Διεθνούς Συνεδρίου Πελοποννησιακών Σπουδών, Κόρινθος 26-28 Σεπτεμβρίου 2008* (= *Πελοποννησιακά, Παράρτημα* 29) [= *Proceedings of the 8th International Conference of Peloponnesian Studies, Corinth 26-28 September 2008*, Athens, 167-79.

Avissar, M. and E. Stern 2005. *Pottery of the Crusader, Ayyubid, and Mamluk Periods in Israel*, Israel Antiquities Authority Reports No. 26, Jerusalem.

Bintliff, J. 2013. Poverty and resistance in the material culture of Early Modern rural households in the Aegean, in: J. Bintliff and M. Caroscio (eds.), *Pottery and Social Dynamics in the Mediterranean and Beyond in Medieval and Post-Medieval Times*, BAR International Series 2557, 41-46.

Bouras, Ch. 2002. *Η ελλαδική ναοδομία κατά τον 12ο αιώνα*, Athens.

Chatzesoteriou, G.D. 1973. *Ιστορία της Παιανίας και των ανατολικά του Υμηττού περιοχών, 1205-1973*, Athens.

Dagron, G. 2002. The urban economy, seventh-twelfth centuries, in: A.E. Laiou (ed.), *The Economic History of Byzantium: from the Seventh through the Fifteenth Century, Vol. 2*, Washington, DC, 393-462.

Dietler, M. 2010. Consumption, in: D. Hicks and M. C. Beaudry (eds.), *The Oxford Handbook of Material Culture Studies*, Oxford, 209-28.

Gerstel S.E.J., 2001, Art and identity in the Medieval Morea, in: A.E. Laiou and R.P. Mottahedeh (eds.), *The Crusades from the Perspective of Byzantium and the Muslim World*, Washington, DC, 263-80.

Gregory, T.E. 1989. Late Byzantine Pottery from Isthmia: New Evidence from the Korinthia, in: V. Déroche and J.-M. Spieser (eds.), *Recherches sur la céramique byzantine*, BCH Suppl. 18, Athens, 201-208.

Gregory, T.E. 1993a. *Isthmia Vol. V: The Hexamilion and the Fortress*, Princeton, NJ.

Gregory, T.E. 1993b. Local and imported Medieval pottery from Isthmia, in: S. Gelichi (ed.), *La ceramica nel mondo bizantino tra XI e XV secolo e i suoi rapport con Italia*, Siena, 11-13 marzo 1991, Florence, 283-306.

Gregory, T.E. 2022. Byzantine and Post-Byzantine pottery, in: J.L. Rife and E. Korka (eds.), *On the Edge of a Roman Port: Excavations at Koutsongila, Kenchreai, 2007-2014*, Hesperia Supplement 52, pp?? [not yet published]

Harvey, A. 1989. *Economic Expansion in the Byzantine Empire, 900-1200*, Cambridge & New York.

Joyner, L. 2007, Cooking pots as indicators of cultural change. A petrographic study of Byzantine and Frankish cooking wares from Corinth, *Hesperia* 76, 183-227.

Laiou, A. 2006. Μεταξύ παραγωγής και κατανάλωσης: Είχαν οικονομία οι βυζαντινές πόλεις;, Public lecture held on June 6th 2006, *Praktika tis Akadimias Athinon* 81, Vol. B, 85-126.

Laiou, A. 2013. The Byzantine city: Parasitic or productive? Paper presented at the XXIst International Congress of Byzantine Studies (London, August 2006), in: C. Morrisson and R. Dorin (eds.), *Economic Thought and Economic Life in Byzantium*, Ashgate Variorum, Chapter XII, Aldershot, 1-35.

Lev-Tov, J. 1999, The influences of religion, social structure, and ethnicity on diet: An example from Frankish Corinth, in: S.J. Vaughan and W.D.E. Coulson (eds.), *Palaeodiet in the Aegean. Papers from a Colloquium Held at the 1993 Meeting of the Archaeological Institute of America in Washington, DC*, Wiener Laboratory Monographs 1, Oxford, 85-98.

Lolos, Y.A. 2011. *Land of Sikyon. Archaeology and History of a Greek City-State*, Hesperia Suppl. 39, Princeton, NJ.

Morgan, C.H. 1942, *Corinth XI: The Byzantine Pottery*, Cambridge, MA.

Nikolaos Methones, Life of Meletios: Νικόλαος επίσκοπος Μεθώνης, Βίος τοῦ ὁσίου πατρός ἡμῶν Μελετίου τοῦ ἐν τῷ ὄρει τῆς Μυουπόλεως ἀσκήσαντος, ed. Ch. Papadopoulos, Συμβολαί εις την ιστορίαν του μοναχικού βίου εν Ελλάδι, ιι. *Ο Όσιος Μελέτιος 'ο νέος' (περ. 1035-1105)*, Athens 1935 (second edition 1949: P. S. Speliopoulos [ed.]), 37-72.

Piéri, D. 2005. *Le commerce du vin oriental à l'époque byzantine (Ve-VIIe siècles). Le témoignage des amphores en Gaule*, Beyrouth.

Sanders, G.D.R. 1987. An assemblage of Frankish pottery at Corinth, *Hesperia* 56, 159-95.

Sanders, G.D.R. 2000. New relative and absolute chronologies for 9th to 13th century glazed wares at Corinth: Methodology and social conclusions, in: J. Koder (ed.), *Byzanz als Raum. Zu Methoden und Inhalten der historischen Geographie des östlischen Mittelmeerraumes im Mittelalter*, Vienna 2000, 153-73.

Sanders, G.D.R. 2002. Corinth, in: A. Laiou (ed.), *The Economic History of Byzantium. From the Seventh through the Fifteenth Century, Vol. 2*, Washington, DC, 647-54.

Sanders, G.D.R. 2003. Recent developments in the chronology of Byzantine Corinth, in: C. K. Williams II and N. Bookidis (eds.), *Corinth Vol. XX: Corinth, The Centenary 1896-1996*, Princeton, NJ, 385-99.

Sanders, G.D.R. 2014. Did ordinary people own pottery?, public lecture held at the lecture series *Byzantium without Twilight: Modest Objects and their Use in the Everyday Life of the Byzantines* of the National Research Foundation at Athens on May 6, 2014. http://helios-eie.ekt.gr/EIE/handle/10442/14416.

Sanders, G.D.R. 2016. Recent finds from Ancient Corinth: How little things make big differences, *Babesch. Tenth Babesch Byvanck Lecture, 29.11.2016, National Museum of Antiquities at Leiden*, 1-31.

Sanders, G.D.R. 2018. Είχαν οι απλοί άνθρωποι κεραμικά; Είδη οικοσκευής των πλουσιότερων και των φτωχότερων βαθμίδων της κοινωνίας, in: A. G. Yangaki and A. Panopoulou (eds.), Το Βυζάντιο χωρίς λάμψη. Τα ταπεινά αντικείμενα και η χρήση τους στον καθημερινό βίο των Βυζαντινών, Athens, 79-107.

Scranton, R.L. 1957. *Corinth XVI. Mediaeval Architecture in the Central Area of Corinth*, Princeton, NJ.

Tzavella, E. 2018. Βυζαντινή κεραμική από την αρχαία Κόρινθο και οι μαρτυρίες της για την οικιστική μορφή της πόλης, in: E. Zymi, A.-V. Karapanagiotou and M. Xanthopoulou (eds.), Το αρχαιολογικό έργο στην Πελοπόννησο (αεπελ 1). *Πρακτικά του Διεθνούς Συνεδρίου, Τρίπολη, 7-11.11.2012*, Kalamata, 811-823.

Tzavella, E. 2020. Corinth: Beyond the Forum. Use of ceramics, social implications, and settlement pattern, 12th-13th centuries, in: Y. Waksman (ed.), *Multidisciplinary Approaches to Food and Foodways in the Medieval Eastern Mediterranean (Proceedings of the final conference of the POMEDOR Project, Lyon 19-21 May 2016)*.

Tzavella, E. 2021. The Middle Byzantine, Frankish and Ottoman periods, in: Y. Lolos (ed.), *The Sikyon Survey Project*, Meletemata Series, Athens, 347-69.

Vezzoli, V. 2011. The Fustat ceramic collection in the Royal Museums of Art and History in Brussels: The Mamluk assemblage, *Bulletin des Musées Royaux d'Art et d'Histoire* 82, 119-68.

Vroom, J. 2011. The Morea and its links with Southern Italy after AD 1204: Ceramics and identity, *Archeologia Medievale* 38, 409-30.

Vroom, J. and E. Tzavella 2017. Dinner time in Athens: Eating and drinking in the Medieval Agora, in: J. Vroom, Y. Waksman and R. van Oosten (eds.), *Medieval Masterchef. Archaeological and Historical Perspectives on Eastern Cuisine and Western Foodways*, MPMAS II, Turnhout, 145-80.

Vroom, J., Y. Waksman and R. van Oosten (eds.). *Medieval Masterchef. Archaeological and Historical Perspectives on Eastern Cuisine and Western Foodways*, Medieval and Post-Medieval Mediterranean Archaeology Series II, Turnhout.

Watson, O. 2004. *Ceramics from Islamic Lands. Kuwait National Museum, the Al-Sabah Collection*, New York.

Wickham, C. 2005. *Framing the Early Middle Ages: Europe and the Mediterranean, 400-800*, Oxford.

Whittaker, C. R. 1990. The consumer city revisited: The vicus and the city, *Journal of Roman Archaeology* 3, 110-18.

Williams II, C.K. and O. Zervos 1990. Excavations at Corinth, 1989: The Temenos of Temple E, *Hesperia* 59, 325-69.

Williams II, C.K. and O. Zervos 1992. Frankish Corinth: 1991, *Hesperia* 61, 133-91.

Williams II, C.K. and O. Zervos 1995. Frankish Corinth: 1994, *Hesperia* 64, 1-60.

Williams II, C.K., L.M. Snyder, E. Barnes and O. Zervos 1998. Frankish Corinth: 1997, *Hesperia* 67, 223-81.

Williams II, C.K. 2003. Frankish Corinth, in: C.K. Williams II and N. Bookidis (eds.), *Corinth XX: The Centenary, 1896-1996*, Athens, 423-34.

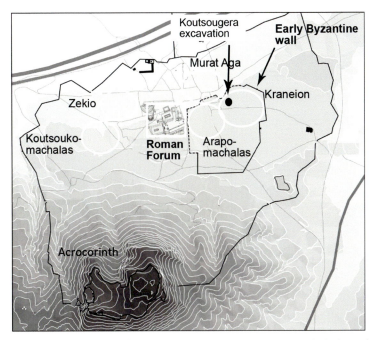

FIG. 1 – Map of Byzantine Corinth (image: James Herbst, American School of Classical Studies in Athens, re-worked by E. Tavella)

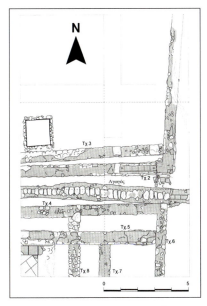

FIG. 2 – Corinth, Koutsougeras plot (ground plan: Yannis Nakas. Τχ = Wall, Αγωγός = Water drain).

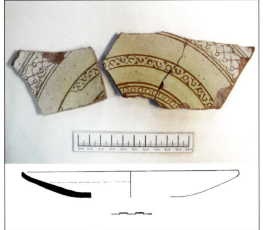

FIG. 3 – Fine Sgraffito dish found in Corinth, Koutsougera plot (E. Tzavella).

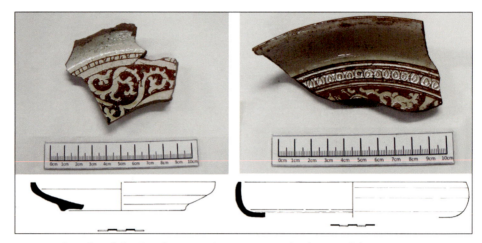

FIG. 4 – Champlévé dishes found in Corinth, Koutsougera plot (E. Tzavella).

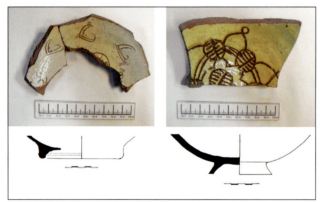

FIG. 5A-B – (A) – Late Sgraffito dish; (B) – Incised Sgraffito dish found in Corinth, Koutsougera plot (E. Tzavella).

FIG. 6 – Mamluk Sgraffiato Ware dish found in Corinth, Koutsougera plot (E. Tzavella).

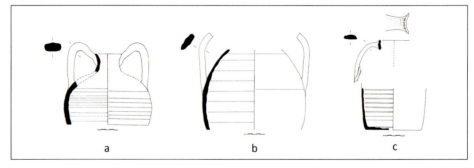

FIG. 7A-C – (A) – Amphora; (B) – *Lageni* (closed storage and transport vessel); (C) – Unglazed White Ware jug, all found in Corinth, Koutsougera plot (drawings: Evangelia Broziouti).

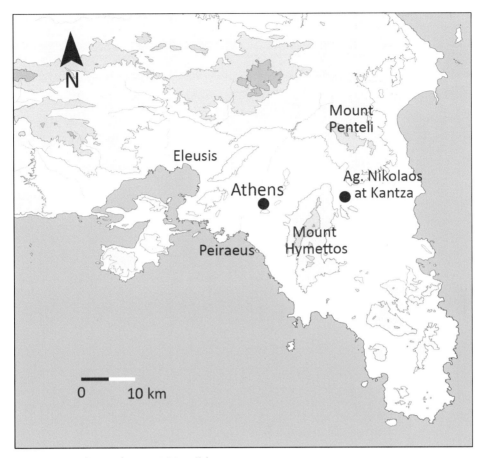

FIG. 8 – Map of Attica (image: E. Tzavella)

FIG. 9 – The church of Agios Nikolaos, Kantza, Attica. View from east (photo: author. Courtesy Ephorate of Antiquities of East Attica © Hellenic Ministry of Culture and Sports).

FIG. 10 – Agios Nikolaos, Kantza. Ancillary room of Byzantine monastery (reprinted from Arapoyanni 1986, fig. 6. Courtesy Dr X. Arapoyanni).

FIG. 11 – Fragments of a Günsenin 3 amphora found in Kantza, Agios Nikolaos (E. Tzavella).

FIG. 12 – Stewpot found in Kantza, Agios Nikolaos excavation (E. Tzavella).

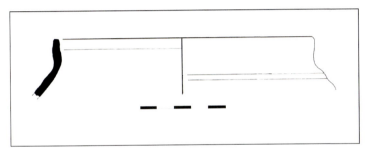
FIG. 13 – Stewpot rim found in Kantza, Agios Nikolaos excavation (drawing: E. Tzavella).

FIG. 14 – Base fragments of Slip-Painted bowls found in Kantza, Ag. Nikolaos excavation (E. Tzavella).

FIG. 15 – Base fragments of a Slip-Painted bowl found in Kantza, Ag. Nikolaos excavation (E. Tzavella).

FIG. 16 – Base fragment of a bowl with Green and Brown Painted decoration found in Kantza, Agios Nikolaos excavation (drawing: E. Tzavella).

FIG. 17 – Fragments of a dish with Sgraffito decoration found in Kantza, Agios Nikolaos (E. Tzavella).

FIG. 18 – Upper part of a jug with bulbous neck and vertical rim from Kantza, Agios Nikolaos excavation (E. Tzavella).

FIG. 19 – Upper part of a jug with narrow neck found in Kantza, Agios Nikolaos excavation (E. Tzavella).

* * *

EARLY BYZANTINE TO LATE BYZANTINE PERIODS

AN OVERVIEW

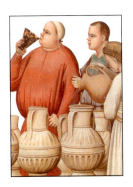

* * *

Medieval person drinking wine from a glass beaker, fresco by Giotto di Bonone, *The Wedding at Cana*, ca. 1304-1306, Scrovegni (Arena) Chapel, Padua, Italy (photo: J. Vroom).

* * *

Production, exchange and consumption of ceramics in the Byzantine Mediterranean (ca. 7th-15th centuries)

Joanita Vroom

*

INTRODUCTION

Although Byzantine pottery is ubiquitous on archaeological sites all over the eastern Mediterranean, it has not always been studied to its full potential. If these wares were studied at all (which was not at all obvious), they were mostly used for dating purposes only, thus leaving unexplored their great potential to capture long-term patterns of production, distribution and consumption of the Byzantine past.[1] In the wide range of interdisciplinary scholarship on consumption studies (for example in anthropology, history, art history),[2] archaeology can nonetheless provide comparative rich evidence of material culture across time and space that is not always available in written texts or in ethnographic research. It can thus offer 'an exceptionally powerful mechanism to examine complicated consumption tactics' (among which improvements of manufacture techniques, innovations in glazed tablewares, spatial distribution of specific goods, changing consumer demands over time etc.).[3]

This chapter sets out to approach Byzantine pottery precisely from this perspective, and aims to offer recent views on Byzantine ceramic manufacture, trade and use (in the sense of consumption). For my approach I will explore the demand for two consumer products in particular, glazed tablewares and amphorae, as they both provide indications on the making, the purchase, and the transfer of various (bulk) goods in the (eastern) Mediterranean. In fact, these vessels were often transported in a mixed cargo by ship in addition to or in combination with (silk) textiles and other exotic commodities along maritime routes.[4] Their manufacture, consumption and re-distribution was typically concentrated in a specific location, such as the Byzantine city. This city could have functioned as a nodal point, a provincial market, as well as a regional consumption centre (which would also service the immediate hinterland).[5]

In order to identify consumption patterns in earthenware vessels, some questions will be raised in this chapter.[6] First of all, is it possible to define levels of ceramic consumption in the Byzantine world? How can we trace changes in demand for consumer's (semi-)durables, such as pottery, during Byzantine times? Were there high-level or rather low-level values of ceramic consumption? When did new ceramic products start to appear? And when did they spread from the capital Constantinople to provincial urban centres, and perhaps even to rural communities in the countryside?

In the first part of this chapter short overviews are presented of crucial innovations in Byzantine pottery manufacture (especially glazed tablewares) in the eastern Mediterranean between the 7th and 15th centuries. It is my intention to present the most common shapes, painted colours and decoration styles used per period, ranging from Early Byzantine to Late Byzantine/Late Medieval times. The focus in the second part of the chapter is on excavated shipwrecks as evidence for distribution mechanisms of Byzantine amphorae and glazed tablewares, and in a broader sense as evidence for sea trade and maritime contacts in the eastern Mediterranean during this time period. Finally, ceramic 'exotic' imports in Byzantium from the Islamic world will be discussed, focussing in particular on new finds from excavated contexts instead of on well-known material of unknown provenance in museum collections. The ultimate objective is to contribute to the understanding of long-term patterns of ceramic production and consumption and its changes over time during the Byzantine period.

PRODUCTION AND CONSUMPTION OF EARLY BYZANTINE GLAZED CERAMICS – (CA. 7TH-9TH CENTURIES)

From an archaeological point of view, the introduction of lead glazed pottery marked the transition from Late Antiquity to Early Byzantine times in the eastern Mediterranean. The relatively easy technique of lead-oxide glazing had already been known in some parts of the Roman Empire, but in the 7th century lead-glazed wares started to be produced in and around Constantinople (modern Istanbul) in substantial quantities. Some areas in Istanbul have been mentioned as possible production sites of these ceramics, among which Arnavutköy and Tekfur Palace.[7] Recent archaeometric analyses show that these first products appear to be more in common with Late Roman glazed pottery manufacture on the Balkans than with Near Eastern glaze technology.[8]

At first the glazing was only covering as a surface treatment the interior of unglazed utilitarian vessels, such as *mortaria*, cooking pots and jugs, in order to make these pots less porous (see left above image in Fig. 1).[9] Very little was actually glazed in the beginning (less than 0,5 percent).[10] During the 8th century the lead glazes became more common on tablewares made of a (whitish) kaolin fabric, producing translucency after firing at low temperatures (700-800° Centigrade). From this time onwards it remained the principal glazing method in the Byzantine capital for many centuries for this group of 'Glazed White Wares' (of which the name is based on fabric, not on glaze colour).[11]

The first Constantinopolitan products, also known as 'Glazed White Ware I' (sometimes shortened into 'GWW I'), included undecorated closed vessels of an utilitarian character (mainly cooking pots), followed by open vessels incised with basic scrollwork, wavy lines, occasionally varied by crosses, fishes and inscriptions in Greek letters (see left below image and right image in Fig. 1). A graph showing the most common incised motifs in Glazed White Ware I makes it clear that animals formed the largest category (particularly fishes) but that human figures were not depicted yet in this period (Fig. 2).

These products were not only distributed from the capital to urban centres along the western and south-western Turkish coasts (among which Ephesus and Miletus), but also reached through vital land routes some inland towns (e.g., Amorion, Kalehöyük). Roads, carts and pack animals (mules, donkeys, camels) were probably used for the transport of pottery by land.[12] At Ephesus, we may notice the dissemination of Glazed White Wares from Constantinople (varying in date from the 7th to the 11th centuries) south-west of the Ayasoluk Hill as well as on the ancient site of Ephesus (Fig. 3). Furthermore, they were mostly recovered so far at ports and coastal sites in the Aegean (e.g., Athens, Aegina), Crete (e.g., Heraklion, Gortyna, Agia Galini, Pseira, Loutres/Mochlos, Itanos),[13] Cyprus, northern Africa (e.g., Tocra, Carthage, Alexandria?), southern Albania (e.g., Butrint) and the Crimea (e.g., Chersonesos; see Fig. 1).[14]

A lead-alkali glaze covered these imports initially for functional reasons as a sealant, later for more decorative purposes on dishes, bowls and chafing dishes.[15] These last ones were vessels with an upper glazed bowl that was set on an unglazed hollow stand with ventilation holes.[16] Glaze White Ware I chafing dishes made in a kaolin fabric started already to appear in the Byzantine Empire around 700. A nicely decorated example from Constantinople was for instance recovered on the island of Samos, which shows similarities with 7th- and 8th-century finds from Crete and Rome (see drawing in Fig. 1).[17] The Glazed White Ware I chafing dishes were soon imitated by examples in more reddish (iron-rich) and coarser fabrics (Fig. 4).[18] These characteristics made this intricate vessel suitable as a multi-functional cooking or heating utensil.[19] Burnt parts in the lower stands of chafing dishes indicate that food in the upper glazed bowl was kept warm by charcoal put in or around the lower parts.

It has been suggested that these chafing-dishes were placed on the table during banquets.[20] According to some scholars, chafing dishes are mentioned in Byzantine texts as *saltsaria, saltsera, gararia* or *garera*, because their main function was to prepare and serve warm sauces and, in particular, warm fish-sauces on the table.[21] However, it now seems clear that chafing-dishes were rather placed next or near the table during meals as portable utensils in combination with a so-called *authepsa* (a hot water samovar), as can be seen on Byzantine 11th-century miniatures (see Fig. 5).[22] These pictures show that chafing dishes were used as multi-purpose braziers on or near an open fire, to keep it hot next to the table in a society where separate kitchens were not yet widely used.[23] In this aspect, their function (both in urban centres and in the countryside) shows similarities with contemporary stoves from the Islamic world (known in Arabic as *kanoun*) for the simmering of food on charcoal.

Authepsa (from the Greek αὐθέψης, which literally means 'self-boiling' or 'self-cooking'), was the name of a kind of metal samovar, which was used for heating water (sometimes supplemented with aromatic substances or herbs), or for keeping it hot to mix it with wine during dinner. Examples made of copper and copper alloy with matching lids (like boiling kettles)[24] were found on various sites in Turkey (Fig. 6). We can distinguish these, for instance, at 7th-century Byzantine shops in Sardis,[25] at Constantinople, at Ephesus,[26] at Pergamon,[27] as well as part of the cabin's or crew's equipment at the 7th-century Yassi Ada shipwreck[28] and at the 9th-century Bozburun shipwreck[29] – the last ones both near the Turkish Coast. In Europe, similar vessels were recovered at Durostorum, Stara Zagora and Golemanovo Kale in Bulgaria,[30] at Amathus and Alassa on Cyprus,[31] at Olympia,[32] Eleutherna (Crete) and Spetses in Greece,[33] and even as far away as the 7th-century Anglo-Saxon princely burial at Princewell (in south-east England).[34] Furthermore, two more examples were spotted in northern Africa: one at Korbous in Tunisia, and an unpublished one at Leptis Magna (Fig. 6).[35]

In the Near East these metal utensils were equally widespread (Fig. 6). We can distinguish examples at Jerusalem, at the monastery of Mount Nebo, at Beth Shean, at three shipwrecks near Dor[36], at the monastery St. Martyrios at Ma'ale Adummim (in Palestine)[37] and at the Byzantine church complex in Pella (in Jordan).[38] Others, made of copper and leaded bronze, were even recovered in 8th-century contexts of the Umayyad period, like the ones from the Citadel of Amman, from Umm al-Walid in Jordan[39] and from Sussita/Hippos in Israel.[40]

Ceramic jugs with double handles and attached lids were clearly imitating these metal *authepsae* with small lids attached to the double handle with a small chain (Fig. 7). Such jugs in a kaolin fabric (which were probably also used for boiling purposes) have been recovered in 7th- and 8th-century contexts of various sites in Turkey, among which Limyra.[41] Analogous examples have been found at excavations at the Saraçhane complex in Istanbul, at Anemurium in Cilicia, as well as outside Turkey: at Pitagoreia on Samos, and even on sites in faraway places as Spain (for instance, at Tolmo de Minateda in the south-east, and at Recopolis near Toledo in the centre of the Iberian Peninsula).[42] Excavations at Xanthos in Lycia, at Salamis on Cyprus and at Elaiussa Sebaste in Cilicia yielded a second jug type of an even more realistic ceramic imitation of a metal *authepsa* (Fig. 7).[43]

PRODUCTION AND CONSUMPTION OF MIDDLE BYZANTINE GLAZED CERAMICS – (CA. 10TH – 12TH/EARLY 13TH CENTURIES)

Pottery finds of Middle Byzantine times are fairly well documented in archaeological publications and reports. This period is mostly taken to stretch from the late 9th/early 10th to the 12th/early 13th century, and is sometimes characterised by archaeologists and historians as an 'era of recovery and development'.[44] It is clear that shapes and volume capacities of glazed tablewares gradually changed in the Middle Byzantine era. In most ceramic samples studied in Greece there were striking differences in pottery shape and technology of the tablewares for each chronological phase (see Fig. 8).

New centres of pottery production developed indeed in this period, experimenting with new shapes and innovative incised decoration-techniques (known as sgraffito, from the Italian word *sgraffiare* for 'scratched'). The distribution of these new glazed products changed rapidly due to a rise in production from the 12th century onwards. Although we are not dealing entirely with luxury products, we may notice the evident change in emphasis from function to decoration in this period. With the appearance of widely used glazed wares with painted or incised decoration, 'a greater uniformity of taste in pottery styles' was emerging in the Byzantine world.[45]

The standard glazed tablewares of the Middle Byzantine era are traditionally divided into two main groups: glazed ceramics with a white (kaolin) fabric and glazed ones with a red (iron-rich) fabric. The first ones, the so-called 'Glazed White Wares' (mentioned above), remained dominating pottery manufacture in the capital. These wares were produced there for a long period of time: from the early 7th to the 13th century, with a peak in the 10th to 12th centuries.

Glazed White Wares from Constantinople – After two reports on the Great Palace finds (which appeared in 1947 and 1954 respectively) and an article on the Agia Eirene material, it took some time until a large deposit of Glazed White Wares (including another Cosmopolitan product, the colourfully painted 'Polychrome Ware') was published in 1992 from excavations at Constantinople/Istanbul.[46] This deposit was recovered in the Saraçhane district, where once the church of St. Polyeuktos was situated.[47]

John Hayes provided the dating framework for Glazed White Wares and Polychrome Ware, the majority being dishes with a high pedestal ring-foot or cups often decorated with impressed or stamped motifs imitating precious metalwork (see Fig. 9).[48] The stratigraphic and numismatic evidence of the Saraçhane excavations contributed greatly to the refinement of the dating of these pottery types. Hayes' publication dealt with circa 20,000 glazed sherds in a white kaolin fabric, suggesting several improvements in the traditional diagnosis and dating of Glazed White Wares. Previous classifications tended to stress the decorative aspects of these ceramics,[49] but Hayes divided these wares into five new groups (dating from the early 7th to the 13th centuries) on the basis of fabric, while Polychrome Ware was treated as a different and smaller group altogether.[50] Due to its occurrence in massive quantities, he assumed that they were made locally – although no unquestionable kilns, wasters or unfinished products have been found yet.

Charles Morgan published already in 1942 small quantities of Glazed White Ware II found at Corinth in central Greece.[51] It is now clear that this imported pottery type was much in use at Corinth in the late 10th and 11th centuries before the local factories became active. In fact, this pottery type was one of the primary stimuli for the local glazed pottery production at Corinth, though it continued to be imported on a smaller scale during the 12th century.[52]

To date, finds of Hayes' Glazed White Ware groups II-IV and Polychrome Ware have been recorded at various Byzantine coastal and inland sites in the Aegean, around the Black Sea shores, in Turkey, in Cyprus, in Italy and even in northern Russia (e.g., Novgorod) and Sweden (e.g., Sigtuna, Lund; see Fig. 9).[53] Some of these Constantinopolitan products were even found at rural settlements in the hinterland of important Byzantine harbours and urban centres, as is shown in the case of Thespiae in Boeotia.[54] In short, they were more widely distributed within the provincial rural economy than the previous Glazed White Ware I products.

The open vessels of Glazed White Ware II-IV and Polychrome Ware were usually incised, painted or stamped on the interior with representations of human figures in a classical style, with animals, with objects (mostly crosses), with vegetal and abstract designs or with scenes of a different character (put in the category 'other'; see Fig. 10). Observing over a longer period, the majority of the designs (humans, animals, objects, vegetal, abstract and other) appear in Glazed White Ware II, and we see that animals form the largest group in the most used motifs (see Fig. 10). However, this time there is a difference in the animal motifs with the previous Glazed White Ware I group of earlier times, because in the Middle Byzantine period birds become by now most favourite. At Constantinople, for instance, animals form the largest group of used motifs in Middle Byzantine times, and birds (specifically the eagle with spread-out wings) form at least 56 percent of these animal motifs (Figs. 11-12). Interesting is also the increase of abstract painted motifs in the later Glazed White Ware IV group, which can be dated to circa mid 12th-(early) 13th centuries, although objects seem to be more favourable as designs in the Polychrome Ware group (Fig. 13).

Looking at the use of these motifs from a larger geographical perspective we may notice another interesting feature. In Fig. 14 we can for instance distinguish pie charts with decorated Glazed White Ware finds from different parts of the Byzantine Empire (the colours in these pie charts indicate the following: humans = dark blue, animals = red, vegetal = green, objects = purple, abstract = light blue, and other = orange). In the northern parts of Byzantium (in particular at Constantinople and around the Black Sea) we see larger percentages of animal decorations, whereas towards the south (on the Peloponnesus) more abstract designs (Corinth) or objects (Sparta) are predominant in the decoration repertoires. The question is how to interpret these differences: are they related to production or rather to consumer behaviour; that is to say, are they related to supply- or demand-driven needs? This is a challenging dilemma, which asks for further study in the near future.

Glazed Red Wares from central Greece – The so-called 'Glazed Red Wares' (formerly named by Morgan as 'Plain Glazed Wares') are the second group of Middle Byzantine tablewares found in significant quantities in the eastern Mediterranean. The first products of Glazed Red Wares appear without much decoration from the late 9th century onward; the most decorative ones start from the late 11th century onward. Many originate from Corinth, but we now start to realize that these wares probably were manufactured at more than one site: Chalcis, Athens, Thessaloniki and Sparta can at present also be named as production centres in central Greece.[55]

Central Greece was the centre of a network of regional and inter-regional trade that developed in the 11th-12th centuries. At the end of the 11th century the Corinthian industry went through a period of transformation. Apparently, the new influences occurred in the years immediately after the mid 11th century, after the battle of Manzikert in 1071 and the conquest of Sicily by the Normans in 1091.[56] The volume of glazed pottery in the Corinthian deposits increased indeed from the 11th century onward, and especially during the 12th and into the 13th century (Fig. 8).[57] The shapes changed (shallow dishes and bowls replaced dishes with a high ring foot), and innovative decoration-techniques were introduced according to new engraving styles in silverware.[58]

From the end of the 11th century onward, the practice of using pottery for table purposes became more widespread in the Byzantine world. The potters took much more trouble to ensure that vessels for the table such as bowls and dishes were pleasing to look at, by covering their inside with an overall coating of white slip and a lead glaze, and further enhancing the surfaces with a colourful variety of incised and painted designs.[59]

In addition, the shapes of these decorated wares are generally very simple. We see thick-walled dishes and shallow bowls, but jugs are unusual. The open and wide dishes and bowls come in similar shapes, but in a wide range of sizes.[60] Looking from the perspective of eating habits, the function of most of these vessels must have been quite practical for communal rather than individual purposes. The open and wide dishes and bowls were sizeable enough to hold food for several diners. However, because of the porosity of their clays these vessels were probably not very suitable for watery dishes.

One notable change was the use of a white slip as an attempt to imitate the imported Glazed White Wares from Constantinople. The Byzantine potters experimented with a white slip (on a red fabric) and various painted and incised designs as decoration, creating the so-called 'Slip-painted Ware' (using the white slip as a decoration-technique), 'Green and Brown Painted Ware' (painting designs with copper and iron oxides on a white slip), 'Fine Sgraffito Ware' (making fine line incisions through the white slip), Incised Sgraffito Ware' (using broader incisions through the white slip) and 'Champlevé Ware' (removing the slip coating in such a way as to make designs in low relief).[61] Furthermore, compasses must have been used by the potters in order to get regular circles in the white slip, because traces of holes caused by the compasses can still be seen in many pottery fragments.[62]

Apart from these new incised decoration techniques, the Byzantine potters also used some sort of 'formulae' for the preparation of glazes and colours. A Medieval treatise from north-western Europe gives us a recipe from Greek potters for glazing vessels in various colours. This manuscript with the title *De diversis artibus* was written in the Rhineland by the monk Theophilus in the first half of the 12th century, showing that 'the Greeks' used all kind of colours and ground each one separately with water.[63] Furthermore, Heraclius' treatise *De coloribus et artibus Romanorum* (III, 3) offered a 12th-century recipe for decorating pottery with a clear lead, or a copper lead glaze. This text was the first mentioning of the use of lead, copper or brass in the manufacture of glazes.[64]

A reconstruction of a pottery kiln can be made of excavated examples from Greece, Turkey, Bulgaria, Rumania and Cyprus.[65] Most of these kilns were of the updraught type, with a cylindrical structure and a crude dome.[66] Furthermore, the Byzantine potters must have known Islamic kiln technology, as is shown by kiln material from Serres, northern Greece.[67] Here clay rods (of ca. 3.5 cm in diameter) were found that formed a shelf in the kiln on which the vessels were placed for firing.[68] This coincides with the description of an Islamic kiln by the 14th-century potter Abu'l-Qaim: '[...] inside [it] has row upon row of fired earthenware pegs, each an *arsh* and a half long, fitted in the holes in the wall. The vessels are placed on them [...]'[69]

Transmission of iconographical styles – Inspiration for the motifs found on the Middle Byzantine incised and painted tablewares perhaps originated from the repertoire of Medieval ornament employed by craftsmen working in other media and in other materials.[70] For example, the spiral painted motifs on Brown and Green Painted Ware are comparable to the ornamental, figural frescoes produced by painters in the crypt of the monastery of Osios Loukas in central Greece.[71]

On the other hand, the potters engraving these Byzantine glazed tablewares undoubtedly drew upon the decorative vocabulary of the Islamic world for their inspiration. One can observe, for example, exactly the same design of so-called 'Pseudo-Kufic script' in Fine Sgraffito Ware, as well as in the abstract wall-masonry created by masons in the walls of Byzantine monasteries and churches.[72] This Oriental influence on decoration motifs and techniques in Byzantine ceramics was increasingly recognized by several scholars working with Islamic pottery since the beginning of the twentieth century.[73]

This is not so strange, because we know that there were links between Byzantium and the Islamic world as Muslim communities lived within the Byzantine Empire and mosques existed in Constantinople and Athens.[74] Apart from 'Pseudo-Kufic script', we can distinguish arabesque ornaments, birds, fantastic creatures and court scenes depicting amusements.[75] Perhaps these motifs came into the Byzantine repertoire through war booty, diplomatic gifts or travellers,[76] although Islamic pottery reached the eastern Mediterranean at many different Byzantine sites in order to imply commercial connections (see Table 2, Fig. 14).

PRODUCTION AND CONSUMPTION OF LATE BYZANTINE/LATE MEDIEVAL GLAZED CERAMICS – (CA. 13TH-15TH CENTURIES)

During the 13th century the locations and types of glazed pottery production changed, resulting in a peak of tableware manufacture and a subsequent rise in pottery trade. It is clear that from the 13th century onward all over the Byzantine Empire many potter's workshops were manufacturing ceramic products, especially glazed tablewares for the use of more liquid foods.[77] These consisted for the greater part of quickly-made mass-produced decorative ceramics in incised and painted decoration styles, as well as their variants or imitations.[78]

The fancy tablewares of Middle Byzantine times seem to have gone out of use in the 13th century, being overtaken in the Late Byzantine/Frankish period by other types of sgraffito wares with sometimes two or more colours in the glaze. In addition to the vast improvement in the quality of the lead glaze (which became thicker and with a more glassy appearance), a fine, thinly-potted ware replaced the previous thick, soft and coarse tablewares.[79]

Changes in shapes and designs – Noteworthy for the transition from the Middle Byzantine to the Late Byzantine/Frankish period is also a change in pottery shapes. The ceramic repertoire of the Middle Byzantine period is, for instance, much more characterized by open shapes of large dishes with large rim diameters (sometimes up to 30 cm), while in the Late Byzantine/Frankish period, much smaller bowls with smaller rim and base diameters form the larger part of the diagnostic forms (Fig. 8a; see also Fig. 8b for the increase of smaller bowls in Late Medieval ceramic assemblages on two Medieval sites).[80] These deep bowls could have been used for more or less liquid mixtures, or perhaps they were even intended as drinking vessels. After all, the consumption of liquids clearly implies vessels with fairly high sides. In the Turkish or Ottoman period, on the other side, the rim diameters of most vessels become much larger again.[81] However, for obvious reasons I will discuss here only the differences in pottery shape of glazed tablewares between the Middle Byzantine and Late Byzantine/Frankish periods.

When one looks at 244 Late Medieval Cypriot ceramic vessels from four museum collections (Nicosia, Larnaca, Stockholm, Paris),[82] it is striking that most of them have open shapes, such as goblets, footed dishes or bowls with small rim diameters (Fig. 15).[83] So, we have to keep in mind that we are dealing in this period with glazed objects with limited dimensions, which permitted only a restricted repertoire of designs. Furthermore, the use of colour on these 244 vessels can be allocated between the ones painted with one colour, two colours and three colours. The next graph makes it evident that ceramics with three colours were most common, especially in the 14th century, followed by three-coloured vessels in the 15th century (Fig. 16).

The motifs on these 244 vessels were divided between designs with human figures, with animals (such as birds and fishes), with objects (such as keys and heraldic shields), as well as with vegetal and finally with (more abstract) geometric motifs (Fig. 17). Of these designs, the vessels with vegetal motifs were most common, especially in the 14th century. If we differentiate the amount of the depiction of the human figures in all four collections over the centuries, it is clear that the motif of a standing single man is most common among the published vessels of the 14th century (Fig. 17). If we take the material from one collection – in this case, the vessels from the Leventis collection in Nicosia, for example – the portrayal of a standing single man is indeed represented by 64 percent of the total of human depictions.[84]

It may be fruitful to look also at dining patterns as far as Late Byzantine/Late Medieval glazed ceramics are concerned. Fig. 18 shows, for instance, the use of colour on pottery per period at excavations in Butrint (southern Albania), and the differences (in colour percentages) over time are quite striking. In order to develop methodologies by which consumption patterns can be recognized in archaeological contexts, it may also be important to record the presence or the absence of decoration on the ceramics. I have, therefore, divided decorated wares with the use of one painted colour, two painted colours, three painted colours and, finally, four (or more) painted colours. Also here the differences over times are clear.

After differentiating these four groups within each period it is obvious that the Late Byzantine/Late Medieval (in the graph described as 'LMED', circa 13th-14th centuries) and Early Venetian periods (in the graph described as 'EVEN', circa late 14th-mid 16th centuries) at Butrint produced by far the most colourful wares, reflecting the taste for colourful everyday objects during these periods. If we look at the colour percentages in the Late Byzantine/Late Medieval period (circa late 13th to 14th centuries), when Butrint was under Angevin domination, we may note further details in this respect (Fig. 18). The large number of decorated wares with three colours (47 percent) – and these are mainly imported fine wares from southern Italy (from southern Apulia, Basilicata and Calabria) – is clear evidence of the complexity of decoration on serving vessels in Late Byzantine/Late Medieval times, and it is quite tempting to relate this to wider socio-economic developments in changing foodways and dining habits in this part of the Mediterranean.[85]

Heterogeneous styles – There was no homogeneity in shapes or decoration in the eastern Mediterranean during this period, but rather a liberal use of styles and motifs, the last ones often being geometric, stylised floral or human beings (among which the introduction of well-equipped soldiers wearing helmets, body armour, mail chausses, spears or lances, pennons and shields, while marching fully armed or combating a dragon). Fig. 19 shows a glazed dish from central Greece (probably made at Chalcis) decorated with broad incised lines, also known as Incised Sgraffito Ware, dated to the late 12th and early 13th centuries.[86] The dish was found during excavations at Vrea on the western coast of Chalkidhiki in Macedonia. The figure portrayed on this vessel is open to interpretation. On the one hand, the soldier seems to be heavily armed in the Byzantine style, wearing features of warrior's uniforms common in the Byzantine world – known for instance from the portrayal of the Byzantine epic hero and border-warrior Digenis Akritas on pottery found in Corinth, Thebes and other places.[87]

On the other hand, he is wearing Western-style shoes and mail stockings as well as a shield of Norman type.[88] It has recently been suggested that the helmet on the warrior dish shows much resemblance with helmets in use in Russia and the Ukraine during the 12th and 13th centuries.[89]

In general, we are looking at vessels with schematic enigmatic images of foot soldiers and warriors made during the Crusader period, often portrayed on Incised Sgraffito Ware (and a few on Fine Sgraffito Ware or Measles Ware) with multi-cultural and hybrid military outfits derived both from myth and everyday experience from different parts of the Mediterranean (see Fig. 19). We see the sudden appearance of a standing single man on bowls of the late 13th and 14th centuries, who is heavily armoured and dressed in chain-mail.[90] In fact, some of these male figures were portrayed as a Crusader warrior in action with a Western-style shield and sword, as one can also find these items in similar looking warrior depictions on vessels from southern Italy, Greece and southern Turkey (Fig. 19).[91]

Whether this presentation is perhaps connected to a new definition of knighthood (in order to distinguish oneself in a battle or in a tournament), to contemporary epic and literary themes (Akritic songs or some other folk tale), or perhaps to historical events, we do not know yet. Undoubtedly, some of these images belong to the era of the Crusades, reflecting the chivalric culture, customs and beliefs of that period. They show a knightly culture in a multicultural society with a blend of French, Italian, Greek and Islamic elements, with an emphasis on personal relations and with a growing interest in an individual's own feelings. They focus on regional history, especially on areas where the Franks were living, as is shown on similar looking frescoes or gravestones with heavily armoured warriors.[92]

Decoration styles on glazed tablewares were in this period also influenced by artefacts made in other materials, such as glass vessels, metalware or printed textiles. Parallels existed, for instance, between textiles and relief-moulded glazed and unglazed ceramics from the Islamic world, in particular those of the Late Ayyubid and Early Mamluk periods (ca. 12th-14th centuries).[93] Shared motifs consisted of elaborate knots, stars, scattered dots, twelve-petalled rosettes and inscriptions (often generic benedictions or blessings to unspecified owners). The use of similar designs has been attributed to the common practice of portable moulds and small stamps, which were perhaps used for the transmission of designs across different media, regions and cultures. For example, heraldic motifs (such as eagles, rosettes and lions) that were prominent in 13th-century Mamluk textile decoration can be seen both on Islamic and Late Byzantine/Frankish glazed pottery.[94]

Various cities and regions stand out as centres of local production in this period (such as Pergamon, Thessaloniki, Thrace, Cyprus), with newly operating pottery workshops making distinctive regional products with the help of innovative techniques (for instance tripod stilts).[95] From the end of the 13th century onwards, tripod stilts (or earthenware supports, supposedly originating from Asia) were used to separate glazed vessels from sticking together in the kiln, when fired.[96] These clay stands made it possible to stack the pots vertically one on top of the other. This allowed better distribution of heat and flow of air around vessels in the kiln, when compared with simple stacking.[97] A thicker vitreous glaze seems to accompany the use of these tripod stilts, which (after taking away) often leave small marks of bare clay on the bottom of the vessels. The introduction of the tripod stand resulted in a tighter packing in the kiln and consequently a substantially increased output.

Distinctive distribution patterns – Imported glazed tablewares show distinctive distribution patterns in different regions and are not seldom important for the dating of archaeological contexts (such as in the case of Ephesus).[98] However, the exchange of ceramics could happen within a small region, and was then more often than not confined to the close vicinity of a production centre or to its immediate hinterland. On the other hand, the distribution patterns of newly fashioned glazed tablewares imported by long-distance trade appear to have been focussed principally on strategically situated (coastal) distribution centres and transit stations, while dispersal of the pottery over land to more inland regions seems an additional aspect.

The historian David Jacoby suggested that – apart from demand and supply – political factors also had an impact upon the channelling of goods (including ceramics) along established maritime lanes after 1204.[99] In particular, the rivalry between two important maritime city-states, Venice and Genoa, resulted in the division of the (eastern) Mediterranean and the Aegean along their shipping routes. According to Jacoby, each of these two Italian mercantile nations 'consolidated its dominance over specific waterways and maritime spaces, Venice on the western and Genoa on the eastern Aegean, a process completed by the mid-14th century'. And he added: 'The two maritime powers promoted the development of their own transit and transhipment stations, whose infrastructure and services furthered the mobility of passing merchants, ships and goods'.[100]

This division is quite evident when one visualizes the transport of certain glazed tablewares of the Crusader period along the Venetian and Genoese trading routes, trading posts, and their colonized territories in the Mediterranean on a map of the eastern Mediterrenean (see Figs. 20-21). The visual representation of the distribution of the first glazed products made in Venice, known as Lead Glazed Ware from the Veneto region (including *ceramica graffita a spirale cerchio* and Roulette Ware),[101] clearly shows the cabotage system that Venice was using along its established maritime trade routes in the Adriatic Sea, in the eastern Mediterranean and in the Black Sea from the 13th century onwards (Fig. 20). Furthermore, it is obvious that within this system over medium-range distances the Venetian glazed imports were understandibly specifically spread in the western Aegean area, where the most vital Venetian trading posts and colonized territories (among which the southern Peloponnese, Crete and Euboea) were located.

It is very well possible that other goods, such as wine, grain or textiles, were also travelling with these Venetian glazed tablewares to ports and islands within this maritime trade system. Indeed, examples of Roulette Ware from the Veneto region were found within the mixed cargo of the Novy Svet shipwreck near Sudak in the northern Black Sea (off the Crimean coast) together with Günsenin 3 amphorae,[102] which were surely carrying wine from the fertile Lelantine Plain through the nearby Venetian transit port of Chalcis on Euboea island.[103]

The mapping of the Genoese trading system is more complicated (Fig. 21). When one visualizes the distribution of two glazed and incised decorated tableware groups since the 13th century along the Genoese trade routes, outposts and colonized territories, it clearly suggests quite different trade incentives, different mercantile considerations and different market demands compared to the Venetian ones. The right part of this map shows the dissemination of the so-called Port Saint Symeon Ware and its regional variants that were produced in the north-eastern Mediterranean, in particular in workshops in Cilicia and in the area of Antioch-on-the-Orontes.[104] Actually, it was in this crossroads region where the most important harbour of Antioch in eastern Mediterranean, Port Saint Symeon (al-Mina), was situated during the Crusader period (the glazed pottery type has been named after this place since 1938).[105]

The diffusion of the Port Symeon Ware Family was not only restricted to the Levant, Egypt and Cyprus, but also stretched out along the Genoese maritime trading routes and colonised territories (Phokaia, Chios, Lesbos, Pera) to western Turkey, the northern Black Sea and even to Genoa and Marseilles in the western Mediterranean (Fig. 21). It is therefore no coincidence that an imitation of Port Symeon Ware was quickly manufactured in the direct hinterland of Genoa. In fact, the main production of this first Ligurian glazed and incised decorated tableware, known as Tyrrhenian Archaic Graffita (or *graffita arcaica tirenica*) took place from the 13th century onwards at Savona in north-western Italy.[106] The distribution of this pottery type is clearly concentrated in Liguria, the Provence, Corsica, Sardinia, Tuscany, Latium, Sicily and western North Africa. These were areas that were definitely commercially controlled by Genoa or by other subordinate regimes (Fig, 21).

It is clear from this map that Genoa was either dealing with pottery exchange on a regional scale (within its immediate backyard) or with long-distance trade (*Fernhan-*

del) of ceramics on longer distances, but always along its trading routes and colonized territories (in particular the Genoese ports and islands in the eastern Aegean). Perhaps this trans-Mediterranean system comprised the shipping of more precious and costly goods (such as silk textiles) or the large-scale supply of grain and industrial raw materials (among which alum, cotton, mastic or kermes) from distant places, as suggested by David Jacoby.[107] It is evident, though, that during the 13th century Genoa was not involved in the dissemination of glazed tablewares in the Adriatic Sea region, which was undeniably under Venetian domination.

Cabotage trade and long-distance shipping with the help of these two Italian maritime nations facilitated the circulation of new ceramic products along their navigation and transit routes to insular and coastal continental regions of the eastern Mediterranean and of the Black Sea, promoted the spread of innovations, and probably favoured mutual cultural influences and commercial competition.[108] This process is illustrated by the discovery of various shipwrecks in the eastern Mediterranean with substantial quantities of glazed tablewares – as profitable ballast or as the main cargo of the ship.

EXCHANGE PATTERNS:
THE VIEW FROM MARITIME ARCHAEOLOGY

Shipwrecks are not only relatively undisturbed time capsules preserved on the bottom of the sea. In the best case they contain besides remains of the cargo also a collection of utilitarian objects, of archaeobotanical and of archaeozoological remains used by the ship's crews. It is, however, the contents which can put us on the trace of possible maritime trade patterns. Textual evidence of the Byzantine period for the movement of pottery is sparse, yet the archaeological evidence suggests that ceramics were distributed on ships, and that specific tastes played a rol in the content and direction of the cargo.

The shipwrecks which have been excavated in the Aegean since the 1970s clearly show that pottery – especially amphorae for the transport of bulk goods (oil, wine, fish sauce etc.) – moved a lot in Byzantine times.[109] Pottery as such was, however, in most ships in the Mediterranean never the major item of the cargo, because it was quite cheap. It was usually stowed on top of the main cargo. Some scholars suggest that ceramics (even tablewares) were more likely to have been space-fillers or ballast for more valuable shipments.[110]

Until now warehouses (*horrea, apothiki*) stacked with pottery (mostly amphorae) have been seldom recovered in Byzantine ports and cities. The only exceptions are a coastal warehouse excavated at Classe (the harbour of Ravenna), which was filled with imported tablewares, lamps and amphorae grouped together in sets,[111] a military storehouse at the fort of Dichin (along the Danube river) which yielded six amphorae of different types (for instance, LRA 1 and LRA 2) stacked in a row,[112] and a warehouse and anchorage at 'Ard el-Mihjar, south of Ashqelon (Israel), packed with local Gaza-type amphorae, apparently ready for inspection and for transport to other Mediterranean harbours.[113] While the latter 7th-century warehouse shows the export of a prized wine from a productive viticultural region, the first two ones show how goods were imported (around 500) and on their way to consumption sites. Furthermore, we know of shops (often within a *stoa*) in Byzantine cities, which housed potters (Justiniana Prima), or which functioned as grocers (*ergasteria*) where amongst many things pottery was sold (Constantinople).[114]

Shipwrecks with amphorae – Several Byzantine shipwrecks with a cargo of 7th-century amphorae were found in the waters of the eastern Mediterranean, such as the ones off Cape Andreas at the north-eastern end of Cyprus, at the port of Dor, or off the Datça Peninsula in south-western Turkey.[115] The best published 7th-century shipwreck was the one recovered off the island Yassı Ada, near Bodrum, with circa 850-900 wine amphorae (mostly LRA 1 and LRA 2/13 types) on board.[116] In addition, the excavations yielded pantry wares found in the galley, including glazed and red-slipped wares, cooking pots, pitchers (sometimes with resin-coated interiors), various jars, a pithos, copperware, a wine thief and a dozen grape seeds from the amphorae.[117]

The 9th-century Bozburun shipwreck sunk off the southwest coast of Turkey to a depth of 30-35 m.[118] It was excavated in the 1990s, containing a cargo of circa 1200-1500 wine amphorae of a globular type.[119] These amphorae were probably manufactured in the eastern Aegean region and not products from the Crimea, as is often assumed.[120]

An increase in 10th/11th-century maritime contacts can be noted by the numerous wrecks found in various parts of the eastern Mediterranean.[121] The most well-known was the one that sank at Serçe Limanı, southwest of Marmaris and north of Rhodes.[122] This 11th-century ship (of 15 m. long) was carrying Syrian/Palestine glazed ceramics, 80 intact glass vessels and three tons of Syrian glass cullet, comprising two tons of raw glass and one ton of broken glassware.[123] The cargo further included piriform-shaped Byzantine amphorae of the Günsenin 1/Saraçhane 54 type from Ganos on the northern coast of the Sea of Marmara.[124] This popular wine container of the Byzantine Empire was, in fact, widely distributed over the Mediterranean and Europe.[125]

At Constantinople's southern harbour in Yenikapı (Istanbul), no less than 37 shipwrecks from Late Antique to Middle Byzantine times were discovered, among which several smaller 10th- to 11th-century ships.[126] Some wrecks such as 'YK12' even contained their cargo, often full with wine amphorae.[127] The role of Constantinople as a large consumer city and as a regional and inter-regional distribution centre of

Ganos wine is shown by thousands of Günsenin 1/Saraçhane 54 amphorae found at Yenikapı.[128] It seems clear that from Late Antiquity onwards, medium- and long-distance cabotage voyages on smaller, low-status merchant ships (such as the ones found at the Yenikapı excavations) were quite prevalent in the Mediterranean.[129]

Another Middle Byzantine amphora type that is found frequently as cargo on 12th-/13th-century shipwrecks has an elongated body shape and handles rising high above the rim (see amphora image in Fig. 22). About 5000 vessels of this so-called Günsenin 3/Saraçhane 61 amphora were, for example, recovered at a wreck off the Syrian coast near Tartus/Tortosa (see Table 1; Fig. 22, no. 14).[130] More examples came from wrecks found near Sudak in the Crimea, in the Sea of Marmara but especially in the western Aegean, such as off Dhia island (near Crete), at Tainaron on the Peloponnese, at the northern Sporades, south of Euboea island, as well as on eight wrecks recovered at the entrance of the Pagasitikos Gulf (Fig. 22).[131]

These amphora finds definitely mark the main sea-lanes of trade from the western Aegean to Constantinople and the Black Sea region as well as to the Levant during the 12th-13th centuries. Günsenin 3/Saraçhane 61 amphorae were recovered all over the Mediterranean and even up to Russia and Sweden, showing its widespread distribution.[132] One of its places of manufacture was in an important harbour in the western Aegean, such as the port city of Chalcis/Euripos/Negroponte (connecting the island of Euboea with the Boeotian mainland), where at recent excavations outside the town walls evidence of amphora production has been detected.[133] It is clear that Chalcis was not only an important production centre for the mass-production of fairly cheap commodities (among which ceramics), but also a nodal point within the long-distance networks between Constantinople, Crete and Italy.[134] As such, it had a mechanism that superseded local production and distribution.

Shipwrecks with glazed tablewares – From the 12th century onwards ships started to carry glazed tablewares as their principal cargoes (see Table 1; Fig. 23). The discovery of two shipwrecks with cargoes of glazed tablewares was especially of importance. One was found off the Island of Pelagonnisos (Pelagos) near Alonnesos in the northern Sporades, and the other was discovered between Kastellorizo and Rhodes in the Dodecanese.[135] These wrecks yielded very diverse finds of the late 12th and early 13th centuries.[136] The Pelagonissos-Alonnesos shipwreck, for instance, transported 1,490 ceramics and other objects, among them 768 complete vessels and 628 fragments of tablewares (mainly Fine Sgraffito Ware) compared to 79 pieces of domestic wares and amphorae.[137] The Skopelos and Kastellorizo shipwrecks were carrying cargoes of (hastily manufactured) Incised Sgraffito Ware, Champlevé Ware and Slip-painted Ware.[138]

Shipwrecks found in de coastal waters near Skopelos, Kavalliani, Izmir, Bodrum, Kumluca, Adrasan Bay and Antalya contained similar late 12th-early 13th-century glazed tablewares, although there is still limited information about these wrecks and their cargoes.[139] The shipwreck of Çamaltı Burnu, near Marmara Island, is a bit later in date, and yielded some 13th-century glazed painted and sgraffito vessels in addition to the main cargo of Günsenin 4 amphorae.[140]

Furthermore, the underwater excavations of the Novy Svet shipwreck near Sudak (Crimea) revealed a substantial quantity and a combination of late 13th-century decorative glazed tablewares from northern Italy, the Levantine coast, Constantinople/Istanbul, Cyprus and from other (yet unknown) regions, as was confirmed by chemical analyses of the pottery.[141] Apart from tablewares, the Novy Svet shipwreck also yielded amphorae (mostly the Günsenin 3 and 4 types), *pithoi*, glass and other items.

This commercialisation and internationalisation of pottery distribution coincides with the emergence of a larger scale pottery production in the Middle Byzantine period, perhaps capable of supplying more extensive markets. In addition, the rise of population numbers and relative wealth in towns and countryside, as well as the more organised circulation of persons and goods between East and West during the 12th and 13th centuries may have created new demands and new markets for these glazed tablewares.[142] From the 13th century onward, one can observe also a more intensive (maritime) circulation of pottery between the western and eastern parts of the Mediterranean.[143]

A decisive factor for this active period of sea trade could have been the Crusades, as well as grants of extensive commercial privileges from the Byzantine Emperor to Venetians, Genoese and Pisans between the late 11th and mid 12th centuries.[144] Communities of these maritime states were often stationed in vital ports in the western Aegean such as Chalcis in Euboea and in Almyros in Thessaly (an important grain supplier for Constantinople) on the trunk sea route connecting the southern (Crete, Peloponnese) and the northern parts of the Byzantine Empire (Thessaloniki, Sea of Marmara, Black Sea region). In these harbours goods (such as wine from Euboea or silk textiles from Thebes) could have been either exchanged for grain from Thessaly, or perhaps redistributed in smaller quantities for secondary ports. The ships were further surely linking Constantinople with Syria and Egypt in the East and with the Italian cities Pisa, Venice and Genoa in the West.[145]

CERAMIC IMPORTS FROM THE ISLAMIC WORLD

It is clear that from the 12th century onwards ships started to transport glazed tablewares all over the Mediterranean.[146] This perhaps explains the occurrence of small quantities of imported Islamic pottery in excavated contexts of Byzantine sites (see Table 2 and Fig. 24). The capital of the Empire, for instance, yielded such finds since the 1920s. At the Great Palace excavations in Constantinople two plates and fragments of a third plate were recovered in 1937, which were described with a 'carved' decoration below a turquoise glaze and recognized as 12th-century 'Raqqa Ware' from Syria.[147] Furthermore, in the same area fragments of Fritware of 'Persian origin' were found, among which one with a turquoise-blue glaze and another one with a cream glaze and carved Kufic script.[148] At the Hippodrome excavations (near the Great Palace) 'a fine piece of Egyptian Fritware' was recovered in 1927,[149] as well as three fragments of Lustreware.[150]

In another part of the city, in the Saraçhane district, fragments of mid to late 12th-century Fritware with carved motifs and Laqabi Ware from Syria were unearthed.[151] The Myrelaion (Bodrum Camii) excavations nearby yielded a bowl fragment of so-called Minaï Ware from Iran with a painted human figure and pseudo-Kufic pattern on the interior rim, dated to ca. 1175-1225.[152] Finally, an 11th-/12th-century fragment of Incised Fritware from Iran? (or rather from Syria?) was found during recent excavations in the Sultanahmet area, showing the depiction of a human figure.[153]

Apart from the capital, Islamic tablewares were recovered in other Byzantine cities as well. Excavations in Thessaloniki yielded a 12th-century glazed closed vessel with painted vertical stripes in black and blue-green that apparently originated from Egypt.[154] Islamic Fritwares of the 12th-/13th-century (sometimes covered with a monochrome turquoise glaze) were also recovered at Chersonesos (Crimea), and even at Russian cities (up to Novgorod).[155]

More to the south, at the Boeotian harbour city of Chalcis (on the island of Euboea) a fragment of Islamic Fritware (but unfortunately without a glaze left) was recently recognized in an excavated industrial area outside the Medieval fortification walls (personal observation).[156] More inland, the city of Thebes yielded parts of a 13th/14th-century jar of the Late Almohad/Nasrid period from Islamic Spain.[157]

In nearby Athens, two 11th-century Lustreware dishes from Fatimid Egypt were built for decorative purposes as '*bacini*' within the façade of the Middle Byzantine church of Agioi Theodoroi (see picture in Fig. 24).[158] Apart from these dishes, further fragments of Lustreware and Painted Wares from Egypt were recently identified among finds from houses and cisterns at the Agora excavations.[159]

On the Peloponnese, a 14th-century glazed closed vessel of the Mamluk period with a carved decoration and Arabic inscription was recovered at the Crusader Castle of Glarentza, but is now on display in nearby Chlemoutsi Castle.[160] A survey in Laconia yielded two pieces of a 12th-century bowl with turquoise glaze from 'Persia'.[161]

In addition, a few sherds of Islamic Fritware were found in 13th-/early 14th-century contexts near the Roman Stoa of Sparta.[162] Furthermore, two Islamic *bacini* immured in the exterior facades of churches have been identified in the Mani (in particular in the Oitylo region): one 11th-century dish with splashed painted decoration (known as 'Fayyumi Ware') from Egypt in the Taxiarchis church at Glazou, and another 11th-century painted bowl from North Africa (known as '*ceramica siculo-maghrebina*') in the Agios Theodoros church at Vamvaka.[163]

At Corinth, Charles Morgan published several Islamic ceramic imports from unknown contexts.[164] Among these imports were a few fragments of Monochrome and Polychrome Lustrewares from Abbasid Iraq, which can be dated in the 9th-10th centuries.[165] Furthermore, we can distinguish in Corinth an 11th- to 12th-century Lustreware fragment from Fatimid Egypt with the painted hand of a lute player,[166] as well as pieces of 12th- to 13th-century Incised Fritware from Fustat in Egypt (or from Syria?) covered with a thick white or bright blue glaze with impressed or incised lines.[167] Apart from more Islamic imports (including red-bodied 10th/11th-century fragments from Aghlabid Tunisia with green and brown paint, and bowls of black paint under a white glaze), the excavators also found a 13th-century Chinese Porcelain vessel.[168]

On the other side of the Aegean, recent excavations at an anonymous Türbe (grave monument) in Ephesus yielded imports of Islamic Fritwares.[169] Some pieces are simply covered with a monochrome turquoise alkali glaze, or decoratively painted with floral motifs in blue/black under a turquoise alkali glaze.[170] The sherds come from Syrian workshops (probably from Raqqa), showing thus contacts between both regions from the 12th to 14th centuries. Similar looking imported Islamic ceramics were also found at the nearby site of Anaia/Kadıkalesi in Kuşadası, as well as on the Island of Rhodes more to the south.[171]

Finally, on the island of Cyprus three 14th-century underglaze painted bowls from Syria were found in Nicosia, together with a fragment of White Chinese Porcelain.[172] More Islamic glazed and painted Fritwares dating to the late 11th to end 12th century were found in Nicosia, in the Paphos area, at the Monastery of Ayia Moni, as well as during a surface survey in the Troodos Mountains.[173]

SOME CONCLUDING REMARKS

If one looks at Byzantine pottery from a broader perspective than mere typo-chronology, the manufacture, distribution and consumption of 7th- to 15th-century ceramics in the eastern Mediterranean reads like a fascinating story. For instance, it now seems quite clear that due to changing consumer demands during this period potters were actively exploring new potting and decoration techniques throughout the entire Byzantine era. One of the most important of these new techniques, and perhaps the one with the most consequences, was the introduction of lead glaze in Constantinople. At first it was applied on the interior of rather mundane utilitarian vessels (among which cooking pots and chafing dishes), but later on footed bowls and dishes of which the function was probably primarily display on the table. These last ones had a limited repertoire of basic incised decoration; that is to say, they had predominantly simplistic-looking animal and vegetal designs (such as fishes and palmettes).

The glazed products from Constantinople were mostly exported to coastal cities and provincial nodal points along important land routes in the eastern Mediterranean. Sometimes their shapes were exact copies of metal vessels, as can be seen in the covered jugs with double handles from Constantinople, Limyra and Elaiussa Sebaste, which were imitating copper or bronze (samovar-like) *authepsae* with attached small lids.

During Middle Byzantine times (ca. 10th-12th/early 13th centuries), the next products in the glazed tableware series from Constantinople were evidently travelling to the West, as the archaeological record shows that they reached the Byzantine territories in (southern) Italy, Sicily and Malta. The decoration on these export products seems to have varied per region, although in the case of Glazed White Ware II the emphasis was on animal designs (in particular stamped or impressed birds), and in the case of Polychrome Ware on objects (mostly painted crosses) and abstract motifs. Perhaps such aniconic themes were inspired by imports of Islamic glazed tablewares in Byzantium from the 11th century onwards. Examples of Islamic pottery were found in various Byzantine urban centres and harbours, as is shown in Table 2.

The centralised production of Glazed White Wares in the capital and their more widespread distribution (even to rural communities) within the Byzantine Empire proved to be a stimulus for regional imitations made for provincial markets during Middle Byzantine times. Among these the most notable were Glazed Red Wares, manufactured in various new production centres in the western Aegean (e.g., Corinth, Chalcis, Athens and Sparta). These specialized workshops started to experiment with new shapes and with new decoration techniques and motifs, which were not only borrowed from metal vessels and from textiles but also from the Islamic world.

During this period the main focus of ceramic productions shifted dramatically from functionality to more high-level innovative decoration, with the introduction of the use of a white slip, of various kiln types (including an Islamic one), of compasses, and of formulae for glazes and colours in Byzantine pottery. There was definitely an increase of exchange of consumer goods between towns and their environs in this period, shown by the penetration of these new ceramic products into the countryside. This regional distribution often happened to rural sites in the immediate hinterland of the urban workshops, thus showing the rise in demand for (semi-)durables.[174]

From the 13th century onwards we see a rapid increase in the number of pottery workshops, especially in new regional centres (such as Thessaloniki, Thebes, Pergamon, Anaia-Kadikalesı, Ephesus, as well as Paphos and Lapithos on Cyprus). An important innovation in this period was the introduction of tripod stilts, which separated glazed vessels during firing in the kiln from sticking to each other. This allowed for a more controlled kiln process, which increased the output for local Byzantine workshops and facilitated mass pottery production all over the eastern Mediterranean.

Hand in hand with this booming production went the development of intermediate- and long-distance trade of amphorae (including the Günsenin 3 type for the transport of bulk goods, such as wine) and of glazed tablewares by sea. Excavated shipwrecks in the Mediterranean and Black Sea offer unique details for our picture of the patterns of this pottery distribution, which was often instigated by the Italian maritime powers (Venice, Genoa and Pisa) in this time period. These last ones were able to distribute from the 13th century onwards glazed tablewares either through a cabotage system (Venice) or through trans-Mediterranean *Fernhandel* (Genoa) along their established trading routes and their colonized territories in the western (Venice) and eastern parts (Genoa) of the Aegean.

It is quite probable that the Italian merchant ships not only carried export ceramic products of Byzantine and Italian potters, but included in their cargoes on the way back from Middle Eastern harbours small quantities of Islamic glazed tablewares. Most imports in Byzantium from the Islamic world originated from Syria and from Egypt, only a few from Iraq, Iran, North Africa and Spain. It has been suggested that these luxury glazed ceramics came as war booty or diplomatic gifts to the Byzantine court at Constantinople.

However, looking at the excavated contexts of most fragments, it is evident that Islamic pottery is not only to be found in the Byzantine capital, but that it was actually widespread all over the Byzantine Empire. Fragments have been recovered in industrial areas, in town houses, in castles, and even in rural communities in the countryside. This wide distribution of Islamic glazed tablewares to Byzantine provincial markets makes it much more plausible that these vessels were perhaps souvenirs of travellers, soldiers and pilgrims, or more probable part of commercial connections between specific areas. The evidence suggests that many of the excavated fragments of Islamic pottery in the Byzantine world came from vessels exported from Syria and Egypt, which were probably transported (through brokering?) via Cyprus, Crete and Rhodes to the western and northern parts of the Byzantine Empire.

From a more food-related consumptive perspective, it is clear that shape and volume of glazed tablewares changed from one period to another, with a gradual development towards smaller and taller open vessels with less volume capacity through time. We can observe in the Late Byzantine period an increased use of small footed bowls, which were decorated with a diversity of colourful motifs. These motifs not only included vegetal designs, but also human beings such as warriors, women and couples, who were sometimes carrying attributes of feasting.

With the improvement of manufacturing techniques and of decoration styles in glazed ceramics, we may notice throughout the Byzantine period an increase in the output of produced items (fuelling thus the growth of a consumer society), as well as a growing demand for exotic decorated serving sets on the table. The responses of potters in their ceramic output were often related to social changes in food preparation and dining habits in the Byzantine world, at first by trendsetting consumers, followed by a much wider group of ordinary consumers in both town and country alike.

FINDS OF AMPHORAE AND GLAZED TABLEWARES ON SHIPWRECKS IN THE EASTERN MEDITERRANEAN

SHIPWRECK	LOCATION	DATE	FINDS
No. 1 Novy Svet, Sudak (2 wrecks) (Figs. 20-21, 1)	Crimea, Black Sea	Ca. late 13th c.	Zeuxippus Ware, Zeuxippus Ware Derivatives, Late Slip-Painted Ware, Glazed White Ware IV, Incised Sgraffito Ware, Cypriot Sgraffito and Slip-painted Wares, Roulette Ware, *Graffita arcaica tirrenica*, Port Saint Symeon Ware, Seljuk Painted Ware, Günsenin 3/ Saraçahne 61 amphorae, Günsenin 4 amphorae (most), Beirut cooking pots and frying pans, pithoi, unidentified amphora (1)
No. 2 Çamaltı Burnu I Marmara Island (Figs. 20-21, 2)	Turkey	Ca. mid 13th- early 14th c.	Glazed White Ware IV, Incised Sgraffito Ware, Polychrome Sgraffito Wares, Günsenin 3/ Saraçahne 61 amphorae (3), Günsenin 4 amphorae (236 complete)
No. 3 Glafki Bank, N. Aegean (Figs. 20-21, 3).	Greece	Ca. 12th-13th c.	Fine Sgraffito Ware; Günsenin 3/ Saraçahne 61 amphora
No. 4 Pelagonissos, N. Sporades (Figs. 20-21, 4).	Greece	Ca. mid-late 12th c.	Fine Sgraffito Ware, Painted Fine Sgraffito Ware
No. 5 Pagasitikos Gulf (8 wrecks) (Fig. 20, 5)	Greece	Ca. 12th-13th c.	Günsenin 3/ Saraçahne 61 amphorae
No. 6 Sporades C, N. Sporades (Fig. 20, 6)	Greece	Ca. 12th-13th c.	Günsenin 3/ Saraçahne 61 amphorae
No. 7 Sporades B, N. Sporades (Fig. 20, 7)	Greece	Ca. 12th-13th c.	Günsenin 3/ Saraçahne 61 amphorae
No. 8 Skopelos, N. Sporades (2 wrecks) (Fig. 20, 8, Fig. 21, 5)	Greece	Ca. late 12th-mid 13th c.	Incised Sgraffito Ware, Champlevé Ware Dhasia islet: Günsenin 3/ Saraçahne 61 amphorae
No. 9 Portolafia, Euboea (Fig. 20, 9)	Greece	Ca. 12th-13th c.	Günsenin 3/ Saraçahne 61 amphora (1x)
No. 10 Kavalliani, Euboea (Fig. 21, 6)	Greece	Ca. late 12th-early 13th c.	Slip-painted Ware, Fine Sgraffito Ware, Incised Sgraffito Ware

No. 11 Thorikos, Attica (Fig. 21, 7)	Greece	Ca. late 12th- early 13th c.	Incised Sgraffito Ware
No. 12 Aegina, Attica (Fig. 20, 10)	Greece	Ca. 12th- 13th c.	Günsenin 3/ Saraçhane 61 amphorae
No. 13 Tainaron, Pelo- ponnese (Fig. 20, 11)	Greece	Ca. 12th-13th c.	Günsenin 3/ Saraçhane 61 amphorae
No. 14 Dhia B=C, Crete (Fig. 20, 12)	Greece	Ca. 12th-13th c.	Günsenin 3/ Saraçhane 61 amphorae
No. 15 Beşadlar, Near Izmir (Fig. 21, 8)	Western Turkey	Ca. late 12th-mid 13th c.	Incised Sgraffito Ware, Champlevé Ware
No. 16 Near Izmir (Fig. 21, 9)	Western Turkey	Ca. late 12th-mid 13th c.	Incised Sgraffito Ware, Champlevé Ware
No. 17 Tavşan adası, Bodrum (Fig. 21, 10)	South-western Turkey	Ca. late 12th-early 13th c.	Fine Sgraffito Ware, Incised Sgraffito Ware, Slip-painted Ware, Brown Painted Ware
No. 18 Rhodes, Dode-canese (Fig. 20, 13)	Greece	Ca. 12th-13th c.	Günsenin 3/ Saraçhane 61 amphorae
No. 19 Kastellorizo, Dodecanese (Fig. 21, 11)	Greece	Ca. late 12th- mid 13th c.	Slip-painted Ware, Incised Sgraffito Ware, Champlevé Ware, Green Painted Ware
No. 20 Kumluca, Cape Gelidonya (Fig. 21, 12)	South-western Turkey	Ca.13th-14th c.	Late Byzantine Sgraffito Wares
No. 21 Göcük Burnu, Adrasan Bay (Fig. 21, 13)	South-western Turkey	Ca. mid-late 12th c.	Fine Sgraffito Ware, Painted Fine Sgraffito Ware
No. 22 Near Antalya (Fig. 21, 14)	South-western Turkey	Ca. 2nd half 12th c.	Painted Fine Sgraffito Ware
No. 23 Slifke (Fig. 21, 15)	South-eastern Turkey	Ca. late 12th-early 13th c.	Fine Sgraffito Ware; Champlevé Ware
No. 24 Tartus (Fig. 20, 14)	Syria	Ca. 12th-13th c.	Günsenin 3/ Saraçhane 61 amphorae (5000), amphora from Acre? (1)
No. 25 North of Tyre (Fig. 21, 16)	Lebanon	?	Glazed tablewares

TABLE 1 – List of shipwrecks transporting 12th- to 14th-century amphorae and glazed tablewares in the eastern Mediterranean mentioned in this chapter and shown in Figs. 20-21 (J. Vroom).

ISLAMIC TABLEWARES ON BYZANTINE SITES IN THE EASTERN MEDITERRANEAN			
SITES	DATE	PROVENANCE	TABLEWARES
Constantinople, Great Palace	Ca. late 11th-late 12th c.	Syria (Raqqa), Iran?	Monochrome Glazed Fritware + with carved motifs (e.g. Kufic script)
Constantinople, Hippodrome	Ca. 11th-12th c.	Egypt	Fritware, Lustreware (Fatimid)
Constantinople, Saraçhane	Ca. mid-late 12th c.	Syria, Iran?	Monochrome Glazed Fritware with incised and carved motifs, Laqabi Ware
Constantinople, Myrelaion	Ca. 1175-1225	Iran	Minaï Ware
Constantinople, Sultanahmet	Ca. late 11th- late 12th c.	Iran? Syria?	Monochrome Glazed Fritware with incised motifs
Thessaloniki	Ca. 12th c.	Egypt	Fritware with painted motifs ('Fayyumi Ware')
Cherson	Ca. 12th-13th c.	Syria	Monochrome Glazed Fritware (turquoise)
Chalcis	?	?	Fritware (worn out)
Thebes	Ca. 13th-14th c.	Spain (Granada?)	Monochrome Green Glazed Stamped Ware (Late Almohad-Nasrid)
Athens, Ag. Theodoroi	Ca. 11th c.	Egypt	Lustreware (Fatimid)
Athens, Agora	Ca. 11th-12th c	Egypt	Lustreware (Fatimid), Fritware with painted motifs
Glarentza Castle	Ca. 14th c..	Egypt?	Fritware with carved motifs and Arabic inscription
Laconia Survey	Ca.12th c.	Iran?	Monochrome Glazed Fritware (turquoise)
Sparta, near Roman Stoa	Ca. late 13th-early 14th c.	Syria?	Monochrome Glazed Fritware (turquoise)
Glazou, Mani Taxiarchis church	Ca. 11th c.	Egypt	Fritware with painted motifs ('Fayyumi Ware')
Vamavaka, Mani Ag. Theodoros church	Ca. 11th c.	North Africa (Tunisia)	Green and Brown Painted Ware (Aghlabid)
Corinth	Ca. 9th-10th c.	Iraq (Basra)	Monochrome and Polychrome Lustrewares (Abbasid)
Corinth, e.g. Panayia Field	Ca. 10th-11th c.	North Africa (Tunisia)	Green and Brown Painted Ware (Aghlabid)

Corinth	Ca. 12th-13th c.	Egypt (Fustat), Syria?	Lustreware (Fatimid), Fritware with incised motifs, Painted Ware
Ephesus, Türbe	Ca. 12th-13th c., 13th-14th c.	Syria (Raqqa)	Underglaze Painted Fritware (black), Underglaze Painted Fritware (black-and-blue), Monochrome Glazed Fritware (turquoise)
Anaia/Kadıkalesi	Ca. 12th-13th c.	Syria (Raqqa)	Underglaze Painted Fritware (black), Underglaze Painted Fritware (black-and-blue), Monochrome Glazed Fritware (turquoise) with carved motifs
Rhodes	Ca 14th c.	Syria	Monochrome Glazed Fritware (turquoise)
Crete, Heraklion	Ca. 9th-10th c.	Syria?	Monochrome Glazed 'Kernschnittware'
Cyprus, Nicosia	Ca. 14th c.	Syria	Underglaze Painted Fritware
Cyprus, Nicosia (Palaion Demarcheion)	Ca. 2nd half 12th c.	Syria	Monochrome Glazed Fritware, + with incised and carved motifs, Underglaze Painted Fritware, Lebanese Sgraffito
Cyprus, Paphos area (Kouklia, Leptos Walls)	Ca. late 11th- late 12th c.	Syria	Monochrome Glazed Fritware, + with incised and carved motifs, Imitation Lustreware (clay)
Cyprus, Ayia Moni Monastery	Ca. late 11th- late 12th c.	Syria	Monochrome Glazed Fritware (turquoise), + with incised motifs, Monochrome Glazed Ware (clay)
Cyprus, Troodos	Ca. 12th-13th c., 13th-14th c.	Syria (Raqqa, Damascus)	Monochrome Glazed Fritware (turquoise), + with carved motifs, Lustreware (Mamluk)

TABLE 2 – Finds list of imported Islamic tablewares on Byzantine sites in the eastern Mediterranean mentioned in this chapter (J. Vroom).

NOTES

1. See Vroom 2003 for such an approach. I would like to express my gratitude to the Netherlands Organisation of Scientific Research (NWO) awarding me with a VIDI research grant for the years 2010-2015 that allowed me to do research on various sites in the eastern Mediterranean.
2. According to Mullins (2011, 133), these studies 'reflect the ways consumers negotiate, accept, and resist goods-dominant meanings within rich, global, historical, and cultural contexts'.
3. Mullins 2011, 133; see also Douglas and Isherwood 1979; Deetz 1972; Miller 1995; Majewski and Schiffer 2001; Dietler 2010.
4. Vroom 2020a, 12.
5. See for the idea of the Byzantine 'consumption city', Laiou 2013.
6. This is not the place to deal extensively with consumption related to 'foodways'; see for this type of research, Vroom 2007; *Idem* 2009; *Idem* 2015a; *Idem* 2016a; *Idem* 2018; *Idem* 2020b; *Idem* 2022b; Vroom *et al.* 2017.
7. Yenişehirlioğlu 1995; *Idem* 2009, 630; Waksman *et al.* 2007.
8. Waksman *et al.* 2008.
9. See Vroom 2014², 62-63.
10. Hayes 1992.
11. Hayes 1992.
12. Vroom 2011, 147-48; see also Zanini 2010, fig. 1a,b and d (showing ancient reliefs of pack animals loaded with amphorae); McCormick 2012, figures 3.7-3.9 (showing a ceramic figurine/bottle and a mosaic of camels loaded with amphorae).
13. See also N. Poulou's contribution in this volume.
14. E.g., Vroom 2014², 63; *Idem* 2012, 357-58 and notes 10-13 with further literature; Costa 2017, fig. 4, GQB – CER 1032.17+18 (Gortyna, Crete, first half of the 8th century).
15. Vroom 2014², 62-63.
16. Bakirtzis 1989, pls. 12-14.
17. Gerousi 1993, 258-59, no. 8050, figs. 7-8, pl. 50; see also Hayes 1992, 14-18.
18. Vroom 2014², 62-65, 72-73.
19. Vroom 2008, 294-95.
20. Morgan 1942, 37; Bakirtzis 1989.
21. Koukoules 1952, 162; Bakirtzis 1989, 55-65; Gourgiotis 1991, 82.
22. Vroom 2007, 339-42, fig. 8.1-8.2; *Idem* 2012a, 348-52, figs. 10-18.
23. Vroom 2008, 295-97; *Idem* 2012b, 294; *Idem* forthcoming. See for the storage of foodstuffs in Byzantine times and in particular in Byzantine Athens, Vroom 2020b.
24. These vessels with carinated shoulders and slightly convex bases are also described in the modern literature as 'pitchers'.
25. Waldbaum 1983, nos. 515-517, 523-526, 528-530; Stephens Crawford 1990, figs. 211, 213 (M67.15.7381), figs. 212, 214 (M67.29.7475), fig. 285 (M67.16.7382) and fig. 522, (M63.56.5871).
26. Birgitte Pitarakis has published copper examples from a private collection in Istanbul and from the Archaeological Museum in Selçuk/Ephesus; cf. Pitarakis 2005.

27 Pitarakis 2005, 16, fig. 7 with further literature.
28 Bass and van Doorninck 1982, 269, object no. MF 5, figs. 12-2, 12-3, wreck plan Vc.
29 See http://inadiscover.com/projects/all/southern_europe_mediterranean_aegean/bozborun_turkey/photo_gallery/
30 Angelova and Buchvarov 2007, 82, fig. 12 (upper right); Cholakov and Ilieva 2005, nos. 7-8, figs. 7-8; Pitarakis 2005, 15.
31 Flourentzos 1996, pl. 42; Mundell Mango 2001, 103, n. 32 and fig. 5.7c; Pitarakis 2005, 18, fig. 11.
32 Pitarakis 2005, 15, fig. 3 with further literature.
33 Brokalakis 2005, 42-43, figs. 12-13; Pitarakis 2005, 14, note 13.
34 See Vroom 2012a, 347 and note 34 with further literature.
35 Jacquest and Baratte 2005, 124 and fig. 2.
36 Mundell Mango 2001, 93, n. 34 and fig. 5.7F.
37 Pitarakis 2005, 16, fig. 6 with further literature.
38 Smith and Preston Day 1989, no. 9, pl. 62.9.
39 Bujard 2005, fig. 1, nos 5-6 and fig. 3. See also for these Umayyad examples from Jordan the permanent collection of the Museum with no Frontiers on http://www.discoverislamicart.org.
40 Segal *et al.* 2003, 29 and fig. 53; Mundell Mango 2009, 232. In addition, she also mentions unpublished ones from Gerasa.
41 Vroom 2012a, 345 and figs. 3-5.
42 Vroom 2012a, 345-46 and figs. 6-7.
43 Vroom 2012a, 346 and fig. 8.
44 Papanikola-Bakirtzis 1999, 18.
45 Hayes 1992, 3.
46 Stevenson 1947; Talbot Rice 1954; Peschlow 1977-78.
47 Hayes 1992.
48 Hayes 1992, 12-34.
49 Vroom 2003, Appendix A2.
50 Hayes 1992, 35-37; Sanders 2001; see Kostova 2009 for its Bulgarian production.
51 Morgan 1942.
52 Morgan 1942, 49; Sanders 1995.
53 See also Armstrong 2001, fig. 3.1; Vroom 2014^2, 75-79; *Idem* 2021a with further literature.
54 Vroom 2003, figs. 6.6 and 6.40 (w8.1).
55 Vroom 2014^2, 80-93; see also the contributions by Kontogiannis and Skartsis, as well as by Vroom, Tzavella and Vaxevanis in this volume.
56 Hayes 1993, 86.
57 Sanders 1995; see also the contribution by Tzavella in this volume.
58 Ballian and Drandaki 2003.
59 Vroom 2003, 232.
60 See in general, Vroom 2000, fig. 2.
61 Morgan 1942; Papanikola-Bakirtzis 1999; Vroom 2003, figs. 3.7-9; *Idem* 2014, 80-93.
62 Vogt 1993.
63 Dodwell 1986, 47.
64 De Boüard 1974, 69; Ilg 1970, 50-51 for the German translation.
65 Vroom 2003, 268, note 18 with further literature.
66 Morgan 1942, fig. 9; Vroom 2003, figs. 9.6 and 9.9.
67 Papanikola-Bakirtzis 1999, 222-23.
68 Thiriot 1995, fig. 13.
69 As cited by Allan 1973, 114.
70 Le Patourel 1986.
71 Vroom 2003, fig. 7.2.

72 Megaw 1931-32; Ettinghausen 1976; Vroom 2003, fig. 7.1.
73 Talbot Rice 1965, 194-95 with references to earlier literature.
74 *ODB*, vol. 2, 1418.
75 Talbot Rice 1965.
76 E.g., Grabar 1997; Cutler 2001; Ballian 2013, 292.
77 Vroom 2003, 233, 329 and table 7.3.
78 Vroom 2014², 108-25.
79 Vroom 2003, 233; *Idem* 2011, 409-10.
80 Vroom 2003, 232-33 and table 7.3; see also *Idem* 2000, 202-204, figs. 2-3; *Idem* 2015c, figs 1, 2 and 5, table 1 with further literature.
81 Vroom 2000, 204-205, fig. 4; *Idem* 2003, 234-46.
82 It concerns here 244 published ceramic vessels from Medieval Cyprus at the Leventis Collection in Nicosia, the Pierides Collection in Larnaca, the Von Post Collection in Stockholm and the Sèvres Collection in Paris; cf. Papanikola-Bakirtzis 1989; *Idem* 2004; Piltz 1996 and Kontogiannis 2003; see also Vroom 2015b, fig. 3-9.
83 Vroom 2014, fig. 1; *Idem* 2015b, figs. 3-4.
84 Vroom 2014, fig. 4b; *Idem* 2015b, fig. 8.
85 Vroom 2011, 425-26.
86 Papanikola-Bakirtzis 1999, 48 with further literature; Vroom 2014², 90, MBYZ 11.2; cf. for more ceramic finds from Vrea, Tsanana 2003, 245-250. See for the Chalcis' workshop manufacturing Incised Sgraffito Ware dishes with similar looking warrior motifs, the contribution by Vroom, Tzavella and Vaxevanis in this volume.
87 E.g., Morgan 1935, 76-78; Frantz 1940-41, 87-91; Morgan 1942, no. 1686, pl. LII;

Notopoulos 1964, 108-133; Ioannikade-Dostoglou 1981, 127-138.
88 Armstrong 2006, 80 and note 18.
89 Armstrong and Sekunda 2006, 18-19.
90 Vroom 2015, fig. 11.
91 See also Vroom 2014, fig. 9.
92 Vroom 2022a.
93 Sardi 2020.
94 Sardi 2020, see also Vroom 2003.
95 E.g., Papanikola-Bakirtzis and Zekos 2010.
96 Papanikola-Bakirtzis 1992, 26, figs. 16-17.
97 Vroom 2003, figs. 9.7-8.
98 Vroom 2005.
99 Jacoby 2001, 226-28; idem 2012, 107-11; see also Haldon 2005, 148-50 and map 11.5
100 Jacoby 2012, 107.
101 See for this type of ware in general, Vroom 2014², 132-33.
102 Cf. for the Novy Svet shipwrecks, Waksman and Teslenko 2010, 362-63 and fig. 13.
103 See the contribution by Vroom, Tzavella and Vaxevanis in this volume.
104 Burlot and Waksman 2020 with literature.
105 Lane 1938; see also Redford 2012.
106 Blake 1986 with further literature.
107 Jacoby 2012, 101.
108 Vroom and van IJzendoorn forthcoming.
109 Parker 1992.
110 E.g., Gill 1991; Stern 2012.
111 Cirelli 2008, 133, figs. 113, 334; see also McCormick 2012, figs. 3.4-3.5.
112 Swan 2007, 252-255.
113 Fabian and Goren 2001.
114 Mundell Mango 2000, 195.
115 Parker 1992, nos. 203, 367, 352.
116 Parker 1992, no. 1239: Bass and Van Doorninck 1982; Doorninck 2014.
117 Bass 1982.

118 Parker 1992, no. 111.
119 Hocker 1995.
120 Vroom 2012b, 292-93.
121 E.g., Zelenko 2009.
122 Parker 1992, no. 1070.
123 Bass and Van Doorninck 1978; Van Doorninck 1989.
124 Günsenin 1989, 268-71; figs 2-3; Hayes 1992, 73-75, fig 24, nos. 1-11, 14.
125 Vroom 2014², 94-95.
126 Kocabaş and Özsait Kosabaş 2007, 196-201; Pulak 2007, 202-15.
127 Denker *et al.* 2013, 204-9, nos. 237-44, 246-540.
128 Asal 2007, 185-187; Kocabaş and Özsait Kosabaş 2007, 200; Pulak 2007, 203-215.
129 Vroom 2016b, table 1.
130 Parker 1992, no. 1136.
131 Parker 1992, nos. 361, 1110-1111, 1128; Günsenin 2001, 118, fig. 9; Waksman and Teslenko 2010; Demesticha and Spondylis 2011, 37-38, nos. 1, 3-6, 8, 10-11; Özdaş *et al.* 2012: Koutsouflakis *et al.* 2012, 53-54, no. 5, fig. 20.
132 Vroom 2014², 99; *Idem* 2021a with further literature; *Idem* 2022.
133 Vroom 2022a; see also Vroom, Tzavella and Vaxevanis in this volume.
134 See also the contributions by Kontogiannis and Skartsis and by Vroom, Tzavella and Vaxevanis in this volume.
135 Kritzas 1971; Parker 1992, nos. 538, 306, 796.
136 Papanikola-Bakirtzis 1999, 118-57.
137 Papanikola-Bakirtzis 1999, 122-42.
138 Philotheou and Michailidou 1986; *Idem* 1989; Ioannidaki-Dostoglou 1989; Loucas 1989; Armstrong 1991, 347 and note 19.
139 Armstrong 1991; Parker 1992, no. 1099; Papanikola-Bakirtzis *et al.* 1999, 81, note 119 and 84, no. 160; Döğer 2007, 52; Dimopoulos 2009, 179-81; Stern 2012, table 8.1; Koutsouflakis *et al.* 2012, 58, no. 11, fig. 24.
140 Günsenin 1989, 274-76, figs. 12-14; *Idem* 2003, figs. 10a-b to 14a-b.
141 Waksman *et al.* 2009; Waksman and Teslenko 2010; Stern 2012, table 8.1.
142 François 1997; Vroom 2022a.
143 François 1995, figs. 23-24; *Idem* 1997.
144 Laiou and Morrisson 2007, 142-144.
145 See for these western contacts, Jacoby 2009; Vroom 2021b.
146 In Vroom 2011, I discuss ceramic imports from the West (such as Proto-Maiolica, RMR Ware, Roulette Ware, Archaic Maiolica etc.) in Byzantine times; therefore I will concentrate hence on ceramic imports from the East. See also for the last Byzantine amphora type of this period, Vroom and Van IJzendoorn forthcoming.
147 Stevenson 1947, 56, pl. 26, nos. 3-4.
148 Talbot Rice 1954, 111-112.
149 Talbot Rice 1930, pl. III.
150 Talbot Rice 1965, 194 and note 2.
151 Hayes 1992, 43-44, fig. 16, pl. 19.
152 Hayes 1981, 36 and 38, no. 1 (BC 59), fig. 82a.
153 *Gün Işığında,* 152, SC14.
154 *Byzantio & Arabes*, 94.
155 Koval 2006; Sedikova 2015.
156 See Vroom, Tzavella and Vaxevanis in this volume.
157 Personal observation.
158 Philon 1980, 186; Korre-Zographou 1995, pls. 116-117.

159 Personal observation.
160 Athanasoulis 2005, 46 and 54; *Byzantio & Arabes*, 100.
161 Armstrong 1996, 130, no. 12, note 44.
162 Dimopoulos 2007, 343.
163 A. Yangaki, pers. comm. in 2018.
164 Morgan 1942, 169-171, figs. 147-151.
165 Morgan 1942, 170, fig. 150; Ballian 2013, fig. 119a; cf. for comparative material in the Benaki Museum, Philon 1980, figs. 195-196 and pl. XI.c.
166 Morgan 1942, fig. 159; Ballian 2013, fig. 118a.
167 Morgan 1942, fig. 147; Ballian 2013, fig. 121a.
168 Morgan 1942, figs. 148b, 149, 151a; see also *Byzantio & Arabes*, 90 for another piece of Aghlabid pottery with Arabic inscription found at the Panayia Field baths in Corinth.
169 Vroom and Fındık 2015.
170 Watson 2004, 295.
171 Mercangöz 2013, 167, fig. X-2; *Byzantio & Arabes*, 98-99.
172 Megaw 1951, 148, nos. A1-5, fig. 2 and pl. 45, 155, nos. B1 and B2a.
173 Von Wartburg 1998, fig. 51, nos. 8-9, fig. 77, no. 48; *Idem* 2003, 155-57, figs. 7-10; 160-61, figs 14-17; Von Wartburg *et al.* 2010; Von Wartburg and Violaris 2009; Vroom 2013, 76-77,
174 See in the case of Chalcis, Vroom 2022a.

BIBLIOGRAPHY

Allan, J.W. 1993. Abu'l-Qasim's treatise on ceramics, *Iran* 11, 111-20.

Angelova, S. and I. Buchvarov 2007. Durostorum in Late Antiquity (fourth to seventh centuries), in: J. Henning (ed.), *Post-Roman Towns, Trade and Settlement in Europe and Byzantium, Vol. II: Byzantium, Pliska, and the Balkans*, Berlin, 61-87.

Armstrong, P. 1991. A group of Byzantine bowls from Skopelos, *Oxford Journal of Archaeology* 10.3, 335-47.

Armstrong, P. 1996. The Byzantine and Ottoman pottery, in: W. Cavanagh, J. Crouwel, R.W.V. Catling and G. Shipley (eds.), *Continuity and Change in a Greek Rural Landscape, The Laconia Survey. Vol. II: Archaeological Data*, The British School at Athens Supplementary Volumes 27, London, 125-40.

Armstrong, P. 2001. From Constantinople to Lakedaimon: Impressed white wares, in: J. Herrin, M. Mullett and C. Otten-Froux (eds.), *Mosaic. Festschrift for A.H.S. Megaw*, London, 57-68.

Armstrong, P. and N.V. Sekunda 2006. A Byzantine soldier from the Crusading Era, *Quaestiones Medii Aevi Novae*, 11-21.

Asal, R. 2007. Istanbul'un ticareti ve Theodosius Limanı, in: *Gün Işığında: Istanbul'un 8000 yılı. Maramaray, Metro, Sultanahmet kazıları*, Istanbul, 180-89.

Athanasoulis, D. (ed.) 2005. *Glarentza / Clarence*, Athens.

Bakirtzis, Ch. 1989. *Byzantine 'Tsoukalolagina'* [in modern Greek, with summary in English], Athens.

Ballian, A. 2013. Exchanges between Byzantium and the Islamic world: Courtly art and material culture, in: A. Drandaki, D. Papanikola-Bakirtzis and A. Tourta (eds.), *Heaven & Earth. Art of Byzantium from Greek Collections* (exhibition catalogue), Athens, 292-96.

Ballian, A. and A. Drandaki 2003. A middle Byzantine silver treasure, *Mouseio Benaki* 3, 47-80.

Bass, G.F. 1982. The pottery, in: G.F. Bass and F.H. Van Doorninck, Jr (eds.), *Yassi Ada I: A Seventh-Century Byzantine Shipwreck*, College Station, Texas, 155-88.

Bass, G.F. and F.H. Van Doorninck, Jr. (ed.) 1982. *Yassi Ada I: A Seventh-Century Byzantine Shipwreck*, College Station, Texas.

Blake, H. 1986. The medieval incised slipped pottery of north-west Italy, in: *La ceramica medievale nel Mediterraneo occidentale, Siena 8-12 ottobre 1984, Faenza 13 ottobre 1984*, Florence, 317-52.

Brokalakis, Y. 2005. Bronze vessels from Late Roman and Early Byzantine Eleutherna on Crete, *Antiquité Tardive* 13, 27-50.

Böhlendorf-Arslan, B. 2013. *Spätantike, byzantinische und postbyzantinische Keramik*, Staatl. Museen zu Berlin – Preußischer Kulturbesitz Skulpturensamml. & Museum für Byzantinische Kunst, Bestandskataloge, 3, Wiesbaden.

Bujard, J. 2005. Les objets métalliques d'Umm al-Walid (Jordanie), *Antiquité Tardive* 13, 135-140.

Burlot, J. and S.Y. Waksman 2020. Provenances and production techniques of the so-called 'Port Saint Symeon ware' (13th-early 14th centuries CE) from Kinet Höyük (Cilicia, Turkey): Witnessing interactions in the medieval north-eastern Mediterranean, *Archaeometry* 64.3, 611-31.

Byzantio & Arabes = 2011. *Byzantio & Arabes / Byzantium & the Arabs* (museum catalogue Museum of Byzantine Culture in modern Greek and in English), Thessaloniki.

Cirelli, E. 2008. *Ravenna: Archeologia di una cittá*, Florence.

Cholakov, J.M. and P. Ilieva 2005. A collective find from the Early Byzantine age found in Stara Zagora (south Bulgaria), *Antiquité Tardive* 13, 51-63.

Costa, S. 2017. An archaeology of domestic life in Early Byzantine Gortyna: Stratigraphy, pots and contexts, in: D. Dixneuf (ed.), *LRCW 5-2. Late Roman Coarse Wares, Cooking Wares and Amphorae in the Mediterranean. Archaeology and Archaeometry*, Études Alexandrines 43, Alexandria, 711-21.

Cutler, A. 2001. Gifts and gift exchange as aspects of the Byzantine, Arab and related economies, *Dumbarton Oaks Papers* 55, 247-78.

De Boüard, M. 1974. Observations on the treatise of Eraclius, de coloribus et artibus Romanorum, in: V.I. Evison, H. Hodges and J.G. Hurst (eds.), *Medieval Pottery from Excavations*, London, 87-76.

Deetz, J. 1972. *In Small Things Forgotten. An Archaeology of Early American Life*, New York.

Dietler, M. 2010. Consumption, in: D.Hicks and M. Beaudry (eds.), *The Oxford Handbook of Material Culture Studies*, Oxford, 207-26.

Demesticha, S. and E. Spondylis. 2011. Late Roman and Byzantine trade in the Aegean: Evidence from the HIMA survey project at Pagasitikos Gulf, Greece, *Skyllis* 11, 34-40.

Denker, A., F. Demirkök, G. Kongaz, M. Kiraz, Ö.K. Kömörcü and T. Akbaytogan 2013. YK12, in: *Stories from the Hidden Harbor. Shipwrecks of Yenikapı* (museum catalogue Istanbul Archaeological Museums), Istanbul, 198-209.

Dimopoulos, J. 2007. Byzantine graffito wares excavated in Sparta (12th-13th centuries), in: B. Böhlendorf-Arslan, A. O. Uysal and J. Witte-Orr (eds.), Çanak. *Late Antique and Medieval Pottery and Tiles in Mediterranean Archaeological Contexts*, Byzas 7, Istanbul, 335-48.

Dimopoulos, J. 2009. Trade of Byzantine red wares, end of the 11th-13th centuries, in: M. Mundell Mango (ed.), *Byzantine Trade, 4th-12th centuries*, Society for the Promotion of Byzantine Studies Publications 14, Aldershot, 179-90.

Dodwell, C.R. (ed. and translated) 1986. *Theophilus: The Various Arts / De Diversis Artibus*, Oxford.

Döğer, L. 2007. Halkın imge dünyasında seramik sanatı / The art of ceramics in the imagination of the folk, in: *'Kalanlar' 12. ve 13. Yüzyıllarda Türkiye'de Bizans / 'The Remnants' 12th and 13th Centuries Byzantine Objects in Turkey*, Istanbul, 48-55.

Douglas, M. and B. Isherwood 1979. *The World of Goods. Towards an Anthropology of Consumption*, New York.

Ettinghausen, R. 1976. Kufesque in Byzantine Greece, the Latin West and the Muslim World, in: *A Colloquium in Memory of George Carpenter Miles (1904-1975)*, New York, 28-47.

Fabian, P. and Y. Goren 2001. A Byzantine warehouse and anchorage site of Ashqelon, *'Atiqot* 42, 211-19.

Fiorillo, R. 2005. *La tavolà dei d'Angiò. Analisi archeologica di una spazzatura reale, Castello di Lagopesole (1266-1315)*, Florence.

Flourentzos, P. 1996. *Excavations in the Kouris Valley, Vol. II: The Basilica of Alassa*, Nicosia.

François, V. 1995. *La céramique byzantine à Thasos*, Paris.

François V. 1997. Céramiques importées à Byzance: Une quasi-absence, *Byzantinoslavica* 58, 387-403.

Frantz, A. 1940-41. Digenis Akritas: A Byzantine epic and its illustrators, *Byzantion* 15, 87-91.

Gerousi, E. 1993. Early Christian ceramics from the area of 'Episkopi' on Samos (in Modern Greek), *Archaiologikon Deltion* 47-48 (A), 251-68.

Gill, D.W.J. 1991. Pots and trade: Spacefillers or objects d'art, *Journal of Hellenic Studies* 111, 29-47.

Gourgiotis, G.K. 1991. Thessalian 'hand washing equipment' and 'chafing dishes' of the Late Byzantine centuries (in modern Greek), *Archaiologia* 38, 81-83.

Grabar, O. 1997. The shared culture of objects, in: H. Maguire (ed.), *Byzantine Court Culture from 829 to 1204*, Washington, DC, 115-29.

Gün Işığında = *Gün Işığında. Istanbul'un 8000 yılı. Maramaray, Metro, Sultanahmet kazıları* (museum catalogue Archaeological Museum Istanbul in Turkish), Istanbul, 180-89.

Günsenin, N. 1989. Recherches sur les amphores byzantines dans les musées turcs, in: V. Déroche and J.-M. Spieser (eds.), *Recherches sur la céramique byzantine*, BCH Supplément 18, Athens & Paris, 267-76.

Günsenin, N. 2001. L'épave de Çamaltı Burnu I (île de Marmara, Proconnese): Resultats des campagnes 1998-2000, *Anatolia Antiqua* 9, 117-33.

Günsenin, N. 2003. L'épave de Çamaltı Burnu I (île de Marmara, Proconnese): Resultats des campagnes 2001-2002, *Anatolia Antiqua* 11, 361-76.

Haldon, J. 2005. *The Palgrave Atlas of Byzantine History*, London

Hayes, J.W. 1981. The excavated pottery from the Bodrum Camii, in: C.L. Striker (ed.), *The Myrelaion (Bodrum Camii) in Istanbul*, Princeton, NJ, 36-41.

Hayes, J.W. 1992. *Excavations at Saraçhane in Istanbul, Vol. II: The Pottery*, Princeton, NJ.

Hayes, J.W. 1993. Les débuts de la céramique vernissée byzantine et omeyyade d'après les fouilles de Saraçhane (Constantinople), in: *Bulletin de l'Association pour l'Antiquité tardive 2, Annuaire 1992*, Paris, 85-89.

Hocker, F.M. 1995. A ninth-century shipwreck near Bozburun, Turkey, *The INA Quarterly* 22.1, 12-14.

Ilg, A. (ed.) 1970². *Heraclius, Von den Farben und Kunsten der Römer*, Osnabrück (2nd new ed.; 1rst ed. Vienna, 1873).

Ioannnidaki-Dostoglou, I. 1989. Les vases de l'épave byzantine de Pélagonnèse-Halonnèse, in: V. Déroche and J.-M. Spieser (eds.), *Recherches sur la céramique byzantine*, Bulletin de Correspondance Hellénique Suppl. 18, Athens & Paris, 157-71.

Jacoby, D. 2001. Changing economic patterns in Latin Romania: The impact of the West, in: A.E. Laiou and R.P. Mottahedeh (eds.), *The Crusades From the Perspective of Byzantium and the Muslim World*, Washington, DC, 197-233.

Jacoby, D. 2009. Venetian commercial expansion in the eastern Mediterranean, 8th-11th centuries, in M. Mundell Mango (ed.), *Byzantine Trade, 4th-12th Centuries*, Farnham & Burlington, 371-91.

Jacoby, D. 2012. The Eastern Mediterranean in the Later Middle Ages: An island world?, in: J. Harris, C. Holmes and E. Russell (eds.), *Byzantines, Latins, and Turks in the Eastern Mediterranean World after 1150*, Oxford, 93-117.

Jacques, H. and F. Baratte 2005. La vaisselle de bronze, dans l'Afrique byzantine: État des questions, *Antiquité Tardive* 13, 121-34.

Kocabaş, U. and I. Özsait Kosabaş 2007. Istanbul Üniversitesi, Yenikapı Bizans batıkları projesi kapsamındaki gemilerin yapım teknikleri ve özellikleri, in: *Gün Işığında. Istanbul'un 8000 yılı. Maramaray, Metro, Sultanahmet kazıları* (museum catalogue Archaeological Museum Istanbul in Turkish), Istanbul, 196-201.

Koilakou, C. 2001-2004. Thebes: Odos Amphionos 18 [in modern Greek], *Archaiologikon Deltion* 6-59, 47-48.

Kontogiannis, N.D. 2003. Κυπριακή Μεσαιωνική κεραμική στο Μουσείο των Σεβρών, in: Επιστημονική Επετηρίδα του Τμήματος Αρχαιοτήτων για το 2003, 311-26.

Korre-Zographou, K. 1995. *Pottery of the Greek Area* (in modern Greek), Athens.

Kostova, R. 2009. Polychrome ceramics in Preslav, 9th to 11th centuries: where were they produced and used?, in: M. Mundell Mango (ed.), *Byzantine Trade, 4th-12th centuries*, Society for the Promotion of Byzantine Studies Publications 14, Aldershot, 97-117.

Koukoules, F. 1947-55 (5 vols.). *Byzantine Life and Civilisation* (in modern Greek), Athens.

Koutsouflakis, G., X. Argiris, Chr. Papadopoulou and J. Sapoundis. 2012. Underwater survey in the south Euboean Gulf (2006-2008) (in modern Greek, with English summary), *Enalia* 11, 40-69.

Koval, V.Y. 2006. Eastern pottery from the excavations at Novgorod, in: C. Orton (ed.), *The Pottery from Medieval Novgorod and its Region*, London, 161-192.

Kritzas, C. 1971. The Byzantine shipwreck of Pelagos near Alonesos (in modern Greek), *Athens Annals of Archaeology* 4, 176-85.

Ladstätter, S. 2008. Römische, spätantike und byzantinische Keramik, in: M. Steskal and M. La Torre (eds.), *Das Vediusgymnasium in Ephesos. Archäologie und Baubefund*, FiE 14,1, Vienna, 97-189.

Laiou, A. 2013. The Byzantine city: Parasitic or productive? Paper presented at the XXIst International Congress of Byzantine Studies (London, August 2006), in: C. Morrisson and R. Dorin (eds.), *Economic Thought and Economic Life in Byzantium*, Ashgate Variorum, Chapter XII, Aldershot, 1-35.

Laiou, A. and C. Morrisson. 2007. *The Byzantine Economy*, Cambridge.

Lane, A. 1938. Medieval finds at Al Mina in North Syria, *Archaeologia* 87, 19-78

Le Patourel, J. 1968. Documentary evidence for the pottery trade in North West Europe, *Medieval Archaeology* 12, 101-26.

Loucas, I. 1989. Les plats byzantins à glaçure inédits d'une collection privée de Bruxelles, in: V. Déroche and J.-M. Spieser (eds.), *Recherches sur la céramique byzantine*, Bulletin de Correspondance Hellénique Suppl. 18, (= Actes du collogue organisé par l'Ecole française d'Athènes et l'Université de Strassbourg II; Athènes 8-10 avril 1987) Athens & Paris, 177-83.

Majeweski, T. and M.B. Schiffer 2001. Beyond consumption: Towards an archaeology of consumerism, in: T. Majewski and D. Gaimster (eds.), *The International Handbook of Historical Archaeology*, New York, 191-207.

McCormick, M. 2012. Movements and markets in the first millennium: Information, containers, and shipwrecks, in: C. Morrisson (ed.), *Trade and Markets in Byzantium*, Washington, DC, 51-98.

Megaw, A.H.S. 1931-32. The chronology of some Middle Byzantine churches, *Annual of the British School at Athens* 32, 90-130.

Megaw, A.H.S. 1951. Three Medieval pit-groups from Nicosia, *Report of the Department of Antiquities, Cyprus* 1937-39 = 1951, 145-68 and 224-26.

Mercangöz, Z. 2013. Kadıkalesi/Anaia ticari "retiminin Latin patronları / Latin patrons of commercial production in Kadıkalesi/Anaia, in: Z. Mercangöz (ed.), *Bizanslı Ustular – Latin Patronlar / Byzantine Crafstmen – Latin Patrons* (in Turkish and English), Istanbul, 161-74.

Miller, D. (ed.) 1995. *Acknowledging Consumption. A Review of New Studies*, New York.

Morgan, C.H. 1935. Several vases from a Byzantine dump at Corinth, *American Journal of Archaeology* 39, 76-78.

Morgan, C.H. 1942. *Corinth, Vol. XI: The Byzantine Pottery*, Cambridge, MA.

Mullins, P.R. 2011. The archaeology of consumption, *The Annual Review of Anthropology*, 133-44.

Mundell Mango, M. 2000. The commercial map of Constantinople, *Dumbarton Oaks Papers*, 54, 189-207.

Mundell Mango, M. 2001. Beyond the amphora: Non-ceramic evidence for Late Antique industry and trade, in: S. Kingsley and M. Decker (eds.), *Economy and Exchange in the East Mediterranean during Late Antiquity*, (Proceedings of a Conference at Somerville College, Oxford, 29th May, 1999), Oxford, 87-106.

Mundell Mango, M. 2009. Tracking Byzantine silver and copper metalware, 4th-12th centuries, in: M. Mundell Mango (ed.), *Byzantine Trade, 4th-12th Centuries. The Archaeology of Local, Regional and International Exchange*, Society for the Promotion of Byzantine Studies Publications 14, Farnham & Burlington, 221-36.

Notopoulos, J. 1964. Akritan iconography on Byzantine pottery, *Hesperia* 33, 108-33.

ODB = A.P. Kahzdan *et al.* 1991. *The Oxford Dictionary of Byzantium*, New York & Oxford.

Omont, H. 1908. Évangiles avec peintures byzantines du XIe siècle (Reproduction des 361 miniatures du manuscrit grec 74 de la bibliothèque nationale), Paris.

Özdaş, H., N. Kızıldağ and E. Okan. 2012. Akdeniz Kıyıları Arkeolojik Sualtı Araştırmaları 2011 / Underwater archaeological Surveys along the Mediterranean coastline 2011, *ANAMED Anadolu Akdenizi Arkeoloji Haberleri / News of Archaeology from Anatolia's Mediterranean Areas* 10, 119-24.

Papanikola-Bakirtzis, D. 1989. Μεσαιωνική Κυπριακή κεραμεική στο Μουσείο του Ιδρύματος Πιερίδη, Larnaca.

Papanikola-Bakirtzis, D. 1992. Serres: A glazed pottery production center during the Late Byzantine period, in: D. Papanikola-Bakirtzis, E. Dauterman Maguire and H. Maguire (eds.), *Ceramic Art from Byzantine Serres*, Urbana & Chicago, 21-35.

Papanikola-Bakirtzis, D. 1996. *Medieval Glazed Pottery of Cyprus: The Workshops of Paphos and Lapithos*, Nicosia.

Papanikola-Bakirtzis, D. (ed.) 1999. *Byzantine Glazed Ceramics. The Art of Sgraffito*, Athens.

Papanikola-Bakirtzis, D. 2004. *Colours of Medieval Cyprus Through the Medieval Collection of the Leventis Municipal Museum of Nicosia* (with essays by Sir David Hunt and Eleni Loizides), Nicosia.

Papanikola-Bakirtzis, D., F.N. Mavrikiou and Ch. Bakirtzis. 1999. *Byzantine Glazed Pottery in the Benaki Museum*, Athens.

Papanikola-Bakirtzis, D. and N. Zekos (eds.) 2010. *Late Byzantine Glazed Pottery from Thrace. Reading the Archaeological Finds*, Thessaloniki.

Parker, A.J. 1992. *Ancient Shipwrecks of the Mediterranean & the Roman Provinces*, BAR International Series 580, Oxford.

Peschlow, U. 1977-78. Byzantinische Keramik aus Istanbul, *Istanbuler Mitteilungen* 27-28, 363-414.

Philon, H. 1980. *Early Islamic Ceramics. Ninth to Late Twelfth Centuries*, Athens.

Philothéou, G. and Michailidou, M. 1989. Plats byzantins provenant d'une épave près de Castellorizo, in: V. Déroche and J.-M. Spieser (eds.), *Recherches sur la céramique byzantine*, Bulletin de Correspondance Hellénique Suppl. 18, Athens & Paris, 173-76.

Piltz, E. 1996. *The Von Post Collection of Cypriote Late Byzantine Glazed Pottery*, Studies in Mediterranean Archaeology Vol. CXIX, Jonsered.

Pitarakis, B. 2005. Une production caractéristique de cruches en alliage cuivreux: (VIe-VIIIe siècles), *Antiquité Tardive* 13, 11-27.

Pulak, C. 2007. Yenikapı Bizans batıkları, in: *Gün Işığında. Istanbul'un 8000 yılı. Maramaray, Metro, Sultanahmet kazıları* (in Turkish & English), Istanbul, 202-15.

Redford, S. 2012. Trade and economy in Antioch and Cilicia in the twelfth ad thirteenth centuries, in: C. Morrisson (ed.), *Trade and Markets in Byzantium*, Washington, DC, 297-309.

Ricci, M. 2007. Elaiussa Sebaste: Context, production & commerce, in: B. Böhlendorf-Arslan, A. O. Uysal and J. Witte-Orr (eds.), *Çanak. Late Antique and Medieval Pottery and Tiles in Mediterranean Archaeological Contexts*, Byzas 7, Istanbul, 169-80.

Romei, D. 1992. La ceramic a vetrina pesante altomedievale nella stratigrafia dell'esedra della Crypta Balbi, in: L. Paroli (ed.), *La ceramica invetriata tardoantica e altomedievale in Italia*, Florence, 378-93.

Sanders, G.D.R. 1995. Byzantine Glazed Pottery at Corinth to c. 1125, *unpublished* PhD Thesis, University of Birmingham, 1995.

Sanders, G.D.R. 2001. Byzantine Polychrome pottery, in: J. Herrin, M. Mullett and C. Otten-Froux (eds.), *Mosaic: Festschrift for A.H.S. Megaw*, London, 89-103.

Sanders, G.D.R. 2003. An overview of the new chronology for 9th to 13th century pottery at Corinth, in: Ch. Bakirtzis (ed.), *VIIe Congrès international sur la céramique médiévale en Méditerranée*, Athens, 35-41.

Sardi, M. 2020. Foreign influences in Mamluk textiles: The formation of a new aesthetic, in: N. Vryzidis (ed.), *The Hidden Life of Textiles in the Medieval and Early Modern Mediterranean*, Medieval and Post-Medieval Mediterranean Archaeology Series III, Turnhout, 83-118.

Sedikova, L. 2015. Glazed Ware from the mid thirteenth-century destruction layer of Chersonesos, in: J. Vroom (ed.), *Medieval and Post-Medieval Ceramics in the Eastern Mediterranean: Fact and Fiction*, Medieval and Post-Medieval Mediterranean Archaeology Series I, Turnhout, 269-82.

Segal, A. et al. 2003. *Hippos-Sussita: Fourth season of Excavations June-July 2003*,

Smith, R.H. and L. Preston Day 1989. *Pella of the Decapolis, Vol. 2: Final Report on the College of Wooster Excavations in Area IX. The Civic Complex, 1979-1985*, Wooster, Ohio.

Stern, E.J. 2012. *Akko I: The 1991-1998 Excavations. The Crusader-Period Pottery, Part 1: Text, Part 2: Plates*, IAA Reports 51/1-2, Jerusalem.

Stevenson, R.B.K. 1947. The pottery, 1936-7, in: G. Brett, W.J. Macaulay and R.B.K. Stevenson (eds.), *The Great Palace of the Byzantine Emperors*, London, 31-63.

Stephens Crawford, J. 1990. *The Byzantine Shops at Sardis*, Cambridge, MA.

Swan, V.G. 2007. Dichin (Bulgaria): The fifth- and sixth-century destruction deposits, and their implications for ceramic chronology, in: M. Bonifay and J.-C. Tréglia (eds.), *LRCW 2. Late Roman Coarse Wares, Cooking Wares and Amphorae in the Mediterranean. Archaeology and Archaeometry*, BAR International Series 1662 (II), Oxford, 835-44.

Talbot Rice, D. 1930. *Byzantine Glazed Pottery*, Oxford.

Talbot Rice, D. 1954. The Byzantine pottery, in: D. Talbot Rice (ed.), *The Great Palace of the Byzantine Emperors, Second Report*, Edinburgh, 110-13.

Talbot Rice, D. 1965. The pottery of Byzantium and the Islamic world, in: *Studies in Islamic Art and Architecture in Honour of Professor K.A.C. Creswell*, Cairo, 194-236.

Thiriot, J. 1995. Les ateliers, in: *Le vert & le brun de Kairouan à Avignon, céramiques du Xe au XVe siècle*, Marseille, 19-39.

Tsanana, A. 2003. The glazed pottery of Byzantine Vrya (Vrea), in: Ch. Bakirtzis (ed.), *VII Congrès international sur la céramique médiévale en Méditerranée*, Athens, 245-50.

Van Doorninck Jr., F.H. 1989. The cargo amphoras on the 7th century Yassi Ada and 11th century Serçe Limani shipwrecks: Two examples of a reuse of Byzantine amphoras as transport jars, in: V. Déroche and J.-M. Spieser (eds.), *Recherches sur la céramique byzantine*, Bulletin de Correspondance Hellénique Suppl. 18, Athens & Paris, 247-57.

Van Doorninck Jr., F.H. 2014. Byzantine amphoras made for war?, *The INA Quarterly* 41.1, 21-27.

Von Wartburg, M.-L. 1998. Mittelalterliche Keramik aus dem Aphroditeheiligtum in Palaiopaphos, *Archäologischer Anzeiger*, 133-65.

Von Wartburg, M.-L. 2003. Cypriot contacts with East and West as reflected in Medieval glazed pottery from the Paphos region, in: Ch. Bakirtzis (ed.), *VIIe Congrès international sur la céramique médiévale en Méditerranée*, Athens, 11-16.

Von Wartburg, M.-L., A. Portmann, F. Wild, S. Stockhause and H. Berke 2010. 'Islamic' table ware found in Cyprus: Study and analysis of fabric and glazes, *Report of the Department of Antiquities, Cyprus 2009*, 389-410.

Von Wartburg, M.-L. and Y. Violaris 2009. Pottery of a 12th century pit from the *Palaion Demarcheion* site in Nicosia: A typological and analytical approach to a closed assemblage, in: J. Zozaya Stabel-Hansen, M. Retuerce Velasco, M.A. Hervás Herrera and A. De Juan García *(eds.)*, *Actas del VIII Congreso Internacional de Cerámica Medieval en el Mediterráneo*, Vol. I, Ciudad, 249-64.

Vroom, J. 2003. *After Antiquity. Ceramics and Society in the Aegean from the 7th to the 20th centuries A.C. A Case Study from Boeotia, Central Greece*, Archaeological Studies Leiden University 10, Leiden.

Vroom, J. 2005. Medieval pottery from the Artemision in Ephesus: Imports and locally produced wares, in: F. Krinzinger (ed.), *Spätantike und Mittelalterliche Keramik aus Ephesos*, Österreichische Akademie der Wissenschaften, Philosophisch-Historische Klasse, Denkschriften, 332. Band, Vienna, 17-49.

Vroom, J. 2007. The changing dining habits at Christ's table, in: L. Brubraker and K. Linardou (eds.), *Eat, Drink, and Be Merry (Luke 12:19) – Food and Wine in Byzantium. Papers of the 37th Annual Spring Symposium of Byzantine Studies, in Honour of Professor A.A.M. Bryer*, Society for the Promotion of Byzantine Studies, Publications 13, Aldershot, 191-222.

Vroom, J. 2008. Dishing up history: Early Medieval ceramic finds from the Triconch Palace in Butrint, *Mélanges de l'Ecole française de Rome – Moyen Âge* 120.2, 291-305.

Vroom, J. 2009, Medieval ceramics and the archaeology of consumption in Eastern Anatolia, in: T. Vorderstrasse and J. Roodenberg (eds.), *Archaeology of the Countryside in Medieval Anatolia*, PIHANS CXIII, Leiden, 235-58.

Vroom, J. 2011. The Morea and its links with Southern Italy after AD 1204: Ceramics and identity, *Archeologia Medievale* 38, 409-30.

Vroom, J. 2012a. Tea and ceramics: New perspectives on Byzantine pottery from Limyra, in: M. Seyer (ed.), *40 Jahre Grabung Limyra. Akten des Symposions, Wien, 3-5 Dezember 2009*, Vienna, 341-55.

Vroom, J. 2012b. Early Medieval pottery finds from recent excavations at Butrint, Albania, in: S. Gelichi (ed.), *Atti del IX congresso internazionale sulla ceramica medievale nel Mediterraneo, Venezia, Scuola Grande dei Carmini, Auditorium Santa Margherita, 23-27 novembre 2009*, Florence, 289-96.

Vroom, J. 2013. Medieval – Modern Fine Wares, in: M. Given, A.B. Knapp, J. Noller, L. Sollars and V. Kassianidou (eds.), *Landscape and Interaction: The Troodos Archaeological and Environmental Survey Project, Cyprus, Vol 1: Methodology, Analysis and Interpretation*, Oxford, 74-80.

Vroom, J. 2014². *Byzantine to Modern Pottery in the Aegean: An Introduction and Field Guide, Second Revised Edition*, Turnhout (2nd and revised ed.; 1rst ed. Utrecht, 2005).

Vroom, J. 2014. Human representations on Medieval Cypriot ceramics and beyond: The enigma of mysterious figures wrapped in riddles, in: D. Papanikola-Bakirtzis and N. Coureas (eds.), *Cypriot Medieval Ceramics: Reconsiderations and New Perspectives*, Nicosia, 153-87.

Vroom, J. 2015a, Food and dining as social display, in: K.B. Metheny and M.C. Beaudry (eds.), *The Archaeology of Food: An Encyclopedia*, Lanham & Boulder & New York & London, 184-87.

Vroom, J. 2015b. 'Strike a Pose': Human representations and gestures on Medieval ceramics from Cyprus (ca. 13th-15th/16th centuries), in: S. Rogge and M. Grünbart (eds.), *Medieval Cyprus: A Place of Cultural Encounter*, Schriften des Instituts für Interdisziplinäre Zypern-Studien 11, Münster & New York, 245-75.

Vroom, J. 2015c. The archaeology of consumption in the Eastern Mediterranean: A ceramic perspective, in: M.-J. Gonçalves and S. Gómez-Martinez (eds.), *Actas do X Congresso Internacional A Cerâmica Medieval no Mediterrâneo, Silves – Mértola, 22 a 27. outubro 2012*, Silves, 359-67.

Vroom, J. 2016a, Pots and pies: Adventures in the archaeology of eating habits of Byzantium, in: E., Sibbesson, B. Jervis and S. Coxon (eds.), *Insight from Innovation: New Light on Archaeological Ceramics. Papers Presented in Honour of Professor David Peacock's Contributions to Archaeological Ceramic Studies*, St. Andrews, 221-44.

Vroom, J. 2016b. Byzantine sea trade in ceramics: Some case studies in the eastern Mediterranean (ca. seventh - fourteenth centuries), in: P. Magdalino and N. Necipoğlu (eds.), *Trade in Byzantium: Papers from the Third International Sevgi Gönül Byzantine Studies Symposium*, Istanbul, 157-77.

Vroom, J. 2018. The ceramics, agricultural resources and food, in: J. Haldon, H. Elton and J. Newhard (eds.), *Archaeology and Urban Settlement in Late Roman and Byzantine Anatolia: Euchaita-Avkat-Beyözü and its Environment*, Cambridge, 134-84.

Vroom, J. 2020a. Preface, in: N. Vryzidis (ed.), *The Hidden Life of Textiles in the Medieval and Early Modern Mediterranean*, Medieval and Post-Medieval Mediterranean Archaeology Series III, Turnhout, 11-12.

Vroom, J. 2020b. Eating in Aegean lands (ca 700-1500): Perspectives on pottery, in: S.Y. Waksman (ed.), *Multidisciplinary Approaches to Food and Foodways in the Medieval Eastern Mediterranean*, Archéologie(s) 4, Lyon, 275-93.

Vroom, J. 2021a. From Xi'an to Birka and back: Constantinople as a nodal point in Early Medieval long-distance contacts (ca. 6th-12th centuries), in: H. Nol (ed.), *Riches Beyond the Horizon: Long-distance Trade in Early Medieval Landscapes (ca. 6th-12th Centuries)*, Medieval and Post-Medieval Mediterranean Archaeology Series IV, Turnhout, 149-200.

Vroom, J. 2021b. Thinking of Linking: Pottery connections, Southern Adriatic, Butrint and beyond, in: M. Skoblar (ed.), *Byzantium, Venice and the Medieval Adriatic. Spheres of Maritime Power and Influence, c. 700-1543*, Cambridge, 45-82.

Vroom, J. 2022a. Shifting Byzantine networks: New light on Chalcis (Euripos/Negroponte) as a centre of production and trade in Greece (ca. 10th-13th c.), in: E. Fiori and M. Trizio (eds.), *The 24th International Congress of Byzantine Studies, Vol. 1: Proceedings of the Plenary Sessions*, Venice, 453-87.

Vroom, J. 2022b. A Byzantine space oddity: The cultural geography of foodways and cuisine in the eastern Mediterranean (700-1500), in: M. Veikou and I. Nilsson (eds.), *Spatialities of Byzantine Culture: From the Human Body to the Universe*, Leiden & Boston, 171-211.

Vroom, J. and E. Fındık 2015. The pottery finds, in: S. Ladstätter (ed.), *Die Türbe im Artemision. Ein frühosmanischer Grabbau in Ayasuluk/Selçuk und sein kulturhistorisches Umfeld* (Österreichisches Archäologisches Institut Sonderschriften Band 53), Vienna, 205-92.

Vroom, J., Y. Waksman and R. van Oosten (eds.) 2017, *Medieval MasterChef: Archaeological and Historical Perspectives on Eastern Cuisine and Western Foodways*, Medieval and Post-Medieval Mediterranean Archaeology Series II, Turnhout.

Vroom, J. and M. van IJzendoorn forthcoming. Sherds, sites and shipwrecks: the last amphora type of Late Byzantine times, in J. Leidwanger and H. Cesteros (eds.), *Regional Convergences: Mass Production and the Development of Roman and Byzantine Amphora Standardization. Proceedings of Workshop at the Danish Institute in Athens held at 16-18 October 2017*.

Waksman, S.Y., A. Bouquillon, N. Cantin and I. Katona 2007. The first Byzantine 'Glazed White Wares' in the Early Medieval technological context, in: S.Y. Waksman (ed.), *Archaeometric and Archaeological Approaches to Ceramics*, BAR International Series 1691, Oxford, 129-35.

Waksman, S.Y., A. Bouquillon, N. Cantin and I. Katona 2008. Approche archéométrique des premières « Byzantine Glazed White Wares » et de productions glaçurées romaines et romaines tardives, *Rei Cretariae Romanae Acta* 40, 531-36.

Waksman, S.Y. and I. Teslenko. 2010. Novy Svet Ware, an exceptional cargo of glazed wares from a 13th-century shipwreck near Sudak (Crimea, Ukraine) – Morphological typology and laboratory investigations, *The International Journal of Nautical Archaeology* 39.2, 357-75.

Waksman, S.Y., I. Teslenko and S. Zelenko 2009. Glazed wares as main cargoes and personal belongings in the Novy Svet shipwreck (13th c. AD, Crimea): A diversity of origins investigated by chemical analysis, in: J. Zozaya Stabel-Hansen, M. Retuerce Velasco, M.A. Hervás Herrera and A. De Juan García (eds.), *Actas del VIII Congreso Internacional de Cerámica Medieval en el Mediterráneo, Vol. I*, Ciudad, 851-56.

Waldbaum, J.C. 1983. *Metalwork from Sardis: The Finds through 1974*, Cambridge, MA.

Watson, O. 2004. *Ceramics from Islamic Lands*, London.

Yenişehirlioğu, F. 1995. Istanbul – Tekfur Sarayı – Osmanlı dönemi çini fırınları ve Eyüp çömlekciler mahallesi yüzey araştırmaları, *XII Araştırma sonuçları toplantısı*, Ankara, 535-66.

Yenişehirlioğu, F. 2009. Les fours et al production des céramiques du Palais de Tekfur a Istanbul, in: J. Zozaya Stabel-Hansen, M. Retuerce Velasco, M.A. Hervás Herrera and A. De Juan García (eds.), *Actas del VIII Congreso Internacional de Cerámica Medieval en el Mediterráneo, Vol. I*, Ciudad, 617-32.

Zanini, E. 2010. Forma delle anfore e forme del commercio tardoantico: Spunti per una riflessione, in: S. Menchelli, S. Santoro, M. Pasquinucci and G. Guiducci (eds.), *LRCW 3. Late Roman Coarse Wares, Cooking Wares and Amphorae in the Mediterranean. Archaeology and Archaeometry*, BAR International Series 2185 (I), Oxford, 139-48.

Zelenko, S. 2009. Shipwrecks of the 9th-11th centuries in the Black Sea near Soldaya, in: J. Zozaya Stabel-Hansen, M. Retuerce Velasco, M.A. Hervás Herrera and A. De Juan García (eds.), *Actas del VIII Congreso Internacional de Cerámica Medieval en el Mediterráneo, Vol. I*, Ciudad, 235-44.

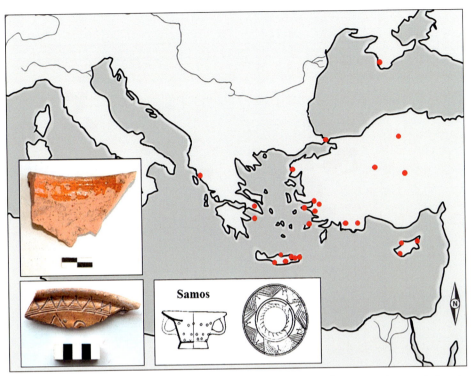

FIG. 1 – Distribution map of Glazed White Ware I in the eastern Mediterranean (map and photo's: J. Vroom; drawing after Gerousi 1993, 258-59, no. 8050, figs. 7-8).

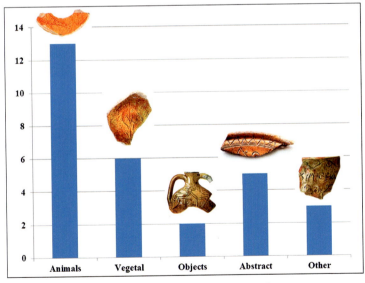

FIG. 2 – The most commonly used motifs of Glazed White Ware I (J. Vroom; pictures: after Talbot Rice 1930 and Böhlendorf-Arslan 2013, pl. 4, nos. 26 and 30).

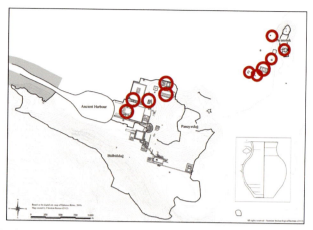

FIG. 3 – Map of Ephesus with distribution of Glazed White Ware I, II and IV (J. Vroom; map: C. Kürtze; drawing: after Ladstätter 2008, pl. 297, K 239).

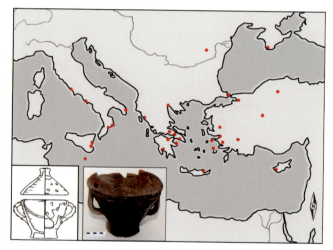

FIG. 4 – Distribution map of glazed chafing dishes in the Mediterranean (map and photo: J. Vroom; drawing: after Romei 1992, figs. 1-2).

FIG. 5 – Miniature from Bibliothèque national gr. 74 Tetraevang., Paris, 3rd quarter of the 11th century (after Omont 1908, fol. 82/1).

328

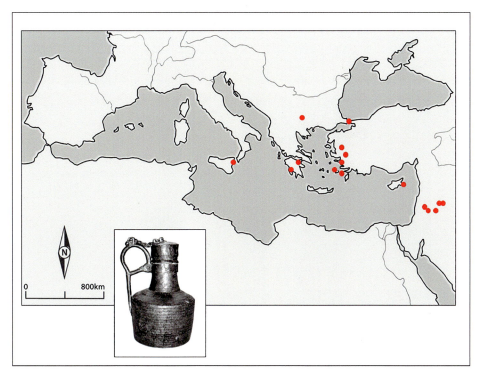

FIG. 6 – Distribution map of metal jugs in the Mediterranean (J. Vroom; after Pitarakis 2005, fig. 3).

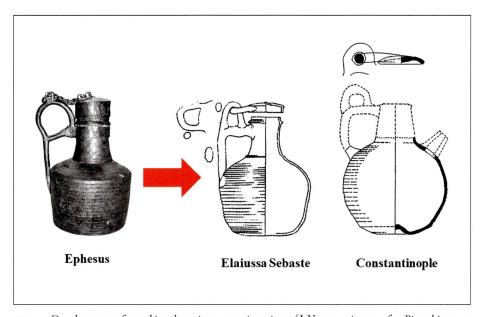

FIG. 7 – Development of metal jug shape into ceramic variants (J. Vroom; picture: after Pitarakis 2005, fig. 3; drawings: after Hayes 1992, fig. 33, 14, 21; Ricci 2007, fig. 3, no. 18).

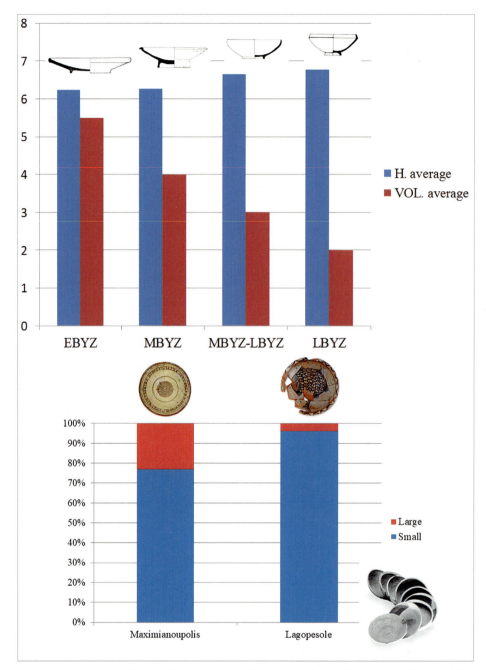

FIG. 8A-B – (A) – Graph showing the average vessel height and volume of Byzantine tablewares (after Vroom 2016a, fig. 13.5); (B) – Graph showing the increase of smaller bowls in Late Medieval ceramic assemblages on two sites: Maximianoupolis (northern Greece) and Lagopesole (southern Italy) – (Graph: J. Vroom; pictures: after Papanikola-Bakirtzis and Zekos 2010 and Fiorillo 2005).

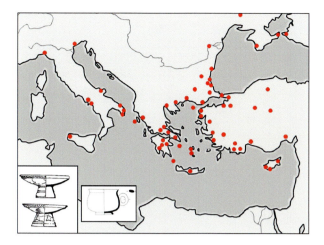

FIG. 9 – Distribution map of Glazed White Wares II-IV and Polychrome Ware in the Mediterranean (map: J. Vroom; drawings: after Peschlow 1977-78, figs. 9 and 12; Sanders 2001, fig. 10.3, no. 12).

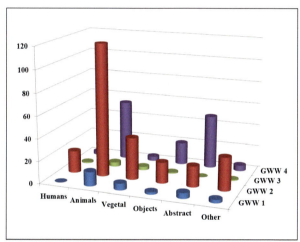

FIG. 10 – The most commonly used motifs of Glazed White Wares I-V (J. Vroom).

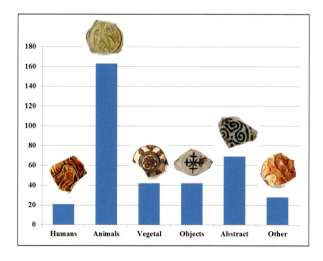

FIG. 11 – The most commonly used motifs of Glazed White Wares II-V and Polychrome Ware at Constantinople (J. Vroom; pictures after Talbot Rice 1930 and Böhlendorf-Arslan 2013).

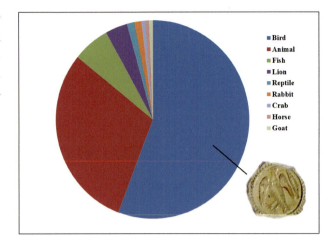

FIG. 12 – The most commonly used animal motifs of Glazed White Wares II-V and Polychrome Ware at Constantinople (J. Vroom; picture: after Morgan 1942).

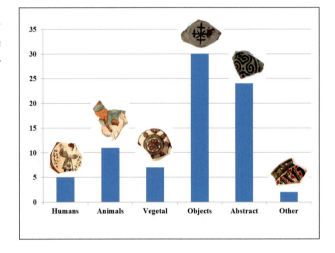

FIG. 13 – The most commonly used motifs of Polychrome Ware (J. Vroom; pictures: after Morgan 1942).

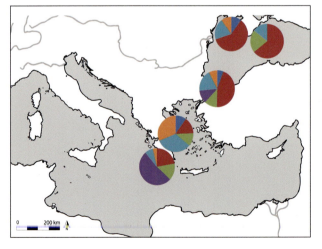

FIG. 14 – Categories of motifs in Glazed White Wares II-V across some sites and regions. From North to South: Chersonesos; Novy Svet Shipwreck; Constantinople; Corinth; Sparta. Blue = humans; red = animals; green = floral; purple = objects; light blue = geometric/abstract; orange = other motifs (J. Vroom).

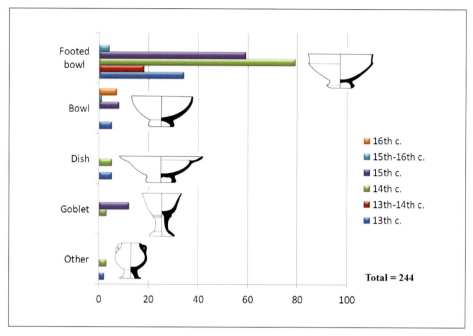

FIG. 15 – Total of main vessel shapes of Medieval glazed decorated tablewares by century from four museum collections (J. Vroom; drawings: after Papanikola-Bakirtzis 1996).

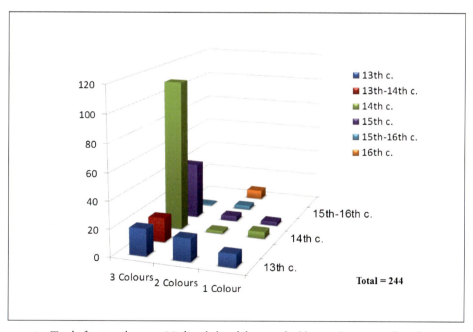

FIG. 16 – Total of main colours on Medieval glazed decorated tablewares by century from four museum collections (J. Vroom).

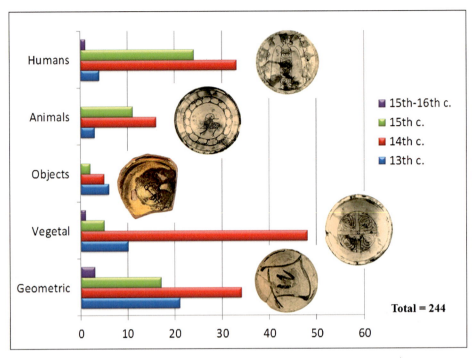

FIG. 17 – Total of main designs on Medieval glazed decorated tablewares by century (J. Vroom; pictures: after Papanikola-Bakirtzis 1989 and *Idem* 2004).

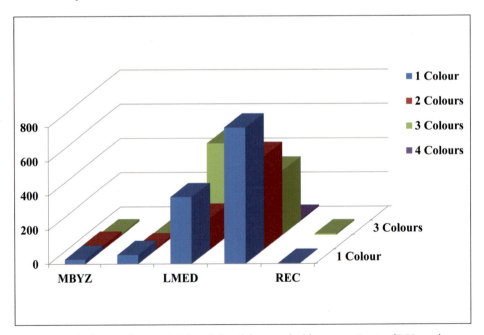

FIG. 18 – Total of main colours on Medieval glazed decorated tablewares at Butrint (J. Vroom).

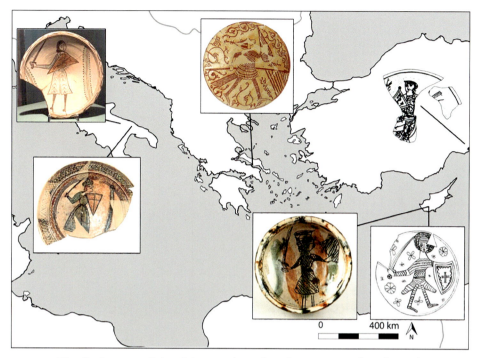

FIG. 19 – Distribution map of glazed decorated vessels with warrior motifs in the Mediterranean according to their provenance (J. Vroom; pictures: after Vroom 2014, 162, fig. 9).

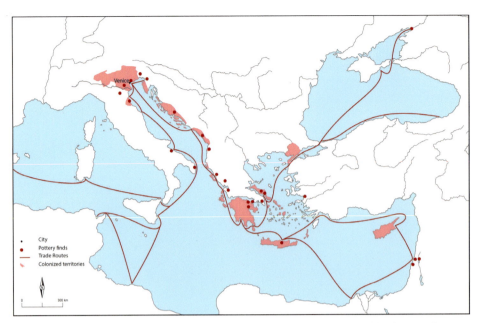

FIG. 20 – Map of Venetian trading routes, Venetian colonized territories, and find spots of Veneto Ware (Pottery finds), including *ceramica graffita a spirale cerchio* and Roulette Ware, in the Mediterranean (J. Vroom; map: after Haldon 2005, map. 11.5).

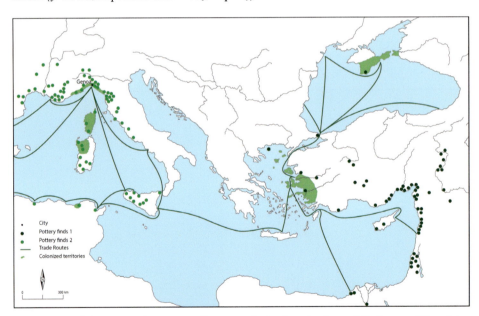

FIG. 21. Map of Genoese trading routes, Genoese colonized territories, and find spots of Port Saint Symeon Ware (Pottery finds 1) and of Tyrrhenian Archaic Graffita / *graffita arcaica tirenica* (Pottery finds 2) in the Mediterranean (J. Vroom; map: after Haldon 2005, map. 11.5).

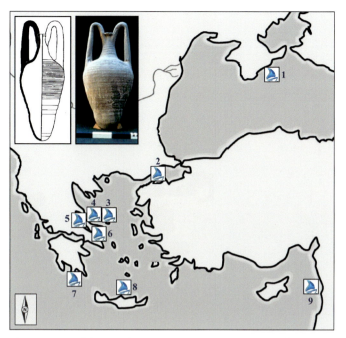

FIG. 22 – Distribution map of shipwrecks transporting Günsenin 3/Saraçhane 61 amphorae in the eastern Mediterranean (map: J. Vroom; drawing and picture: after Günsenin 1989, fig. 8).

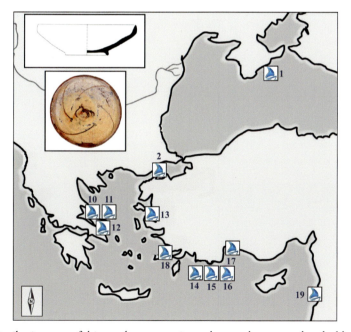

FIG. 23 – Distribution map of shipwrecks transporting 12th- to 14th-century glazed tablewares in the eastern Mediterranean (map: J. Vroom; pictures: after Papanikola-Bakirtzis 1999, 47, no. 168).

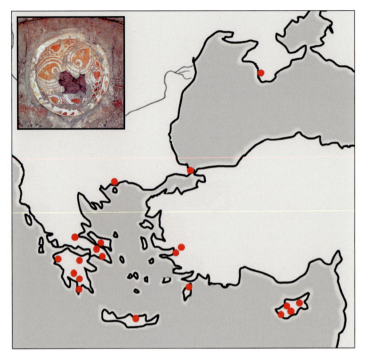

FIG. 24 – Distribution map of imported Islamic tablewares found on Byzantine sites in the eastern Mediterranean (map and photo of Fatamid Lustreware dish in wall of the Agioi Theodoroi church in Athens: J. Vroom).

✳ ✳ ✳

List of figures

✳

JOANITA VROOM

FIG. 1 – Map with most important regions mentioned in the contributions in this volume, ordered by chapter sequence: 1 – Eastern Macedonia (e.g., Thessaloniki); 2 – Serbia (e.g., Caričin Grad); 3 – Epirus; 4 – Crete; 5 – Bulgaria; 6 – Western Anatolia (e.g., Miletus); 7-9 – Central Greece (e.g., Thebes, Chalcis, Corinth, Athens); 10 – Eastern) Mediterranean (drawing J. Vroom).

ARCHIBALD DUNN

FIG. 1 – South-eastern Macedonia (part): Lakes and wetlands (fisheries) ca. 1900 (Archibald Dunn).

FIG. 2 – Thessaloniki: Records of regional products (Archibald Dunn).

FIG. 3 – South-eastern Macedonia: Medieval Byzantine towns and cities (Archibald Dunn).

VESNA BIKIĆ

FIG. 1 – Caričin Grad and neighbouring sites (after Ivanišević 2016b, fig. 2).

FIG. 2A-B – Caričin Grad: Cooking ware (1-6), and baking cover; (A) – photo; (B) – drawings (Institute of Archaeology, Belgrade).

FIG. 3A-B – Caričin Grad: *Maison aux pithoi* on the Acropolis; (A) – general overview; (B) – detail of a pithos (photo: Institute of Archaeology, Belgrade).

FIG. 4 – Caričin Grad: Pithoi (photo: Institute of Archaeology, Belgrade).

FIG. 5A-B – Caričin Grad: Tableware; (A) – photo; (b) – drawings (Institute of Archaeology, Belgrade)

FIG. 6 – Caričin Grad: Handmade pottery; (A) – photo; (B) – drawings (Institute of Archaeology, Belgrade)

FIG. 7 – Caričin Grad and the movement of goods as evidenced by ceramics (after Haldon 2005, 45).

FIG. 8 – Caričin Grad: Imported pottery (photo: Institute of Archaeology, Belgrade).

MYRTO VEIKOU

FIG. 1 – Map of western Greek mainland, marking the location of the four archaeological sites discussed in this chapter (M. Veikou; the background is courtesy of Google Maps).

FIG. 2 – Archaeological evidence of consumption in Epirote Byzantine 'urban environments' during the 7th century (after Veikou 2012, map 16; the background is courtesy of Google Maps).

FIG. 3 – Archaeological evidence of consumption in Epirote Byzantine 'urban environments' during the 8th century (after Veikou 2012, map 16; the background is courtesy of Google Maps).

FIG. 4 – Archaeological evidence of consumption in Epirote Byzantine 'urban environments' during the 9th century (after Veikou 2012, map 16; the background is courtesy of Google Maps).

FIG. 5 – Archaeological evidence of consumption in Epirote Byzantine 'urban environments' during the 10th century (after Veikou 2012, map 16; the background is courtesy of Google Maps).

FIG. 6 – Archaeological evidence of consumption in Epirote Byzantine 'urban environments' during the 11th century (after Veikou 2012, map 16; the background is courtesy of Google Maps).

FIG. 7 – Archaeological evidence of consumption in Epirote Byzantine 'urban environments' during the 12th century (after Veikou 2012, map 16; the background is courtesy of Google Maps).

NATALIA POULOU

FIG. 1 – Map of Crete (N. Poulou).

FIG. 2 – Gortyna fortification, polygonal tower (photo: N. Poulou).

FIG. 3 – Itanos, Basilica A (after Tsigonaki 2009, fig. 7).

FIG. 4 – Painted bowl produced in Gortyn. Excavation of Pseira (PS 3623, after Poulou-Papadimitriou 2011-13, fig. 3).

FIG. 5 – Jug with slip painted decoration and traces of glaze. Eleutherna, Sector I (after Poulou-Papadimitriou 2004, fig. 7).

FIG. 6 – Basin. Fabric from Mochlos area. Excavation of Pseira (PS 4180, after Poulou-Papadimitriou 2011-13, fig. 6).

FIG. 7 – Chafing dish. Fabric from Kalo Chorio area. Excavation of Pseira (PS 493, after Poulou-Papadimitriou 2011-2013, fig. 8).

FIG. 8 – Byzantine globular amphora. Fabric from Mochlos area. Excavation of Pseira (PS 2727, after Poulou-Papadimitriou 2011-2013, fig. 25).

FIG. 9 – Ovoid amphora. Fabric from South Coast. Excavation of Pseira (PS 2646, after Poulou-Papadimitriou 2011-2013, fig. 18).

FIG. 10 – Amphora survival of LRA 1 type. Excavation of Pseira (PS 1407, after Poulou-Papadimitriou 2011-2013, fig. 30).

FIG. 11A-B – (A) – Bronze belt buckle. Heraklion Archaeological Museum (after Poulou-Papadimitriou 2011-2013, fig. 61); (B) – Golden belt buckle from Crete. Ashmolean Museum (after Poulou-Papadimitriou 2005, fig. 11).

FIG. 12 – Palestinian amphora. Heraklion Archaeological Museum (after Poulou-Papadimitriou 2003, fig. 3).

FIG. 13 – Jug with impressed decoration and green glaze. Heraklion (after Poulou-Papadimitriou 2008, fig. 6).

FIG. 14 – Glazed dish with green and brown painted decoration. Heraklion, excavation at the Dominican monastery of St. Peter (after Poulou-Papadimitriou 2008, fig. 7).

FIG. 15 – Amphora from Mochlos (after Poulou-Papadimitriou and Konstantinidou 2016).

FIG. 16 – Golden earrings from Messonissi, Rethymnon (after Sidiropoulos and Vasileiadou 2011, 43).

FIG. 17A-B-C – Cup, Polychrome ware. Heraklion (after Poulou-Papadimitriou 2008, figs. 11, 12).

FIG. 18 – Dish, Polychrome ware. Heraklion (after Poulou-Papadimitriou 2008, fig. 13).

FIG. 19A-B – Byzantine silk textile decorated with elephants (above) and inscription (below). Aachen Cathedral's Treasury (after Wilckens 1991, pl. 49).

EVELINA TODOROVA

FIG. 1 – Initial map of amphora distribution (E. Todorova).

FIG. 2 – Quantitative distribution of the 7th- to 14th-century amphorae from present-day Bulgaria (E. Todorova).

FIG. 3 – The quantitative distribution of contemporaneous amphorae (E. Todorova).

FIG. 4 – Distribution of amphora stamps found in present-day Bulgaria (E. Todorova).

FIG. 5 – Distribution of diagnostic amphora stamps in the Aegean and the Black Sea area (E. Todorova).

FIG. 6 – Chronology of amphorae found in present-day Bulgaria: (1) – 7th to 9th/10th century; (2) – 9th/10th to 11th/12th century; (3) – 11th/12th to 14th century (E. Todorova).

FIG. 7 – Distribution of the 7th- to 9th/10th-century amphorae in present-day Bulgaria (E. Todorova).

FIG. 8 – Distribution of the 9th/10th- to 11th/12th-century amphorae found in present-day Bulgaria (E. Todorova).

FIG. 9 – Distribution of 11th/12th- to 14th-century amphorae found in present-day Bulgaria (map by E. Todorova).

PHILIPP NIEWÖHNER

FIG. 1 – Ciborium arch that depicts a ciborium and numerous roses, Archaeological Museum Konya in Lycaonia, inv. 201 (Niewöhner 2020).

FIG. 2 – Closure slab with a base profile, interlace that encloses a griffon, an eagle, a lion, as well as a deer, and a handrail with a scroll, Archaeological Museum Konya (J. Kramer).

FIG. 3 – Small impost capital of a knotted column with four shafts, lion heads and bird protomes at the corners, as well as a rose and a palmette in the middle, from Kidyessos/Çayhisar in Phrygia, Archaeological Museum Afyon inv. E1589-3930 (J. Kramer).

FIG. 4 – Knotted column with two shafts and vine capitals, Archaeological Museum Edirne in Thrace, inv. 17 (Niewöhner 2016).

FIG. 5 – Flanking ambo slab with interlace, lozenge, roses, and post, Güdük Minare Camii at Akşehir in Pisidia (Niewöhner 2020).

FIG. 6 – Closure slab with interlace, lozenge, roses, and handrail with astragal, an arcade, four palmettes, and a central cross (erased), Ulu Camii at Akşehir (Niewöhner 2020).

FIG. 7 – Closure slab with interlace, lozenge, roses, and handrail with an arcade, two palmettes, and a central cross (erased), Archaeological Museum Afyon (Niewöhner 2020).

FIG. 8 – Closure slab with cross, interlace, lozenge, and handrail with a scroll, Church of St Nicholas at Myra/Demre in Lycia (Niewöhner 2020).

FIG. 9 – Closure slab with cross, interlace, lozenge, and roses, Archaeological Museum Antalya, inv. 185 (J. Kramer).

FIG. 10 – Closure slab with interlace, lozenge, and roses, Denizli in west Asia Minor (J. Kramer).

FIG. 11 – Closure slab with interlace, lozenge, and roses, Archaeological Museum Edirne (Niewöhner 2016).

FIG. 12 – Eagle and head capital, Archaeological Museum Istanbul, inv. 4722 (J. Kramer).

FIG. 13 – Eagle and head capital, bearded, Archaeological Museum Konya, inv. 1980.12.1 (Niewöhner 2008).

FIG. 14 – Same as FIG. 13 (eagle and head capital), other side with fountain and pair of drinking birds (Niewöhner 2008).

FIG. 15 – Impost capital with a pair of bearded goats (?) that drink from a central chalice or fountain, Archaeological Museum Edirne (Niewöhner 2016).

FIG. 16 – Same as FIG. 15, other side with a pair of doves and a central plant (Niewöhner 2016).

FIG. 17 – Same as FIG. 15, other side with a dog (?) and an ivy leaf (Niewöhner 2016).

FIG. 18 – Same as FIG. 15, other side with a pair of birds and a central plant (Niewöhner 2016).

FIG. 19 – Closure slab with fountain (node?) and flanking peacocks, Archaeological Museum Kütahya in Phrygia (Niewöhner 2010).

FIG. 20 – Closure slab with a pair of hunting lions and a pair of peacocks that drink from a central fountain with node, Archaeological Museum Kütahya, inv. 698 (Niewöhner 2002).

FIG. 21 – Closure slab with a pair of griffons and a central plant, Archaeological Museum Antalya (J. Kramer 1970-1971).

FIG. 22 – Left fragment of a templon epistyle with a central (?) cross, interlace, roses, arcade on twin columns, palmettes, and lozenges, Archaeological Museum Afyon (Niewöhner 2020).

FIG. 23 – Fragment of a templon epistyle with interlace, roses, arcade, palmettes, lozenge, and donor inscription, Archaeological Museum Afyon (Niewöhner 2020).

STEFANIA S. SKARTSIS & NIKOS D. KONTOGIANNIS

FIG. 1 – Map of central Greece showing the location of the main sites mentioned in the text (drawing by the authors).

FIG. 2A-B – Unglazed Incised Ware: (A) – from Thebes; (B) – from Chalcis (Chalcis production) (photo by the authors).

FIG. 3 – Champlevé plate from Thebes (photo by the authors).

LIST OF FIGURES

FIG. 4 – Green and Brown Painted, Slip Painted, Champlevé and Incised Ware from Chalcis (photo by the authors).

FIG. 5 – Green and Brown Painted, Champlevé and Aegean Ware from Chalcis (photo by the authors).

FIG. 6 – Amphora from Dokos (Euboea) (photo by the authors).

FIG. 7 – Sgraffito with Concentric Circles from Chalcis (photo by the authors).

FIG. 8 – Sgraffito bowl from Chalcis (photo by the authors).

FIG. 9 – Venetian Renaissance Sgraffito from Thebes (Archive EFA Boeotia).

FIG. 10 – Partially glazed bowls from Chalcis (photo by S.S. Skartsis).

FIG. 11A-D – Rings: (A-C) – from Thebes; (D) – from Xeronomi (Boeotia) (Archive EFA Boeotia).

FIG. 12 – Circular earrings from Thebes (Archive EFA Boeotia).

FIGS. 13A-B – Lunate-type earrings from Thebes (Archive EFA Boeotia).

FIG. 14 – Pendant crosses from Thebes (Archive EFA Boeotia).

FIG. 15A-B – Pendants from Thebes: (A) – steatite icon with a mounted warrior saint; (B) – circular bronze pendant with a lion (Archive EFA Boeotia).

FIG. 16A-D – Jewelry from Xeronomi (Boeotia): (A) – steatite cross; (B) – bronze ring; (C) – bronze circular earrings; (D) – basket type earring (Archive EFA Boeotia).

FIG. 17A-B – Bronze buttons (A) and buckle (B) from Thebes (Archive EFA Boeotia).

FIG. 18 – Bronze box cover (?) from Thebes with repousse scene of the Annunciation (Archive EFA Boeotia).

FIG. 19 – Silver bowl from Thebes (ext., int.) (Archive EFA Boeotia).

FIG. 20 – Gold earring (lunate type) and ring from Thebes (Archive EFA Boeotia).

FIG. 21A-B – Gold earrings from the treasure of Chalcis (British Museum London, © Trustees of the British Museum).

JOANITA VROOM, ELLI TZAVELLA & GIANNIS VAXEVANIS

FIG. 1 – Map of the eastern Mediterranean with the location of Chalcis on the island of Evvia in central Greece (J. Vroom).

FIG. 2 – Detail of engraved map of Medieval Chalcis with its fortification walls, ca. 1566-1574 (from the atlas of Camocio 1570-1573, Citta di Negroponte, 16,5 x 22,5 cm).

FIG. 3 – Map of modern Chalkida with relocation of the ancient city to a more western part, next to the Euripus Strait (G. Vaxevanis; J. Vroom; the background is courtesy of Google Maps).

FIG. 4 – Old photograph of the *Kastro* of Chalcis with its original fortifications, general view from the north-east, between 1884 and 1890 (see http://square.gr/newlight-on-Negropont/4396); Remaining section of fortification walls with ethnographic museum (photo: J. Vroom).

FIG. 5 – Plan of Medieval Chalcis: location of excavation at Orionos Street (map after Kontogiannis 2012, fig. 1).

FIG. 6 – The excavated plot at Orionos Street in Chalcis (photo: G. Vaxevanis).

FIG. 7 – Chalcis, Orionos Street plot: total numbers of various wares. Total = 66.390 sherds (J. Vroom).

FIG. 8 – Chalcis, Orionos Street plot: total weights of various wares. Total = 2.414.75 kg (J. Vroom).

FIG. 9 – Photograph of Lelantine Plain with dug out clay bed (J. Vroom).

FIG. 10 – Chalcis, Orionos Street plot: Günsenin 3 amphora (J. Vroom).

FIG. 11 – Chalcis, Orionos Street plot: distribution of Günsenin 3 amphorae shown in green in pie charts (J. Vroom).

FIG. 12 – Map showing shipwrecks with mixed cargoes of Günsenin 3 amphorae and Fine Sgraffito Ware: 1 = Alonissos-Pelagonissos; 2 = Glafki (J. Vroom).

FIG. 13A-B – Chalcis, Orionos Street plot: Günsenin 3 amphora variants and their fabric (J. Vroom).

FIG. 14A-B – Chalcis, Orionos Street plot: Champlévé Ware dishes with incised depictions of various animals (J. Vroom).

FIG. 15 – Map showing shipwrecks with Champlevé Ware: 1 = Alonissos-Pelagonissos; 2 = Near Izmir; 3 = Kastellorizo; 4 = Silifke (J. Vroom).

FIG. 16 – Chalcis, Orionos Street plot: unfinished fragment of Champlévé Ware showing a rabbit or hare in a tondo (J. Vroom).

FIG. 17 – Chalcis, Orionos Street plot: reconstructed Incised Sgraffito Ware dish with warrior (J. Vroom).

FIG. 18 – Map showing shipwrecks with Incised Sgraffito Ware: 1 = Novy Svet; 2 = Çamaltı Burnu I; 3 = Kavalliani; 4 = Thorikos; 5 = Near Izmir; 6 = Tavşan Adası; 7 = Kastellorizo (J. Vroom).

FIG. 19 – Map showing shipwrecks with mixed cargoes of Günsenin 3 amphorae and Incised Sgraffito Ware: 1 = Novy Svet; 2 = Çamaltı Burnu I; 3 = Alonissos-Pelagonissos (J. Vroom).

FIG. 20 – Chalcis, Orionos Street plot: rim fragment of a cooking pot (J. Vroom).

FIG. 21 – Euboea, Dokos (near Chalcis): transitional (Günsenin 2-3) amphora type (after Waksman *et al.* 2016, Fig. 2, BZY801).

FIG. 22A-B – Chalcis, Orionos Street plot: upper part of an Unglazed Gouged jug (J. Vroom).

FIG. 23 – Almost complete shape of an Unglazed Incised jar (after Papanikola-Bakirtzis 1999, 17 and Vroom 2014², fig. MBYZ 2.3).

ELLI TZAVELLA

FIG. 1 – Map of Byzantine Corinth (image: James Herbst, American School of Classical Studies in Athens, re-worked by E. Tavella)

FIG. 2 – Corinth, Koutsougeras plot, ground plan (ground plan: Yannis Nakas. Τχ = Wall, Αγωγός = Water drain).

FIG. 3 – Fine Sgraffito dish found in Corinth, Koutsougera plot (E. Tzavella).

FIG. 4 – Champlévé dishes found in Corinth, Koutsougera plot (E. Tzavella).

FIG. 5A-B – (A) – Late Sgraffito dish; (B) – Incised Sgraffito dish found in Corinth, Koutsougera plot (E. Tzavella).

LIST OF FIGURES

FIG. 6 – Mamluk Sgraffiato Ware dish found in Corinth, Koutsougera plot (E. Tzavella).

FIG. 7A-C – (A) – Amphora; (B) – *Lageni* (closed storage and transport vessel); (C) – Unglazed White Ware jug, all found in Corinth, Koutsougera plot (drawings: Evangelia Broziouti).

FIG. 8 – Map of Attica (image: E. Tzavella)

FIG. 9 – Church of Agios Nikolaos, Kantza, Attica. View from east (photo: author. Courtesy Ephorate of Antiquities of East Attica © Hellenic Ministry of Culture and Sports).

FIG. 10 – Agios Nikolaos, Kantza. Ancillary room of Byzantine monastery (reprinted from Arapoyanni 1986, fig. 6. Courtesy Dr X. Arapoyanni).

FIG. 11 – Fragments of a Günsenin 3 amphora found in Kantza, Agios Nikolaos excavation (E. Tzavella).

FIG. 12 – Stewpot found in Kantza, Agios Nikolaos excavation (E. Tzavella).

FIG. 13 – Stewpot rim found in Kantza, Agios Nikolaos excavation (drawing: E. Tzavella).

FIG. 14 – Base fragments of Slip-Painted bowls found in Kantza, Agios Nikolaos excavation (E. Tzavella).

FIG. 15 – Base fragments of a Slip-Painted bowl found in Kantza, Agios Nikolaos excavation (E. Tzavella).

FIG. 16 – Base fragment of a bowl with Green and Brown Painted decoration found in Kantza, Agios Nikolaos excavation (drawing: E. Tzavella).

FIG. 17 – Fragments of a dish with Sgraffito decoration found in Kantza, Agios Nikolaos excavation (E. Tzavella).

FIG. 18 – Upper part of a jug with bulbous neck and vertical rim from Kantza, Agios Nikolaos excavation (E. Tzavella).

FIG. 19 – Upper part of a jug with narrow neck found in Kantza, Agios Nikolaos excavation (E. Tzavella).

JOANITA VROOM

FIG. 1 – Distribution map of Glazed White Ware I in the eastern Mediterranean (map and photo's: J. Vroom; drawing after Gerousi 1993, 258-59, no. 8050, figs. 7-8).

FIG. 2 – The most commonly used motifs of Glazed White Ware I (J. Vroom; pictures: after Talbot Rice 1930 and Böhlendorf-Arslan 2013, pl.4, nos. 26 and 30).

FIG. 3 – Map of Ephesus with distribution of Glazed White Ware I, II and IV (J. Vroom; map: C. Kürtze; drawing: after Ladstätter 2008, pl. 297, K 239).

FIG. 4 – Distribution map of glazed chafing dishes in the Mediterranean (map and photo: J. Vroom; drawing: after Romei 1992, figs. 1-2).

FIG. 5 – Miniature from Bibliothèque national gr. 74 Tetraevang., Paris, 3rd quarter of the 11th century (after Omont 1908, fol. 82/1).

FIG. 6 – Distribution map of metal jugs in the Mediterranean (J. Vroom; picture: after Pitarakis 2005, fig. 3).

FIG. 7 – Development of metal jug shape into ceramic variants (J. Vroom; picture: after Pitarakis 2005, fig. 3; drawings: after Hayes 1992, fig. 33, 14,21; Ricci 2007, fig. 3, no. 18).

FIG. 8A-B – (A) – Graph showing the average vessel height and volume of Byzantine tablewares (after Vroom 2016a, fig. 13.5); (B) – Graph showing the increase of smaller bowls in Late Medieval ceramic assemblages on two sites: Maximianoupolis (northern Greece) and Lagopesole (southern Italy) (J. Vroom; pictures: after Papanikola-Bakirtzis and Zekos 2010 and Fiorillo 2005).

FIG. 9 – Distribution map of Glazed White Wares II-IV and Polychrome Ware in the Mediterranean (map: J. Vroom; drawings: after Peschlow 1977-78, figs. 9 and 12; Sanders 2001, fig. 10.3, no. 12).

FIG. 10 – The most commonly used motifs of Glazed White Wares I-V (J. Vroom).

FIG. 11 – The most commonly used motifs of Glazed White Wares II-V and Polychrome Ware at Constantinople (J. Vroom; pictures after Talbot Rice 1930 and Böhlendorf-Arslan 2013).

FIG. 12 – The most commonly used animal motifs of Glazed White Wares II-V and Polychrome Ware at Constantinople (J. Vroom; picture: after Morgan 1942).

FIG. 13 – The most commonly used motifs of Polychrome Ware (J. Vroom; picture: after Morgan 1942).

FIG. 14 – Categories of motifs in Glazed White Wares II-V across some sites and regions. From North to South: Chersonesos; Novy Svet Shipwreck; Constantinople; Corinth; Sparta. Blue = humans; red = animals; green = floral; purple = objects; light blue = geometric/abstract; orange = other motifs (J. Vroom).

FIG. 15 – Total of main vessel shapes of Medieval glazed decorated tablewares by century from four museum collections (J. Vroom; drawings: after Papanikola-Bakirtzis 1996).

FIG. 16 – Total of main colours on Medieval glazed decorated tablewares by century from four museum collections (J. Vroom).

FIG. 17 – Total of main designs on Medieval glazed decorated tablewares by century (J. Vroom; pictures: after Papanikola-Bakirtzis 1989; and *Idem* 2004).

FIG. 18 – Total of main colours on Medieval glazed decorated tablewares at Butrint (J. Vroom).

FIG. 19 – Distribution map of glazed decorated vessels with warrior motifs in the Mediterranean according to their provenance (J. Vroom; pictures: after Vroom 2014, 162, fig. 9).

FIG. 20 – Map of Venetian trading routes, Venetian colonized territories, and find spots of Veneto Ware (Pottery finds), including *ceramica graffita a spirale cerchio* and Roulette Ware, in the Mediterranean (J. Vroom; map: Haldon 2005, map. 11.5).

FIG. 21 – Map of Genoese trading routes, Genoese colonized territories, and find spots of Port Saint Symeon Ware (Pottery finds 1) and of Tyrrhenian Archaic Graffita / *graffita arcaica tirenica* (Pottery finds 2) in the Mediterranean (J. Vroom; after: Haldon 2005, map. 11.5).

FIG. 22 – Distribution map of shipwrecks transporting Günsenin 3/Saraçhane 61 amphorae in the eastern Mediterranean (map: J. Vroom; drawing and picture: after Günsenin 1989, fig. 8).

FIG. 23 – Distribution map of shipwrecks transporting 12th- to 14th-century glazed tablewares in the eastern Mediterranean (map and photo's: J. Vroom after Papanikola-Bakirtzis 1999, 47, no. 168).

FIG. 24 – Distribution map of imported Islamic tablewares found on Byzantine sites in the eastern Mediterranean (map and photo of Fatamid Lustreware dish in wall of the Agioi Theodoroi church in Athens: J. Vroom).

*

COVER ILLUSTRATION

FRONT COVER – Job's Childern – Miniature, St. Catherine's Monastery gr. 3 (fol. 17v), Sinai – 11th century. After K. Weitzmann and G. Galavaris 1990, *The Monastery of Saint Catherine at Mount Sinai; The Illuminated Greek Manuscripts. Vol. 1: From the Ninth to the Twelfth Century*, Princeton, NJ, 37 and J. Vroom 2003, *After Antiquity. Ceramics and Society in the Aegean from the 7th to the 20th Century A.C. A Case Study from Boeotia, Central Greece*, Leiden, 318, fig. 11.17.

EARLY BYZANTINE & MIDDLE BYZANTINE PERIODS

PAG. 55 – Slip-painted Ware dish of Middle Byzantine times (after J. Vroom 2014². *Byzantine to Modern Pottery in the Aegean: An Introduction and Field Guide, Second & Revised Edition*, Turnhout, 80, fig. MBYZ 6.2).

MIDDLE BYZANTINE & LATE BYZANTINE PERIODS

PAG. 169 – Elaborate Incised Ware bowl of Late Byzantine times (after D. Talbot Rice 1930, *Byzantine Glazed Pottery*, Oxford, pl. 1 and J. Vroom 2014², *Byzantine to Modern Pottery in the Aegean: An Introduction and Field Guide, Second & Revised Edition*, Turnhout, 122, fig. LBYZ/fr 8.2).

EARLY BYZANTINE TO LATE BYZANTINE PERIODS: AN OVERVIEW

PAG. 281 – Medieval person drinking wine from a glass beaker, fresco by Giotto di Bonone, *The Wedding at Cana*, ca. 1304-1306, Scrovegni (Arena) Chapel, Padua, Italy (photo: J. Vroom).

BACK MATTER

pag. 348 – *The Wedding at Cana*, Detail of fresco in the Church of Saint Nicholas Orphanos, Thessaloniki, 14th century (photo: J. Vroom).

* * *

The Wedding at Cana,
Detail of fresco in the Church of Saint Nicholas Orphanos, Thessaloniki, 14th century
(photo. J. Vroom).

Index

OF GEOGRAPHICAL NAMES

Aachen 121, 138
Aegina 285
Aezani 174, 175
Afrati 202
Afyon 173, 189, 194
Aghia Galini 115, 116, 285
Akşehir 173, 189
Alassa 286
Alexandria 285
Aliveri 232
Almyros 300
Amathus 286
Amman 286
Amorion 285
Anaia-Kadikalesi 304
Ancyra 176
Antalya 173, 190, 194, 300
Anthedon 232
Antioch 296
Ard el-Mhjar 297
Argos 234
Arta 84, 86, 94
Athens 12, 16, 89, 146, 196, 234, 261, 263-264, 267-268, 285, 289, 291, 303

Belgrade 12
Beth Shaen 286
Bodrum 300
Butrint 16, 285, 293

Cadir Höyük 177
Candia / Chandax (cf. Herakleion / Heraklion)
Carcin Grad / Justiniana Prima 12, 13, 58,-66, 74-77, 298
Caria 173
Carthage 285
Chalcis (Aetolia-Acarnania) 84, 85, 149
Chalcis / Chalkida (cf. Euripos/ Evripos/Egriboz/

Negroponte) 12, 15, 195, 151-206, 215-218, 221-240, 253-260, 289, 293, 296, 299, 300, 301, 303
Cherson (Crimea) 35, 36
Chersonesos 114, 285, 301, 332
Chersonesus 146
Cherven 151
Chios 296
Cilicia 173
Classe 297
Constantinople / Istanbul 11, 12, 14, 15, 21, 22, 23, 26, 27, 29, 113, 115, 121, 122, 146, 148, 172, 173, 177, 191, 196, 198, 201, 205, 224, 225, 230, 231, 235, 236, 239, 265, 284-287, 289, 291, 298-304, 332
Cordoba 117
Corinth 12, 16, 36, 86, 198, 234, 236, 261, 268, 275, 276, 288, 289, 293, 301, 332
Cydonia/Chania 114

Debelt 148
Demre / Myra 173, 190
Denizli 173, 190
Dichin 297
Djadovo 151, 152
Dobrich 144
Docimium 15, 172, 173, 175
Doha 89
Dokos 217, 236, 260
Dor 286, 298
Durostorum 286

Edirne 146, 173, 189, 190, 192
Elaiussa Sebaste 287, 301
Eleutherna 114, 115, 120, 122, 134, 286
Ephesus 16, 175, 285, 286, 301, 304
Eretria 202

Euripos / Evripos / Egriboz (cf. Chalcis / Chalkida; Negroponte) 12, 15, 195, 151-206, 215-218, 221-240, 253-260, 289, 293, 296, 299, 300, 301, 303
Fustat 301

Ganos 30, 149, 232, 298, 299
Genoa 123, 238, 295-297, 300, 304
Golemanovo Kale 286
Gomatou 26
Gortyna 114, 115, 118, 122, 134, 285

Haskovo 141
Herakleion / Heraklion (cf. Candia/Chandax) 14, 114,-116, 119, 120, 122, 135-137
Hippos / Sussita 286
Huma 150

Ierapetra 114
Istanbul / Constantinople 11, 12, 14, 15, 21, 22, 23, 26, 27, 29, 113, 115, 121, 122, 146, 148, 172, 173, 177, 191, 196, 198, 201, 205, 224, 225, 230, 231, 235, 236, 239, 265, 284-287, 289, 291, 298-304, 332
Itanos 115, 116, 133
Izmir 300

Jerusalem 286

Kaisaroupolis 28
Kalehöyük 285
Kantza 277, 279
Kastorion / Thisvi 201
Kavalliani 300
Kefalos 84, 87
Khrysoupolis 13, 28, 34, 42
Kidyessos 188

349

Kimluca 300
Kladentsi 144, 150
Knossos 115
Konya 172, 173, 188, 191
Korbous 286
Kümbet 175
Kusadasi 301
Kütahya 173, 193

Lagopesole 330
Lapithos 304
Larnaca 292
Lefkada 85
Lentas 114
Leptis Magna 286
Limyra 286
Liopetro 114
Loutres / Mochlos 115, 116, 118, 120, 136, 285
Lycaonia 173, 188
Lycia 173, 287
Lyktos / Lyttos 114

Ma'ale adumim 286
Marseilles 296
Maximianopolis 330
Melnik 151, 152
Messonissi 136
Miletus 12, 15, 176, 285
Mochlos / Loutres 115, 116, 118, 120, 136, 285
Monemvasia 33, 38, 41
Mount Athos 31
Mount Varassova 84-86
Mylopotamos 232
Myra / Demre 173, 190

Nafpaktos 83-89, 94, 96,-98
Naissus / Nis 58
Nauplio 234
Negroponte (cf. Chalcis / Chalkida; Euripos / Evripos / Egriboz) 12, 15, 195, 151-206, 215-218, 221-240, 253-260, 289, 293, 296, 299, 300, 301, 303
Nessebar 141, 148, 150, 151

Nicaea 176
Nichoria 237
Nicosia 292, 293, 301
Nikopolis 84-86, 94
Nis / Naissus 58

Odartsi 150
Olympia 286
Oxa / Oxia 114

Paphos 304
Paris 89, 292
Patara 176
Pella 286
Pergamon 36, 286, 294, 304
Pernik 151
Perperikon 151, 152
Petras / Siteia 120, 122
Philippopolis / Plovdiv 141, 151
Phokaia 296
Pisa 123, 300, 304
Pitagoreia 287, 301
Pliska 143, 148-150
Plovdiv / Philippopolis 141, 151
Pomorie 150, 151
Preslav 143, 145, 149-151
Prilep 15
Princewell 286
Priniatikos Pyrgos 115, 120, 122
Proconnesus 172, 173
Pseira 116, 120, 122, 134, 135, 285

Radolivos 31
Raqqa 117, 301
Ravenna 297
Rethymnon 118
Rome 285

Sagalassos 57, 176
Samarra 117
Sardis 286
Sarkel 146
Scupi 58
Serres 28, 38, 199, 290
Shiraz 117
Shumen 141
Side 176
Sikyon / Vasilika 266

Silistra 141-145, 149-151
Siteia / Petras 120, 122
Sivec 15
Skala 149, 150
Skopelos 300
Smyrna 37
Sofia 12, 141
Sozopol 141-144, 148, 149, 150
Sparta 199, 289, 301, 302, 303, 332
Spetses 286
Stara Zagora 150, 286
Stockholm 292
Sudak 300
Sussita / Hippos 286
Svistov 141, 145

Tainaron 299
Tarsus 16, 88
Tartus / Tortosa 199
Taurision 58
Thebes 15, 20, 195, 196-206, 215, 216, 218-221, 225, 239, 293, 300, 304
Thespiae 288
Thessaloniki 13, 26, 27, 29, 31, 33, 35, 41, 58, 83, 87, 146, 149, 199, 225, 236, 289, 294, 300, 304
Thisvi / Kastorion 201
Tocra 285
Toledo 287
Tolmo de Minateda 287
Toxompous 28
Trebizond 21
Tsoutsouros 114

Ücayak 175
Umm al-Walid 286

Vamvaka 301
Varna 141, 143, 145, 149, 150
Vasilika / Sikyon 266
Veliko Tarnovo 141, 151, 152
Venice 123, 196, 204, 238, 295, 300, 304
Vrea 293

Xeronomi 202, 219, 220

MEDIEVAL AND POST-MEDIEVAL MEDITERRANEAN ARCHAEOLOGY SERIES

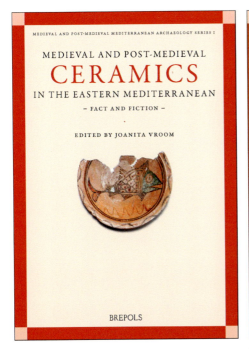

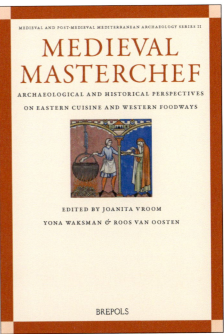

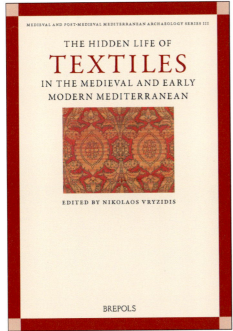

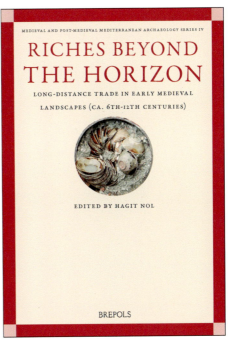

* * *